'I applaud Roy Millar's endea[...] most profound books of the [...] and soundly examines the te[...] impressive.'

Dr R T Kendall, Bible Teacher and Author; formerly Minister, Westminster Chapel, London

'*Come and See* gave me many new and precious insights into John's unique Gospel. Roy's excellent book is theologically faithful and thought-provoking – an invaluable guide to anyone seeking to understand and enjoy this profound Gospel.'

Reverend Lyndon Bowring, Chairman, CARE

'Dr Roy Millar has been a follower of Jesus for many years and has sent much time in study of His Word. *Come and See* is the fruit of a gifted teacher's sustained meditation and careful exposition on John's gospel. Staying faithful to the text, with a deep grasp of first-century Jewish context, Jesus and His teaching is vividly presented to us. Whether you are a seasoned scholar, a growing follower or even a new enquirer, this rich study will help you "come and see" and meet and know, Jesus the Messiah.'

Simon Ponsonby - Teaching Pastor St Aldates Church, Oxford, and Author

'It is hard to believe that this is Roy Millar's first book. Not only is it beautifully written in clear, lucid prose, it is amazingly perceptive from beginning to end. In chapter nine, speaking about his methodology, Roy says, "We need to read forwards from the Hebrew roots of the Bible and from the standpoint of those who heard the words in their original context." So like modern-day, Messianic Jews, this is exactly what the author does in a knowledgeable and perceptive way. I can honestly say that rarely have I read a book on Scripture which displays such a profound spiritual understanding of the meaning and implications of God's word. It is a veritable tour de force and I wholeheartedly recommend it to all who wish to know Jesus better, including fellow-Catholics.'

Pat Collins CM, MA, STL Evangelist, Scholar and Author

'In this book, Roy Millar shares some of the fruit of a lifetime's immersion in the Scriptures: reading them, studying them, praying them and living them. His writing weaves together rich background context and grounded insight on what it is to be human, offered together as a very accessible narrative commentary, unfolding in line with the Gospel itself. Roy's book will be of benefit not only to those who preach and help others to learn, but also to all who are looking for an accessible way to deepen their Biblical understanding and Christian faith. It enabled me to read familiar passages in a new and life-giving light. It will help all readers to *Come and See* in a fresh and deeper way the grace and generosity of God.'
(Revd Canon Dr) Jonathan Kimber, Director of Ministry and Discipleship, Diocese of Worcester

'The Word having been made flesh continues to be made fresh in these pages. Like a well-matured wine, this book is to be savoured. Chapter by chapter it lends itself to weekly tastings. As the French have crystallised the concept of "terroir" in describing the distinctives of a particular wine, so Roy Millar helps us discern the unique aspects of the Fourth Gospel. He demonstrates a particular sensitivity to the Jewish matrix out of which John shaped his material and uses this to lead his readers into a deeper understanding of Jesus, God's Word in and to the world.'
Desmond Maxwell, Founder and Director of Xplorations Teaching Ministry

'Some ideas come via information, but transformational truth comes by revelation. Through the invitation to "come and see", the author not only invites us into the deep waters of John's magnificent Gospel, but he also reveals something of the depth of his own soul. In these pages you will feel his passion for Jesus through his love and reverence of the text, and I pray you too will catch the life-changing power of his message. If you love the Lord and His Word, this book will serve to encourage and enrich your relationship with both.'
Dr John Andrews, Leader, Teacher and Author

'Roy Millar's new book, *Come and See*, makes Jesus, John and the whole New Testament landscape come alive for twenty-first-century readers. Theologically astute and yet also devotionally apt and eminently readable, this mini-commentary serves as a veritable roadmap to John's Gospel, and to Jesus Himself as its subject, within its historical, canonical and spiritual life context. Jesus as divine, Jesus as truly Jewish, Jesus as the One who meets us in unexpected ways... and then never lets us remain the same: all are here, in the mystery of this Man unlike any other!

'I can think of no better introduction to Jesus for seekers and mature believers alike!'
Rev Lance Wonders, DPhil, DMin, Academic Dean, ACTS International Bible College, Blaine, Minnesota, USA

'Having known Roy Millar for 25 years it was a delight to use his commentary on John's Gospel for my daily devotions. It reflected his own depth of scriptural knowledge by providing both wonderful insights into the text and practical encouragement for daily living. It is accessible to the youngest Christian and at the same time draws more seasoned believers into fresh revelation and personal dedication to Christ. I used it on a daily basis but it would be great for a small group to work through. I thoroughly commend it to you.'
Paul Reid, Pastor Emeritus, Christian Fellowship Church, Belfast

'Roy has been a personal friend for a number of years and I have seen his desire to help people to have a clearer understanding of God's Word, in a way that leads to a deeper relationship with Him. *Come and See* is a particular example of this, illuminating the Gospel of John like a floodlight and revealing the mysteries of God and of His Son the Lord Jesus Christ, and inviting readers to follow Him as disciples. I recommend it to everyone but especially to my brothers and sisters from a Muslim background, both those who currently believe in Jesus and also those who are willing to investigate His claims to be the Messiah and the Son of God.'
Davood Mahmoodi, Pastor Iranian Ministry Ireland

'Roy Millar has provided us with a thoughtful and accessible narrative commentary on John's Gospel. He has, as it were, taken us by the hand to "come and see" the Jesus whom John wants us to see. The narrative takes us to creation and incarnation, to historically significant locations and to the deepening and disturbingly sharp conflict between Jesus and the pervasively influential, non-relational, legalistic and dedicated religious establishment and then to self-interested political power, to the cross, death, burial and resurrection.

'John's Gospel finds its origin in God's generous love for the world. In contrast to the world's darkness, Jesus, the Light of the world, came among us, was one of us, triumphed with cosmic significance and still shines brightly. Here is John's good news about Jesus for people everywhere to believe.'
Rev John Dunlop, Minister Emeritus, Rosemary Presbyterian Church, Belfast; formerly Moderator of the General Assembly of the Presbyterian Church in Ireland

'A number of features mark this commentary as a very useful resource for those seeking to understand the Gospel of John. On a practical level, it is useful to have the biblical text of the Gospel included in the publication. However, it is the content of the commentary that makes a particularly valuable contribution. The Introduction: the Journey, is a concise overview of the message of the Gospel and is a helpful foundation on which the main commentary builds and develops. Connections between the Gospel and the Old Testament are highlighted and the key words and themes such as "authority" are clearly explicated. Aspects of Jewish culture and practice that shed light on the Gospel are also explored and explained. Moreover, the commentary is not just a historical study of an ancient text but it also emphasises the relevance and importance of this powerful message for today. Overall, this is an insightful and thought-provoking commentary that will be a useful addition to any Christian's library.'
Dr James McKeown, Fellow of the Higher Education Academy and member of the Board of the Institute of Theology, Queen's University Belfast

'*Come and See* is a clear, careful and comprehensive exposition of John's Gospel. It contains many original and helpful insights into the life and work of Jesus. It is particularly strong in seeing Jesus as the fulfilment of the Old Testament Scriptures and in setting His ministry in its original Jewish context. All Christians, young and old, will benefit from it, and the serious enquirer will discover who Jesus is and what it means to follow Him. I am delighted to be able to recommend this book.'

Pastor Leslie Hutchinson, former President of the Association of Baptist Churches in Ireland; Lecturer in Ethics at the Irish Baptist College

'There is an exciting renaissance in biblical studies, yielding blessing after blessing for disciples of Jesus of Nazareth. The simple but profound truth that our Christian roots run deep into the soil of Hebrew language and culture nourishes every area of faith and practice. Roy Millar draws on the best of this scholarship to help paint, from John's context, a portrait of the Jewish Messiah in continuity with Israel's prophetic history and God's redemptive purposes in the world. The startling result helps us recapture the sense of awe in the inspired invitation, "come and see".

'Roy's writing displays the clarity of a scholar, the passion of a shepherd, and the skill of an artist. These gifts work in harmony to accomplish the author's goal of offering you, the reader, a fresh invitation to intimacy with your great Creator. I invite you to read this book.'

James Whitman, President, Center for Judaic–Christian Studies, Dayton Ohio

COME AND SEE

An invitation to journey with Jesus and His beloved disciple John

Roy Millar

instant
apostle

First published in Great Britain in 2019.

Instant Apostle, The Barn, 1 Watford House Lane, Watford, Herts, WD17 1BJ

British Library Cataloguing-in-Publication Data

A catalogue record for this book is available from the British Library.

This book and all other Instant Apostle books are available from Instant Apostle:

Website: www.instantapostle.com

E-mail: info@instantapostle.com

ISBN 978-1-912726-07-3

Printed in Great Britain.

Dedicated to my wife Rosemary

and to

Sarah

Matthew

Chloe

Annabel

Katie

Lucas

Barney

Seven young disciples

To my dear friends Peter and Sharon Yarr, whose steadfast faith, in the midst of extreme circumstances, has demonstrated what it means to truly believe that Jesus is the Son of God.

These [things] are written, that you may believe that Jesus is the Christ, the Son of God, and that believing you may have life in his name. (John 20:31)

CONTENTS

Author Note...13

Acknowledgements 15

Preface...17

Foreword 21

Introduction: The Journey..23

1 John 1:1-5: In the Beginning Was the Word............................29

2 John 1:6-13: The Word, the Witness and the World..............34

3 John 1:14-18: The Word Became Flesh.....................................39

4 John 1:19-28: John the Baptist and the Jewish Leaders 47

5 John 1:29-39: Seeing Jesus..55

6 John 1:40-51: Come and See...60

7 John 2:1-12: A Wedding and the First Sign...............................67

8 John 2:13-25: Jesus in His Father's House 75

9 John 3:1-10: Born of the Spirit – Born from Above 82

10 John 3:11-21: Son of Man – Son of God...................................88

11 John 3:22–4:3: The Bridegroom and the Bride........................96

12 John 4:4-26: Living Water 103

13 John 4:27-43: Telling Good News 112

14 John 4:43-54: Jesus Lord of Space and Time..........................118

15 John 5:1-14: Jesus in the House of Mercy...............................122

16 John 5:15-30: Two Competing Sources of Authority............127

17 John 5:31-47: The Only Possible Witness 134

18 John 6:1-29: Passover and the Sign of Multiplied Bread.......139

19 John 6:30-52: The Bread of Life...145

20 John 6:53-71: Parting of the Ways 151

21 John 7:1-36: A Feast of Mystery and Suspense 158

22 John 7:37-52: An Offer and a Challenge 167

23 John 7:53–8:11: Jesus Shames the Pharisees........................... 173

24 John 8:12-29: The Light of the World 180

25 John 8:30-59: Which Father, Which Freedom? 186

26 John 9:1-19: A Spectacular Miracle 194

27 John 9:20-41: The Blind Who Claim To See 199

28 John 10:1-21: The Good Shepherd and the Sheep 204

29 John 10:22-41: A Setup and an Attempted Stoning 211

30 John 11:1-31: Mysterious Love 217

31 John 11:32-40: Grief and Groaning 224

32 John 11:41-53: Glory! 229

33 John 11:54–12:19: Anointing and Acclamation 234

34 John 12:20-36: Death and Glory 242

35 John 12:37-50: Final Offer and Warning.................................. 248

36 John 13:1-30: A Unique Passover Meal.................................... 252

37 John 13:31–14:11: A Temporary Parting.................................. 260

38 John 14:12-31: The Promise of the Spirit 268

39 John 15:1-11: The True Vine... 276

40 John 15:12-25: Servants, Friends and Martyrs....................... 281

41 John 15:26–16:15: The Spirit Of Truth 286

42 John 16:16-33: The Father Himself Loves You...................... 291

43 John 17:1-12: Father and Son Are One.................................... 297

44 John 17:13-26: Eternal Glory and Love 302

45 John 18:1-27: Jesus Is Betrayed and Denied........................... 307

46 John 18:28-40: Jesus Confronts Pilate 315

47 John 19:1-16: No King But Caesar 321

48 John 19:17-37: Finished! 328

49 John 19:38-42: Secret Disciples No More 337

50 John 20:1-18: Who Are You Looking For? 341

51 John 20:19-31: My Lord and My God 348

52 John 21:1-25: Feed My Sheep 355

Appendix 1: Inverse Parallelism: The Literary Structure of John 2:1-12 365

Appendix 2: John 1:14: The Only Begotten Son of God 367

Appendix 3: Jesus' Attitude to and Treatment of Women 374

Appendix 4: Was Jesus Born at the Feast of Hanukah? 377

Appendix 5: Did Jesus Die at Passover? 380

Appendix 6: What Were the Times of the Morning and Evening Offerings? 382

AUTHOR NOTE

All profits from this book will be used to support Kiwoko Hospital in rural Uganda:

Kiwoko Hospital had its origin about thirty years ago, in the aftermath of a civil war that left the district devastated and without medical help of any kind. It now has 200+ beds and provides a high standard of medical care to a community of mostly poor people. External support is still required in order to maintain its work of healing and Christian mission.

For further information about Kiwoko Hospital please visit: http://www.fokh.org.uk/

Free audio and written Bible study material by Roy Millar is available at: www.treeoflifebiblestudies.org/

'Wisdom…is a tree of life to those who lay hold of her.' (Proverbs 3:13, 18)

ACKNOWLEDGEMENTS

In writing this book I have chosen to draw on material that has accumulated in my mind over the course of many years. Some of this has its origins in the insights of others, gleaned from oral presentations on different occasions, and I now gratefully acknowledge those whose input I can currently identify. Chief among these is Professor David W Gooding who showed me how to recognise the literary structure of a sacred text and thus to better understand it from the author's point of view. He pointed out how various events at the wedding in Cana of Galilee had important symbolic significance. He explained how two other miracle-signs revealed Jesus as Lord of space and time, and also how His power to raise the dead prefigured the ultimate renewal of the whole creation. He also highlighted the clash of two kingdoms, based alternately on truth and power, as revealed in the encounter between Jesus and Pilate.

Barry Kissell provided an important insight when, speaking about Jesus' conversation with the Samaritan woman, he pointed out that Jesus was being guided by His Father in a moment-by-moment way, rather than following an agenda. I then realised that this dynamic applied to all the other events of Jesus' life. My good friend Alan George suggested an alternative understanding of the background of the Samaritan woman, and I have incorporated this into my discussion of this incident.

I am also grateful to the late Dr Dwight A Pryor for drawing my attention to the fact that, consistently throughout John's Gospel, water functions as a metaphor for the Holy Spirit, and for explaining how the Pharisee Nicodemus would have reacted to Jesus' teaching about new birth.

On several occasions, Leon Morris' discussions of difficult points of exegesis were very helpful.[1]

I gratefully acknowledge the contributions of a number of friends in bringing this book to its final form. Ian Taylor designed the initial format of the text and spent very many hours restoring it on the numerous occasions when technical difficulties occurred. Richard Kimber acted as critical reader of the text, clarifying expressions and making necessary amendments, helping me to discard superfluous material and challenging my ideas, and his expertise on the Greek text has been invaluable. Such virtues as the book possesses owe much to Ian's and Richard's honest and kindly critiques, and to Jonathan Kimber's robust and kindly criticism which resulted in a major rewrite of the text. Other friends, including Jim and Pamela Ferguson, Anne Flynn and Eugene Boyle, also read the text, correcting errors, offering encouragement and making suggestions, and I am most grateful to all of them. I am also grateful for the professional input and personal encouragement of the Instant Apostle team and, in particular, for the patient and insightful work of Nicki Copeland, the editor.

It is usual at this point to express thanks to one's spouse. I do so, not as a matter of routine, but because of the immense amount of encouragement that I received from my wife Rosemary during almost three years it took to complete writing the book, including times when progress was slow or stationary. Without her love and patience the process of climbing this particular mountain would have been much more daunting.

All Bible references are from the World English Bible British English (WEBBE). This version is in the public domain, which makes it possible to include the whole text of John's Gospel within the text of the book. The WEBBE is an updated and thoroughly modernised version of the 1901 American Standard Version..

---

[1] Leon Morris, *The Gospel according to John* (Grand Rapids: William B Eerdmans, 1995).

PREFACE

John's Gospel has a unique place in my affections. When I was a young Christian, seeking a more personal knowledge of God, He responded to my prayer in a very dramatic and immediate way. Soon after this I began to read John's Gospel and, although I already knew much of the content, it was like a new book. The person of Jesus emerged in a fresh and vivid way and I also discovered the reality of God as my Father. This book, entitled *Come and See*, is the product of much reflection during several decades, augmented with insights from many sources.

'Come and see' was how Jesus invited Andrew and John, His first two followers, to join Him on a journey that would lead to increasing intimacy with Him. This invitation was extended, implicitly or explicitly, to many other people during the following two to three years and was met with very different responses. Some realised that Jesus was the Messiah whom they had been seeking and joined Him on His journey as disciples. Others were taken by surprise but gladly recognised that He was the answer to the situations in which they were trapped. Another group had vested interests in denying Jesus' identity and turned against Him in anger and fear. As we follow the journey of Jesus through John's eyes we are confronted with the same challenge, for there is ultimately no neutral position.

Jesus also received the invitation to 'come and see' the tomb of Lazarus, His friend. It was a moment of deep emotion, for it was a place of death and corruption and despair that encapsulated the condition of the broken creation. It also portrayed the imminent events of His own crucifixion and resurrection.

I have had the opportunity to teach extended courses on this Gospel, initially in a midweek class at Christian Fellowship Church, Belfast, and then with a group of young Christians. These experiences, together with teaching many other study groups, have convinced me that many Christians have a desire for a deeper engagement with the Word of God than is possible in the context of Sunday services where many items compete for limited time. The option of Bible or theological college courses is impracticable for many people, and they may find it difficult to identify suitable written material in the space between popular devotional books and academic commentaries whose style and intricacy of content may be intimidating.

It is with such people in mind that I have written this book. I have provided a detailed exegesis of each part of the text, without the use of technical language. I have also explained the thought flow of the Gospel as a whole and how it connects with the rest of Scripture, so those engaged in theological studies may also find useful insights. Where appropriate, I have made connections and applications for us in our current world situation. The book could therefore also be relevant to Jews and Muslims, an increasing number of whom are becoming open to study the life of Jesus of Nazareth. His claim to be the Son of God is contradicted by their strict interpretations of monotheism, as was also the case for the Pharisees during Jesus' lifetime. Perhaps they may be helped to see that Jesus is the revelation of the Father, emphasising rather than diminishing the glory of the one true God.

John's world also contained sceptics and pagans. The Sadducees, although dressed in religious clothing and performing associated rituals, were the sceptics of their day. They did not believe in the supernatural world, denied Jesus' claims to have come from another world, discounted the evidence that He provided, and were determined to silence Him one way or another. Modern sceptics, dressed in scientific clothing, often do the same.

Pontius Pilate was a pagan who believed in many gods, also not unusual in our contemporary world. He was disconcerted in the presence of Jesus, who was claiming to be the representative of absolute truth.

Perhaps some members of these two groups, if willing to reconsider their positions, would also find direction to the One who is the way and the truth and the life, as a result of understanding John's account of the life of Jesus.

The portion of the Gospel text being considered is included within each chapter of the book, so that it can be read without the need to refer to a separate Bible text. This should facilitate reading in situations where this would be inconvenient or impossible; the book is designed to be read initially as a narrative rather than as an intensive study. Individual chapters were deliberately kept short in order to facilitate a daily-reading programme.

The finished text turned out to have fifty-two chapters. An initial reading through the book could be followed by more detailed study during the course of a year, making use of the many biblical cross references in the footnotes to explore connections with other scriptures. References to non-biblical sources have been kept to a minimum, as this book is not intended as an academic treatise.

I am very mindful of John's purpose in writing his Gospel: 'these [things] are written, that you may believe that Jesus is the Christ, the Son of God, and that believing you may have life in his name'.[1] I pray that you will encounter Jesus and come to a new awareness of God as your Father, for this is the reason why Jesus became flesh and lived among us.

---

[1] John 20:31.

FOREWORD

I have had the privilege of knowing Roy Millar for most of my life, initially meeting him when I attended a Scripture Union summer house party. I subsequently came to know him better in the context of a Bible class, and then at informal Bible study groups where my love for the Bible was nourished. Over the years, God has enabled Roy to influence many other people, including a number of other young teenage men and women who are now involved in Christian leadership in different parts of the world.

One of the root meanings of the word 'disciple' is 'learner'. Roy has always been a learner with an enquiring mind, asking questions and searching for answers. His commitment to understanding Scripture, interpreting it faithfully and applying it ruthlessly has always impressed me. His approach has always been that to understand Scripture we stand under it. You will see all of this as you read *Come and See*.

I am delighted that he has stepped out into new paths and has written this book. He has approached John's Gospel with humility, knowing it to be God's inspired and authoritative Word. It has been said that the Bible is as up to date as this morning's newspaper, and this book is a good illustration of that statement. It is not some cold academic exercise but rather it will both inform and inspire you. This book has been birthed in Roy's personal Bible study and extensive reading and also through listening attentively to others. The long pregnancy of study and writing has now reached the point of delivery, and I have no doubt that this 'new birth' will be a blessing. *Come and See* has both spiritual and intellectual depth and provides much food for thought and material for quiet reflection. Roy has opened up this Gospel in fresh and intriguing ways and has pointed to the life-related and life-changing implications of John's narrative. We will certainly be made to think, and at times we will be stopped in our tracks.

Roy has always been a humble explorer of God's Word, and this book is tangible evidence of those explorations. He is like a miner of the gold mine of the Bible who digs deep and brings out gold nuggets of biblical truth. He is like a travel guide who takes us on a journey of learning so that we see things we have never previously noticed. He is a teacher who communicates with sincerity from his lifetime of learning. Most of all, he leads us into a deeper relationship with the 'Author' of the Bible, which was John's stated purpose when writing his Gospel. As we read we will want to know Him better and worship and adore Him. Thank you, Roy, for pointing us to Him!

I have no hesitation whatsoever in commending this book. It will stretch our minds, warm our hearts and feed our souls. As we come and see the One who is the subject of John's Gospel, we will discover more of what it means to believe that Jesus is the Messiah, the Son of God, and as we do so we shall truly experience life in His name.

Take time to graze and gaze!

Bishop Ken (Fanta) Clarke, formerly the Church of Ireland Bishop of Kilmore Elphin and Ardagh

INTRODUCTION

The Journey

In July 1969 Neil Armstrong completed the first stage of an epic journey and touched down safely on the surface of the moon. He had lived in a very different kind of world for all of his previous existence. The lunar environment in which he now found himself was bleak and barren and colourless and was devoid of the life and beauty of the world from which he had come. Neil Armstrong's visit coincided with his strong personal desire to make the journey, but the mission had its origins elsewhere: in the mind of President John F Kennedy. Armstrong was a volunteer, but he was also an agent of a higher authority and his mission was on behalf of the human race, as expressed in his historic words, 'One small step for [a] man, but one great leap for mankind.' When his mission had been completed, he ascended from the surface of the moon and returned to the 'parent world', where he was received with honour and glory.

This historical sequence has many features in common with the journey of Jesus as John describes it in his Gospel. Jesus, the Word through whom all things were made, came from another world which was the source of this one. He repeatedly stated that He came on the initiative of the Father and with His authority. Jesus stayed in communication with the Father and closely followed His instructions, for His ambition was to fulfil the purposes of the One who had sent Him. He travelled an inner and spiritual path in parallel to His outer and physical journey, as He was constantly guided by the Father through the Holy Spirit. When He had completed His assignment, climaxing in His death and resurrection, He returned to the glory that He had had with the Father before the world was made.

This is the heart of the journey that John describes, but within it he includes carefully selected events and particular milestones that provide a map for the journey. These milestones consist of a series of visits to Jerusalem in order to participate in the annual festivals, as was required of a Jewish man. It was in this context that most of the recorded events took place. This alerts us to the fact that the journey of Jesus was the culmination of a much longer journey, stretching back to Abraham and encompassing the entire history of the Jewish people. In fact, it also extended back to creation and the great disaster that overtook mankind and the world when man the creature disobeyed his Creator.[1]

As *Come and See* was approaching completion, I read Tom Wright's biography of the apostle Paul, and I realised that John viewed the nature and purpose of Jesus' life on earth in a similar way to Paul, as recorded in the Acts of the Apostles and in his epistles.[2] Both John and Paul understood that Jesus was the culmination of the story of Israel, with all its covenant promises and all the prophecies of the coming Messiah. Jesus was the embodiment of all that Israel should have been but failed to be, and He was also its hope of ultimate deliverance and of becoming the channel of blessing for the world.

Tom Wright identified the Torah (strictly speaking the first five books in the Bible but sometimes used more loosely to include the remainder of the Hebrew Scriptures) and the Temple as the two loci around which the narrative of Jesus' life turns. This is clearly the case with John's Gospel in the context of major confrontations between Jesus and the religious leaders. Representatives of the two main factions appear early in John's record as they each interrogate John the Baptist about his identity. First to come were the senior priests who regarded the Temple as 'our place', followed by the Pharisees who considered themselves as experts in interpretation of the Torah. Much of John's Gospel focuses on interactions between these two groups of protagonists and Jesus, on the issue of His identity and authority.

---

[1] Gen. 1:27; 1 Tim. 2:13-14.

[2] Tom Wright, *Paul: A Biography* (SPCK, 2018).

As was required of a Jewish man, Jesus attended the great pilgrim feasts in the Temple. These festivals recalled seminal events in the nation's history and were also enacted prophecies concerning the coming Messiah who would redeem His people from oppression and would pour out the Holy Spirit on Israel. It was in the context of these festivals that controversy was stirred as Jesus revealed Himself as Lord of the Temple and of the Sabbath, as the source of the living water of the Spirit, as the Light of the world, as the Good Shepherd (in contrast to the bad shepherds), as the Passover Lamb, as the Messiah King, and as the Resurrection and the Life. In the context of Passover season He also revealed Himself as the One greater than Moses and as the true manna. He was thus claiming to be the culmination and goal of all of Israel's history and hope, the living Temple and the embodiment of Torah.

John described five distinct stages in this journey. Jesus' incarnation was the first stage, when, 'The Word became flesh'.[3] His subsequent growth to mature manhood was documented in Luke's Gospel but not explicitly by John.[4]

The second stage began when Jesus visited with John the Baptist. In this context He was baptised and anointed with the Holy Spirit, and He also received His first disciples. This second stage, lasting for almost three years, continues to the end of John chapter 12. During this period many other people were on journeys that interconnected with Jesus' journey. Those who were open to receive His words remained with Him, and their inner and spiritual journeys gradually bent and converged towards His. In Jesus' own words, they became 'children of light'.[5]

Also during this second stage, Jesus interacted with a number of individuals whose reactions revealed the varying conditions of their hearts. All *came and saw* the same person but with differing and contrasting responses. One was a highly esteemed Pharisee and teacher whose initial and tentative inquiry finally blossomed into committed faith over a period of three years. Another was a

---

[3] John 1:14.

[4] Luke 2:40-52; 3:23.

[5] John 12:36.

complete outsider, a Samaritan woman with a troubled background, whose heart opened to Jesus when He revealed Himself to her as the Messiah for whom she had been waiting. A third was a beggar who moved, in the course of a single day, from physical blindness to physical and spiritual sight, worshipping Jesus as the Son of God.

Others, principally from the ruling religious elite, were incensed by what they saw and heard. Jesus performed a number of miracle-signs that pointed to His identity as the Son of God. In the light of this evidence He challenged them to believe in Him as the One whom the Father had sent into the world. (Most of Jesus' recorded words in this section were primarily directed towards this group, although they also contained excellent instructions for the disciples who were also present.) Sadly, the majority of the leaders refused the light that Jesus brought and they became increasingly hostile towards Him, determined to stop Him in His tracks. By rejecting His words in favour of a version of truth that was convenient to themselves, they moved progressively, and ultimately irreversibly, into ever-increasing spiritual darkness. This choice, of darkness rather than light and power rather than truth, would finally lead to the destruction of everything that those leaders treasured and cherished.

This stage of the journey concluded with a final appeal from Jesus to the Jewish leaders. It fell on deaf ears and their time of opportunity was now at an end. John's Gospel acts as a warning that to encounter Jesus on the journey of life is not a neutral experience. We are either drawn closer to the light in company with Jesus, or plunged deeper into darkness if we choose to reject or ignore Him.

The third stage of the journey was very short but intense. It lasted for only a few hours but it occupies five chapters, from 13 to 17. Jesus' entire focus was now on the faithful disciple band, as He prepared them for immediate challenges and also for the subsequent mission that they would undertake after being empowered by the Holy Spirit. At the conclusion of this stage Jesus was able to say to the Father, 'I glorified you on the earth. I have accomplished the work which you have given me to do.'[6] At that time He prayed for His followers as they faced a traumatic few days without Him, and contemplated His return in glory to the world from which He had come. Sadly, Judas, who had closely observed Jesus and had seen much evidence for His identity, left the company of the disciples and went out into the night, having previously chosen the path of darkness.

The fourth stage was the most challenging of all for Jesus and His followers. Jesus was betrayed and arrested and the disciples were scattered and devastated. Peter suffered additional emotional trauma, for he denied Jesus after having promised to remain faithful at any cost to himself. Jesus was put on trial before Pilate, the Roman Governor, during which time He was scourged, mocked and rejected by the leaders of Israel. As the trial neared its end, the contest between truth and power and between light and darkness reached its crescendo in the shocking words of the High Priest, 'We have no king but Caesar!'[7] This part of Jesus' journey was one of agony and deep darkness, both physical and spiritual, but as it ended He re-emerged into the light with a cry of completion and victory: 'It is finished!'[8]

The last stage of the journey involved Jesus' resurrection and reunion with His followers, when He reassured and restored their troubled hearts. Thomas, who had been absent when Jesus appeared to the others, demanded visible proof before he would believe. Jesus graciously extended the invitation to come and see, to physically inspect the wounds in His hands and feet and side, and Thomas responded in worship.

After Jesus had ascended to the Father the disciples would continue the same journey that they had begun in company with Jesus, for that had always been His intention from the time that He had called them. He commissioned them for their task with the words, 'As the Father has sent me, even so I send you', and He then breathed on them saying, 'Receive the Holy Spirit!'[9]

---

[6] John 17:4.
[7] John 19:15.
[8] John 19:30.
[9] John 20:21-22.

These words and the accompanying action were in token of the promise of the Father to pour out the Holy Spirit upon them. Jesus' earthly mission had now been completed and He would soon ascend to the glory at the Father's right hand, but He would continue His work in and through them. When He had spoken of the coming of the Spirit, He informed them that this would be equivalent to His own presence within them. They, together with those who would receive their words, would continue His journey until the end of the age and would thus complete the mission that the Father had entrusted to Him.

John recorded a final and very touching incident, describing how Peter was fully restored and recommissioned for the journey ahead. This is a sign of hope for any of us who have faltered and assumed, incorrectly, that our journey with Jesus is all over.

1

John 1:1-5
In the Beginning Was the Word

> *1:1-3* *In the beginning was the Word, and the Word was with God, and the Word was God. The same was in the beginning with God. All things were made through him. Without him, nothing was made that has been made.*

With these majestic words John commenced his account of the man whose disciple he had been for more than three years. John had been present at all the significant events and teachings of those years, and he was one of only three apostles who were chosen to accompany Jesus on the Mount of Transfiguration and also to stay close to Him in the Garden of Gethsemane. He stood at the cross in company with Jesus' mother and he was the first apostle to arrive at the empty tomb. He had been in a close and intimate relationship with Jesus and had come to understand that He is the only begotten Son of God.[1]

The opening phrase in Greek, *en arche*, echoes the first word in the Hebrew Bible, *b'reshit* ('in the beginning'), announcing the unfolding events of creation by the Word and the Spirit of God. The events that John was about to describe were nothing less than the beginning of the new creation through that same agency of the Word and the Spirit. John's opening statement, 'In the beginning was the Word', was made without context or explanation, provoking questions that demand answers. Who or what is this Word and what is His/Its relationship to the God of Genesis 1? Was John simply saying that God communicates and that He

---

[1] Luke 9:28-29; John 13:21-26; Mark 13:32-34; John 19:25-27; 20:1-10.

created the world by speaking it into existence? Was it just a description of how God had chosen to act in creating the universe?

The second statement, 'the Word was with God', implies that God and the Word are not identical but are in an association of some kind. In the book of Proverbs, Wisdom made a similar claim in the context of creation:

> The LORD possessed me in the beginning of his work, before his deeds of old. I was set up from everlasting, from the beginning, before the earth existed ... then I was the craftsman by his side. I was a delight day by day, always rejoicing before him.[2]

As in John's introduction of the Word, Wisdom appears to be a person rather than merely a personal attribute. The motif of Wisdom personified as a royal counsellor at God's side continues throughout Jewish wisdom literature, and is the context within which Jesus is identified here in John's Gospel and also throughout the New Testament as the wisdom of God.

John's third statement – 'the Word was God. The same was in the beginning with God. All things were made through him. Without him, nothing was made that has been made' – clearly indicates that the Word is none other than the Creator God Himself. Does this mean that 'Word' is simply a synonym for 'God', or does this statement express some complex and more profound truth? John would have been mindful of the outlook of first-century Jewish readers and their passionate belief in the truth that God is one. Their core creedal assertion was expressed in the Shema: 'Hear, Israel: the LORD is our God. The LORD is one.'[3] Many of their forefathers had died as martyrs as a result of persecution by a Greek king, Antiochus IV Epiphanes (167–164 BCE). In order to sanctify the name of God they had accepted death rather than agree to worship pagan gods. Any suggestion of polytheism would thus have been anathema to John's contemporaries.[4]

---

[2] Prov. 8:22-23, 30.
[3] Deut. 6:4; Mark 12:28-34.
[4] 1 Maccabees 1:10-63.

This creedal statement can be understood in a different way that is also consistent with the Hebrew text: 'The Lord is our God, the Lord alone.'[5] This insists that there is only one God but does not define His personal nature. The Scriptures contain many allusions to relationship within the Godhead.[6] This was recognised by Jewish scholars prior to the time of Jesus and also at the time when John wrote his Gospel.[7] John's purpose in writing was to reveal that Jesus is the mysterious person to whom those writings referred, the Son of God and the One whose mission on earth was to give eternal life to all who would believe in Him:

> Therefore Jesus did many other signs in the presence of his disciples, which are not written in this book; but these are written, that you may believe that Jesus is the Christ, the Son of God, and that believing you may have life in his name.[8]

In the process John would reveal how the religious leaders, who held to a rigid and exclusive interpretation of the Shema, had rejected Jesus and had dismissed His claims as blasphemous.[9]

The opening verses of Genesis 1 indicate that God launched the whole process of creation with the command, 'Let there be light.' John was giving a radically new interpretation of this scripture. God the Father did not create the universe simply by a spoken word but through the willing agency of His Son, of whom John wrote, 'All things were made through him. Without him, nothing was made that has been made.' He it was who had released all the energy that was required for the universe to come into existence in all its grandeur and complexity.[10] In his Gospel, John describes the Father's purpose to restore the broken creation, again through His Son, now revealed in the person of Jesus, the Word made flesh.

---

5 Deut. 6:4 ESVUK alternative translation.

6 For example, Prov. 30:4; Isa. 48:16; Ps. 110:1, c.f. Matt. 22:41-45.

7 Risto Santala, *The Messiah in the Old Testament in the Light of Rabbinical Writings* (Jerusalem: Keren Ahvah Meshihit 1992), pp. 86-92.

8 John 20:30-31.

9 John 8:58-59; 10:30-31.

10 Gen. 1:3; Heb. 1:1-3.

> **1:4-5** *In him was life, and the life was the light of men. The light shines in the darkness, and the darkness hasn't overcome it.*

In John's understanding, life and light are intimately connected. The light that flooded the primeval darkness flowed from the eternal and self-sustaining life of God. As human creatures our lives are contingent on sources outside of ourselves, such as food, air, water, other people, and ultimately on God Himself. Jesus was fully human and His biological life was sustained from the resources of the earth, but He also possessed the same life as the Father for, 'In him was life'.[11]

As the eternal Word, Jesus created the physical light that still pervades the universe. As the incarnate Word, He radiated the glory of God and brought spiritual illumination to all those who would receive Him, for 'the life was the light of men'. In this way John identified Jesus as the great light that had come in order to shine on those who sat in darkness, as the fountain of life and in whose light we see light, as the Lord who is our light and our salvation and who would also shine His light upon the Gentiles.[12]

John made twenty-four references to light in the first twelve chapters of the Gospel, but there are none at all in the subsequent ones. Life features thirty-nine times in the first twelve chapters but only seven times in the remainder. Love occurs twelve times in the first twelve chapters and forty-five times in the final nine chapters. This change of emphasis occurs at the point when Jesus switched His attention from what John calls 'the world', those who have resisted and rejected His word, to His disciples, who are 'not of this world', because they have believed and received His word. Jesus spoke repeatedly of love to those who gladly received the light that He brought to them through His words and actions. The true light, which enlightens everyone, had indeed come into the world.[13]

The apostle Paul used the same imagery of light and darkness, creation and new creation, in a way that mirrors John's

---

[11] See also John 1:14; 5:25-27; 8:42, 58, 10:30; 11:25-26; 15:1-5; 17:24.

[12] John 1:4-5, 8:12, 9:5; Ps. 36:9; Isa. 9:2; 49:6.

[13] John 1:9.

introduction to his Gospel: 'seeing it is God who said, "Light will shine out of darkness," who has shone in our hearts to give the light of the knowledge of the glory of God in the face of Jesus Christ'.[14] The disciples in the Upper Room did not require further instruction about light and darkness, but they did need to know how to live in relationship with Jesus and with one another in the context of the surrounding hostile world.[15]

The Jewish leaders were exposed to the same light as the disciples but were so blinded by their own prejudices and agendas that they did not perceive Jesus as light. They did not comprehend (understand) His words because those words did not fit with their understanding of reality and truth, thus precipitating a collision between light and darkness. Paul also wrote:

> Even if our Good News is veiled, it is veiled in those who are dying, in whom the god of this world has blinded the minds of the unbelieving, that the light of the Good News of the glory of Christ, who is the image of God, should not dawn on them.[16]

Light ultimately prevailed over darkness, for Jesus fulfilled the Father's purpose when, in perfect obedience, He laid down His life and was raised again in triumph.[17]

We live at a time in history when there is increasing hostility to the Gospel and severe persecution from those who love darkness rather than light. Those who remain true to the light may suffer for their faithfulness, but they too will ultimately be vindicated.[18]

---

[14] 2 Cor. 4:6.

[15] John 14:23; 15:4-10, 17, 18; 16:26-28; 17:20-26; 21:15-17.

[16] 2 Cor. 4:3-4.

[17] John 19:30; 20:14-17; Phil. 2:5-11.

[18] 2 Tim. 4:6-8; Rev. 2:10; Rev. 6:9-11; Rev. 7:9-17.

2

John 1:6-13
The Word, the Witness and the World

> *1:6-9 There came a man, sent from God, whose name was John. The same came as a witness, that he might testify about the light, that all might believe through him. He was not the light, but was sent that he might testify about the light. The true light that enlightens everyone was coming into the world.*

John has begun to reveal that this Supreme Being, the Creator of the universe, the Eternal Word, has come into the world in order to shine light into the darkness. He is about to explain that the Word became flesh in order to live among His creatures, and yet he pauses to introduce a lesser, though esteemed, person: John the Baptist. There are at least two possible explanations for this apparent digression.

The first is that John's preaching and baptising activity continued in parallel with Jesus' public ministry. Disciples continued to follow John, and some of them even regarded Jesus as a competitor. John remained popular with the people and was highly esteemed as a prophet, and some of his disciples continued to follow him for many years after his death.[1] Jesus made His first appearance in the context of this well-established and popular ministry. The Gospel makes it clear that Jesus and John the Baptist were not on the same level, being respectively Creator and creature. John the Baptist was happy to agree with this.[2]

Perhaps the most compelling explanation for the interposition of John the Baptist into the text is that he provided a connecting

---

[1] John 3:25-26; Matt. 9:14; Luke 7:18-19; Matt. 21:24-27; Acts 19:1-5.
[2] John 1:27, 34; 3:28-30.

link between the statements, 'In the beginning was the Word', and 'The Word became flesh, and lived amongst us'.[3] The eternal Word had entered space and time in human flesh. He had also stepped into the Jewish world as a Jewish man and in fulfilment of the Jewish Scriptures. Those Scriptures had concluded some 400 years before, with the prophecy of Malachi who recorded God's promise to send the prophet Elijah. He would prepare the hearts of the people to receive the Messiah. John was that Elijah figure, to whom Isaiah had also alluded.[4] God had sent John in advance of Jesus to complete the work of the previous prophets and to usher in the age of the Messiah, thus acting as the final bridge between promise and fulfilment.

> *1:10-13 He was in the world, and the world was made through him, and the world didn't recognise him. He came to his own, and those who were his own didn't receive him. But as many as received him, to them he gave the right to become God's children, to those who believe in his name: who were born not of blood, nor of the will of the flesh, nor of the will of man, but of God.*

The word 'world' appears three times in the first sentence of verse 10. On the first two occasions 'the world' described the place that the Word had made and which He was now visiting. Specifically, it referred to the land of Israel as promised to Abraham, Isaac and Jacob, and confirmed by the prophets. The third usage, 'the world didn't recognise him', referred to the world of human beings and, in particular, to the people of Israel, His own people.

At one point Jesus stated that He had been sent only to the lost sheep of the house of Israel (although, for particular reasons, He made a few exceptions to this rule). During the period of His life on earth, until His saving work had been accomplished, He placed a similar restriction on His apostles. The ultimate plan was that Gentiles would also be included in one flock with one shepherd.[5]

---

[3] John 1:1, 14.
[4] Mal. 4:5-6; Isa. 40:3-5; Matt. 3:10-12; Luke 7:18-23; Matt. 17:10-13; Luke 7:26-27.
[5] Matt. 15:24; John 4:22; Matt. 10:6; John 10:16.

Initially both John the Baptist and the Pharisees were ignorant of Jesus' identity, but this situation would soon change. When John saw a miraculous sign from heaven, he identified Jesus as the Messiah and received Him with acclamation and joy.[6] In contrast, when Jesus subsequently performed miraculous signs from heaven, most of the religious leaders rejected these signs as constituting evidence for His identity. Jesus later described such people as being 'of the world'. Conversely, Jesus described those who chose to receive Him as Messiah as being 'not of the world', for they believed the truth that He had come from and belonged to, another world.[7] The distinction between these two groups progressively sharpened as events moved towards their conclusion in Jesus' trial and crucifixion.

Jesus' followers are said to have believed in His name. In the Jewish culture of Jesus' day, 'The Name' (Hebrew *Hashem*) was used as a synonym for God, expressing His very nature, all that He is. When the disciples believed in Jesus' name they were not merely giving formal recognition to His identity, but were committing themselves to Him as their Lord and their God. In return they received a new life and a new identity as God's children.

The expression 'God's children' would have had special significance for Jewish people. When the nation was about to emerge from slavery in Egypt, God referred to Israel as His firstborn son. In his prophetic song Moses affirmed this: 'Isn't he your father who has bought you? He has made you and established you.' The prophet Hosea recalled this relationship: 'When Israel was a child, then I loved him, and called my son out of Egypt.' He also described Israel as a son whom God, as a father, fed and taught to walk. Israel failed to live up to that high calling, but even as God was about to judge them for their unfaithfulness, He still called them His dear son. Likewise, Isaiah's impassioned prayer for mercy on God's erring people was based on the assertion that 'you are our Father'.[8] What was largely an unfulfilled aspiration now

---

[6] John 1:29-34.

[7] John 8:23; 12:31; 14:30; 15:19; 17:6, 14, 16.

[8] Exod. 4:22; Deut. 32:6, 18; Hos. 11:1, 3; Jer. 31:20; Isa. 63:15-16; 64:6-12.

became an actual relationship, through the sending and sacrifice of the beloved Son.[9]

John gave two complementary descriptions of how we can become children of God. Firstly, a child can be adopted into an existing family. God called Abraham from the Gentile nations to become the foundation stone for the new nation of Israel. In a similar way, Gentiles could join the nation as proselytes and become equal members in the family of Israel. When anyone receives Jesus in faith, he or she is adopted into the family of God and has all the rights of a son and heir within His Kingdom.[10]

Birth, with the implication of new life, is the second description of how a person can enter into the family of God. This life comes from heaven and it has no connection with blood, family, nationality or ethnicity. It cannot be achieved by the will of the flesh, personal works or human effort, nor can it be imparted or imposed by the will of a human being or by any external human agency. New birth will be the subject of a later chapter when Nicodemus, a prominent religious expert, came to visit Jesus and discovered, to his surprise, that he needed to be born again from above.[11]

Before we conclude this section, we should take note of a highly significant word, 'authority', which becomes one of the central themes of the Gospel. 'But as many as received him, to them he gave the right to become God's children'.[12] The issue of authority and its source was at the heart of the conflict between Jesus and the leaders of Israel. They claimed jurisdiction and the right to call Him to account. He refused that claim, and insisted that He had absolute authority as the Son of Man and by virtue of His relationship with the one He dared to call 'my Father'. Near the end of the narrative it seemed that they had prevailed in the battle of wills, but they would be proved wrong. Jesus made this clear when He said, many months prior to His death:

---

[9] John 14:6, 21-23, 16:26-28.
[10] Isa. 56:3-8; Acts 2:10; Rom. 9:4; Gal.4:5; Eph. 1:3-6; Rom. 8:15.
[11] John 3:1-12.
[12] John 1:12.

'Therefore the Father loves me, because I lay down my life, that I may take it again. No one takes it away from me, but I lay it down by myself. I have power to lay it down, and I have power to take it again. I received this commandment from my Father.'[13]

---

[13] John 10:17-18.

3

John 1:14-18
The Word Became Flesh

> *1:14 The Word became flesh, and lived amongst us. We saw his glory, such glory as of the one and only Son of the Father, full of grace and truth.*

This verse begins with an awesome statement. The Word, whom John has previously identified as the Creator God Himself, has now appeared in human flesh. Jesus was a human being like us but, unlike us, His conception did not initiate His life and existence. The tense of the verb that is translated 'became' implies an action at a point in time, a real space–time event. Jesus came from heaven as Son of God and now was also fully human. The incarnation is the great miracle without which the rest of the story is mere illusion.[1]

Paul described the fact that 'the mystery of godliness is great: God was revealed in the flesh'.[2] In Scripture, a mystery is a statement or promise that cannot be understood without further revelation. The fact that God Himself would come in the person of the Messiah was implicit in many prophetic words, being interpreted as such in many Targums (ancient Aramaic paraphrases of the Scriptures), but the implications were too daring and outrageous to imagine.[3] The fact that Jesus was fully human while remaining fully God constitutes the 'mystery of godliness', for it is a paradox that defeats human reason (1+1=1). The eternal Word

---

[1] Luke 1:31-35; Matt. 1:20-23; John 3:13.

[2] 1 Tim. 3:16.

[3] Risto Santala, *The Messiah in the Old Testament in the light of Rabbinical writings*, pp. 84-92.

created man, but as Messiah He was made of woman.[4] The human mind cannot comprehend this mystery; the proper response combines faith, trust and worship.

Greek philosophers considered human beings to be composed of flesh and spirit, the former being bad and the latter being good. By contrast, the Bible teaches that the physical body was part of God's good creation, so Jesus could take on human flesh, bone of our bones and flesh of our flesh, without being corrupted in the process.[5]

David was a prophet of the coming Messiah both through the things that happened to him as well as the things he wrote. In Psalm 40 he made a statement that was subsequently taken up by the writer to the Hebrews as being Jesus' words to the Father prior to His incarnation.[6] The Father had prepared a body for His Son and Jesus accepted it, together with the similar possibilities and limitations of our own bodies. His body began on earth as a single cell in Mary's womb. In anticipation of this He must have known that, for a significant period of time, His existence in an unconscious state would be totally dependent on the Father's faithfulness.[7] This relationship of trust in and obedience to the Father was the basis of everything that He did on earth.

The angels who witnessed His birth may have wondered how to address the One whom they had worshipped from the time of their own creation, but who now lay helpless and dependent in the arms of a teenage girl. The answer was that they must worship Him, for He was still fully God.[8] The baby Jesus remained vulnerable and totally reliant on His mother for sustenance. He was a real human baby and not engaged in thinking 'God-thoughts'. We must assume that, as He grew in wisdom and stature, the Holy Spirit somehow awakened the consciousness of His deity. It is clear that, for the remainder of His earthly life, He lived at ease in the

---

[4] Gen. 2:7, 21-23; 3:15; 1 Cor. 11:7-12; Luke 1:34-35.

[5] Gen. 2:23, Luke 24:38-39; Eph. 5:30.

[6] Ps. 40:6-8; Heb. 10:5-10.

[7] John 17:5; Ps. 16:8-11; Acts 2:25-31.

[8] Heb. 1:6; Luke 2:13-14.

awareness of that dual nature, speaking of God as both His Father and His God.[9]

'The Word became flesh' implies a real physical body and a real human nature. Jesus was not God living in the façade of a human body, pretending to be a man, like an actor dressed for a part. Paul's use of language in Philippians 2:7-8 might cause us confusion, using as it does the terms 'form' of a servant, 'likeness' of men, and 'in human form', as if describing human resemblance but not the substance. However the same phrase, 'in the form of God', is used in verse 6 of the same chapter, where it obviously refers to Jesus' eternal and divine nature. Similar language is used when referring to ordinary human beings: Adam begot a son, 'in his own likeness, after his image' – meaning another human being.[10]

Jesus' outward appearance corresponded to His fully human nature. He shared our humanity in every respect: choosing, eating, drinking, sleeping, becoming weary, feeling hungry, speaking, seeing, praying, weeping, suffering pain, being angry, feeling moved with compassion, being tempted in every conceivable way (but without acquiescence), and so forth. Had He not been made like us in every respect, then His offering of Himself for us would have been invalid in relation to God, and He would have been disqualified from acting on our behalf as the great High Priest.[11]

The Word stepped from the eternal state into our space–time continuum. Now, as Messiah, Jesus also stepped out of the pages of the Scriptures, the One who had walked with Adam in the garden, who had visited with Abraham and had wrestled with Jacob, and who had revealed Himself to Isaiah in overwhelming glory.[12]

The phrase 'and lived among us' connects with the Exodus account: the Greek word *(skenoo)* used here and translated 'lived' means to pitch a tent or to live in a tent. Following the departure of the Israelites from Egypt, God revealed His desire to live in their midst and He instructed Moses in the following words: 'Let them

[9] Luke 2:45-52; John 20:17; c.f. Heb. 1:8-9.

[10] Gen. 5:3.

[11] Heb. 2:17-18; 4:14-16; 5:6-10.

[12] Gen. 2:8; 3:8; 18:1-33; 32:24-30; Isa. 6:1-5; c.f. John 12:37-41.

make me a sanctuary, that I may dwell amongst them.' This arrangement was designed to make it possible for God, in His purity and holiness, to coexist with the people in their sin and corruption without destroying them, a problem that became acute when they worshipped the golden calf. This incident provoked God to say, 'I will not go up amongst you, for you are a stiff-necked people, lest I consume you on the way.'[13] Yet even before that dreadful event had occurred, God in His grace had already revealed His solution: the Tabernacle.

The Tabernacle was a sacred and protected space at the centre of the camp where God in His holiness could live in the midst of His redeemed but still imperfect people. They still had to keep at a certain distance in order to protect it from contamination and themselves from danger, but nevertheless God was present among them. The glory of God, the Shekinah (linguistically related to 'dwell'), came down on the Tabernacle and rested on the Ark of the Covenant in the Holy of Holies, which was separated from the outer part of the tent by a dividing curtain. Repeated rituals and sacrifices were required in order to maintain the holiness of the Tabernacle, keeping it fit for the continuing presence of God. Each year, on the Day of Atonement, blood was sprinkled on the Ark, symbolically covering the peoples' sin and purifying them from its pollution.

John drew on this prophetic picture when he indicated that the Word pitched His tent among us. It is important not to misinterpret the metaphor and think of Jesus as being God camouflaged in a human body. Paul used the same analogy of a tent to describe his own body, in order to emphasise that He was on a journey from the visible to the invisible, the temporal to the eternal. Jesus came from the eternal and invisible realm and took on flesh in order to live in this temporal and visible world.[14] Jesus' physical body was the true sanctuary, containing the very presence of God. Many years later, John wonderingly recalled that he and others had seen, heard and examined the Word of Life and had

---

[13] Exod. 25:8; 29:42-46; 32:4-6; 33:3.
[14] 2 Cor. 5:1-9; John 17:5, 24; 2:19-22.

even touched the one who was God incarnate in human flesh.[15] Only those who really desired to see could recognise the glory that Jesus displayed through His words and actions. It was hidden from those who chose darkness rather than light, blinded by their prejudices and personal ambitions.[16]

Jesus did not need to keep people at a distance in order to preserve their safety, nor did He fear contamination. Holiness and health flowed from Him when He touched those suffering from conditions that would cause ritual uncleanness (leprosy, bodily discharge and death).[17] He welcomed and interacted with people whose sinful behaviour or reputations had made them outcasts in society. In consequence, He was criticised for being a friend to tax collectors and sinners.[18]

Jesus offered His sinless human body on the cross on our behalf in order to provide permanent cleansing, forgiveness, and life for us. When He died, the great dividing curtain that barred the way to the Holy of Holies in the Temple was torn in two from top to bottom. The writer to the Hebrews explained that Jesus' body in death became the torn curtain that opened the new and living way into the Father's presence, the holiest place of all. He died, the just for the unjust, in order to bring us to God.[19]

Jesus is the glory of the God of Israel. Moses was not permitted to see the face of God, but the glory of God was revealed in the face of Jesus the Messiah.[20] John was one of three disciples who saw Jesus transfigured. This event was probably on John's mind when he wrote the words, 'we saw his glory', and also when he penned the introduction to his first epistle.[21] John was also present at the cross and saw Jesus being lifted up. It was probably only after Jesus' resurrection that John understood the crucifixion as the means by which He would be lifted up in glory. Many years later

---

[15] 1 John 1:1-3.
[16] John 3:19-21; 5:36-44; 9:39-41.
[17] Hag. 2:11-14; Luke 5:12-13; 8:43-56.
[18] John 8:2-11; Luke 19:1-10; Matt. 11:19.
[19] Matt. 27:50-53; Heb. 10:19-22; John 14:6; 1 Pet. 3:18.
[20] Exod. 33:17-23; John 12:41; 2 Cor. 4:6.
[21] Luke 9:28-36; John 1:14; 1 John 1:1-3; 2 Pet. 1:16-18.

John would have a revelation of Jesus as the glorified Son of Man, and would be completely overwhelmed.[22]

> **1:15-18** *John testified about him. He cried out, saying, 'This was he of whom I said, "He who comes after me has surpassed me, for he was before me."' From his fullness we all received grace upon grace. For the law was given through Moses. Grace and truth were realised through Jesus Christ. No one has seen God at any time. The one and only Son, who is in the bosom of the Father, has declared him.*

John again refers to John the Baptist, this time in the company of Moses, and now sandwiched between the two references to grace and truth. 'The law ... given through Moses' seems to refer to the covenant that God made with the nation of Israel and which they undertook to obey, as recorded in Exodus. It was initially described as the Book of the Law, to which further instructions were added in Leviticus, Numbers and Deuteronomy, together with accounts of how that Law was transgressed. Israel's destiny involved being the channel through which the Messiah, the Seed promised to Abraham, would come, and He would then bring blessing to the whole world. This necessitated that Israel be kept separate from the pagan nations; this was one of the chief purposes of the Law, which defined them as a holy nation that lived in loyalty to the covenant with their God. The era of the Law was, therefore, time limited and moving towards its appointed goal through the succeeding centuries.[23]

John reminds his readers, and us, that the era of the Law extended from Moses to John the Baptist, and contained many prophecies and promises of the coming Messiah. John the Baptist testified that a new age had dawned in the person of the One who had existed before him in eternity and in glory.[24] Jesus, the prophet like Moses, had arrived in flesh, and John was the appointed witness to this dramatic and climactic event. Moses had faithfully played his God-given role in the process of salvation history that had now reached its goal.

---

[22] Rev. 1:10-18.

[23] Gal. 3:16-19; 4:4-5.

[24] Deut. 18:15, 18-19; Mal. 4:4-5; John 5:46; 7:40.

The translators of some English translations of the Bible – such as the King James Version, the New King James Version and the Amplified Bible – have inserted 'but' between 'the law was given through Moses' and 'grace and truth came by Jesus Christ', as if a negative point is being made. This is to misunderstand the dynamic of the single story of the Bible. A necessary phase had now come to a conclusion and, having served its purpose, gave way to the following chapters for which it had been the essential preparation. Paul wrote, 'For Christ is the fulfilment [Greek *telos*] of the law for righteousness to everyone who believes.' *Telos* means either 'goal' or 'end/completion', or both as here in Romans and also in John's Gospel.[25]

The God of Moses and of Israel is one and the same as the God and Father of the Lord Jesus; grace and truth figure prominently in the account of God's dealings with Israel. In the aftermath of the great sin of worshipping the golden calf, Moses asked God for a revelation of His glory. The LORD responded by making all His goodness pass before Moses and proclaiming:

> 'The LORD! The LORD, a merciful and gracious God, slow to anger, and abundant in loving kindness and truth, keeping loving kindness for thousands, forgiving iniquity and disobedience and sin; and who will by no means clear the guilty, visiting the iniquity of the fathers on the children, and on the children's children, on the third and on the fourth generation.' [26]

Grace and truth were by no means absent in the former days, but now the author of grace and truth had come, embodying them and revealing their full extent.

The Greek mindset that pervades western culture tends to emphasise truth as accurate information. John, with his Hebrew worldview, would have embraced a wider range of meaning. Truth as we encounter it in the Hebrew Scriptures also emphasises faithfulness within a covenant relationship. The Hebrew word *emet*, in the passage quoted from Exodus 34, is variously rendered 'truth'

[25] Rom. 10:4.
[26] Ps. 103:1-14; Exod. 34:6-7.

or 'faithfulness' in different English versions of the Bible.[27] By living a life of faithful love, complete trust and total obedience to the Father, Jesus modelled the true and appropriate relationship between creature and Creator.[28] Jesus asserted that He, personally, *is* that truth and that He had come to bear witness to the truth – namely, how the Father purposed to restore His Kingdom on earth through the obedience of His Son.[29]

The metaphor in John's statement 'in the bosom [leaning on the breast] of', had its origins in his own personal experience at the Passover supper where he describes how the disciple whom Jesus loved reclined next to Jesus and physically leaned against Him. Other leading disciples such as Peter and Andrew are included by name, but John's name does not appear in the text. It seems that John preferred anonymity and chose to describe himself simply in terms of his relationship to Jesus.[30] This human picture helps us to understand the nature of the unity between the Father and the Son.[31] The one and only Son, 'who is in the bosom of the Father',[32] has declared him.

Prior to the crucifixion Jesus promised His disciples that it would soon be possible for them to share that same intimacy with the Father.[33] Paul explained that God dwells 'in unapproachable light, whom no man has seen, nor can see'. We now see the glory of God (the Father) in the face of Jesus the Messiah. John was subsequently given a revelation that, at the end of time, the Father Himself will make His dwelling with us and we shall see His face.[34]

---

[27] Among many other instances, see Gen. 32:10 and Ps. 108:4.

[28] John 17:4; 18:37-38; 5:19-20.

[29] John 14:1-11; 19:36-37.

[30] John 13:23.

[31] John: 17:24.

[32] John 1:18.

[33] John 14:23; 16:25-28; 17:24-26.

[34] 1 Tim. 6:13-16; 2 Cor. 4:6; Rev. 21:1-7; Rev. 22:1-5.

4

John 1:19-28
John the Baptist and the Jewish Leaders

> ***1:19-23*** *This is John's testimony, when the Jews sent priests and Levites from Jerusalem to ask him, 'Who are you?'*
> *He declared, and didn't deny, but he declared, 'I am not the Christ.'*
> *They asked him, 'What then? Are you Elijah?'*
> *He said, 'I am not.'*
> *'Are you the prophet?'*
> *He answered, 'No.'*
> *They said therefore to him, 'Who are you? Give us an answer to take back to those who sent us. What do you say about yourself?'*
> *He said, 'I am the voice of one crying in the wilderness, "Make straight the way of the Lord," as Isaiah the prophet said.'*

In writing his introduction to the narrative of the Gospel, John had already mentioned John the Baptist on two occasions. Now he is featured in the full flow of his prophetic activity in the wilderness. The location was highly symbolic in connection with his prophetic calling, which was to summon Israel to repentance and to a restored relationship with their God, in preparation for the moment when the Messiah would be revealed. The wilderness was the place where significant leaders, and also the whole nation, had previously encountered God and had been transformed.

The Patriarchs and Moses had spent much of their lives in that same context. Israel had accepted a covenant with the Lord in the wilderness of Sinai and He had provided for them and protected and tested them there. David sought refuge in the wilderness, and it was there that he learned to trust in God and was prepared for his future reign.[1] On one occasion when God was calling Israel back to Himself, He reminded them of the time when, as a betrothed wife, she had gladly followed Him in the wilderness. He also promised her that one day He would bring her there again and betroth her to Himself forever.[2]

In response to a question from the priests and Levites, John the Baptist referred to a passage in Isaiah that begins with God's desire to comfort His people,

> 'Comfort, comfort my people,' says your God. 'Speak comfortably to Jerusalem; and call out to her that her warfare is accomplished, that her iniquity is pardoned, that she has received of the LORD's hand double for all her sins.'[3]

The following verse that John quoted takes the form in Hebrew of a single statement followed by two couplets:

> The voice of one who calls out, 'Prepare the way of the LORD in the wilderness! Make a level highway in the desert for our God.'[4]

John was summoning people to come to the wilderness and meet with the God who loved them dearly and who was coming to them in the person of His Son in order to bless them. John's prophetic preaching and unconventional practice of baptising those who responded to his message were also beginning to sound alarm bells with the religious authorities in Jerusalem. Among the crowds were a number of people who had been sent to investigate John's unconventional activities. They represented the religious leaders of the nation, who should have been the first to recognise and submit to God's authority as expressed through His prophet John. Sadly, this was not the case. Their encounter with John the Baptist was the opening scene in the drama that was about to

---

[1] Ps. 18:1-6, 16-19; 34:1-7; 42:1-11; 54:1-7; 1 Sam. 30:1-20.

[2] Luke 1:80; 3:2; Jer. 2:2; Hos. 2:14-20.

[3] Isa. 40:1-2.

[4] Isa. 40:3.

unfold as a major theme in the Gospel: the conflict between light and darkness.

The first delegation from Jerusalem consisted of priests and Levites. Apart from Luke's Gospel we would not know that John himself was in the priestly succession, his father Zechariah having been given the honour to offer prayers on behalf of the nation within the Holy Place in the Temple. This was the setting for the angel Gabriel's announcement that Zechariah and his wife Elizabeth were, at last, to have the son for whom they had longed and yet had ceased to expect. In other circumstances John would have followed his father into the priestly office. God's purpose for John was very different, for he was to be a prophet rather than a priest. This could have been a disappointment for Zechariah but he responded with delight and prophetic understanding of the even greater dignity of his son's appointed role.[5] John never served in the Temple in Jerusalem but he served the One who was the true Temple, God in human flesh – Immanuel.[6] We too must remember that God's plans for our children may not coincide with our dreams for them.

The chief priests were from the party of the Sadducees who did not believe in the supernatural world: they denied the existence of angels and the reality of the final resurrection. They were the ruling elite whose power base was the Temple, and they were also the experts in religious rituals. They thus held a monopoly on access to God through the sacrificial system and were uniquely placed to acquire great wealth, both from the sale of suitable animals and from currency exchange between secular and sacred coinage.

Annas, the former High Priest who was known for his greed and corruption, remained the most powerful figure and exerted his influence through his son-in-law Caiaphas, the current High Priest.[7] The office of High Priest was at the discretion of the Roman authorities, who made it clear that continuance in the office was contingent on maintaining order among a population that was seething with anger over the occupation and crippling taxation.

---

[5] Luke 1:5-25, 39-45, 57-79.

[6] John 2:18-19; Matt. 12:3-6.

[7] John 1:19; 18:12-13; 11:47-50.

Caiaphas and other senior priests used their religious positions as a means of exercising power and enriching themselves.

The sudden appearance of a popular and charismatic prophet presented a threat to the status quo that had to be carefully managed in order to maintain the delicate balance with the Romans. Their question to John the Baptist was both a challenge and a veiled threat: 'Who are you?' ('Who do you think you are?') Within John's lifetime there had been messianic pretenders who had roused popular feeling, and the Romans had responded with brutal suppression. The ruling class had much to lose in this situation so they were anxious to prevent any disturbance to the status quo.[8] It may seem curious that the priestly authorities had forgotten the startling events that surrounded the birth of Zechariah's son about thirty years previously, the son who would have recently reached the qualifying age for entering the priesthood. Luke's Gospel suggests that John had spent many years in seclusion in wilderness places, in preparation for his unique prophetic ministry.[9]

John the Baptist had commenced his public ministry around CE 27–28, a Sabbatical Year (this calculation is based on Jesus' statement about the progress of Temple construction).[10] Every seventh year the land was to remain uncultivated and debts were to be cancelled, recalling Israel's deliverance from slavery in Egypt. It was thus a favoured time to expect the Messiah to appear. John's preaching and his baptising were attracting large crowds of people, which was deeply worrying. Being free of personal ambition and any hidden agenda, John replied to their question with simple and unambiguous words: 'I am not the Christ.'

John's denial was welcome, but the issue of his identity remained unresolved. He was popular and his activities were potentially very destabilising. His unusual dress, lifestyle and uncompromising call for repentance resembled that of the prophet Elijah, which connected with the belief that Elijah would reappear just before the Messiah arrived.[11] John might have had the crazy

[8] Acts 5:36-37.

[9] Luke 1:80; 7:24-28.

[10] John 2:20.

[11] Matt. 3:1-12; 1 Kgs. 17:1; 18:17-40; 21:17-26; Mal. 4:5-6.

notion that he was a reincarnation of Elijah, which would certainly be dangerous, and hence their next question: 'Are you Elijah?' John's answer was even shorter and to the point: 'I am not.' Of course, John was correct in a literal sense, but Jesus subsequently affirmed that John had come 'in the spirit and power of Elijah', and had thus fulfilled the Scriptures.[12]

Their next question, 'Are you the prophet?' connected with the belief that the Messiah would be a prophet like Moses, to whom God would speak in a direct and intimate way as foretold in the Torah.[13] John's response was an emphatic denial, using a single word: 'No.' He neither desired nor intended to engage with these self-important men whom he regarded as 'offspring of vipers'. He subsequently showed the same carelessness for ungodly human power and authority when he rebuked Herod for his adulterous relationship.[14]

John's threefold denial left the problem unresolved. The facts on the ground indicated that John was a force to be reckoned with, and yet he claimed to be a nobody. If so, he was indeed a dangerous nobody! The delegation could not return to their masters empty-handed, hence their desperate appeal: 'Who are you? Give us an answer to take back to those who sent us. What do you say about yourself?' ('You have told us who you are not; please tell us who you are!') John's reply, 'I am the voice of one crying in the wilderness, "Make straight the way of the Lord"', did nothing to assuage their fears, as this statement had strong messianic associations.

We are left to imagine how the delegation was received when they returned to Jerusalem. Subsequent events would reveal the corrupt hearts of the chief priests who would play a key role in the process that led to the cross. On two occasions Jesus cleansed the Temple over which they claimed to hold supreme authority – 'our place' – and on both occasions they challenged His authority to behave in this way.[15] On the second occasion Jesus counter-challenged with a question: 'The baptism of John, was it from

---

12 Mark 9:11-13; Luke 1:17.

13 Deut.18:15, 17-19; John 7:40-43.

14 Matt. 3:7; Mark 6:18.

15 John 11:48; 2:13-20; Luke 19:45–20:2.

heaven, or from men?' The Sadducees were caught between foolishness and fear and did not answer, thus revealing their moral and spiritual bankruptcy.[16]

> **1:24-28** *The ones who had been sent were from the Pharisees. They asked him, 'Why then do you baptise, if you are not the Christ, nor Elijah, nor the prophet?'*
>
> *John answered them, 'I baptise in water, but amongst you stands one whom you don't know. He is the one who comes after me, who is preferred before me, whose sandal strap I'm not worthy to loosen.'*
>
> *These things were done in Bethany beyond the Jordan, where John was baptising.*

The second delegation came from the Pharisees, who shared the leadership of the ruling council with the Sadducees. They had heard about the Sadducees' interrogation of John and about his enigmatic responses and his strong rebuke.[17] Pharisees, unlike the Sadducees, did believe in the supernatural world and they enjoyed a considerable measure of popularity and respect among the people on account of their learning and outward piety. They placed strong emphasis on holiness and they engaged in detailed study of the Scriptures, together with commentaries by previous generations of scholars. The Pharisees had begun as a protest movement in the aftermath of attempts by Greeks to enforce paganism on the Jewish people. The movement had begun with the best of motives but, sadly, it had degenerated into a legalistic system with a multitude of detailed regulations that were impossible for ordinary people to follow. In consequence, the Pharisees had become a religious elite, with a tendency to self-righteousness and pride of position.[18]

Although the Pharisees and the Sadducees differed in many respects, their central question – the source of John's authority – was identical. John's practice of baptising people was of core concern to the Pharisees because they placed great emphasis on ritual washing as a way to maintain holiness. Ritual immersion was

[16] Luke 20:3-8.
[17] John 3:1, 10; 7:45-52; Matt. 3:7.
[18] Matt. 23:1-36.

a common practice – for example, prior to marriage, or to deal with an acquired state of impurity or when preparing to present an offering.[19]

John's baptism signalled a rival movement that posed a threat to their authority. John claimed that he was preparing the way for the coming of the Lord by preaching about repentance and then immersing in the Jordan River those who responded. A long time previously, the nation of Israel had entered into a new life in the Promised Land through the waters of the Jordan, thus recapitulating deliverance from slavery in Egypt through the waters of the Red Sea.[20] These two seminal events in Israel's history marked crucial stages in the fulfilment of God's covenant promises to them. John's baptism was no mere ritual, but was rather a powerful symbolic statement about a new phase in salvation history. John was bypassing the experts in holiness as he called people to a new relationship with God in heart and in behaviour, outwardly expressed in baptism. Subsequently, Jesus' disciples baptised even more disciples than John, which would create additional problems for the Pharisees.

John challenged the Pharisees to repent and to receive his baptism, but they refused to do so as it would have placed them in the same category as the common people. Jesus rebuked the Pharisees for having rejected John – '[They] rejected the counsel of God, not being baptised by him themselves' – and attributed a demonic source to John's ministry. John, a model of humility and deference, described himself in terms of the lowliest servant, unworthy even to attend to the Messiah's feet. Jesus would later take a similar role in washing His own disciples' feet.[21]

John's answer to their question could only have served to increase the Pharisees' concern. The Messiah, who was much more important than he, was already physically present! When John said, 'whom you don't know', he was making a statement that was obviously true of them in a physical sense, as it was for himself.[22] When Jesus came into the world He made light available and

---

19 Matt. 15:1-2; 23:25-26; John 2:6; Acts 21:26.
20 John 4:1-31; 1 Cor. 10:1-2.
21 Luke 7:30-35; John 13:3-6.
22 John 1:31.

possible for all, but the way divided when some chose darkness rather than light. John gladly embraced the light of revelation that he received concerning the identity of the Messiah. In contrast, the Pharisees subsequently joined forces with the disciples of Herod, the murderer of John the Baptist, in their quest to destroy Jesus and to extinguish the light that He brought.[23]

John the writer thus set the scene for the conflict of light and darkness that he subsequently documented in detail. The first episode of this would take place in the Temple when Jesus confronted the senior priests.[24] Then, for a considerable time, the Pharisees would take centre stage in a controversy. Finally, the two groups of antagonists would unite in a common plan to condemn Jesus and have Him crucified. Happily, not all of the religious leaders joined in this conspiracy, and John subsequently identified two such exceptions.[25]

---

[23] John 3:19-21; 9:40-41; Matt. 22:15-22.
[24] John 2:13-21.
[25] John 3:1-2; 7:45-52; 19:38-42.

5

John 1:29-39
Seeing Jesus

> **1:29-34** *The next day, he saw Jesus coming to him, and said, 'Behold, the Lamb of God, who takes away the sin of the world! This is he of whom I said, "After me comes a man who is preferred before me, for he was before me." I didn't know him, but for this reason I came baptising in water: that he would be revealed to Israel.' John testified, saying, 'I have seen the Spirit descending like a dove out of heaven, and it remained on him. I didn't recognise him, but he who sent me to baptise in water said to me, "On whomever you will see the Spirit descending and remaining on him is he who baptises in the Holy Spirit." I have seen, and have testified that this is the Son of God.'*

John described a series of incidents that took place on three successive days, thereby conveying a sense of the speed at which events were now moving and of their importance to the purpose of his narrative. On the first of these three days, the Pharisees took their leave of John the Baptist. John had informed them that one who was greater than he was actually present among them, but they did not think it worthwhile to wait and see what this meant in practice. So they came and they saw, but probably left on the day preceding Jesus' arrival on the scene, thus missing the opportunity to hear John's testimony about Him.

On the second day in the series, John saw Jesus coming towards him and recognised Him as the 'man who is preferred before me, for he was before me', about whom he had previously spoken. John explained that he had come into the wilderness because God had sent him there, in order to reveal the Messiah to Israel. God had instructed him to baptise people (as a sign of their repentance), so that they would be ready to receive the One whom God was sending to them. God had also informed John that he would see the Spirit descend on the promised One, empowering Him for His mission in the world.

John had been filled with the Spirit from the womb of his mother Elizabeth and he had leaped within her when Jesus, in the womb of Mary, came near to him. Jesus now took the initiative and purposefully walked towards him. John instantly recognised Jesus as the One about whom God had spoken to him. John had obeyed God's call to come into the wilderness and baptise, and now he saw the promised One whom he was to reveal to Israel. John had come in obedience to God's call and had now seen the One of whom God had spoken. John's response, in a spirit of deep personal humility, was to divert attention away from himself and to direct all eyes towards Jesus. Although Jesus was six months younger than he was, John insisted that Jesus had existed before him and that He was in every respect greater.

This was a very dramatic moment, as John ceased to speak about the One who was to come and now proclaimed His arrival with the words, 'Behold, the Lamb of God, who takes away the sin of the world!' The Synoptic Gospels indicate that John's preaching had hitherto focused on the need for repentance and the prospect of coming judgement. He had previously described the Messiah as the One who would lay the axe to the root of the trees and would burn up the chaff with unquenchable fire.[1] John's choice of words, as he now introduced Jesus, is very significant. These words did not cancel John's previous statements, for Jesus will one day judge the world, but first He had come into the world to remove the sin that made such judgement necessary and otherwise inevitable. As we will see later, the apparent conflict between Jesus as judge and Jesus as saviour would cause problems for John the Baptist when he languished in prison.[2]

The description, 'Lamb of God, who takes away the sin of the world', obviously arose from John's Jewish worldview, as formed by the Scriptures and the contemporary understanding of them. The words would have had a specific reference point for people in

---

[1] Matt. 3:1-10; Luke 3:7-9.
[2] Luke 7:18-23.

the crowds who heard John speak. They would no doubt have connected the phrase with the animals that were sacrificed in the Temple for cleansing and forgiveness. The more popular expectation of the Messiah was as the king who would reign on David's throne, subsequently demonstrated in the events of Palm Sunday. However, there was also a recognition that the Scriptures spoke of a suffering Messiah, most vividly revealed in Isaiah's prophecy.[3] John's stated mission was to reveal the Messiah to Israel but, consciously or unconsciously, his words also revealed a wider purpose that included the Gentile world as well.

When Jesus was baptised, John saw the sign that God had promised him. This was not in order to identify Jesus as the Messiah, for John was already aware of this, but to reveal the way in which Jesus would live as a man on earth and how He would make it possible for His followers to follow His example. John saw the Spirit not only descend upon Jesus but also remain on Him. This was different from past times when the Spirit would come upon a chosen person for a particular season and purpose. Jesus' work in death and resurrection would allow the Spirit to come and live within God's people in intimate relationship. They would be guided and empowered by the Spirit in the same way as Jesus was.

So John had come into the wilderness in obedience to God's word and had been given several revelations of Jesus' identity and role as Messiah. Having seen all of this he responded with worship and witness: 'This is the Son of God.'

> *1:35-39 Again, the next day, John was standing with two of his disciples, and he looked at Jesus as he walked, and said, 'Behold, the Lamb of God!'*
>
> *The two disciples heard him speak, and they followed Jesus. Jesus turned and saw them following, and said to them, 'What are you looking for?'*
>
> *They said to him, 'Rabbi' (which is to say, being interpreted, Teacher), 'where are you staying?'*
>
> *He said to them, 'Come, and see.'*

---

[3] Isa. 53:1-12.

They came and saw where he was staying, and they stayed with him that day. It was about the tenth hour.

The third day is often significant in Scripture, and this new day that had dawned was the third day in the sequence of events.[4] On the previous day Jesus had approached John, but now He walked away never to return. As John stood watching the retreating figure, he knew that he had one last task to perform. He had declared that the coming One, now revealed to be Jesus, was much greater than he himself was. Now his actions had to match up to those spoken words, for he would have to give away his ministry and also his devoted disciples. This was costly, but John did not hesitate to call out, 'Behold, the Lamb of God!' There is a discrepancy within the account of the *Akeda* (the binding of Isaac) in Genesis 22 that was noted by Jewish scholars and is relevant here. In response to Isaac's question, 'Where is the lamb for a burnt offering?' Abraham replied, 'God will provide himself[5] the lamb for a burnt offering, my son.' Curiously, God, on this occasion, provided a ram caught in a thicket by its horns rather than the lamb that Abraham and Isaac had envisaged. This incident was prophetic of the Messiah through whom God provided the sacrifice, to Himself, of a willing lamb rather than an involuntary ram.[6]

John and Andrew, as yet unnamed, also had to make an instant choice, one that would shape their lives and destinies. Should they leave the charismatic prophet and his proven and successful ministry and follow the unfamiliar person of Jesus, with no guarantee of the outcome? Moments later, John watched them hurry after Jesus and then disappear with Him into the distance. It was simultaneously the climax and the beginning of the end of his own ministry: a corn of wheat had to fall into the ground and die if the long-awaited harvest was to materialise. John had come and he had seen; now his response was clear and unreserved and fixed.[7]

Jesus turned and asked the two men, 'What are you looking for?' Clearly they were looking for the Messiah and, prompted by

---

[4] See note on John 2:1.
[5] Lit. 'to himself'.
[6] Gen. 22:7-8, 13; Isa. 53:7.
[7] John 3:30; 12:24.

John, they had set out in pursuit of Jesus, but they were not yet ready for this simple but searching question. They had heard John's witness to Jesus but they were not yet comfortable to share the deepest longings of their hearts with Him. They addressed Jesus as 'Rabbi', employing an honorific but non-committal title and, in typically Jewish fashion, they replied with a question of their own, 'Where are you staying?' Jesus took their question at face value and replied in a way that was both disarming and revealing: 'Come, and see.' He did not give information, but rather He opened a door to relationship.

They came, they saw, and they remained. Although their remaining was temporary at this stage, it served to define the nature of true discipleship as being with Jesus.[8] They arrived at the house at the tenth hour (4pm). John's Gospel contains many references to precise times, pointing to the fact that John was present at the various events described therein. Presumably they stayed for the night. There is no record of what was said and done during that evening or on the following morning, but it was sufficient to convince them that the Rabbi was indeed the Messiah whom they had been seeking, and of whom John the Baptist had been speaking.[9] Of course, their understanding of Jesus' identity as the Messiah would have been very limited at this stage, and would have been coloured by current expectations that the Messiah would be a political leader. They would discover the true situation as they journeyed with Him during the next two to three years.

---

[8] John 6:66-69; Mark 3:13-14; Matt. 19:27.
[9] John 7:6-8, 30, 32, 44; 12:27; 13:1; 17:4.

6

John 1:40-51
Come and See

> *1:40-42 One of the two who heard John and followed him was Andrew, Simon Peter's brother. He first found his own brother, Simon, and said to him, 'We have found the Messiah!' (which is, being interpreted, Christ). He brought him to Jesus.*
>
> *Jesus looked at him, and said, 'You are Simon the son of Jonah. You shall be called Cephas' (which is by interpretation, Peter).*

Very soon after this Andrew sought out his brother Simon and, breathless with excitement, blurted out, 'We have found the Messiah!' That's what (who) they had been looking for. The implication is clear: a group of young men from Galilee had been on a quest to find the Messiah. John the Baptist seemed to be the 'Elijah who was to come', so they followed him in the hope and expectation that the Messiah would soon be revealed.[1] This is the first in a series of incidents that include the word 'found', which raises the question, who was seeking and who was finding? The usual Jewish answer to a question of this sort is that everyone was both a seeker and a finder. Andrew personified the archetypical disciple/evangelist as he shared the good news that he had just discovered. He did not just share information but also introduced Simon to Jesus.

This information about how Jesus first met Peter, Andrew and John helps to explain the accounts in the Synoptic Gospels (Matthew, Mark and Luke). The impression from Matthew and Mark is that a complete stranger called a group of fishermen to follow Him and, without further ado, they immediately left their

---

[1] Dan. 9:24-27.

nets and families and accompanied Him. Luke's expanded version includes the miracle of a huge catch of fish, focusing on Peter's awestruck and terrified response as the identity of Jesus suddenly overwhelmed him. He became acutely aware of his sinfulness and the danger of being close to such power and holiness. This mismatch of sin and holiness was the problem that the people of Israel had faced in the wilderness, and God had provided the solution in the form of the Tabernacle. Jesus' human body was God's true tabernacle, allowing people like Peter to come close to Him. Jesus reassured him with characteristic words, 'Don't be afraid.'[2]

When Jesus first encountered Simon, He 'looked at him' with prophetic insight and gave him a new name that marked a transition point in his life. Changing names was an ancient practice in Israel. God gave Abram a new name at a critical point in his life, when the promised son Isaac was about to be conceived. Abram meant 'high father' and Abraham meant 'father of a multitude'. Similarly, Jacob was renamed Israel when he had a close encounter with God and was about to re-enter the Promised Land after a long exile in Haran. As would be the case with Simon/Peter, both names continued to be used while character transformation was under way.[3] *Cephas* is equivalent to 'stone' or 'rock', suggesting 'firm/unyielding/stable', which were not native qualities in impulsive and reactive Simon. Jesus saw what Simon was not yet but would become as they journeyed together.[4]

It is surely significant that John chose to retain three Hebrew or Aramaic words rather than simply use the Greek equivalents. By so doing he is emphasising the Jewish culture of which Jesus, humanly speaking, was a product. It also reveals John's own Hebrew roots and worldview. *Rabbi* is simply a transliteration from Hebrew into Greek, and is explained as meaning 'teacher'. *Cephas* has Aramaic origins, but a similar word meaning 'rocks' is found in two Hebrew texts in the Scriptures.[5]

---

[2] Matt. 4:18-22; Mark 1:16-20; Luke 5:1-11.

[3] Gen. 17:5, 15-16; 32:28;. 46:2, 5.

[4] Matt. 16:16, 18, 22-23; 26:33; Luke 22:31-34, 54-62; John 21:15-19.

[5] Job 30:6; Jer. 4:29.

John's use of a transliterated version of the Hebrew word *Messiah* is particularly significant to his purpose of revealing Jesus' identity, for He was the embodiment of all the promises of the former Scriptures. The Greek word *Christ* also means 'Anointed One', but it lacks the historical and prophetic roots of the Hebrew word. In the apostolic era, when John's Gospel was written, the word *Christ* could be used interchangeably with *Messiah*, but it gradually lost much of its original content as the predominantly Gentile church became increasingly divorced from its Hebrew roots. This eventually became a deliberate policy in response to Jewish rejection of Jesus as Messiah.

Many contemporary Christians appear to regard Jesus Christ as the founder of a new religion – Christianity – whereas He is the fulfilment of and central person in the one faith that began with Abraham and will persist until the end of time.

1:43-51 On the next day, he was determined to go out into Galilee, and he found Philip. Jesus said to him, 'Follow me.'

Now Philip was from Bethsaida, of the city of Andrew and Peter. Philip found Nathanael, and said to him, 'We have found him, of whom Moses in the law, and the prophets, wrote: Jesus of Nazareth, the son of Joseph.'

Nathanael said to him, 'Can any good thing come out of Nazareth?' Philip said to him, 'Come and see.'

Jesus saw Nathanael coming to him, and said about him, 'Behold, an Israelite indeed, in whom is no deceit!'

Nathanael said to him, 'How do you know me?'

Jesus answered him, 'Before Philip called you, when you were under the fig tree, I saw you.'

Nathanael answered him, 'Rabbi, you are the Son of God! You are King of Israel!'

Jesus answered him, 'Because I told you, "I saw you underneath the fig tree," do you believe? You will see greater things than these!' He said to him, 'Most certainly, I tell you all, hereafter you will see heaven opened, and the angels of God ascending and descending on the Son of Man.'

The next day Jesus set out for Galilee. It is not clear whether He travelled to Bethsaida on the north shore of the lake or met with Philip and Nathanael elsewhere in the region. What does seem clear is that this first group of disciples consisted of friends who shared a common quest to find the Messiah. Jesus now took the initiative and found Philip, who responded to His invitation to follow Him. At first sight this may seem strange, but perhaps there is a clue in Philip's subsequent statement to Nathanael: 'We have found him, of whom Moses in the law, and the prophets, wrote: Jesus of Nazareth, the son of Joseph.' Philip had been convinced as a result of his personal interaction with Jesus, and from listening to Him as He explained the Scriptures. Probably Andrew and John had previously experienced something similar during their overnight stay with Jesus. Later, following His resurrection, He said to them, 'This is what I told you, while I was still with you, that all things which are written in the law of Moses, the prophets, and the psalms, concerning me must be fulfilled.'[6] These men were hungry to discover the truth and they had set no preconditions on how they would respond when they found it. They had no personal agendas to protect, in contrast with others whom we will meet again later in the Gospel.

Philip's immediate thought was similar to Andrew's: I must share this news with my friend Nathanael who is also seeking the Messiah. Nathanael's logic suggested that the second part of Philip's news, 'Jesus of Nazareth, the son of Joseph', cancelled out the first part, 'We have found [the Messiah].' It seems that Nazareth did not enjoy a good reputation, so 'good news' combined with 'Nazareth' constituted an oxymoron. Philip could have argued with Nathanael about this but, wisely, he chose a different strategy and invited him to 'Come and see'. Perhaps Philip took his cue from the way Jesus had extended a similar invitation to Andrew and John.[7] Philip's friendship and honest testimony overcame Nathanael's prejudice and scepticism and he was willing to investigate the matter for himself. This may be the earliest example of friendship evangelism; we should not reject

---

6 Luke 24:44.
7 John 1:39.

people who do not immediately respond to our offer of the good news.

So Nathanael came to see for himself. Jesus interacted with Nathanael in a fascinating way that had deep roots in the Scriptures. He began by disarming Nathanael with the statement, 'Behold, an Israelite indeed, in whom is no deceit!' Jesus saw a heart that thirsted for integrity and truth.

Nathanael knew that this was no mere flattery, and was hooked and drawn in by this unexpected insight: 'How do you know me?'

Jesus replied in a way that seems strange unless something else was going on under the surface: 'Before Philip called you, when you were under the fig tree, I saw you.'

Nathanael's response, coming from an erstwhile sceptic, was nothing short of astounding, and at first sight it seems inexplicable: 'Rabbi, you are the Son of God! You are the King of Israel!'

The mystery deepened as Jesus said (in effect), you think that's amazing, but you haven't seen anything yet! 'Most certainly, I tell you all, hereafter you will see heaven opened, and the angels of God ascending and descending on the Son of Man.'[8]

We have to ask ourselves, 'What is going on here? There must be more than meets the eye.' Of course there was and, as usual, the keys are contained in the Scriptures. Nathanael was sitting under a fig tree, a place of *shalom* and a good place to meditate on the Word of God.[9] Possibly he was reflecting on the story of Jacob, whose name implied deceit but who was transformed into Israel by a direct encounter with God. It seems likely that Nathanael had been pondering on the meaning of the dream that Jacob had seen at Bethel, when heaven and earth were joined by a mysterious stairway, thus creating access to God.[10] It was some kind of

---

[8] Throughout the text of the Gospels the WEBBE translates *amen, amen* as 'most certainly', whereas in other parts of the New Testament the same two Hebrew words are retained, as is the case in the Greek text. This translation reduces the force of the words from a statement of absolute and final authority to an expression of assurance. Jesus is the Amen: Rev. 3:14. *Amen, amen* is utilised in all of my subsequent comments.

[9] Mic. 4:4; Zech. 3:10.

[10] Gen. 27:36; 32:24-32; 28:10-22.

prophecy, but what could it mean? Could it be pointing to the Messiah for whom they were earnestly looking?

Jesus had seen Nathanael's location before Philip had spoken to him, and He had read his thoughts and knew the deepest longings of his heart. Who else could do such things except the Messiah, the Son of God and the King of Israel![11] Nathanael had been willing to accept the invitation to 'come and see', and now the former sceptic was lost in wonder, love and praise. His scepticism evaporated when he encountered Philip's new friend, and he was willing to listen to what He had to say and give Him a fair hearing. Jesus subsequently promised that the truth would be revealed to anyone who has a genuine desire to do God's will.[12] It is sad that many people are unwilling to make the radical changes that faith and commitment will require; others are not prepared to devote the time and effort that a thorough examination of the evidence would require, preferring to respond with stock objections.

Nathanael said to Jesus, 'You are the Son of God', but Jesus referred to Himself as the 'Son of Man'. We will explore the significance of this title in a later chapter.

The stairway connecting earth and heaven could not be constructed from below, for man's attempts to do this always end in failure and disaster.[13] Jesus came down from heaven, as Son of God and Son of Man, so that we could share fellowship with the Father here on earth, and then live in His immediate presence forever.[14]

Nathanael also called Jesus the 'King of Israel'. Nathanael, like other Jews of his day, expected that the Messiah would come as king. The angel Gabriel confirmed this when he informed Mary that her son would be conceived by the Holy Spirit. Jesus was acclaimed as king by the crowds who welcomed Him to Jerusalem on Palm Sunday. Pilate, perhaps in an act of retaliation against the

---

[11] These three aspects of the Coming One are present in the account of the visit of the wise men to Herod, Matt. 2:1-4.

[12] John 7:17.

[13] Gen. 3:5-6; 11:1-9.

[14] John 3:13-17, 6:33, 51, 58, 14:1-6; 17:24-26.

Jewish leaders, placarded this title on the cross.[15] Immediately before Jesus ascended to heaven, the disciples asked Him if He was about to restore the Kingdom to Israel. The question was not relevant to the immediate mission on which He was about to send them, which was to proclaim the good news of salvation to ever widening circles of people. At that moment the question was theoretical rather than practical and the answer could await its appointed time.

The disciples, like John the Baptist, correctly anticipated that all the promises concerning the Messiah would be literally and physically fulfilled, including His reign as the King of Israel, but they did not understand that this would happen in two stages.[16]

When a prophecy in the Hebrew Scriptures was couched in physical terms it was usually fulfilled in a physical way, such as Jesus' birth in Bethlehem and His coming out of Egypt.[17] Prophecies that were clothed in metaphorical language were also usually fulfilled in literal and physical ways, even if the manner was not initially apparent.[18] We who live in the interval between His first and second comings have the advantage of identifying those prophecies of Scripture that still await their fulfilment. There is no reason to assume that the as yet unfulfilled prophecies have only an allegorical or metaphorical sense, as some do, rather than the physical and literal sense that characterised His first coming. The prophet Zechariah predicted that the feet of the Messiah would stand on the Mount of Olives, and this was affirmed by the angels when Jesus ascended from that site. Jesus said to Jerusalem that He would only return there when its inhabitants were ready with the words of greeting from Psalm 118: 'Blessed is he who comes in the LORD's name! We have blessed you out of the LORD's house.'[19]

---

15 Luke 1:31-33; John 12:12-15; 19:19-22.

16 Acts 1:3, 6-7; Luke 7:18-23.

17 Mic. 5:2 and Matt. 2:4-6; Hos. 11:1 and Matt. 2:13-15.

18 Jer. 31:15 and Matt. 2:16-18.

19 Zech. 14:3-4; Acts 1:9-12; Luke 13:33-35; Ps. 118:26.

7

John 2:1-12
A Wedding and the First Sign

> *2:1-5 The third day, there was a wedding in Cana of Galilee. Jesus' mother was there. Jesus also was invited, with his disciples, to the wedding.*
>
> *When the wine ran out, Jesus' mother said to him, 'They have no wine.'*
>
> *Jesus said to her, 'Woman, what does that have to do with you and me? My hour has not yet come.'*
>
> *His mother said to the servants, 'Whatever he says to you, do it.'*

As previously noted, the third day marks a specific period of time and also has major symbolic significance in Scripture, with its climax in the resurrection on the third day.[1] The miracle here described would become the launching pad for Jesus' journey to the cross and the empty tomb. Biblical writers of stories, parables and poetry frequently used literary structures to underscore the truth that they presented. The present section is crafted in the form of inverse parallelism as a means of highlighting two dramatic transitions that were taking place.[2] Jesus was redefining His most important relationships, from being a son and a brother in a nuclear family to becoming the leader of a new kind of family. He was also demonstrating the character of the new movement that He was inaugurating: the Kingdom of God.

Jesus' baptism, His anointing by the Holy Spirit and the affirmation by the Father were the background events to these

---

[1] Gen. 22:4; 40:20; 42:18; Exod. 19:1-16; Josh. 1:11; Hos. 6:1-2; Jonah 1:17; Matt. 12:40; John 2:19-20; Mark 9:31.

[2] See Appendix 1.

radical changes in relationships. Jesus would have celebrated His bar mitzvah (son of the Law) at the age of around twelve or thirteen. Following this, a Jewish boy is considered to be personally responsible to God for His choices and actions. Jesus would probably have taken this step during the same year in which He remained in the Temple with the teachers after the Feast of Passover, while His parents set out on the return journey to Nazareth. At that age Jesus was already aware that He was God's Son in a unique sense, but He still remained subject to His parents as the process of maturing through adolescence into manhood continued.[3] He arrived at the wedding courtesy of His mother, but departed in the leading role of a group that comprised His mother, His brothers and His fledgling disciples. His natural family were welcome to be part of His journey, but from now on primary relationships would depend on faith and loyalty rather than kinship. At a later time His brothers became sceptical and attempted to manipulate Him, but Jesus responded by sending them on their way while He followed His Father's instructions, in company with His committed disciples.[4]

We have already been introduced to some of the members of this new family: John, Andrew, Peter, Philip and Nathanael (Cana was his home town). Their relationships with Jesus were still at an early stage. They had affirmed belief in Him as Messiah, and Nathanael had described Him in even more exalted language, but Jesus had not formally called them and they continued in their previous occupations.

The words 'believe' and 'disciple' are both used in a variety of ways in John's Gospel; the particular context is important in determining the actual level of faith and commitment. Just prior to the events at the wedding, these five men had embarked on the process of becoming disciples and already had a measure of true faith. That faith was about to be strengthened by the revelation of Jesus' glory, and this would help them to face the challenges that lay ahead and to become truly His disciples.[5] As the account in the

---

[3] Luke 2:45-52.

[4] Mark 3:20-21, 31-35; John 7:1-10; 11:14-16.

[5] John 21:2; Luke 5:1-11, 27-28; John 8:31-32.

Gospel unfolds, we shall meet other people who were also called disciples and who were said to have believed in Jesus, but their commitment was superficial and temporary and they deserted Him when they took offence at His words. The reality of the faith that we initially profess is either confirmed or contradicted by whether or not we continue in the path of discipleship, wherever it leads. Jesus assures us that if we walk the journey of life with Him, then there will be abundant evidence that we have chosen the right path.[6]

As in other parts of the Gospel, John referred to time in two senses: clock time and symbolically important time. When Mary prompted Jesus to take action, He replied, 'My hour [time] has not yet come.' During the entire period of His ministry He remained conscious of His destiny, and He was also conscious of the significance of each stage as He encountered it. Jesus did not have a prearranged schedule, like a journal written in advance or a route marked on a map. The way the events unfolded at this wedding illustrate how the Holy Spirit revealed the details of the Father's purposes to Jesus in a dynamic and ongoing way. In this way He was demonstrating how His followers would also live and function after they had received the Holy Spirit.[7]

By now Mary would now have been about forty-five years old, but memories from her teenage years must have remained strong and vivid. She would have been aware that the prophetic words spoken in those days were beginning to be fulfilled.[8] Jesus had arrived at the wedding accompanied by some recently acquired disciples, and no doubt she was aware of the events that had occurred during the previous week at the Jordan River.

Wine was a symbol of joy (the Aramaic word for wedding feast is *mistila*, literally, 'drink festival'), so the failure in supply was very embarrassing.[9] Mary seems to have perceived the providential nature of a situation that others would have regarded as a disaster. We may wonder whether her words to Jesus, 'They have no wine', were simply the result of a mother's intuition or were inspired by

---

[6] John 6:53-71; 11:21-27, 39-40.

[7] Luke 4:1, 14; 6:12-16; Mark 1:35-38; John 5:19-20; 20:19-23.

[8] Luke 1:31-35; 2:25-35.

[9] Ps. 104:15; Isa. 16:10.

the Holy Spirit. Probably both were involved, for she was very sensitive to God.[10] It seems that Jesus received His prompt from the Father slightly later than Mary.

On two occasions prior to the miracle John referred to Mary as 'Jesus' mother', in a context that suggested her position of seniority. At this point of transition in His life Jesus needed to establish that He no longer accepted direction from any other human being, however much He respected and loved him or her. Jesus revealed this in His response: 'Woman, what does that have to do with you and me? My hour has not yet come.' Jesus' words were respectful, but the message was clear: their relationship was changing. For her part, Mary was beginning to experience the reality of Simeon's prophecy to her when he saw her infant son, the approach of the sword that would pierce her heart. Later, as she stood by the cross, that sword inflicted a deep wound in her soul, and Jesus lovingly committed her to John's care. A short time later, Jesus committed Himself to the Father, and then a Roman spear pierced His own side.[11]

Mary responded to Jesus' words without argument or bitterness, just as she had done as the teenage girl who had said 'Let it be done to me according to your word.'[12] She accepted Jesus' claim to independence, recognising that the time for this had come. The ancient instruction about marriage was being invoked: 'Therefore a man will leave his father and his mother, and will join with his wife, and they will be one flesh.' In a sense, Jesus had previously left His Father when He came to earth; now He was leaving His mother, in order to be betrothed to His bride, the church, the disciples who were already gathering to Him and all those who would follow in their train.[13] Mary then issued the only instruction attributed to her in the Gospels: 'Whatever he says to you, do it.'

---

10 Luke 1:38; 1:46-55; 2:51.

11 Luke 2:34-35; John 19:25-27, 34.

12 Luke 1:38.

13 Gen. 2:24; Matt. 19:5-6; 2 Cor. 11:2; Eph. 5:31-32; Rev. 19:7-9; Rev. 21:2, 9.

2:6-12 Now there were six water pots of stone set there after the Jews'
way of purifying, containing two or three metretes apiece. Jesus said to
them, 'Fill the water pots with water.' So they filled them up to the brim.

He said to them, 'Now draw some out, and take it to the ruler of the
feast.' So they took it.

When the ruler of the feast tasted the water now become wine, and
didn't know where it came from (but the servants who had drawn the
water knew), the ruler of the feast called the bridegroom and said to him,
'Everyone serves the good wine first, and when the guests have drunk
freely, then that which is worse. You have kept the good wine until now!'

This beginning of his signs Jesus did in Cana of Galilee, and revealed
his glory; and his disciples believed in him. After this, he went down to
Capernaum, he, and his mother, his brothers, and his disciples; and they
stayed there a few days.

Six large stone water pots formed the centrepiece of the action.
They had recently held about 150 gallons of water but now stood
empty. The water would have been used for symbolic purification
of the bride by full immersion in a ritual bath (*mikveh*). This was
not a requirement of the Law but was 'after the Jews' way of
purifying'. 'The Jews' (Gk. *hoi iudaioi*, meaning 'the Judeans') is a
descriptive term with more than one meaning. It originated from
the name Judah, one of the sons of Jacob. His descendants were
known as the tribe of Judah, and the name was also applied to the
geographical area, including Jerusalem, where that tribe settled.
The term eventually came to be used more loosely, as it is today,
to include the whole people of Israel, the Jewish people. Almost
always John used the term in a more restricted and special sense,
to designate the religious leaders whose authority Jesus threatened.
We have already encountered them in the delegations to John the
Baptist from the priests (Sadducees) and the Pharisees. If we do
not understand this usage we may even conclude that John was
anti-Semitic, as some have suggested or, mistakenly, believe that
the nation as a whole was responsible for Jesus' death. In fact, Jesus
remained popular to the end. It was the leaders who felt
threatened, by His preaching, His miracle-signs and His claims
about His identity, and who engineered His death.

Water is described in two different ways in the Hebrew language. Static water collected in a cistern or container was considered less valuable than flowing water (living water, Heb. *mayim hayim*), and in John's Gospel it functions as a symbol for the Holy Spirit.[14] The empty water pots that had contained static water acted as symbols for the old order of tradition and human authority that was passing away. The Torah required people to undergo cleansing rituals following contact with dead bodies or contact with people who had some form of discharge from their bodies and in other specified situations. Additional regulations had been added by religious authorities: some were in the spirit of the original ones, but the Pharisees had gone to extremes, multiplying detailed rules and regulations. External rituals, which ordinary people were unable to keep, often replaced humility, generosity and love as the essence of holiness.

God had given the Torah as an exclusive gift to the nation of Israel, as is evident from the repeated command to Moses, 'Speak to the children of Israel', but this was for a limited period of time, until the Messiah would come.[15] Jesus was born into this religious environment and lived as a Torah-observant Jewish man.[16] He did not come in order to destroy that heritage but to bring it to its destiny and fulfilment, being Himself the goal of all the promises and prophecies contained in the Scriptures.[17] Thus the laws and rituals were about to become obsolete.

Jesus instructed the servants to refill the pots with water, which seem to have been stored out of sight, having served their purpose; the master of the feast appears to have been unaware of this part of the proceedings. The static water was not merely transformed into a better form of water but into wine, for Jesus was announcing the longed-for arrival of the Messianic kingdom. In the Scriptures this is characterised as a banquet with rich and abundant wine, the biblical symbol for joy. This miracle was a sign that the long-

---

[14] Prov. 5:15; Jer. 2:13; John 4:10-14; 7:37-39.

[15] Lev. 1:2, for example; Gal. 3:21-25; 4:1-7; Heb. 8:13; 9:11-15; 10:1-4.

[16] E.g., Luke 2:21-24, 41-42; John 2:13; 5:1; 7:1-10; Mark 1:40-44.

[17] Luke 24:25-27, 44-47; John 5:45-47; 6:30-35; Rom. 10:1-4; Heb. 9:19-28.

expected Messiah had finally come, full of the Holy Spirit and offering blessing, joy and abundant life to His people.[18]

At this wedding Jesus did not create wine *de novo*; Christianity is not a new, stand-alone religion, but continues the revelation that God gave to Israel. Israel's prophets form a vital part of the foundation of the church. Similarly, Paul likened Israel to an olive tree into which new branches have been grafted. God did not discard the olive tree and plant a Christmas tree![19] Jesus was inaugurating a new movement, 'the Kingdom of God', which was the culmination of all that had gone before. This was the Father's appointed time and Jesus was acting on His instructions and with His authority.[20]

The bridegroom at a wedding was responsible for providing the wine. When Jesus stepped in and supplied what was missing, He was making a prophetic statement. He is the heavenly bridegroom who will be the host at the marriage supper of the Lamb. It did not cost Him anything to supply wine for this earthly banquet, but He knew that He must drink the cup of suffering before the heavenly wedding banquet could begin. This He would do on the cross fewer than three years hence, paying an incalculable price in order to be in relationship with a purified and holy bride, the church that will last forever.[21]

This miracle also revealed Jesus' glory as the Creator of the world, now incarnate as a man. As the creative Word, He had made trees with the potential to transform water, in combination with other ingredients, into fruit. In the case of wine this requires a vine, a period of time for grape production and a further period for the process of fermentation. Jesus revealed His glory as the Word who made everything by completing the process in a moment, without intermediate and secondary means. He Himself is 'the true vine', the source of the full and abundant life of which the physical wine was but a symbol. Jesus promised that those who remain united with Him, as branches to a vine, will share the fullness of His joy.[22]

18 Isa. 25:6; Jer. 31:12; Joel 2:19, 24; 3:18; Amos 9:13-14.

19 1 Cor. 10:1; Eph. 2:20; Rom. 11:16-29.

20 Matt. 4:17; 12:25-28; Acts 1:3, 6; John 3:3.

21 Matt. 20:22; 26:27-29, 36-42; Eph. 5:25-32; Rev. 19:7-9.

22 Gen.1:11-13; Ps. 104:14-16; John 1:1-3, 10; 15:1-12.

A short time later Jesus moved on, leading a company that included His mother, His brothers and His disciples. They had all come to the wedding and had seen the miracle, but it seems that there were differing responses. They all travelled together to Capernaum but Jesus did not stay there for long. It is not clear whether or not His family continued to journey with Him when He left the town and, sometime later, travelled south to Jerusalem to keep the Passover. Mary does not appear in the record until, along with John, she is present at the cross. John's only further mention of Jesus' brothers is in the context of the Feast of Tabernacles, perhaps around two years later, when they reacted to Him in unbelief.[23]

Mark recorded an incident which probably took place in Capernaum; Jesus was speaking to a crowd of people indoors when His mother and brothers requested Him to come out and speak with them. A little earlier in his account Mark records that the family had come with the intention of seizing Him, believing that He was out of His mind. Jesus did not go out to them, and instead answered, 'Who are my mother and my brothers?" Looking around at those who sat around him, he said, "Behold, my mother and my brothers! For whoever does the will of God is my brother, my sister, and mother."'[24]

Jesus began to establish these priorities at the wedding in Cana as He began His public ministry. His new family consisted of His committed disciples, and His natural family would have been welcome to participate on the same terms, within this wider family. Happily, this did happen following the resurrection, and both His mother Mary and His brother James are named as members of the early church family. Jesus taught that, in a similar way, Jewish disciples would be joined by Gentile believers to form a common flock, one great family of faith throughout the earth.[25] The spiritual blessings promised to Abraham and his natural family would be extended to embrace the world, Jew and Gentile alike.

---

[23] John 19:25-27; 7:1-5.
[24] Mark 3:19b-21, 31-35.
[25] Acts 1:14; 15:13-19; John 3:16; 6:51; 10:16; Gen. 12:1-3; Gal. 3:6-9, 13-14.

8

John 2:13-25
Jesus in His Father's House

> *2:13-16* *The Passover of the Jews was at hand, and Jesus went up to Jerusalem. He found in the temple those who sold oxen, sheep, and doves, and the changers of money sitting. He made a whip of cords, and threw all out of the temple, both the sheep and the oxen; and he poured out the changers' money and overthrew their tables. To those who sold the doves, he said, 'Take these things out of here! Don't make my Father's house a marketplace!'*

Passover was the first of the three great annual pilgrim feasts of Israel. It recalled the redemption of Israel from slavery in Egypt, deliverance from death through the Passover Lamb and the birth of Israel as a nation. At Passover, tens of thousands of pilgrims would ascend to Jerusalem from the land of Israel and from the diaspora, together with proselytes and other Gentiles who were attracted to the God of Israel.

Jesus had been brought up in an observant Jewish family and would often have participated in the great pilgrim feasts in Jerusalem. As a twelve-year-old boy, Jesus had remained in the Temple after the festivities had ended and His family had departed for home. His worried parents subsequently found Him among the teachers, discussing the Scriptures with them. Jesus' explanation for this contained the expression 'my Father's house'. Jewish people were happy to speak of God as our Father, but this use of the first person singular was a very different matter, implying a unique relationship with God.[1] Now, as a mature man, He repeated the same words.

---

[1] Luke 2:41-50; Isa. 63:16; Isa. 64:8; Matt. 6:9.

Jesus travelled to this Passover celebration with the new family of His disciples. He had begun His ministry in Galilee so this visit to Jerusalem and the Temple was highly significant. Malachi had prophesied that the Lord, the messenger of the covenant, would suddenly come to His Temple and would take steps to purify it.[2] Jesus' action at this Passover fulfilled this prophecy and provoked a hostile reaction from the chief priests which would culminate in His death at another Passover, two or three years hence.

In describing the event as 'the Passover of the Jews', John was not merely stating the obvious fact that Passover was a Jewish festival as prescribed in the Torah (in contrast to other versions as celebrated by Samaritans and the Essenes). As previously explained, 'the Jews' does not refer to the Jewish people in general but has a narrower definition: the Jewish leaders. In the present case, the chief priests were a section of 'the Jews' who arranged and controlled affairs in the Temple and used them as a means to personal enrichment and advantage. The Temple was the only place where Passover lambs could be slaughtered and other sacrifices offered. All animals required inspection and approval by the Temple authorities. Also, at Passover, the obligatory Temple tax of half a shekel had to be paid in specified coinage.[3]

All of this was in the hands of the high priestly family and they took full advantage of this monopoly, charging a percentage for all financial transactions. The business area of the Temple had become known as the bazaars of the sons of Annas. Annas had been appointed as High Priest by the governor Quirinius in 6 CE and was deposed in CE 15. However, he kept the honorary title and remained the power-broker, a godfather figure, while five of his sons and his son-in-law Caiaphas successively held the official position. (There is an interesting suggestion that Jesus was making use of an old Jewish folk tale in the parable involving the rich man and Lazarus. People who heard the parable might have identified Annas, Caiaphas and the five brothers as counterparts to the characters in the traditional story.[4])

[2] Mal. 3:1-3.

[3] Deut. 16:5-6; Exod. 30:13; Matt. 17:24-27.

[4] Luke 16:19-31.

The senior priests were thus exceedingly rich. A large and luxurious 'millionaire's mansion', believed to have been the house of Caiaphas, has been uncovered in Jerusalem. Meanwhile, the heavily taxed peasantry were struggling simply to survive. The common people hated the chief priests on account of their ruthless avarice, and would take the opportunity to drive them from office during the Jewish revolt of CE 67–70.

Multitudes of people thronged the Temple courts in an atmosphere of noise and commotion, a veritable Middle Eastern bazaar. Animals were mooing and bleating and sellers were touting for business and haggling with customers, and meanwhile there was little concern for justice and mercy or for the sanctity of the place. It is significant that Jesus chose the occasion of this feast to commence His public activities in Jerusalem. John the Baptist had declared Jesus to be the Lamb of God, and here He was among the animals that were being selected for slaughter. His final visit to the Temple just prior to the crucifixion would be even more poignant and significant.

When Jesus came to the Temple and saw the desecration of the house where His Father had put His Name, He was horrified and enraged.[5] Jesus' voice would have been lost among the cacophony of sounds so, as Lord of the Temple, He took decisive and violent action. Jesus did not seek human permission because He carried all authority within Himself. There may also have been an element of tit-for-tat justice, for the servants of the senior priests were known to assault people while extorting money from them. Jesus would encounter a similar situation at His final Passover visit and would again be outraged, this time because the unscrupulous commerce was corrupting the Court of the Gentiles, where non-Jewish people should have been welcomed to share in the prayers of Israel.[6]

Jesus' action was totally unexpected, highly dramatic and shocking, and, with this initial confrontation, He was deliberately challenging the status quo and was claiming a unique identity and authority. The priests were probably aware that the oppressed and defrauded people would have secretly approved of His

[5] Gen. 6:5-7; 11:5-9; 18:20-21; Exod. 3:7-10; 32:19-20.
[6] Luke 2:41-50; Mark 11:15-18.

intervention. This may explain why they did not arrest Jesus or take other strong measures against Him. The ever-watchful eyes of the Romans in the Fortress Antonio were trained on the Temple courts, so the Jewish authorities could not risk provoking public disorder at this sensitive time; their positions depended on keeping things under wraps.

Jesus' words to the dove sellers were very significant: 'Don't make my Father's house a marketplace!' His use of the expression 'My Father's house' constituted a direct challenge to the leadership of the Temple, who later described it as 'our place'.[7] At this early stage in His ministry, Jesus thus defined the issues, His identity and His critique of their ungodly and corrupt leadership that would provoke them to a murderous hatred of Him. John's Gospel describes the stages through which this progressed to its conclusion.

> **2:17-22** *His disciples remembered that it was written, 'Zeal for your house will eat me up.'*
>
> *The Jews therefore answered him, 'What sign do you show us, seeing that you do these things?'*
>
> *Jesus answered them, 'Destroy this temple, and in three days I will raise it up.'*
>
> *The Jews therefore said, 'It took forty-six years to build this temple! Will you raise it up in three days?'*
>
> *But he spoke of the temple of his body. When therefore he was raised from the dead, his disciples remembered that he said this, and they believed the Scripture, and the word which Jesus had said.*

John described two contrasting responses to what Jesus had done. On the one hand, the disciples connected His words and actions with a statement in one of David's psalms: 'For the zeal of your house consumes me'.[8] As Jewish men they would have been aware that many of David's words, although immediately personal to himself, were also prophetic of the coming Messiah. This incident in the Temple helped them to see how Jesus was fulfilling the

---

[7] John 11:48.
[8] Ps. 69:9.

Scriptures, and reinforced their growing conviction that He was indeed the One who was to come.

The Jewish religious leaders, on the other hand, were unimpressed and deeply offended. In their eyes Jesus had acted in a totally outrageous way, and had done so in the place where they were officially in charge. It was a challenge to their authority, so they demanded that He must provide proof of His authority by performing a spectacular miracle. They would then pass judgement on whether or not the sign was sufficient to justify His actions. This was a futile demand, for they demonstrated later that no sign, even the resurrection of Lazarus who had been dead for four days, would be sufficient to convince them. On the contrary, this miracle was the event that would launch their final strategy to eliminate Jesus and the threat that He posed to their cherished position.[9] Jesus always refused to perform miracles to order, for He only acted at His Father's bidding. Following the resurrection He would send His disciples out to behave in a similar way.[10]

Instead of a sign, Jesus gave the priests an enigmatic reply, as was the case in His future debates with the Pharisees. He spoke to both groups of leaders in this way, in response to their attitudes and motivations. The Sadducean priests were corrupt and had a vested interest in the ungodly commerce that Jesus had disturbed. They were offended, not by the improper trade, but by Jesus' intervention to suspend it. His statement, obviously absurd if intended in a literal sense, should have led them to seek a possible deeper and spiritual meaning of His words. Instead, they reacted with disdain and ridicule and treated Jesus as a fool.

We know that the chief priests remembered Jesus' words and later used them in a devious way to accuse Him of threatening to destroy the Temple. They fulfilled the first part of His prediction by engineering His death, and Jesus then fulfilled the second part by rising from the dead. After this, Caiaphas the High Priest would attempt to suppress the evidence for the resurrection, and would silence witnesses in order to conceal the truth.[11]

---

9 John 11:48.
10 Matt. 12:38-39; 16:1-4; Luke 23:6-11; John 6:30-31; 20:21-22.
11 Matt. 26:59-61; 28:11-15; Acts 6:13-14.

In the days of Solomon, the Temple of stones had been filled with the glory of God, but that was short-lived and was also unique in the history of Israel. This incident pointed to a different sort of Temple: Jesus' body was now the true and appointed place for the presence of God to be fully revealed. Following His death and resurrection, that Temple would expand to include all those who would, in faith, be organically joined to Him. They would be living stones built up as a spiritual house on the chief cornerstone, Jesus Himself.[12]

Caiaphas plotted to kill Jesus because of his desire to preserve the Temple, which the members of the Council described as 'our place', not realising that Jesus' death was the one thing that would make that structure redundant. The building was only completed in CE 63, and seven years later it lay in ruins, as Jesus had predicted.[13] There is no consensus among scholars as to whether John wrote his Gospel before or after CE 70, but this has no bearing on how we read the text as fulfilment of Jesus' prophetic statement or on our understanding and experience of the spiritual Temple, in which we participate through relationship with Jesus.

Like the religious leaders, the disciples did not understand the hidden meaning of Jesus' words. They would only do so after He rose from the dead and then explained the relevant scriptures to them. Nevertheless, their response to Jesus was very different from that of the leaders. As had been the case with Nathanael, the disciples were open to the significance of the signs that He did. They had embarked on a relationship with Him and were prepared to trust Him and receive further evidence as and when He chose to supply it.

In contrast, the leaders occupied entrenched positions of privilege and power, and potentially they had much to lose. They viewed Jesus through a lens of personal interest, and this perspective increasingly blinded them to the truth. The disciples' eyes were gradually being opened while the Jewish leaders were simultaneously descending into darkness. This self-imposed blindness would lead them to choose a murderer rather than the

---

[12] 2 Chron. 5:13-14; John 1:14; 1 Pet. 2:4-8; Eph. 2:19-22.
[13] John 11:48; Matt. 24:1-2; Heb. 8:13.

Prince of Life and a pagan emperor in place of the Messiah King. Yet, in their wickedness and as priests, they would offer Jesus in sacrifice: the Lamb of God for the sins of the world.[14]

The Temple in Jerusalem had been corrupted by those who should have maintained its sanctity, but Jesus nevertheless called it 'My Father's house'. God had chosen the Temple as the place of His presence, where He said He would put His Name. It was also the central shrine where all Israel assembled to worship and where they gathered as a community of faith.[15] Human frailty, foolishness and sin meant that these blessings were not fully realised. Nevertheless, the Temple remained as a prophetic witness that one day, in the person of the Messiah, God would come into the midst of His people. So John wrote, 'The Word became flesh, and lived amongst us.' Jesus is the true Temple through whom we enter the presence of God.[16]

> **2:23-25** *Now when he was in Jerusalem at the Passover, during the feast, many believed in his name, observing his signs which he did. But Jesus didn't entrust himself to them, because he knew everyone, and because he didn't need for anyone to testify concerning man; for he himself knew what was in man.*

Jesus offered no signs in response to the priests' demands, but He did perform a number of miracle-signs in Jerusalem during the feast and many people believed in His name. At first sight this seems very positive, but Jesus did not appear to be impressed. He saw beneath the outer veneer of words into the condition of the people's hearts. He did not overestimate the significance of initial professions of faith and commitment, but neither did He give up on those who, like Peter, failed but longed for restoration. He does not commit Himself to those who follow the signs, but to those who sign up for the long haul.

---

[14] John 18:39-40; 19:15; 11:49-52.
[15] Deut. 12:4-5; 1 Chron. 22:1; 2 Chron. 6:18-21.
[16] Mal. 3:1; John 1:14.

9

John 3:1-10
Born of the Spirit – Born from Above

> *3:1-4* Now there was a man of the Pharisees named Nicodemus, a ruler of the Jews. The same came to him by night, and said to him, 'Rabbi, we know that you are a teacher come from God, for no one can do these signs that you do, unless God is with him.'
>
> Jesus answered him, 'Most certainly, I tell you, unless one is born anew, he can't see God's Kingdom.'
>
> Nicodemus said to him, 'How can a man be born when he is old? Can he enter a second time into his mother's womb, and be born?'

Two main groups of Jewish leaders – Sadducean priests and Pharisees – were introduced in the context of official visits to investigate the activities of John the Baptist. Jesus had confronted the senior priests within their place of authority – the Temple – at a time of maximum public exposure – the Feast of Passover. The priests do not appear again in John's Gospel until the final Passover of Jesus' ministry. During that interval their disquiet about Jesus' activities and His claims about Himself would intensify.

The Pharisees now became the main public antagonists of Jesus, and they would become increasingly angry and frustrated when their best attempts to discredit Him failed. Their dual focus was on Jesus' refusal to comply with their very strict interpretation of the Sabbath laws and on His claims to have a unique relationship with the God of Israel. There was another unspoken agenda: the claims that Jesus made about Himself and the accompanying miracle-signs were a threat to their self-appointed role as guardians of truth. Eventually the two groups – Sadducees and Pharisees, who were not natural friends or allies – would unite in the face of a common threat to their status as religious leaders. By that stage both parties would have descended deeply into the same spiritual and moral condition where they could not distinguish darkness from light.

Nicodemus was the first Pharisee to have a face-to-face encounter with Jesus. This did not take place in public but was intentionally private, under cover of darkness. Nicodemus was an elite member of his group, being described both as a ruler and as a member of the ruling council. Jesus was aware of Nicodemus' reputation as a teacher in Israel; as a twelve-year-old boy He would probably have encountered similar people when engaged in the question-and-answer session in the Temple. The present interaction was similar in nature except that Jesus assumed the role of authority.

Nicodemus opened the discussion by paying Jesus a compliment, the final words even hinting at the Hebrew word *Immanuel*. He, a distinguished teacher, was giving Jesus an honoured position alongside himself, so he must have been taken aback when Jesus brushed the compliment aside, claimed to speak with ultimate authority and challenged Nicodemus to act in accordance with what he had just said: 'Rabbi, we know that you are a teacher come from God, for no one can do these signs that you do, unless God is with him.' John subsequently recorded that other Pharisees would see similar evidence in abundance but refuse to reach the obvious conclusion because of the consequences that this would have for their way of life.

As previously noted, 'most certainly' corresponds to the Hebrew *Amen, Amen*.[1] On three occasions Jesus used this formula as He responded to Nicodemus' statements or questions. Jesus did not appeal to the sayings of famous scholars or even to Scripture, but spoke directly on His own authority, as He did on other occasions, such as the Sermon on the Mount.[2]

Jesus' initial reply contained two phrases that would have challenged Nicodemus at the core of his identity: 'born anew' and 'God's Kingdom'. These concepts contradicted his worldview and

---

[1] See chapter 6, footnote 8.
[2] Matt. 5:18 20, 22, 26, 28, 32, 34, 39, 44.

caused him confusion and discomfort. As a Jewish scholar, Nicodemus would have understood the Kingdom of God as referring to the period of the Messiah's reign on earth. As an observant and pious Jew, he would have considered himself to be an insider, a member of that Kingdom and awaiting its visible manifestation in the days of the Messiah. Jesus appeared to be treating him as an outsider, alongside impious Jews, Samaritans and Gentiles!

Pharisees engaged in mission to win Gentiles as converts to the Jewish faith, who would then qualify to enter the family of Israel as proselytes. The final stage in that process was immersion in a ritual bath (*mikveh*), from which a Gentile would emerge as one newly born and would be considered as equal to natural-born Jews in every important respect. Jesus was claiming that everyone, Jews and Gentiles alike, required a new birth in order to be part of the Kingdom of God. His words were incomprehensible and insulting, and they contradicted Nicodemus' view of his special status as one of God's chosen people.[3]

The phrase 'born anew' could equally be translated 'born from above'.[4] The former expression refers to an event on earth and the latter to its source in heaven. Jesus seems to have intended both of these, with the main emphasis on the second, but Nicodemus recognised only the earthly component and its physical dimension. Perhaps he was hoping to avoid the issue altogether for, if interpreted in a literal way, these words were nonsensical. He had no other frame of reference by which to understand them, so he was totally foxed.

> *3:5-8 Jesus answered, 'Most certainly I tell you, unless one is born of water and spirit, he can't enter into God's Kingdom. That which is born of the flesh is flesh. That which is born of the Spirit is spirit. Don't marvel that I said to you, "You must be born anew." The wind blows where it wants to, and you hear its sound, but don't know where it comes from and where it is going. So is everyone who is born of the Spirit.'*

---

[3] Matt. 23:15; John 8:31-42.

[4] Leon Morris, *The Gospel according to John,* p. 188.

For the second time Jesus answered with the emphatic, *'Amen, Amen* I say to you.' He reasserted the complete impossibility of becoming part of the Kingdom of God apart from this mysterious birth experience, and He now raised the issue to a higher and spiritual plane. Jesus often cloaked spiritual truths in physical metaphors that were then frequently misunderstood – for example, water, bread, sleep, leaven and even His flesh.[5] He now explained to Nicodemus that the new birth meant an inner spiritual transformation, the infusion of a new life that would give rise to a new way of living. Nicodemus' systematic learning and settled religious practices could contribute nothing to the process. Physical birth reproduces physical flesh; birth by the Holy Spirit gives rise to spiritual nature in the likeness of God. This was, of course, supremely and uniquely true of Jesus, who was conceived by the Holy Spirit before being physically born of a virgin mother.[6]

Beliefs about the new birth vary in different sections of the church. Some Protestants use the expression 'born-again Christian' to mean a person who has made a decision for Christ. This may indeed be the beginning of a genuine spiritual transformation, but it is not always the case. This definition also tends to emphasise human choice rather than the sovereign action of the Spirit. Other groups insist that believers' baptism is essential for salvation. Roman Catholic and similar churches consider that new birth is mediated through the sacrament of water baptism, to some extent relying on Jesus' words in John 3.

These different approaches highlight the problems that arise from reading the New Testament backwards through the lens of church history and tradition, both ancient and modern. We need to read forwards from the Hebrew roots of the Bible and from the standpoint of those who heard the words in their original context. By doing so we will discover that the new birth is neither the application of a sacrament nor agreement with a statement of doctrine, but is rather the infusion of spiritual life by a sovereign act of God the Holy Spirit.

---

[5] John 4:10-11; Matt. 16:5-12; John 11:11-14; Matt. 13:33-35; John 6:51-52.
[6] 1 Cor. 6:17.

We also need to understand how Jesus used the symbolism of water, as John recorded in this Gospel. 'Born of water and spirit' should be regarded as parallel statements rather than as two separate categories. John's baptism in water was God's way of preparing for the coming of His Saviour, the Messiah. It was also a prophetic picture and promise of how the Messiah would, after His ascension, baptise His disciples in the Holy Spirit. Jesus' life, death and resurrection would open the way for the Spirit to be poured out on all who would believe and receive. The Spirit *is* the living water that Jesus promised to the Samaritan woman and also proclaimed at the Feast of Tabernacles.[7]

The proud Pharisees had investigated and rejected John's baptism and had thus refused God's offer of new life.[8] Nicodemus and his colleagues needed to humble themselves, just as other people had done. Jesus was challenging him to change his attitude, in other words to repent. In order to experience such spiritual transformation, Nicodemus needed to submit his whole being to the unfettered and sovereign Spirit of God. The Holy Spirit is like the wind – beyond human control and utterly free and unconstrained by human tradition.

> **3:9-10** *Nicodemus answered him, 'How can these things be?'*
>
> *Jesus answered him, 'Are you the teacher of Israel, and don't understand these things?'*

Perhaps now Nicodemus, having abandoned the absurd physical interpretation of Jesus' words, was still thinking, 'How can a man be born when he is old?' Now perhaps he was feeling the sense of regret that is common in the latter stages of life and in the awareness of many failures and missed opportunities. Was Jesus suggesting that the past, with all of this, could be wiped out and a fresh new life begun? That too would be an astonishing miracle, beyond the power of imagination.

Mary asked a parallel question when Gabriel informed her that the baby would be conceived in her womb without a human father.

---

[7] John 4:10, 13-14; 7:37-39.
[8] Luke 7:30.

She was humble and trusting and easily satisfied with the angel's simple statement, 'For nothing spoken by God is impossible', and his explanation that the Holy Spirit would bring it about.[9] The fulfilment of God's covenant promises to Israel had regularly required intervention 'from above'. Ordinary flesh-and-blood people had been transformed as a result of direct encounters with God and when they were anointed by His Spirit. The birth stories of Isaac and Samuel, and, more recently, of John the Baptist, bore striking witness to this great truth. Before she bore Isaac, God had asked Sarah, 'Is anything too hard for the LORD?' The Patriarch Jacob had become Israel as a result of his encounter with the angel of the Lord. [10] This truth was also demonstrated in the great national deliverances that God had sent through people such as Deborah, Gideon and Samson.[11] God had promised that, in the days of the Messiah, He would pour out His Spirit on all flesh.

The 'teacher of Israel' knew the stories but he had not connected them with the practicalities of life or with possibilities for radical change in himself. As a Pharisee, Nicodemus believed in the supernatural but, perhaps like some church members, only as a doctrine. Jesus' words, 'So is everyone who is born of the Spirit', contain a challenge for His followers in every generation. How quickly a real and experiential encounter with God the Holy Spirit can lapse into religious routine and come under human control. Outward manifestations of a previous spiritual renewal or revival may persist in the absence of current intimacy with God. Also, the beneficiaries of one move of the Spirit may become critics of the next, because it differs in external appearance. We all need to expect that the supernatural power and presence of God will actually break into human lives and transform them, physically or spiritually or both.

---

[9] Luke 1:30-38.
[10] Gen. 18:14; 32:24-31.
[11] Judg. 4:4-10; 6:11-14; 14:19; 16:28-30.

John 3:11-21
Son of Man – Son of God

> **3:11-13** *'Most certainly I tell you, we speak that which we know, and testify of that which we have seen, and you don't receive our witness. If I told you earthly things and you don't believe, how will you believe if I tell you heavenly things? No one has ascended into heaven but he who descended out of heaven, the Son of Man, who is in heaven.'*

The interview had now taken an unforeseen and very uncomfortable direction for Nicodemus. He was used to deferential treatment, but now found himself in the presence of someone who deeply challenged him and spoke with an authority that was both profound and very disturbing. What was about to follow – a revelation of the amazing love of God and of the danger of ignoring the light that he had already received – would give him much food for thought during the next couple of years.

In response to Jesus' teaching about new birth/birth from above, Nicodemus had asked Jesus, 'How can these things be?' He seemed to consider 'these things' to be remote and out of reach, belonging to the heavenly realm. Jesus brought him down to earth with a bump. The new birth is an 'earthly' thing that takes place on earth, in people with physical bodies. Through this dynamic experience, people who were 'born of the flesh' are now also 'born of the Spirit', and will thus live as spiritual beings, although still with physical bodies. The new birth is accessible to people of flesh and blood, such as Nicodemus, if they are willing to believe and receive.

Nicodemus' first words to Jesus, 'a teacher come from God, for no one can do these signs that you do, unless God is with him', if genuinely intended, implied that Nicodemus was ready to believe and submit to Jesus' words. However, despite the witness of Jesus, he did not currently believe these earthly things. For the third time, therefore, Jesus emphasised His final and unique authority, '*Amen, amen,* I say to you', and now based that authority on His personal experience: 'we speak that which we know, and testify of that which we have seen'. (The first person plural 'we' probably indicates the relationship between the Father, the Son and the Spirit.)

Jesus spoke of Himself with reference to three time frames and two different places – 'descended out of heaven', 'ascended into heaven', and 'is in heaven'. For Him, all three aspects of time were part of the same indivisible reality. He was physically present on earth and, at the same time, enjoyed a continuous relationship with His Father in heaven. His human body was the Temple, the place where heaven and earth met as one. Jesus was not willing to talk to Nicodemus about 'heavenly things', realities in the heavenly realm that are inaccessible except to the One who 'descended out of heaven'. He can only share such things with those who are spiritually alive.[1]

Previously, in conversation with Nathanael, Jesus had identified Himself as 'the Son of Man' who would be the connecting stairway between earth and heaven, as in Jacob's dream.[2] Now Jesus spoke about the Son of Man who is in heaven. Nicodemus would no doubt have connected this with Daniel's vision of the glorious Son of Man upon whom the Ancient of Days, seated in the heavenly court, conferred an everlasting Kingdom. He could not have missed the significance of Jesus' words, in effect claiming to be the Messiah King who would one day judge the world.[3] This pushed Nicodemus into an extremely tight corner where compromise was not a permanent option.

C S Lewis summed up the dilemma that Nicodemus would have faced on that fateful night:

> You must make your choice. Either this man was, and is, the Son of God, or else a madman or something worse. You can

---

[1] John 14:25-26; 16:13-14; 1 Cor. 2:7-16; Rev. 4:1-11.

[2] John 1:51; 14:6.

[3] Dan. 7:13-14.

shut Him up for a fool, you can spit at Him and kill Him as a demon, or you can fall at His feet and call Him Lord and God. But let us not come with any patronising nonsense about His being a great human teacher. He has not left that open to us. He did not intend to.[4]

3:14-18 '*As Moses lifted up the serpent in the wilderness, even so must the Son of Man be lifted up, that whoever believes in him should not perish, but have eternal life. For God so loved the world, that he gave his one and only Son, that whoever believes in him should not perish, but have eternal life. For God didn't send his Son into the world to judge the world, but that the world should be saved through him. He who believes in him is not judged. He who doesn't believe has been judged already, because he has not believed in the name of the one and only Son of God.*'

Having alluded to His identity as the Son of Man who will judge the world, Jesus, with wonderful grace and tenderness, now began to woo Nicodemus with the revelation of the Son of Man as Saviour. The Son of Man had come down from heaven and would ascend to heaven again, so what, then, was the purpose of His coming? Jesus reminded Nicodemus of an incident from Israel's journey in the wilderness when the people had rebelled against God and were being bitten by poisonous snakes. Many people had already died and, in desperation, others cried out to God, who responded with mercy and prescribed the solution. He instructed Moses to make an effigy of a snake and lift it up on a pole, and then instruct the suffering people to look at it. The message was clear: God could easily deal with the snake problem; they needed to return to a proper relationship of trust and obedience towards Him.[5]

Jesus now invited Nicodemus to interpret this incident in Israel's history as a prophecy about Himself. He informed Nicodemus that He, the Son of Man, would be lifted up and that anyone who believed in Him would, like those Israelites, be saved from death and receive eternal life. To us, with the benefit of

---

[4] C S Lewis, *Mere Christianity* (Fontana Books, 1952, reprinted 1964), pp. 52-53.
[5] Num. 21:4-9; Exod. 20:4-6.

hindsight, the connection is clear, but it must have been something of a conundrum for Nicodemus. After all, Jesus had just referred to this 'lifting up' in the context of His ascension to heaven, and at this stage Nicodemus had no reason to anticipate a literal fulfilment of Jesus' words in the form of crucifixion.

Being a scholar of Scripture, another passage about the serpent may have come to Nicodemus' mind: 'He will bruise your head, and you will bruise his heel'. If so, he would have understood the identity of the snake as none other than Satan.[6] Nicodemus would probably have also been aware of a passage in the Wisdom of Solomon, probably dating from the first or second century BCE, with reference to the brass serpent on a pole: '... having a token of salvation to put them in remembrance of the commandment of your law; for he who turned towards it was not saved because of that which was seen, but because of you, the Saviour of all'.[7]

The snake on the pole was not being lifted up as a god but was rather exposed as powerless and defeated. In a future generation the brass snake became an idol and had to be destroyed. This serves as a permanent warning not to divert our gaze from the Lord Himself and transfer our trust to religious techniques or traditions or relics.[8] Jesus was undoubtedly claiming to be the Messiah/Son of Man, the fulfilment of this promise concerning the seed, but what could it all mean?

Jesus was planting a seed thought in Nicodemus' mind that would bear fruit much later, when Nicodemus and Joseph took the body from the cross on which Jesus had been lifted up and reverently placed it in Joseph's tomb.[9] Verses 16 and 17 are perhaps the best known and most frequently quoted texts in the whole Bible, but they are less often understood in their original context. When Jesus spoke of God, Nicodemus as a learned Pharisee would have correctly understood that He was referring to the God of Israel. This is important because some Christians seem to hold to the belief, or at least give the impression, that the God of the Scriptures that we call the Old Testament is not quite the

---

6 Gen. 3:14-15.
7 Wisd. 16:6-7.
8 2 Kings 18:4.
9 John 19:38-42.

same as the God who is revealed in the person of Jesus. We must not create a God in our own image by selecting out those parts of Scripture that support our presuppositions while rejecting or ignoring the rest. The God of Israel is holy, holy, holy, and He also abounds in steadfast love, compassion, mercy and grace, not only towards Israel but also towards the whole world.[10]

Nicodemus' intensive study and close attention to religious practices may have resulted in a rather detached or distant view of God. Jesus now revealed that His Father's heart burned with love for His human creatures, including, of course, Nicodemus. Indeed, everything of which Jesus had been speaking had been initiated and orchestrated by God in consequence of that love. He had responded to the plight of the Israelites long ago by means of a symbol, but now in reality in the person of His only begotten Son. The symbol had cost Him nothing, but now He had given His beloved Son in order to save a perishing world. The Son of Man, the beloved and unique Son of God, would soon be lifted up for the salvation of sinful, rebellious humanity, of which Nicodemus was but an ordinary member. He needed to humble himself and receive God's love and salvation as a gift of grace.

There was a flip side to this wonderful good news: Jesus came as the agent of salvation and not judgement, but those who proudly brushed aside the proffered help would continue headlong to destruction. Nicodemus had been blissfully unaware of the fact that he was part of a lost humanity. His encounter with Jesus had turned out to be much more serious than he had anticipated, for now he could not even hide behind the excuse of ignorance on the Day of Judgement.[11] The proper and required response to this amazing revelation of God's love would be the choice to believe.

The tense of the verb 'believe', here and otherwise in the Gospel, implies a continuous and determined commitment of life. The Bible does not treat unbelief as an unfortunate condition in which we are trapped, but as a sin from which we need to repent. Nicodemus now had sufficient evidence to enable him to take

---

[10] 1 John 5:21.
[11] 1 Tim. 1:12-14; Acts 17:29-31.

action, but for personal reasons he was unwilling to do so at this time.

> **3:19-21** *This is the judgement, that the light has come into the world, and men loved the darkness rather than the light; for their works were evil. For everyone who does evil hates the light, and doesn't come to the light, lest his works would be exposed. But he who does the truth comes to the light, that his works may be revealed, that they have been done in God.'*

In verse 18 Jesus had stated that condemnation was a consequence of failing to believe in Him. Now He identified the reason for that failure. Often the suggested reason is intellectual – that there is insufficient evidence – but Jesus diagnosed a deeper and more serious problem: an unwillingness to face up to the truth. When an issue has no implications for a person's life and behaviour, it is usually not difficult to change that person's opinion by reasoned presentation of suitable evidence. When a change in viewpoint would cause a radical upheaval in behaviour, lifestyle and relationships, things can be very different. Jesus had not only come as the light of the world but, more pointedly, into the world of Nicodemus. Nicodemus held a high position among people with whom Jesus was about to come into conflict, in a clash between light and darkness, so there was much at stake for him.

A popular assumption is that Nicodemus came to Jesus as a prospective disciple. Several features of the text admit the possibility of an alternative interpretation, and one for which there appears to be more textual evidence. John described Nicodemus as 'a man of [or from] the Pharisees', and as 'a ruler of [or from] the Jews [the Jewish leaders]': the Greek text and the English translations are ambiguous. These leaders may have commissioned him, as a distinguished teacher, to suss out this young prophet and miracle worker from Nazareth, in the same way that they had sent others to question John the Baptist. In keeping with this, there is a striking and perhaps deliberate parallel between how John introduced John the Baptist and then Nicodemus:

> There came a man, sent from God, whose name was John. The
> same came as a witness, that he might testify about the light,
> that all might believe through him.
> (John 1:6-7)

> Now there was a man of [from] the Pharisees named
> Nicodemus … The same came to him by night, and said to
> him, 'Rabbi, we know that you are a teacher come from God,
> for no one can do these signs that you do, unless God is with
> him.'
> (John 3:1-2)

Nicodemus had initiated the conversation with the plural, 'we know'. Jesus subsequently referred to Nicodemus and his associates as 'you' (plural), suggesting that He knew that Nicodemus was a spokesman for others as well as himself. Nicodemus began the conversation by paying Jesus an enormous compliment, a technique subsequently used by Jewish leaders who tried to entrap Jesus.[12] Of course, this may or may not have been Nicodemus' purpose, as it may simply have been a respectful approach, consistent with Middle Eastern culture. Jesus cut Nicodemus off after those few words so we do not know what he would have said next. However, Jesus would surely have been aware of the state of his heart for He 'knew everyone, and … he didn't need … anyone to testify concerning man; for he himself knew what was in man'.[13]

None of these considerations is conclusive in determining why Nicodemus came to Jesus that night, but together they do suggest that he was an emissary of the Pharisees. Stronger evidence comes from consideration of the text as a whole. Most commentators consider that there is a break somewhere in the text, a point at which the dialogue between Jesus and Nicodemus ceases and a reflection by John begins.[14] There is no clear reason for this opinion and no consensus as to where the supposed break occurs. In fact, the thought flow appears to continue to the end of the

---

[12] Matt. 22:15-17.

[13] John 2:24-25.

[14] Leon Morris, *The Gospel according to John*, p. 202.

passage. The theory of a break probably has its roots in a perception of Nicodemus as an open-hearted seeker after truth to whom Jesus would not have spoken such negative things.

Jesus presented Nicodemus with a wonderful offer – to enter the Kingdom of God and to possess eternal life through a supernatural new birth by the Holy Spirit. He concluded the interview with a stark and stern warning about the consequences of rejecting the light that Nicodemus had just received. Jesus would subsequently use similarly blunt and uncompromising language when addressing groups of Pharisees who rejected His words.[15] Pharisees claimed to worship the God of Israel, but how would they react when they met Him in person in flesh and blood? The light that shone from God incarnate would expose the hidden things of their hearts and what they really lived for: self-righteousness, public approval and position in society.

Jesus put heavy emphasis on *deeds* and *doing*, for belief that does not change behaviour is empty of meaning. The scene was now set for an inevitable conflict. Jesus' disciples had chosen the light, and many of the Pharisees would soon set their faces towards the darkness.

When Nicodemus took his leave of Jesus he must have been deeply unsettled by the surprising turn that the conversation had taken. A decision to follow Jesus would cause massive disruption to Nicodemus' life and relationships; refusal to do so would mean rejecting the light that Jesus brought. He had come and he had seen. How would he respond? This quandary was to dog Nicodemus' footsteps during the next couple of years, until he eventually emerged into the light of faith.[16]

---

[15] John 5:19-47; 8:13-59; 12:42-50.
[16] John 7:45-52; 19:38-42.

11

John 3:22–4:3
The Bridegroom and the Bride

> *3:22-26 After these things, Jesus came with his disciples into the land of Judea. He stayed there with them and baptised. John also was baptising in Enon near Salim, because there was much water there. They came, and were baptised; for John was not yet thrown into prison. Therefore a dispute arose on the part of John's disciples with some Jews about purification. They came to John and said to him, 'Rabbi, he who was with you beyond the Jordan, to whom you have testified, behold, he baptises, and everyone is coming to him.'*

Jesus had angered one section of the Jewish leadership – the Sadducees – and was about to antagonise another party – the Pharisees – while simultaneously attracting followers from among the common people. At this point He moved to the Judean countryside, not far from Jerusalem but away from its hustle and bustle. More people were joining the original nucleus of disciples, who baptised the newcomers in a way that reflected the practice of John the Baptist, whom Andrew and John had previously followed as disciples. Jesus had commenced His preaching ministry with the same message as John: 'The time is fulfilled, and God's Kingdom is at hand! Repent, and believe in the Good News', so the disciples must have considered baptism appropriate for those who responded to the message. Jesus evidently approved of this, but John subsequently informs us that He did not personally engage in the process.[1]

John the Baptist had moved further north in the Jordan valley and continued to baptise those who repented. Repentance was

---

[1] Mk 1:14-15; John 4:1-2.

even more urgent now that the Messiah had been revealed. In practice, this meant that two similar movements were overlapping, although in different locations, which was bound to create problems of apparent competition. The situation came to a head in an indirect manner as a result of a dispute between some of John's disciples and the Jews, later revealed in John 4:1 to be Pharisees, who were the experts in purification.

The emergence of the new Jesus movement had probably intensified the Pharisees' concerns about unauthorised practitioners of water baptism. This may have alerted John's disciples, who were concerned about competition with their Rabbi. They had heard John testify about Jesus, 'He is the one who comes after me, who is preferred before me', but the implications had not fully registered with them.[2] We may think this strange, but even today many people who acknowledge Jesus as Lord seem much attached to particular Christian leaders and virtually treat their interpretations and applications of Scripture as infallible truth.

> *3:27-30 John answered, 'A man can receive nothing, unless it has been given him from heaven. You yourselves testify that I said, "I am not the Christ," but, "I have been sent before him." He who has the bride is the bridegroom; but the friend of the bridegroom, who stands and hears him, rejoices greatly because of the bridegroom's voice. This, my joy, therefore is made full. He must increase, but I must decrease.'*

Recording the incident, John, in typical Hebrew fashion, used the convention of substituting the word 'heaven' for 'God', in order to avoid writing the sacred divine Name. The report, 'Rabbi, he who was with you beyond the Jordan, to whom you have testified, behold, he baptises, and everyone is coming to him', although exaggerated, would have unsettled a lesser man. John's disciples were jealous for his position, but John was perfectly content and secure in his identity and calling. They were anxious because their meaning and purpose currently depended on their relationship with John, but he himself was at peace because he knew that his life and service came from heaven, and that he had

---

2 John 1:23-27.

God's approval. The Messiah and His Kingdom were John's chief priorities rather than the success and persistence of his own ministry. We also need to have a Kingdom perspective that eliminates competition between denominations, local congregations and 'ministries'.

John used a beautiful analogy, comparing himself to the friend of the bridegroom (the best man). John loved the bridegroom, and his overriding ambition was to honour Him and promote His happiness, so he harboured no conflicting or competitive thoughts. He felt privileged to have played his subsidiary role in the process and was now happy to stand to one side and leave the bridegroom centre stage. To desire the bride for himself would be tantamount to adultery and an act of base treachery towards his friend. John had no such thoughts or ambitions.

In the Scriptures, God is portrayed as being in a love relationship with Israel. The betrothal took place when He rescued His people from Egypt, and she became His wife at Mount Sinai when He gave Israel His commandments and they entered into a covenant to keep them. The relationship was troubled, marred by Israel's repeated unfaithfulness and spiritual adultery, to the point where God suspended the relationship. The prophets promised eventual restoration after a period of corrective justice, and John was the last in the line of these prophets.[3] Jesus called him, 'A prophet ... and much more than a prophet', because it was John's privilege to declare the arrival of the bridegroom and to personally introduce Him to His bride. At that stage the bride consisted of the faithful remnant in Israel, those who recognised and followed Jesus.[4]

Jesus described the Kingdom of God in terms of a wedding banquet, already begun and to be completely revealed when He returns as the Messiah King and the glorified Son of Man.[5] John, having fulfilled his appointed task, continued to witness about the One who had come and to rejoice at His coming. He understood his place in the process and gladly accepted the role that God had

---

[3] Jer. 2:32; Ezek. 16:7-14; Jer. 3:1, 14; Isa. 54:6; 65:2; Ezek. 16:32; Hos. 2:2, 14-20.

[4] Luke 7:26; Mic. 7:18-20; Rom. 9:27; Rom. 11:5.

[5] Matt. 25:1-13; Mark 2:19; Rev. 21:2, 9; Rev. 22:17.

assigned him. He had brought the previous line of prophets to its appointed end and had ushered in the new age of the Kingdom of God, and the soon beginning of the Last Days. Jesus had risen as the Sun of Righteousness, the Dayspring from on high and the Morning Star, so John was content to retreat into the evening shadows and the setting sun.[6] That he was willing to do so is evidence of his greatness.

Christian leaders sometimes hold tightly to status and position and are reluctant to let go when the growth of the Kingdom demands someone else. We need grace to take on the role of John the Baptist in relation to younger people who have begun to carry a spiritual anointing, so that Jesus in them may shine forth, even if we are diminished in the process. We do not merely run an individual race but are part of a great relay race. We have been given a baton that needs to be passed on: this is one of the important messages of Hebrews 11.

> ***3:31-34*** *'He who comes from above is above all. He who is from the earth belongs to the earth and speaks of the earth. He who comes from heaven is above all. What he has seen and heard, of that he testifies; and no one receives his witness. He who has received his witness has set his seal to this, that God is true. For he whom God has sent speaks the words of God; for God gives the Spirit without measure.'*

This section echoes Jesus' words to Nicodemus, affirming His own heavenly origins and status and His unique authority to speak from that perspective. At first it seemed that His testimony had been universally rejected – 'no one receives his witness' – but this was immediately qualified – 'he who has received his witness' – as in the prologue.[7] John was making a statement of enormous significance and challenge within a Jewish context, and one that Jesus would later reinforce. Jesus claimed that the Father had sent Him, and that He was God's Son and His personal representative on earth. The Father testified to this truth by means of the miracle-

---

6 Mal. 4:2; Luke 1:78-79; Rev. 2:28; 22:16.
7 John 1:10-12.

signs that Jesus performed through the power of the Spirit within Him.[8]

The religious leaders refused to recognise the contradiction inherent in their claim to believe in the God of Israel while rejecting Jesus as His Son.[9] In receiving Jesus, we are witnessing to the fact that God is true and faithful and that He has kept His covenants and promises by sending Jesus as the Messiah. If we reject the Son, we necessarily deny the character of the Father.

> **3:35-36** *'The Father loves the Son, and has given all things into his hand. One who believes in the Son has eternal life, but one who disobeys the Son won't see life, but the wrath of God remains on him.'*

We cannot be sure if the concluding sentences were from the mouth of John the Baptist or a commentary by the apostle John, but either way they present a serious warning. The Father has placed His whole creation in the hand of His beloved Son. He achieves His purposes through the agency of His Son and the Spirit who dwells within Him: our response to this truth has both present and eternal consequences. Jesus told Nicodemus that the reason for His coming was to prevent people from perishing and to bestow the gift of eternal life upon them. To believe 'in the Son' is to believe in Him in the context of His saving work. Not to believe 'the Son' is to reject His identity, and thus to reject the truth and integrity of the One who sent Him.

John the Baptist had asked the Pharisees and Sadducees, 'who warned you to flee from the wrath to come?'[10] This wrath is a present reality that awaits full expression: he who does not believe, 'the wrath of God remains on him'. This is a great mystery: the love that impelled the Father to send His Son for the salvation of the world coexisted with His wrath, and still does. It is such an uncomfortable paradox that we are tempted to exclude the latter truth in favour of the former, but the overwhelming witness of Scripture forbids us to do so. Everlasting life is both a present and

---

[8] John 8:58-59; 10:30; 5:36-38.
[9] John 5:39-40.
[10] Matt. 3:7.

future reality for those who believe; judgement awaits those who refuse to believe.

> **4:1-3** *Therefore when the Lord knew that the Pharisees had heard that Jesus was making and baptising more disciples than John (although Jesus himself didn't baptise, but his disciples), he left Judea and departed into Galilee.*

The Pharisees had rejected the baptism of John, and Jesus did not choose to discuss the matter further with them. He did not require human authorisation, and on His own authority as Lord He ignored them and travelled north towards Galilee with those who had received Him. Jesus' chosen route would have taken Him close to where John was baptising, but there is no suggestion that their journeys coincided.

John, the writer of the Gospel, had previously, in an aside, mentioned that 'John was not yet thrown into prison'.[11] This is another indication that the contents of the Synoptic Gospels were already familiar to John's readers. He reminded his readers that Herod had imprisoned John the Baptist, and they would also have known about his violent death. Luke informs us that, from his dungeon, John subsequently sent disciples to ask Jesus, 'Are you he who comes, or should we look for another?'[12] This question contrasted with his previous glowing testimony about Jesus that he had maintained in the face of his disciples' concern about Jesus' growing popularity.

Was John's question simply a consequence of the depressing circumstances of his imprisonment and his uncertain future? John seems rather to have been concerned that he had made a mistake and had, perhaps, wasted his life on an illusion. He had declared that Jesus would lay the axe to the root of the tree and burn up the chaff with unquenchable fire, but it did not seem that He was about to fulfil this programme.[13] Luke places John's question in the context of Jesus' focus on the outsider (the Roman soldier), the neglected (the poor widow) and the sinners (the prostitute). John

---

[11] John 3:24.
[12] Luke 7:20.
[13] Matt. 3:10-12.

may have wondered if this was really all that the Messiah had come to achieve.[14]

John did not understand that the Messiah would come on two separate occasions and for different purposes. John was unaware that the fulfilment of some of the truths that he had proclaimed would be delayed until the end, when the Messiah will return as judge. The first appearance of the Coming One did not coincide with the wrath to come. This misconception, together with his own isolation and suffering, led John to doubt Jesus' identity.

Jesus did not explain the way in which the final judgement would take place but He provided lavish evidence of His identity as Messiah. He had raised a young man from death to life just before John's disciples arrived and He continued to perform many miraculous signs.[15] This shows that Jesus considered John to be in a quite different category from the Pharisees and from Herod, whose demands for authenticating signs He refused. They had rejected John's message and Jesus knew that their hearts were dark and their motives sinister.

We also may experience times of discouragement, depression and honest doubt.[16] We should follow John's example and take up the issues with God rather than running away in bitterness and offence. Honest doubt, if we respond appropriately, can draw us nearer to God to receive the answers that we need, even if they are not the answers for which we originally hoped. Jesus warned John of the dangers of being offended in the face of confusing circumstances and when he did not have complete knowledge of God's agenda.[17] There are many as yet unfulfilled prophesies concerning Jesus' reign on earth as Messiah that, like John, we do not clearly understand. We do know that He will return in glory as the Son of Man to judge and renew the creation and to rejoice with His bride at the marriage supper of the Lamb.[18] Jesus affirmed that John was the greatest of the prophets, and no doubt he will have an honoured place at the table.

---

14 Luke 7:1-20, 36-50.
15 Luke 7:21-22.
16 Ps. 13; 88; John 20:24-29.
17 Luke 7:23.
18 Matt. 25:31-32; Titus 2:11-14; Rev. 21:1-5; 19:7-9.

12

John 4:4-26
Living Water

> *4:4-9 He needed to pass through Samaria. So he came to a city of Samaria, called Sychar, near the parcel of ground that Jacob gave to his son, Joseph. Jacob's well was there. Jesus therefore, being tired from his journey, sat down by the well. It was about the sixth hour.*
>
> *A woman of Samaria came to draw water. Jesus said to her, 'Give me a drink.' For his disciples had gone away into the city to buy food.*
>
> *The Samaritan woman therefore said to him, 'How is it that you, being a Jew, ask for a drink from me, a Samaritan woman?' (For Jews have no dealings with Samaritans.)*

Jesus had left Jerusalem some time previously and now decided to continue north to Galilee, possibly prompted to do so by the hostile attitude of the Pharisees. Two alternative routes existed: a more direct one through Samaria and a longer one skirting around it. Jews tended to use the indirect route in order to avoid Samaritans, so John's statement that Jesus 'needed to pass through Samaria' is intriguing. It is not necessary to suppose that He knew what He would encounter there. John's Gospel portrays Jesus as responding to the Father's guidance in an ongoing way rather than following a prearranged schedule. He simply needed to know that this was the route that His Father had chosen.

After walking for some hours He arrived with His disciples at Jacob's well, which was located at the foot of Mount Ebal and at the crossing point of several roads. The village of Sychar was about half a mile to the north, close to the town of Shechem. Shechem was the site of many foundational events in Israel's history. This fact would be highly significant in the conversation that Jesus was about to have with the woman. Abraham and Jacob had lived at

Shechem and Jacob had bought a plot of land there, in token of God's promise that his descendants would possess the whole land. (In a similar way, Abraham had purchased and acquired title deeds to the field at Hebron, where the three Patriarchs would later be buried.) Jacob's sons conquered Shechem in battle (albeit in a dubious way), prefiguring the subsequent conquest of the land. Joseph's bones were preserved and carried from Egypt to be buried at Shechem in the field that Jacob had bequeathed to him.[1] Soon after the Israelites entered Canaan, Joshua brought them to Mount Ebal, where they built an altar and renewed the covenant that they had previously made with God at Sinai. Shechem was also the place where the ten tribes revolted against the House of David, thus dividing the nation. Jeroboam then made it his capital city and led the nation into idolatry, rejecting the Temple in Jerusalem as God's exclusive place of worship.[2]

The Samaritans were descendants of Gentiles who had been sent to the land of Israel by the Assyrian king after the exile of the ten northern tribes.[3] Some Israelites who subsequently returned from exile intermarried with these settlers. Together they followed the religious beliefs and practices contained in the first five books of the Bible and rejected the other Jewish Scriptures. Using the Pentateuch for their authority and legitimacy, they constructed a historical narrative that began with the Patriarchs but excluded the House of David. They substituted Mount Gerizim for Mount Ebal as the first place of Israelite worship in the Land and built their temple there, in opposition to the one in Jerusalem.[4]

Although the Samaritans were strictly observant of the requirements of the Torah of Moses, most Jews regarded them as inferior because of their origins and because they rejected the other Jewish Scriptures and the Temple in Jerusalem. 'Samaritan' was used as a term of abuse; Jesus was insulted in this way.[5] Nevertheless, Samaritans were not considered to be pagans, and

---

[1] Gen. 12:6; 33:18-19; 34:26; 37:12-14; 48:22; Josh. 24:32.
[2] Deut. 27:1-13; Josh. 8:30-35; 1 Chron. 22:1; 2 Chron.3:1-2; 6:1-11; 1 Kgs. 12:25-31.
[3] 2 Kings 17:24-41.
[4] Deut. 27:4-7.
[5] John 8:48.

during the lifetime of Jesus their food was regarded as clean. It is interesting that the Good Samaritan in Jesus' parable revealed his love for the injured man by prioritising the man's need over the purity regulations in the Torah, in contrast to the priest and the Levite who kept at a safe distance and avoided contamination.

Jesus arrived at the well near Sychar after a long journey in the early summer heat. It was probably noon (although 6pm is also possible if Roman time was being used). Being fully human, Jesus was tired and weary and probably also thirsty. He sat beside the well while the disciples walked the half-mile to the village in search of food. In their absence, a woman arrived at the well. Her clothing would have identified her as a Samaritan. She must have encountered the group of Jewish men walking towards Sychar and had probably found this intimidating. Probably they passed her without speaking, for they were later surprised to find that Jesus was talking with her.

Jesus, an obviously Jewish man, was sitting beside the well from which she needed to draw water. This would have been disconcerting for her, an unaccompanied woman and a Samaritan. She was at a disadvantage in many ways, being inferior in status and vulnerable, and perhaps she feared that this man would reject and insult her. Jesus broke the awkward silence with a simple and genuine request: 'Give me a drink.' This initiative reversed the customary social conventions of male–female and Samaritan–Jewish interactions, causing her to react in amazement, '"How is it that you, being a Jew, ask for a drink from me, a Samaritan woman?" (For Jews have no dealings with Samaritans.)'

Jesus surprised her by His willingness to ask for help from one such as she, rather than standing aloof or making a contemptuous demand. She was also aware that Jesus lacked the means to provide for His own needs. This elevated her to a position of power because she could refuse His request. Jesus' approach enabled her to enter into dialogue as an equal and thus opened the way for her to receive from Him. His attitude intrigued her and she was emboldened to ask questions that would pave the way for her to receive the truth.

4:10-15 *Jesus answered her, 'If you knew the gift of God, and who it is who says to you, "Give me a drink," you would have asked him, and he would have given you living water.'*

The woman said to him, 'Sir, you have nothing to draw with, and the well is deep. So where do you get that living water? Are you greater than our father, Jacob, who gave us the well and drank from it himself, as did his children and his livestock?'

Jesus answered her, 'Everyone who drinks of this water will thirst again, but whoever drinks of the water that I will give him will never thirst again; but the water that I will give him will become in him a well of water springing up to eternal life.'

The woman said to him, 'Sir, give me this water, so that I don't get thirsty, neither come all the way here to draw.'

The woman had power to supply Jesus with water from the well, He having no bucket for the purpose. He claimed power to supply her with a superior kind of water by means of an identity of which she was as yet unaware, and a grace that she had never previously experienced. By the end of the conversation she would know that God is a gracious and generous Father and that Jesus is the true Messiah, not only of the Jewish people but also of Samaritans like herself.

As with Nicodemus, she initially interpreted Jesus' words in a strictly literal way, possibly regarding them as far-fetched or ridiculous. Also, His words pointed to a source other than Jacob's well, and an implied superior status and authority as compared to the great Patriarch who was at the roots of Samaritan history and identity. Certainly, Jews could be arrogant and contemptuous of Samaritans, but this was outrageous, and it was also threatening to their culture and heritage.

Jesus ignored all of these undercurrents and renewed His offer, now making it universal: 'whoever'. He was claiming power and authority that went far beyond the present encounter. He reminded the woman that He was not offering static water from a well – water such as Jacob had been able to provide – but living and flowing and bubbling water, an endless and limitless fountain of life. This water can quench the thirst of the human heart for meaning and identity and satisfaction, and is the very essence of joy.

Perhaps, on later reflection, she might have thought that Jacob, like herself, had been striving to obtain what could only be received as a gift from God. Before Jacob's birth, God had promised that he would be the one who would receive the inheritance of Abraham and Isaac, but Jacob did not trust God to bring this about. Instead he schemed and lied in an attempt to make it happen. Only when he had been stripped down to a state of utter helplessness could he receive the blessing from the hand of God.[6] The woman responded to Jesus in a respectful way, for His words had touched a chord in her heart. His words intrigued her but the deeper significance remained elusive.

> **4:16-18** *Jesus said to her, 'Go, call your husband, and come here.'*
> *The woman answered, 'I have no husband.'*
> *Jesus said to her, 'You said well, "I have no husband," for you have had five husbands; and he whom you now have is not your husband. This you have said truly.'*

At this point Jesus shot an arrow into her heart. No doubt there were many issues in her life, but He identified the one that overshadowed everything else. It coloured all other aspects of her life and had determined her present circumstances, her feelings and her very identity. Jesus only spoke about this one aspect of her life, but it was 'the one thing' that was her constant companion. She expressed this later when she informed her neighbours about 'a man who told me everything that I did', and they saw no reason to disagree.[7] Two questions arise: how did Jesus know about her marital status, and what circumstances had caused it to be as it currently was?

John previously informed us that Jesus 'didn't need for anyone to testify concerning man; for he himself knew what was in man'.[8] However, this does not mean that, at every moment in time, He carried in His mind the details of every human being. He lived in

---

[6] Gen. 25:21-23; 27:18-29, 41-46; 32:24-31.
[7] John 4:29.
[8] John 2:23-25.

intimate relationship with His Father and received guidance through the Holy Spirit in a dynamic and ongoing way. The process may have simply involved a word of knowledge, the impression on His mind of a few words – 'five husbands ... not your husband'. This is important to us because Jesus is the model for His followers. After His resurrection He would say, '"As the Father has sent me, even so I send you." When he had said this, he breathed on them, and said to them, "Receive the Holy Spirit!"'[9]

It is commonly believed that this woman had been in a series of marriages, each of which had ended in divorce, and that she was now living in an immoral relationship. This was why she was shunned by the other women and came to the well alone. This is a possible explanation, but it is not necessarily true, and it actually seems less probable than the alternative. Jesus did not deny the validity of these five relationships, describing all the men as having been her husbands. The Law of Moses required a surviving male relative to marry a childless widow and raise up children to inherit the deceased man's property. Samaritans shared this portion of Scripture with the Jews and probably followed the same practice. On one occasion the Sadducees challenged Jesus with a question about a woman who had, in succession, been the wife of seven brothers. Their question ignored the tragic life of the woman who had been passed from one man to another and yet remained childless, a cause of great shame.[10]

Western categories typically operate within the framework of truth/falsehood and innocence/guilt, but the overriding factor in many Eastern situations is honour/shame, as is still clearly seen in issues to do with marriage. A woman with this history would probably have been seen as undesirable and dangerous, and possibly as being under some sort of curse. The man with whom she was now living may have been a relative who was unwilling to marry her but who was prepared to provide her with practical support. What a burden she would have carried, a deep pain in her heart, a crippling sense of shame and a daily experience of

---

[9] 1 Cor. 12:8; John 20:21-22.
[10] Deut. 25:5-10; Ruth 4:1-12; Matt. 22:23-28.

rejection. Samaritans experienced a similar corporate wound because they were despised by the Jews.

> **4:19-20** *The woman said to him, 'Sir, I perceive that you are a prophet. Our fathers worshipped in this mountain, and you Jews say that in Jerusalem is the place where people ought to worship.'*

Jesus' words had exposed the hurt at the centre of the woman's heart, too painful to discuss with a stranger. She could not deny the truth of His words and she received them as evidence that He was a prophet. She now deftly moved the conversation to the subject of religion, which was much safer ground! This, of course, is still a common device to deflect from sensitive personal issues. She referenced a core theological dispute, no doubt pointing to nearby Mount Gerizim, where the Temple had stood until it was destroyed by John Hyrcanus, one of the Maccabean rulers of Judah, in 130 BCE. Which side of the dispute was correct? Who were orthodox and who were the heretics?

If Jesus was a true prophet then He should know, and perhaps He would vindicate the Samaritan position. After all, the Pentateuch did not specify Jerusalem as the correct place for worship. God had promised to reveal this to the people after they entered the Land. Samaritans believed (incorrectly) that Mount Gerizim was the initial place of sacrifice, giving it priority over Jerusalem. They also appealed to historical connections with Jacob and Joseph.[11]

> **4:21-24** *Jesus said to her, 'Woman, believe me, the hour comes, when neither in this mountain, nor in Jerusalem, will you worship the Father. You worship that which you don't know. We worship that which we know; for salvation is from the Jews. But the hour comes, and now is, when the true worshippers will worship the Father in spirit and truth, for the Father seeks such to be his worshippers. God is spirit, and those who worship him must worship in spirit and truth.'*

---

[11] Deut. 12:5, 13-14; 27:4-6.

Jesus saw through the façade of religious language into her aching and longing heart. He addressed her gently in the same way as He did His mother, 'Woman', and then firmly required her to accept His authoritative word, 'believe me'. The focus was no longer on externals, including the place of worship. What mattered now was to know God as Father, in relationship with Jesus through the Holy Spirit, for Whom living water was a metaphor. The Spirit was currently present with her in the person of Jesus, and He would come within her as a result of the work that Jesus would complete in His death and resurrection. Of course, Jesus did not explain the details of this to her; all that she needed to know now was that the Father welcomed genuine worshippers, those who would draw near to His presence regardless of their origins or personal histories.

Jesus is not the final destination of our journey of faith but is the way to the Father. Christians often stop short, happy to be in a love relationship with Jesus, but this was not His ultimate purpose. I have often heard people use the expression, 'It's not about us; it's all about Jesus!' The first part is certainly true, but Jesus would have denied the second, for His quest is to bring us to the Father.[12]

Jesus stated that true worshippers would – indeed, must – worship the Father in spirit and in truth. They must come on His terms and not on their own. The woman needed to reject a tribal religious narrative that was based on a selective reading of Scripture, and accept God's sovereign choice of Israel as His channel of salvation. Jesus identified Himself as a Jew: 'We worship that which we know; for salvation is from the Jews.' Some Samaritans had a deep antipathy concerning this truth, and subsequently one village would not receive Jesus because His face was set to go to Jerusalem. In so doing they were opposing the purposes of God, for His Messiah must be offered there for their sins and for the sins of the world.

When Philip subsequently travelled to Samaria to preach the gospel, many people responded, but the Holy Spirit was not poured out until Peter and John came from Jerusalem to lay hands

---

[12] John 14:6; 16:26-27; 1 John 3:1-3; 1 Pet. 3:18.

on them. God required the Samaritans to acknowledge His choice and submit to His divinely ordained order.[13]

> ***4:25-26*** *The woman said to him, 'I know that Messiah comes, he who is called Christ. When he has come, he will declare to us all things.' Jesus said to her, 'I am he, the one who speaks to you.'*

The woman shared with her community a belief that one day the Messiah would come, and then all the problems and issues would be resolved. The Jewish stranger's words were intriguing and His knowledge about her was uncanny and disturbing. What could it all mean? Then Jesus said, 'I am he, the one who speaks to you.' Others had and would call Jesus Messiah, but she was the only human being ever to hear this direct testimony from His own lips. He had said, 'The hour comes, and now is, when the true worshippers will worship the Father in spirit and truth.' A doctrinal belief in a future event had now been transformed into a present encounter, with the Promised One who stood before her and gazed into her eyes with understanding and compassion. A veil suddenly lifted from her inner eyes, her wounded heart was healed, and she suddenly became uniquely qualified to bring healing to the wounded community of her Samaritan village.

---

[13] Luke 9:51-53; Acts 8:12-17, 25.

John 4:27-43
Telling Good News

> **4:27-34** *At this, his disciples came. They marvelled that he was speaking with a woman; yet no one said, 'What are you looking for?' or, 'Why do you speak with her?'*
>
> *So the woman left her water pot, went away into the city, and said to the people, 'Come, see a man who told me everything that I did. Can this be the Christ?'*
>
> *They went out of the city, and were coming to him. In the meanwhile, the disciples urged him, saying, 'Rabbi, eat.'*
>
> *But he said to them, 'I have food to eat that you don't know about.'*
>
> *The disciples therefore said one to another, 'Has anyone brought him something to eat?'*
>
> *Jesus said to them, 'My food is to do the will of him who sent me and to accomplish his work.'*

Jesus and the woman, deep in conversation, had probably not noticed the approaching group of disciples who were bearing food for their rabbi. They came within hearing range just after the climax of the dialogue, when Jesus had revealed that He was the Messiah. The scene that met their eyes was confusing and probably also embarrassing, for it was a complete break with convention. A religious Jew would never speak with a woman in public, particularly if she was unaccompanied. Some religious Jews only spoke with their wives when it was necessary to do so.

The woman took their arrival as her cue to leave. Jesus' words had brought her an inner freedom and she was eager to share good news with her fellow villagers. She left the physical burden of the water pot where it was and returned to the village with a light heart. The well water that had been her priority had been sidelined by the offer of living water. It would have taken the woman between ten and fifteen minutes to walk the path to Sychar. Bursting with excitement, she issued an invitation – 'Come, see' – gave a short personal testimony – 'A man who told me everything that I did' – and then asked a relevant question – 'Can this be the Christ?'

No doubt this is an abbreviated version of what she said. Her excited words and emotions conveyed something of the life-changing encounter with Jesus that she had just had. Her fellow villagers all knew her well and also knew the misfortunes that had overtaken her, so something very unusual must have happened to her. They were so impressed by the visible change in her demeanour that they were eager to accept her invitation to meet the person who had brought it about. Soon she was on her way up the path again, with everyone following behind. Jesus had raised her up to a place of dignity within her society; the problem villager had been transformed into the village prophet!

The disciples, probably now relieved that the strange woman had disappeared, urged Jesus to eat. His appetite seemed to have disappeared and He explained the reason in one of His enigmatic statements: 'I have food to eat that you don't know about.' As usual, they interpreted this in a literal way, assuming that someone must have supplied Him better food than they could obtain. Actually, as He went on to explain, they were in a sense correct: 'My food is to do the will of him who sent me and to accomplish his work.'

Desire for food had been displaced by the opportunity to engage with His Father's current agenda, just as the woman's priority to obtain physical water had been displaced by the news about living water. In this statement Jesus revealed the passion that energised Him and also made known the motivation for His every activity. Jesus' awareness of His identity, and His conviction that the Father had sent Him on a mission to bring life to the world, pervades the whole of John's Gospel. As He contemplated His final act of self-giving on the cross, He would say to His Father, 'I glorified you on the earth. I have accomplished the work which you have given me to do.' When about to release His spirit to the Father He cried out triumphantly, 'It is finished.'[1]

> **4:35-39** *'Don't you say, "There are yet four months until the harvest?" Behold, I tell you, lift up your eyes and look at the fields, that they are white for harvest already. He who reaps receives wages and gathers fruit to eternal life; that both he who sows and he who reaps may rejoice together. For in this the saying is true, "One sows, and another reaps." I sent you to reap that for which you haven't laboured. Others have laboured, and you have entered into their labour.'*
>
> *From that city many of the Samaritans believed in him because of the word of the woman, who testified, 'He told me everything that I did.'*

The villagers would not have arrived on the scene for quite some time after the woman had left, but they may have been visible in the distance after half an hour or so. Presumably Jesus had been conversing with the disciples during this time and only introduced the quotation when the delegation came into view. It seems to have been a well-known saying in the form of a proverb that, presumably, meant something like, 'Be patient; things happen in accordance with their own built-in time frame, so don't be impatient and expect results right away.' Some of Jesus' parables included the sequence of planting and harvesting.

While in Sychar the disciples had had no inkling that those who were selling them food were themselves hungry for the food that Jesus could provide. The disciples were involved in an everyday transaction with Samaritans whom they would have judged as not being interested in such spiritual issues. Jesus, on the other hand, saw them as ripened sheaves ready to be harvested. Presumably, at this point in the conversation, the disciples were facing Jesus, who was looking towards the village. He invited them to turn and look at what He alone could see: 'Lift up your eyes and look at the fields, that they are white for harvest already.' ('Lift up your eyes' is the English translation of a Hebrew idiom retained in the Greek text.) Jesus was not calling attention to the state of the surrounding

---

[1] John 17:4; 19:30.

fields, but to the approaching Samaritan villagers, whose white robes were glistening in the afternoon sun.

The Samaritan villagers were a portion of God's harvest fields. Sowing and planting had indeed occurred through the labours of prophets, probably including John the Baptist, who had preached in the vicinity (at Aenon near Salim). The woman had recently added her testimony about Jesus. The villagers, who had responded to the woman's invitation to come to see Jesus for themselves, would not be disappointed. Jesus promised His disciples that, if they recognised the significance of what was happening and were willing to play their part in the process, then they would share the rewards of those who had ploughed the ground before them and had planted the seed.[2]

The disciples must no longer consider the Samaritans as enemies and heretics, but rather as people whom God loved and whom He included in His harvest. Whatever their reservations, the disciples had no choice but to accompany Jesus to the village and stay there with Him for two days. They would never have imagined being thrust into this situation, one that was well outside their comfort zones, but as disciples they were obliged to follow Jesus wherever He led. Much later, Peter would face a similar issue when God called him to go to a Gentile house and share the good news of Jesus.[3]

It is important not to make inappropriate judgements about who might or might not be open to receiving an invitation to meet Jesus, or miss opportunities to share the gospel in the context of everyday activities. God may already be at work in the lives of people whom we judge to be uninterested in or even opposed to the gospel.[4]

> **4:40-43** *So when the Samaritans came to him, they begged him to stay with them. He stayed there two days. Many more believed because of his word. They said to the woman, 'Now we believe, not because of your*

---

[2] Matt. 13:3-39; c.f. 1 Cor. 3:5-9.

[3] Acts 10.

[4] Acts 9:10-20.

speaking; for we have heard for ourselves, and know that this is indeed the Christ, the Saviour of the world.'

After the two days he went out from there and went into Galilee.

The disciples had urged Jesus to eat the food they had brought from the village, but He had refused, setting His own comfort to one side. Now He readily accepted hospitality from the villagers and stayed with them for two days. He was in pursuit of the food that His heart desired. The woman's simple testimony of what Jesus had done for her was the key that had opened the doors of the Samaritans' hearts and homes. We do not know exactly what Jesus said or if He performed any miracles, but during the course of those two days they were thoroughly convinced that He, the Jewish Messiah, was indeed the Saviour of the world. Salvation was from the Jews but was now available to all humankind, including Samaritans. The fountain of living water flowed to them as well.

It is instructive to pause here and compare the two encounters that are placed almost side by side in John's Gospel. Nicodemus and this woman could scarcely have been more different. He was a man, a Jew, a Pharisee, a distinguished teacher of the Law and a member of the ruling class. He would almost certainly not have taken this route through Samaria and would have avoided social contact with Samaritans. He would have considered himself to be highly orthodox, and an 'insider' with respect to the Kingdom of God. The woman was a Samaritan, part of a rejected community; she had also probably suffered from rejection within that community. Her life, for whatever reason, was marked by failure and it is likely that she, an outsider, suffered from low self-esteem.

Jesus challenged both of them, but He treated the woman more gently than He did Nicodemus. She, the outsider, was assured that she was part of the world that God loved and from which He was seeking worshippers. Nicodemus needed to be made aware that he was not, in fact, an insider and must take his place as an ordinary member of the world of human beings whom the God of Israel loved. He needed to know that God loved a world that included Jews, Samaritans and Gentiles, whereas she needed to acknowledge God's sovereignty in choosing the Jewish people to be the unique channel of His salvation. Nicodemus and the woman shared a common humanity before God, each of them needing to be brought into relationship with the Father through the Son whom He had sent into the world, and needing to receive new life through the Holy Spirit.

Jesus used different metaphors – birth from above and living water springing up within the heart – but the meaning and experience are one and the same. The Samaritan woman, bowed down under the burden of her sad history, responded at once to the revelation that Jesus brought and the residents of Sychar were, in their turn, willing to receive the light of truth that shined through her artless testimony.

Nicodemus had even greater encumbrances – position, status, wealth, peer pressure and religious orthodoxy – all of which inhibited him from making a similar commitment to Jesus. He would not, of course, have recognised these things as disadvantages. Nicodemus will reappear in John's narrative at the Feast of Tabernacles about two years later, as a part of the Council that was judging Jesus in absentia, following a failed attempt to arrest Him. Nicodemus was rudely rebuffed when he pointed out the illegality of the process and he did not then indicate any personal allegiance to Jesus. Only when confronted by the cross would he find the courage to nail his colours to the mast.

14

John 4:43-54
Jesus Lord of Space and Time

4:43-54 *After the two days he went out from there and went into Galilee. For Jesus himself testified that a prophet has no honour in his own country. So when he came into Galilee, the Galileans received him, having seen all the things that he did in Jerusalem at the feast, for they also went to the feast. Jesus came therefore again to Cana of Galilee, where he made the water into wine.*

There was a certain nobleman whose son was sick at Capernaum. When he heard that Jesus had come out of Judea into Galilee, he went to him, and begged him that he would come down and heal his son, for he was at the point of death. Jesus therefore said to him, 'Unless you see signs and wonders, you will in no way believe.'

The nobleman said to him, 'Sir, come down before my child dies.'

Jesus said to him, 'Go your way. Your son lives.'

The man believed the word that Jesus spoke to him, and he went his way. As he was now going down, his servants met him and reported, saying 'Your child lives!' So he enquired of them the hour when he began to get better. They said therefore to him, 'Yesterday at the seventh hour, the fever left him.' So the father knew that it was at that hour in which Jesus said to him, 'Your son lives.' He believed, as did his whole house.

This is again the second sign that Jesus did, having come out of Judea into Galilee.

Jesus and His disciples stayed only two days in Sychar, but it appears to have been one of the most successful episodes in His entire ministry, for good seed fell on good ground. This was in contrast to another Samaritan town whose inhabitants turned Him away because He was moving resolutely towards Jerusalem.[1] Unlike the people of Sychar, they were deeply prejudiced against a Jewish Messiah. What a pity that, in defending an entrenched position, they deprived themselves of the opportunity to hear the message of salvation from Jesus' own lips, even as He travelled to the cross to die on their behalf.

The next incident in Cana is not included in any of the other three Gospels, and it is the only healing miracle that John recorded from Jesus' Galilean ministry. This prompts the question, why did John include this particular miracle?

Jesus was aware that the people of Cana had become highly dependent on a diet of signs and wonders to sustain their belief in Him. The man at the centre of this story was a nobleman, a political figure, and was therefore a comparative outsider in religious terms (like the Samaritan woman). His importunate faith is contrasted with the outlook of the local population, and this emphasises one of John's major themes: the nature of the connection between miraculous signs and true faith. A second possible reason for including this miracle is that Jesus had previously revealed in Cana that He is the Lord of creation. Now He is revealing Himself as the Lord of space and time.

Jesus had been welcomed in Galilee as a direct result of the miraculous signs that the Galileans had witnessed at the recent Passover Feast in Jerusalem. News had preceded Him and there were high expectations that similar things would now happen in the north of the country. The text implies that, before arriving in Cana, Jesus had travelled around other parts of Galilee and He had probably performed some of the miracles that are recorded in the other Gospels.[2] When Jesus said that 'a prophet has no honour in his own country', He was probably referring to Nazareth rather than to Galilee in general.

John's use of the word 'sign' is very specific to miracles that had the potential to reveal Jesus' identity as the Son of God. Miracles per se were not exclusive to Him, and He was very aware that many

---

[1] Matt. 13:23; Luke 9:51-53.

[2] John 2:23-25; Luke 4:23.

people did not respond in real and lasting faith, even to those miracles that were designed to act as signs.[3]

On the previous return from Judea to Galilee, following His baptism and temptations, Jesus had visited Cana and performed the first of these signs by turning water into wine. Jesus had attended the wedding as part of His mother's family, but now He returned as a prophet and miracle worker; no doubt, the town was abuzz with excitement and expectation. As on the previous occasion, a sudden crisis became the occasion for a special miracle of this sort. The instigator was, somewhat surprisingly, a royal official who was presumably in Herod's service and who was living in Capernaum. Perhaps the subsequent report of this miracle would feed into Herod's fear of Jesus as being a reincarnation of John the Baptist, and also fuel his desire to see the captive Jesus perform a miracle for His entertainment; this, of course, would be refused.[4] The official would have been aware of the miracles that Jesus had performed in Jerusalem as well as in Galilee. In a state of despair about his son's critical condition, he hurried the fourteen miles to Cana and, with urgency and anxiety, pleaded with Jesus to help him.

Of course, Jesus was ready to respond to his cry for help, but first He addressed a more general problem: 'Unless you see signs and wonders, you will in no way believe.' This, of course, made no sense to the worried father, who had come because of acute concern for his son. His journey and his urgent plea witnessed to the fact that he was reaching out to Jesus in faith. Jesus could easily have healed the boy at once, but first He addressed another group of people whose condition was equally or even more serious. He was not rebuking the anxious father but rather the bystanders, who enjoyed seeing spectacular signs but remained unconvinced and uncommitted.

Faith that responds to Jesus' words is more reliable than belief based on visible phenomena.[5] The bystanders' attitude was

---

[3] Matt. 12:27; Mark 9:38; John 20:30-31.

[4] Luke 9:7-9; 13:31-32; 23:8.

[5] Matt. 7:24-27.

extremely dangerous and would have eternal consequences but, if they were willing, change was still possible

Understandably, the father had an altogether narrower focus. He urged Jesus to intervene before it was too late and also prescribed how He should act. Of course, Jesus responded with compassion, but in choosing a different method He both rewarded and stretched the man's faith and also gave him an overwhelming revelation of His glory. The nobleman believed Jesus' words, and he clung to those words as he walked the long journey home. When he saw these words fulfilled, his initial faith was strengthened, and many other people who learned of the miracle also received grace to believe in Jesus. This servant of Herod was, like the Samaritan woman, the unlikely but chosen channel of that grace.

The former miracle in Cana had revealed Jesus as the Lord of creation who could produce wine without the usual intermediate stages. This miracle revealed Him as the sovereign Lord whose power to act is not limited to a particular location, as is the case for human beings. Jesus is truly the Lord of everything and we should concentrate on our relationship with Him rather than pursuing human agents of signs and wonders. God is sovereign and cannot be imprisoned within human schedules and programmes.

Quite properly, we may have a narrow focus on what we need the Lord to do for us, but we should be aware that He has larger plans. He may act differently from what we expect in pursuit of His glory, and in order to bless other people as well as ourselves.

15

John 5:1-14
Jesus in the House of Mercy

> ***5:1-9a*** *After these things, there was a feast of the Jews, and Jesus went up to Jerusalem. Now in Jerusalem by the sheep gate, there is a pool, which is called in Hebrew, 'Bethesda', having five porches. In these lay a great multitude of those who were sick, blind, lame, or paralysed, waiting for the moving of the water; for an angel went down at certain times into the pool and stirred up the water. Whoever stepped in first after the stirring of the water was healed of whatever disease he had. A certain man was there who had been sick for thirty-eight years. When Jesus saw him lying there, and knew that he had been sick for a long time, he asked him, 'Do you want to be made well?'*
>
> *The sick man answered him, 'Sir, I have no one to put me into the pool when the water is stirred up, but while I'm coming, another steps down before me.'*
>
> *Jesus said to him, 'Arise, take up your mat, and walk.'*
>
> *Immediately, the man was made well, and took up his mat and walked.*

The occasion of this miracle was an otherwise unspecified 'feast of the Jews', possibly not one of the three great pilgrim festivals. A pattern is emerging in the structure of the Gospel: most of the incidents that John has included took place in the context of one or other of the annual festivals, each involving a journey to Jerusalem. The interval between successive visits was often six months or more, indicating the careful and purposeful way in which John selected his material.

The first public conflict between Jesus and certain Jews – the senior Sadducean priests – happened at the Feast of Passover when He cleansed the Temple. Following this, He returned to Galilee where He performed many miracles and gave extensive teachings.

This had aroused opposition from another group of Jews – the Pharisees – and news of His activities had probably preceded Jesus to Jerusalem. The local Pharisees seemed to be keeping Him under scrutiny, particularly in respect of two vital issues: His interpretation of the Law, especially in relation to Sabbath, and His claim to act and speak with the authority of God.[1]

For many years scholars doubted the authenticity of John's account of this miracle because there was no evidence that such pools had ever existed. The accuracy of John's description, however, was confirmed in the mid-twentieth century when the site was sufficiently excavated to reveal the pools with their five porches. Two large pools provided water to the city, including the Temple, and one of them may also have served as a ritual bath pool (*mikveh*).

The oldest manuscripts do not include the text of verses 3 and 4, about the angel and the moving of the water, but the man whom Jesus healed did subsequently refer to this phenomenon. It may have been a natural and intermittent event to which a supernatural explanation had been attached. This would explain why so many desperate people had gathered in search of healing. Adjacent to the pools the Romans had built a temple, dedicated to Asclepius, the god of medicine, and to Fortuna, the goddess of fortune. Some religious people combine truth with superstition and this may have been the case with some of those lying around the pool, hoping that this might prove to be their lucky day.

Bethesda, where the miracle took place, had powerful associations from former times as it was the location of the upper pool where the prophet Isaiah met Ahaz, a wicked king of Judah, and challenged him to ask for a sign from heaven as confirmation that God would save Judah and Jerusalem from invasion. Ahaz had proudly refused to do this, resulting in Isaiah's declaration of God's chosen sign: 'Behold, the virgin will conceive, and bear a son, and shall call his name Immanuel.' Now that sign was being fulfilled in the person of Jesus in that very place. It was also the place where an Assyrian commander had arrogantly threatened King Hezekiah and the city of Jerusalem, and had insulted the God of Israel. The

---

[1] Matt. 9:1-7; 12:1-8; Mark 3:1-6.

Lord then judged the Assyrians for their insolence and rescued the city.[2] The Father had chosen this place, steeped in salvation history, as the location for another powerful sign that would testify to the identity of His Son and would also challenge the leadership of Israel.

'Bethesda' means 'house of mercy, grace or faithful love'. Jesus came on this particular day in order to reveal the Father's love for a man who had all but given up hope for change. At that time, Bethesda was outside the city wall so Jesus would have entered through the nearby Sheep Gate (modern St Stephen's or Lion Gate). This was the gateway through which animals were led to be sacrificed at the Temple. Jesus' intervention on the Sabbath day was part of a chain of events that would eventually lead to the cross, to which He was led as a lamb to the slaughter.[3]

The precincts of the pool were thronged with people, like a large hospital waiting area. They had many different and serious afflictions, a sea of suffering humanity. All were equally helpless and hopeless, with everyone anticipating an event that was not only unpredictable but also inaccessible for many of them. Unusually, Jesus fixed His eyes on one man and ignored all the others. Jesus addressed the man with a challenging question that must have sounded strange to him: 'Do you want to be made well?' He had probably been carried to the poolside each day for many years, knowing that if the waters chanced to move he would be unable to enter the pool. His attendance at the pool was irrational but had become a fixed habit. His response to Jesus' question was indirect, suggesting that he had given up hope.

Jesus cut though his passivity and pessimism with a crisp and straightforward three-part command that called for faith and accompanying action: 'Arise, take up your mat, and walk.' To the man, the situation had appeared complicated and insoluble. Jesus' word of command bypassed all the arguments from past disappointments, current circumstances and the surrounding atmosphere of resignation and unbelief. He was left with a simple choice: either to retreat into a passive victim mentality or to trust

---

[2] Isa. 7:3-4, 10-14; 36:1-7, 17-20; 37:36-38.
[3] Matt. 1:18-25; Luke 1:30-35, 67-75; Isa. 53:7.

and obey. Faith flowed into his heart and, before he had time to think, he was on his feet, rolling up his mat and heading for the city.

> **5:9b-14** *Now it was the Sabbath on that day. So the Jews said to him who was cured, 'It is the Sabbath. It is not lawful for you to carry the mat.'*
>
> *He answered them, 'He who made me well said to me, "Take up your mat and walk."'*
>
> *Then they asked him, 'Who is the man who said to you, "Take up your mat, and walk"?'*
>
> *But he who was healed didn't know who it was, for Jesus had withdrawn, a crowd being in the place.*
>
> *Afterward Jesus found him in the temple, and said to him, 'Behold, you are made well. Sin no more, so that nothing worse happens to you.'*

The fact that these events took place on the Sabbath day was not a coincidence but was the Father's specific choice. God created the Sabbath after completing His perfect creation. The man's physical affliction reflected the fact that the creation had been broken by sin, and the state of Sabbath (rest/harmony/peace) had been shattered. Sabbath had now been restored to this man's body, in token of the coming restoration of the whole creation. The healing was also a visible sign that pointed to the identity of Jesus as the Lord of the Sabbath and the Prince of Shalom.[4]

The Pharisees, the religious police of the day, took a different view and charged the man with Sabbath-breaking. This did not relate to the fact that he was walking, but that he was carrying his mat. They classified this as work and they also claimed the right to enforce their narrow interpretation of the Law. The man countered this by referring to the obviously superior authority of the one who had been able to heal him. The Pharisees refused to accept his testimony because it contradicted their theology, and because the man had been unable to identify the One who had broken the Sabbath.

---

4 Gen. 2:1-3; 3:14-19; Matt. 12:8.

The man continued on his journey to the Temple, perhaps to give thanks to God, and Jesus found him there. The man's body had been healed, but Jesus was conscious of a deeper problem. He was in a dangerous position, having experienced the joy of his newfound physical freedom, but there was still an unresolved issue. Jesus' words, 'Sin no more, so that nothing worse happens to you,' did not require elaboration in order for the man to understand. Jesus knew that the root cause of the man's illness would resurface when the emotions that accompanied his healing had begun to fade. His will needed to be engaged to walk in the ways of God, while drawing strength from the grace that he had so recently received. The grace of God should lead to holiness; to neglect this truth is to court disaster.[5]

[5] Rom. 12:1-2; Heb. 2:1-4; 2 Pet. 2:20-22; Titus 2:11-14; 1 Cor. 11:27-32; 1 John 5:16; Matt. 12:43-45.

16

John 5:15-30
Two Competing Sources of Authority

> *5:15-16 The man went away, and told the Jews that it was Jesus who had made him well. For this cause the Jews persecuted Jesus, and sought to kill him, because he did these things on the Sabbath.*

The man who had been healed was no doubt joyful but he was also naïve. Perhaps he believed that when the Pharisees met Jesus they would be so impressed that they would adapt their interpretation of the Law accordingly. If so, he was to be sadly disappointed. Jesus was accused of having broken the Law by instructing the man to pick up and carry his bedroll. At worst, this constituted a minor infringement of a very strict interpretation of the Law. It was certainly not a high-handed and rebellious act, worthy of punishment by death.[1]

Given the supernatural nature of the miracle, the Pharisees should have paused to consider whether their interpretation of the Law might perhaps be defective. Their disproportionate response may have been fuelled by reports from Galilee of previous incidents when Jesus had been in conflict with certain Pharisees. He had claimed not only to be Lord of the Sabbath but also to have authority to forgive sins.[2] The Pharisees could not compete in the area of miracles so they resorted to pulling rank. They were in a position of power and could not afford to lose in the battle with this upstart young man with His radical message and inconvenient miracles.

---

[1] Num. 15:30-31.
[2] Matt. 12:1-14; 9:2-7.

We need to recognise that such conflicts have been a feature of church history down to the present day. When a fresh breath of the Spirit blows there is always resistance by those whose theological interpretations and vested interests are threatened. Treasured beliefs come to be regarded as sacrosanct and are jealously guarded against challenge, resulting in further divisions in the body of Christ and diminished witness in the world. Revivals have been spoken against, even by those who experienced previous ones, because the current one is different in form and of a kind that they cannot lead.

> **5:17-23** *But Jesus answered them, 'My Father is still working, so I am working, too.' For this cause therefore the Jews sought all the more to kill him, because he not only broke the Sabbath, but also called God his own Father, making himself equal with God. Jesus therefore answered them, 'Most certainly, I tell you, the Son can do nothing of himself, but what he sees the Father doing. For whatever things he does, these the Son also does likewise. For the Father has affection for the Son, and shows him all things that he himself does. He will show him greater works than these, that you may marvel. For as the Father raises the dead and gives them life, even so the Son also gives life to whom he desires. For the Father judges no one, but he has given all judgement to the Son, that all may honour the Son, even as they honour the Father. He who doesn't honour the Son doesn't honour the Father who sent him.'*

Far from submitting to their authority and retreating, Jesus dismissed the accusations in a single sentence: 'My Father is still working, so I am working, too.' This statement was highly inflammatory, like pouring petrol on a fire, and was spoken at a time when the Jewish leaders were already contemplating judicial murder. In using the words 'My Father', Jesus was claiming a unique relationship with the Holy One of Israel. Jews were comfortable with the language of God as 'Our Father', but 'My Father' was radically and qualitatively different and was the exclusive property of the Messiah King, God's only begotten Son.[3]

---

[3] Is. 63:16; Ps. 2:7; 89:26.

Jesus' brief statement had major implications for the correct understanding and application of Sabbath law. Following the six days of creation, God rested from all of His creative acts, but this did not mean that He had ceased to work. He continued to act in dynamic relationship with His creation, upholding everything by His powerful word and sending forth His Spirit to renew the face of the earth. When Jesus engaged in acts of redemption and restoration, He was acting as the Father's agent. Sabbath spoke of *shalom*, wholeness and peace, so there could be no better day for such works of mercy.[4] All of Jesus' actions were the fruit of His intimate love relationship with the Father, His perfect submission to the Father's authority and His complete reliance on the Father's faithfulness. The Father revealed Himself through the works that Jesus did by the power of the Holy Spirit. The most recent of these works was this healing miracle, and this had included Jesus' instruction to carry the mat.

Jesus lived by a simple and God-given strategy: He listened to the Father and followed His promptings. This was fitting and appropriate for Him as the perfect and obedient Son of Man. It also formed a pattern for the way His followers should behave. When, later in the Gospel, He declared that He was the Good Shepherd, He defined His sheep as those who hear His voice. After His resurrection Jesus breathed on His disciples and sent them out to function in the same way as He had done, in dynamic relationship with the Holy Spirit.[5]

Much of the stress and strain in our lives results from multiple agendas that compete and collide: the agendas of the world, of personal ambition, of other people's expectations and even of the organised church. These can conspire to crowd out the Spirit's voice. On another occasion Jesus spoke about His relationship with the Father and then called His disciples into a similar relationship with Himself, in which they would experience true rest. The writer to the Hebrews reminds us that God ceased from one variety of His works – creation – and now calls us also to

---

4 Gen. 2:1-3; Heb. 1:1-3; Ps. 104:30; Luke 14:1-6.
5 John 10:11; 10:3-5; 20:21-22.

abandon one type of activity – our own works – so that we too can enter into His Sabbath rest.[6]

When Jesus made the statement, 'My Father is still working, so I am working, too,' He was putting the Pharisees on notice that He did not intend to retreat in the face of their opposition. His words fuelled a contest that would eventually climax in His death and would also bring to an end the religious life that they so much treasured. Ignoring their hostility, Jesus spelt out the implications of this statement: His visible life on earth was exactly in line with the invisible purposes of the God of heaven. He was one with the Father as the source of life, in having the right to judge and to receive honour. The Pharisees honoured the version of God that they believed they found in Scripture, but they were rejecting the God of Israel who had now come among them in flesh and blood. Jesus had already provided abundant evidence for His identity by means of miracle-signs, and even greater ones still lay ahead. If they continued to stubbornly reject Him then they would be sinning against the light that God was shining on them and they would be without excuse.

> **5:24-30** *Most certainly I tell you, he who hears my word and believes him who sent me has eternal life, and doesn't come into judgement, but has passed out of death into life. Most certainly I tell you, the hour comes, and now is, when the dead will hear the Son of God's voice; and those who hear will live. For as the Father has life in himself, even so he gave to the Son also to have life in himself. He also gave him authority to execute judgement, because he is a son of man. Don't marvel at this, for the hour comes in which all who are in the tombs will hear his voice, and will come out; those who have done good, to the resurrection of life; and those who have done evil, to the resurrection of judgement. I can of myself do nothing. As I hear, I judge, and my judgement is righteous; because I don't seek my own will, but the will of my Father who sent me.'*

Once again Jesus used the authoritative formula, 'Amen, amen I say to you'. This section commences with a powerful proclamation

---

[6] Matt. 11:25-30; Heb. 4:8-10.

of the nature, source and offer of life. This life flows eternally from the Father to the Son. The statement, 'For as the Father has life in himself, even so he gave to the Son also to have life in himself', challenges our understanding of the essential nature of God and of the relationships within the Trinity. Jesus is the eternal Son of God who never had a beginning, and yet His life flows constantly and eternally from the Father. This is the essential meaning of His designation as the only begotten Son. We cannot resolve this mystery; the Son has life in Himself, but not independently of the Father who is the source and fount of all things.[7]

When John writes about eternal life he is not merely saying that it is unending, but that it is a different kind of life from natural life; it is God's life imparted to us and implanted within us. It is made available to us now through the Son as we hear His word and believe in Him. Lesslie Newbigin expressed it in this way:

> Because the one who is both life-giver and judge is present in person, there is already given to believers ('the hour is coming and now is,' v.25) an actual experience of life from the dead and deliverance from judgement in the present time. But there is also a real future ('the hour is coming,' v.28) when the life-giver and judge will have the final word in respect of all that has been, is, and will be. And this is none other than Jesus who is speaking these words (v.24).[8]

Jesus' words to the Pharisees recall His previous conversation with Nicodemus, including the several promises that He had made and the warnings that He had given on that occasion. Having spoken of the Father and the Son in relation to life and judgement, Jesus now proceeded to apply these truths directly to the leaders, who were already incensed against Him and who seem to have been rendered speechless with shock at what He had just said. Jesus claimed that eternal life is available only to those who are willing to receive His message as being the very words of God. From God's point of view there are only two categories of human

---

[7] See Appendix 2 for further discussion of Jesus as the only begotten Son.
[8] Lesslie Newbigin, *The Light Has Come: An Exposition of the Fourth Gospel* (Grand Rapids: William B Eerdmans, 1997) p. 68.

beings. On the one hand there are those who are spiritually dead and who, in consequence of their sins, are currently living in a state of condemnation. On the other hand are those who, by believing in the One whom God sent, have escaped from condemnation and have received new life. Eternal life is a present reality as well as a future hope; those who believe have already passed from death into life.

Having addressed the present dimension, Jesus now spoke dramatically about the future one. A time is coming when both those who are spiritually alive and those who are spiritually dead will hear His voice, and will be physically raised from their graves. That resurrection will have two different outcomes – life or condemnation – depending on their deeds in this life. At first sight this seems to differ from Jesus' earlier saying that the qualifying requirement for life is hearing and believing His word. This is a false dichotomy, for deeds are both the fruit and the demonstration of a transformed heart. Intellectual assent without intentional action does not constitute true faith. Jesus spoke of the power of His voice to raise the dead; He would subsequently and powerfully demonstrate this power when He commanded Lazarus to come forth from the tomb. At the end of time, all will hear His voice, for condemnation or for life.[9]

In relation to the resurrection and judgement, Jesus spoke of His dual identity as the Son of God and the Son of Man. As the obedient Son of Man, Jesus demonstrated His complete commitment to the purposes of God the Father, up to and including death on the cross, in order to redeem sinful human beings.[10] As the glorious Son of Man, revealed in the prophecy of Daniel, Jesus has received authority to judge everything in all creation.[11]

The Pharisees would have been aware of that scripture where Daniel spoke of a time when, 'Many of those who sleep in the dust of the earth will awake, some to everlasting life, and some to shame and everlasting contempt'.[12] They, unlike the Sadducees, strongly

---

[9] John 11:43; 10:4-5.
[10] Ps. 8:4-6; Heb. 2:6-9; Phil. 2:5-11.
[11] Dan. 7:13-14.
[12] Dan. 12:2.

believed in the resurrection of the dead. Probably they also believed that, on account of their extreme piety, they would be among those who would rise to everlasting life. Jesus was claiming that on judgement day He would be their judge. It was quite preposterous, and if true it did not bode well for them. There could be no appeal to a higher court, for Jesus' judgement would accurately correspond to the Father's judgement, whose word He hears and with whom He is in perfect agreement. These were stupendous claims. How could they know that they were true?

Jesus then proceeded to establish the validity of His witness about Himself.

17

John 5:31-47
The Only Possible Witness

> ***5:31-38*** *'If I testify about myself, my witness is not valid. It is another who testifies about me. I know that the testimony which he testifies about me is true. You have sent to John, and he has testified to the truth. But the testimony which I receive is not from man. However, I say these things that you may be saved. He was the burning and shining lamp, and you were willing to rejoice for a while in his light. But the testimony which I have is greater than that of John, for the works which the Father gave me to accomplish, the very works that I do, testify about me, that the Father has sent me. The Father himself, who sent me, has testified about me. You have neither heard his voice at any time, nor seen his form. You don't have his word living in you, because you don't believe him whom he sent.'*

In order to secure a conviction for a crime, the Law required two or, preferably, three witnesses. Jesus refused to condemn a woman accused of adultery in the absence of such witnesses. This safeguard was especially important when the alleged crime was serious, attracting the death penalty. The Jewish leaders had made two accusations against Jesus – Sabbath breaking and making Himself equal with God – each of which was regarded as a capital offence.[1] The first of these charges depended on the testimony of a single witness and his testimony of healing was actually in Jesus' favour, thus rendering the charge doubly invalid. The second charge was much more significant because it flowed from Jesus' own voluntary and public statements. He had not defended Himself and nor had He backed down in the face of their accusations. Instead He had responded three times with a claim to

---

[1] Deut. 17:6; Deut. 19:15; John 8:1-11; Exod. 31:14.

supreme authority, 'Amen, amen, I say to you', and had repeatedly claimed the God of Israel to be His Father.

To the Jewish leaders, these claims constituted blasphemy. Rather than cancelling the offence of Sabbath breaking they created an additional offence. Jesus had not provided any suitable witnesses to support His claims so they were not even legally valid. Jesus anticipated this objection, but went much further: 'If I testify about myself, my witness is not valid [true].' This was a very profound statement about truth itself, and not just about legal valid testimony. If Jesus' claim to relationship with the Father arose simply from His own opinions, then the claim itself would be self-contradictory, for the essence of His claim was that the Father inspired everything that He said and did. Jesus was making the claim that there was 'another who testifies about me'. The invisible and indivisible unity between the Father and the Son was being revealed in the visible world by the works of power and love that the Father gave the Son to do.

Jesus likened John the Baptist to a lamp that burned for a time, as a witness to the true light that was coming into the world. Although everything that John had said about Him was factually true, Jesus did not rely on John the Baptist's witness to authenticate His claims to relationship with the Father. Only the Father could validate His claims, for mortal man is not qualified to authenticate the Son of God.

Jesus did not require a seal of approval from John the Baptist but, as an act of mercy, He made a concession in order to give His opponents a fresh opportunity to believe in Him and enter into life. He reminded them of how they had listened to John's message and that some of them at least had recognised John's testimony as authentic. He now called them back to that light from which they had turned away. Jesus longed that they would be saved before they became so entrenched in darkness that there would be no remedy.

Jesus was totally convinced of His intimate and unique relationship with the Father, but without visible expression this was inaccessible to other people. He pointed out to the leaders that, in the nature of things, they were unable to receive the Father's testimony by direct encounter: 'You have neither heard his voice at any time, nor seen his form.' As Jews they were strictly forbidden from portraying God in any visible way and they were aware that, because of His awesome holiness, God always made Himself known by some intermediate means.[2] The Father was the only one who could authenticate Jesus and the message that He brought, but how could this happen? The incarnate Son Himself was the only one who could do this, by doing the works that the Father gave Him to do and by the power with which the Father had anointed Him.

This testimony was adequate and it was also available to all who had eyes to see and hearts to respond. Sadly, the leaders refused to recognise any evidence that contradicted their cherished belief systems or threatened their status, particularly in relation to their peer group. They filtered out anything that conflicted with their worldview. This was a dangerous choice and it would lead to ever-increasing spiritual blindness, to the point where they would be totally unable to see.[3]

By rejecting Jesus the light of the world, they were thereby rejecting the God of Israel whom they claimed to worship. Jesus interpreted their unbelief in Him as evidence that God's Word did not live within them. This was a startling conclusion about scholars whose principal activity was study of the Scriptures. Yet their approach was academic and analytical, an end in itself, and when God broke into their world in powerful fulfilment of His covenant promises, they defended their territory. They answered to the prophecy that Simeon had spoken over the infant Jesus, that He would be 'a sign which is spoken against' so that the hearts of many would be revealed.[4] Jesus, by contrast, had no need to defend His position and simply responded to everything that the Father revealed to Him.

> *5:39-47* *'You search the Scriptures, because you think that in them you have eternal life; and these are they which testify about me. Yet you will not come to me, that you may have life. I don't receive glory from men. But I know you, that you don't have God's love in yourselves. I*

---

[2] Exod. 20:4; Num. 12:6-8; Exod. 33:20-23.

[3] Isa. 6:9-10; John 12:37-41.

[4] Luke 2:34.

have come in my Father's name, and you don't receive me. If another comes in his own name, you will receive him. How can you believe, who receive glory from one another, and you don't seek the glory that comes from the only God? Don't think that I will accuse you to the Father. There is one who accuses you, even Moses, on whom you have set your hope. For if you believed Moses, you would believe me; for he wrote about me. But if you don't believe his writings, how will you believe my words?'

Jesus recognised the diligence with which the Pharisees studied the Scriptures, but He also knew that they rejected Him because God's Word did not live in them. They were fascinated by the text, with all its interconnections and nuances and grammatical structures, its history and poetry and its prophetic programmes. They engaged in stimulating debates that rehearsed the arguments of previous scholars. Study, and its application within a rigid legalistic framework, had become a pathway to salvation. The process was like examining a window rather than seeing through it, or studying a menu and eating it rather than treating it as an offer of food. Thus, when the incarnate Word appeared, they did not recognise Jesus and thereby rejected the One who was the central theme of the Scriptures that they studied. Torah studies took pride of place and Moses was the hero in whose shadow they lived.

The books of Moses contained many pointers to the person and work of the Messiah, but the Pharisees' eyes were blinded by personal prejudice and prevailing opinions. They should have been in the vanguard of those who welcomed the Messiah but, in contrast to simpler folks, they failed to recognise Jesus as the One whom God had promised to raise up as the prophet like Moses. In rejecting Jesus they also rejected Moses and his recorded words witnessed against them.

Jesus diagnosed the root of their problem: 'I know you, that you don't have God's love in yourselves.' They were blinded by a self-love that was sustained and strengthened by mutual admiration and the desire for praise and position within their religious world. They would gladly receive men of reputation who would add kudos to their religious circle, but regarded Jesus as a dangerous maverick who did not follow the accepted rules. They regarded Him as a threat to the status quo on which their way of life depended. In their quest for human approval they were blinded to the fact that God's opinion is ultimately the only one that matters and that, by means of the works that He had given Jesus to do, the Father had made His opinion crystal clear.

Their blindness was self-inflicted and stemmed from their perceived self-interest. They were unwilling to come to Jesus because they preferred the approval of their peers. This challenge continues in every generation and even in the church.

18

John 6:1-29
Passover and the Sign of Multiplied Bread

> **6:1-4** *After these things, Jesus went away to the other side of the sea of Galilee, which is also called the Sea of Tiberias. A great multitude followed him, because they saw his signs which he did on those who were sick. Jesus went up into the mountain, and he sat there with his disciples. Now the Passover, the feast of the Jews, was at hand.*

'After these things' suggests a fairly close temporal sequence, but clearly this was not the case. More than six months had elapsed since the last recorded incident and many things had taken place during that period. The Synoptic Gospels record numerous miracles that Jesus performed in the area around the lake of Galilee. John includes only two of these in his Gospel: the miracle of the loaves and fishes, and the succeeding one when Jesus walked on water. He did so in a very brief and economical way, leaving out much of the detail that the other writers had already described. Two questions naturally arise: 'Why did John record these particular miracles?' and 'Why did he use the introductory phrase "After these things"?'

The answer to the former question appears to be that the miracle of multiplied loaves and fishes took place around the time of the Feast of Passover. John clearly intended to highlight the prophetic significance of that festival because Jesus' miraculous provision of bread echoed the provision of the manna, and the Passover bread recalled the great act of deliverance from bondage in Egypt.[1] The answer to the second question is that there is continuity of theme rather than that of time. The miracle, and

---

[1] Exod. 16:35; 12:19; 13:3.

Jesus' subsequent teaching based upon it, reignited the confrontation with the Jewish leaders that had begun in Jerusalem and intensified their hostility towards Him.

> **6:5-13** *Jesus therefore lifting up his eyes, and seeing that a great multitude was coming to him, said to Philip, 'Where are we to buy bread, that these may eat?' He said this to test him, for he himself knew what he would do.*
>
> *Philip answered him, 'Two hundred denarii worth of bread is not sufficient for them, that every one of them may receive a little.'*
>
> *One of his disciples, Andrew, Simon Peter's brother, said to him, 'There is a boy here who has five barley loaves and two fish, but what are these amongst so many?'*
>
> *Jesus said, 'Have the people sit down.' Now there was much grass in that place. So the men sat down, in number about five thousand. Jesus took the loaves; and having given thanks, he distributed to the disciples, and the disciples to those who were sitting down; likewise also of the fish as much as they desired.*
>
> *When they were filled, he said to his disciples, 'Gather up the broken pieces which are left over, that nothing be lost.' So they gathered them up, and filled twelve baskets with broken pieces from the five barley loaves, which were left over by those who had eaten.*

John describes what Jesus saw and His response to it. A large crowd of people were approaching Him, some hoping to be healed and many others eager to see spectacular miracles. Jesus attended to their physical and spiritual needs and then asked Philip an ambiguous question, 'Where are we to buy bread, that these may eat?' It could mean 'Where is the nearest bakery?' or alternatively it could be taken as a way of saying that the problem defied current solution. John informs us that Jesus was testing Philip to see how he viewed the crisis in the light of all that he had seen and experienced during the previous two years.

Philip and Andrew were among the first disciples whom Jesus had called and they had recognised Him as the Messiah. They had witnessed many miraculous signs and had personally performed similar miracles by means of the authority of Jesus' name.[2] Philip now retreated into a naturalistic solution to the problem, a tendency with which we can probably identify. Andrew sounded almost apologetic when he mentioned the meagre natural resources that were available. The fact that he mentioned them at all suggests a sense that Jesus just might have something in mind to do. Perhaps the boy had greater faith in Jesus than the disciples appear to have had. Children are often like this, unencumbered by prejudices and disappointments.

The words, 'he himself knew what he would do', have a double application. On the one hand it was a simple statement of fact, but it becomes clear from Jesus' subsequent teaching that He was also aware of the prophetic significance of His actions. He fed the five thousand without cost to Himself, the basic elements having been provided by a boy in the crowd. He performed the miracle in the knowledge that, exactly a year later, His own body would be like the broken bread that the people were about to eat.[3] All of His miracles were performed in obedience to the Father, and this particular act of obedience would find its ultimate expression at the cross.

Jesus shared the task with His disciples, in prospect of the time when they would carry on His mission and share the bread of life with the world. We do not know if the multiplication of the food took place in Jesus' hands or in theirs, but their faith and obedience were crucial to the outcome.

> **6:14-15** *When therefore the people saw the sign which Jesus did, they said, 'This is truly the prophet who comes into the world.' Jesus therefore, perceiving that they were about to come and take him by force to make him king, withdrew again to the mountain by himself.*

John added a postscript that is not included in the other Gospels, revealing another reason for retelling this well-known story. Some people identified Jesus as 'the prophet who comes into the world' and decided to 'take him by force and make him king'. They

---

[2] Mk. 6:30-44; Mk. 6:7-13.
[3] Matt. 26:26.

understood Jesus to be 'the prophet ... like you' about whom God had spoken to Moses, otherwise known as the Messiah, God's anointed King. They had come to Jesus and had seen and experienced His power and they responded by seeking to capture Him for their own selfish purposes. They seemed oblivious of the incongruity of their proposal to make Him a puppet king who would do their bidding. They used Scripture in a selective way and ignored the context. God had said of that prophet:

> 'I will raise them up a prophet from amongst their brothers, like you. I will put my words in his mouth, and he shall speak to them all that I shall command him. It shall happen, that whoever will not listen to my words which he shall speak in my name, I will require it of him.'[4]

Jesus did not argue with them and found a place where He could be alone with His Father, whose voice alone He heeded. We may criticise these people for their arrogant ambition to harness God's power for their own purposes, but we need also to recognise that this attitude still exists, in subtle, or not so subtle forms, in the church. We too can be deceived by a selective reading of Scripture, choosing passages that emphasise the kindly aspects of God's nature while ignoring those that speak of His holiness and our proper response of obedience. Alternatively, like some of the Pharisees, we can err in the opposite direction and, with self-righteousness, fail to recognise the wonderful grace and compassion of the Lord towards all who look to Him for mercy. These self-centred approaches lead to teaching either that God exists for our happiness, comfort and prosperity, or that He is stern, forbidding and inaccessible towards those whose behaviour falls short of respectable standards. Lust for power and control, attitudes as old as the human race, loomed large in the events leading to the crucifixion of Jesus. This will continue to corrupt personal, religious and political life until Jesus returns, so we need to guard our hearts against its insidious influence.

---

[4] Deut. 18:18-19.

6:16-27 When evening came, his disciples went down to the sea. They entered into the boat, and were going over the sea to Capernaum. It was now dark, and Jesus had not come to them. The sea was tossed by a great wind blowing. When therefore they had rowed about twenty-five or thirty stadia, they saw Jesus walking on the sea, and drawing near to the boat; and they were afraid. But he said to them, 'It is I. Don't be afraid.' They were willing therefore to receive him into the boat. Immediately the boat was at the land where they were going.

On the next day, the multitude that stood on the other side of the sea saw that there was no other boat there, except the one in which his disciples had embarked, and that Jesus hadn't entered with his disciples into the boat, but his disciples had gone away alone. However boats from Tiberias came near to the place where they ate the bread after the Lord had given thanks. When the multitude therefore saw that Jesus wasn't there, nor his disciples, they themselves got into the boats, and came to Capernaum, seeking Jesus. When they found him on the other side of the sea, they asked him, 'Rabbi, when did you come here?'

Jesus answered them, 'Most certainly I tell you, you seek me, not because you saw signs, but because you ate of the loaves, and were filled. Don't work for the food which perishes, but for the food which remains to eternal life, which the Son of Man will give to you. For God the Father has sealed him.'

John gave a brief summary of the disciples' hazardous journey and Jesus' dramatic intervention, not even pausing to mention how Peter, at Jesus' invitation, had walked on the water. John may only have mentioned the boat journey in order to explain how Jesus mysteriously disappeared and then reappeared at Capernaum, thus causing confusion among the crowd. John captured the atmosphere of excitement and the determination of the crowd to catch up with Jesus. No doubt they hoped to see yet more spectacular miracles, and also to share in the fringe benefits of these activities. Jesus made decisions in a free and unpredictable way, as guided by the Holy Spirit. This caused problems for people who regarded Him as their prophet and at their beck and call, so they demanded an explanation for His behaviour. Of course, they were to be disappointed, for Jesus would never submit to the requirements of human beings. He ignored their question and responded with His regular claim to ultimate and absolute authority, 'Amen, amen, I say to you'.

Jesus revealed their real motives for pursuing Him, for He knew what everyone was thinking and also understood human nature.[5] They wanted Him not only to serve their agendas but also to satisfy their appetites. Jesus said that His food and drink was to do the will of the One who had sent Him and finish His work. He would do so even when this involved thirst, pain and humiliation.[6] They wanted a successful Messiah who would provide food for the mortal body, but they had no place for the suffering Messiah who could give spiritual food that would sustain life forever. They were like Esau, whose demand for the immediate satisfaction of his appetite led him to sell his birth right for a hot meal. By so doing he demonstrated the low value that he placed on more-substantial and permanent blessings.[7] Jesus reminded them that the signs that He provided were a seal of God's approval. The recent one confirmed His identity as the prophet like Moses, the anointed Messiah. He alone could lead them into life and freedom.

> **6:28-29** *They said therefore to him, 'What must we do, that we may work the works of God?'*
>
> *Jesus answered them, 'This is the work of God, that you believe in him whom he has sent.'*

They had failed to see the purpose of the sign and had expended much energy in pursuit of a very transient physical benefit. Jesus had worked the works of God in performing the miracle and they wanted to know the secret so that they could do the same. He explained that the way to life does not lie in human works but is only possible in relationship with the One whom God has sent. In order to find true rest they must believe in Him, with all the implications of this for relationship, commitment and obedience.[8]

---

[5] John 2:23-25.

[6] John 4:34; 17:4; 19:28-30.

[7] Gen. 25:29-34; Heb. 12:14-17.

[8] Matt. 11:28-30.

19

John 6:30-52
The Bread of Life

> ***6:30-35*** *They said therefore to him, 'What then do you do for a sign, that we may see and believe you? What work do you do? Our fathers ate the manna in the wilderness. As it is written, "He gave them bread out of heaven to eat."'*
>
> *Jesus therefore said to them, 'Most certainly, I tell you, it wasn't Moses who gave you the bread out of heaven, but my Father gives you the true bread out of heaven. For the bread of God is that which comes down out of heaven, and gives life to the world.'*
>
> *They said therefore to him, 'Lord, always give us this bread.'*
>
> *Jesus said to them, 'I am the bread of life. Whoever comes to me will not be hungry, and whoever believes in me will never be thirsty.'*

Jesus' challenge to believe was met with a call for more evidence: what sign, what work? Their objection had to do with scale. Manna, associated in their minds with Moses, had sustained the whole nation for forty years in the wilderness; what Jesus had done was, by comparison, trivial in nature. Of course, they were aware that the Scriptures attributed the manna to God, but Moses was the human agent, thus demonstrating his superiority to Jesus. Jesus must meet their demand for incontrovertible proof before they would follow Him in faith. Jesus would never acquiesce to demands of that sort. They had forgotten that their ancestors had rebelled and had refused to believe, despite the numerous signs that God had provided during the wilderness journeys.[1]

Jesus prefaced His reply with another statement of His unique authority: 'Amen, amen, I say to you'. They were making the wrong

---

[1] Exod. 16:4-6, 14-15; Ps. 78:24-25; Num. 14:20-23.

comparison, for God was the source of the manna. Jesus was the bread and not just the agent of its provision, as was the case with Moses. The manna in the desert was a prophetic sign that God would one day send the true bread, His gift of life to the world.

Jesus referred to God as His Father and to the bread from heaven as a person, but they still didn't get it. The recent sign had been sufficient to convince them, in theory, that Jesus was the prophet who was to come into the world, but they had deeply ingrained prejudices and refused to make the logical connection and response.

We may wonder at this, but it is actually a common phenomenon. Even in the physical world we filter out information that does not conform to our worldviews or expectations. When a change of belief would have major implications for behaviour, many people are likely to be very resistant to such evidence and inclined to ignore or discredit it. On another occasion when people demanded a sign, Jesus refused, describing them as an 'evil and adulterous generation'.[2]

When they said, 'Lord, always give us this bread,' it is not clear whether they still thought of the bread in purely physical terms or if they now interpreted it as a more satisfying and fulfilling kind of life. Either way, they still did not seem to grasp the vital connection between gift and giver, the blessing and the blesser. They called Jesus 'Lord' but they did not realise that receiving the bread meant receiving Him, for the two were in fact one and the same. Jesus now made a series of dramatic claims that would force them to make a radical choice: either to follow Him in true faith and total commitment or to reject Him and walk away. Sitting on the fence would no longer be an option.

'I am the bread of life' is such a familiar and encouraging statement that we do not experience the shock that those who heard Him speak would have experienced, including as it did an allusion to the divine name, I AM. The Father, the God of Israel, had given bread from heaven to sustain the lives of His people in the wilderness. Jesus was now claiming that this same Father God

---

2 Matt. 16:4.

had sent Him as the true bread from heaven, to give life to the whole world.

Clearly this miracle eclipsed the other two, both the one in the wilderness and the recent one on the hillside. Jesus was claiming to be the unique and ultimate answer to the quest for life in all its fullness. Hunger and thirst for meaning and purpose, which are part and parcel of the human condition, are symptoms of our disconnection and alienation from the Father. Jesus came to bring us back to the Father, in relationship with whom we discover our true identity and the purpose of our existence. We can only find the answer to our deepest longings in relationship with the One to whom we belong.

> **6:36-47** *'But I told you that you have seen me, and yet you don't believe. All those whom the Father gives me will come to me. He who comes to me I will in no way throw out. For I have come down from heaven, not to do my own will, but the will of him who sent me. This is the will of my Father who sent me, that of all he has given to me I should lose nothing, but should raise him up at the last day. This is the will of the one who sent me, that everyone who sees the Son, and believes in him, should have eternal life; and I will raise him up at the last day.'*
>
> *The Jews therefore murmured concerning him, because he said, 'I am the bread which came down out of heaven.' They said, 'Isn't this Jesus, the son of Joseph, whose father and mother we know? How then does he say, "I have come down out of heaven?"'*
>
> *Therefore Jesus answered them, 'Don't murmur amongst yourselves. No one can come to me unless the Father who sent me draws him, and I will raise him up in the last day. It is written in the prophets, "They will all be taught by God." Therefore everyone who hears from the Father and has learnt, comes to me. Not that anyone has seen the Father, except he who is from God. He has seen the Father. Most certainly, I tell you, he who believes in me has eternal life.'*

The sceptics had demanded another sign so that they might see it and believe, but Jesus would have none of it. They had seen (and heard) evidence far better than an impersonal sign, but sadly they refused to believe and would not come to Him. Their human wills were in opposition to the will of God. Jesus made three statements about His Father's will. In the first place, Jesus said that the Father had sent Him to do His Father's will. This required Him to accept everyone who came to Him in faith and to receive them as gifts from the Father. In the second place, it was the Father's will that Jesus would keep secure all those whom He had given to Him, until the day of resurrection. In the third place, it was the Father's will that those who looked to Jesus in faith would receive eternal life and would be raised up on the last day.

It is obvious that those who are given to Jesus and those who believe are identical, but Jesus did not further explain the interplay between divine sovereignty and human choice. We are not required to fully understand the mind of God but are rather commanded to believe in His Son, with the assurance that He will not turn us away.

At some point, possibly now, Jesus moved to the synagogue, so the numbers of people now involved would have been much smaller.[3] It also becomes clear that those present were not one homogeneous group. Two distinct sections emerge: 'the Jews', and 'Jesus' disciples'.[4] Here in Galilee, 'the Jews' were almost certainly Scribes and Pharisees, of the same party as those who confronted Jesus in Jerusalem.[5] They seem to have been wary of publicly opposing Jesus, and preferred to grumble and argue among themselves. They were shocked at Jesus' claim to be the bread that came down from heaven, in contrast to what they assumed were His humble origins. Familiarity had bred contempt and His teaching was unpalatable, so they had no wish to dig deeper and possibly uncover another version of truth – like the Scribes who directed the wise men to Bethlehem but did not bother to walk three miles to see for themselves. The grumbling discontent of these Jewish leaders was reminiscent of the behaviour of their ancestors in the wilderness.[6]

Far from retreating, Jesus reasserted the things that He had already said, and added comments that were likely to cause further offence. He implied that their unwillingness to receive Him was a

---

[3] John 6:59.

[4] John 6:41, 52, 61-66.

[5] John 5:10, 16-18.

[6] Matt. 2:1-12; Exod. 16:1-9; Num. 14:29; Phil. 2:14-15; Jude 1:16.

consequence of two things. The first seems surprising, 'No one can come to me unless the Father who sent me draws him', as this would appear to absolve them of responsibility. The second reason explains the first: 'It is written in the prophets, "They will all be taught by God." Therefore everyone who hears from the Father and has learnt, comes to me.' Jesus was addressing scholars of Scripture. They were in a similar condition to their colleagues in Jerusalem whom He had rebuked for failure to believe what God had taught through His servant Moses.[7] God had graciously given them much evidence that Jesus was indeed the prophet like Moses, in order to lead them to faith in Him.

The Pharisees had failed to hear and learn from the Father through His written Word, and were now becoming increasingly blind through persistent rejection of the incarnate Word. Jesus warned them of the danger of continuing to do this, for, in that case, a time would come when they would be totally unable to see.

It is a dangerous deception to believe that we can come to the Creator God at a time of our choosing; it is our responsibility to come when He calls and draws us, and not at our convenience.[8] Jesus' stern message was mingled with hope. If, even now, they would respond to Him, they would receive everlasting life and would be raised up on the last day.

> **6:48-52** '*I am the bread of life. Your fathers ate the manna in the wilderness and they died. This is the bread which comes down out of heaven, that anyone may eat of it and not die. I am the living bread which came down out of heaven. If anyone eats of this bread, he will live forever. Yes, the bread which I will give for the life of the world is my flesh.*'
>
> *The Jews therefore contended with one another, saying, 'How can this man give us his flesh to eat?'*

They had grumbled at Jesus' assertion that He was the bread that came down from heaven. He now repeated that statement, and then added to the offence by explaining the metaphor. Bread

---

[7] John 5:39-47.
[8] Ps. 32:6; Isa. 55:1-7; 49:8; 2 Cor. 6:2; Ps. 95:7-8; Heb. 3:7-19.

actually referred to His physical flesh that He would offer up for the life of the world, and access to eternal life would depend on eating His flesh. This statement would have been utterly abhorrent to Jewish people, implying, as it did, close contact with and consuming a corpse![9] An animated discussion then ensued as to the possible meaning of this revolting, repulsive, nonsensical and heretical statement.

---

[9] Num. 19:11-13.

20

John 6:53-71
Parting of the Ways

> *6:53-59 Jesus therefore said to them, 'Most certainly I tell you, unless you eat the flesh of the Son of Man and drink his blood, you don't have life in yourselves. He who eats my flesh and drinks my blood has eternal life, and I will raise him up at the last day. For my flesh is food indeed, and my blood is drink indeed. He who eats my flesh and drinks my blood lives in me, and I in him. As the living Father sent me, and I live because of the Father; so he who feeds on me, he will also live because of me. This is the bread which came down out of heaven – not as our fathers ate the manna, and died. He who eats this bread will live forever.'*
>
> *He said these things in the synagogue, as he taught in Capernaum.*

Jesus now added a final and most offensive element to His teaching. He stated that, in addition to eating His flesh, it was also essential to drink His blood. This was absolute anathema to Jews and was totally forbidden in Scripture. Blood was symbolic of life and was considered to belong exclusively to God. Thus it had to be drained out on the created earth or offered to Him in sacrifice. Jesus would be physically lifted up on the cross and there would be a cruel rending of His flesh and shedding of His blood before the work of salvation was complete.[1]

Jesus spoke of four ways in which eating His flesh and drinking His blood are connected with life, both physical and spiritual. In the first instance, this eating and drinking would supply life where none previously existed: 'Unless you eat the flesh of the Son of Man and drink his blood, you don't have life in yourselves. He who

---

[1] Lev. 7:22-27; 17:10-12; John 19:1-2, 17-18, 34; Heb. 10:10, 19-22.

eats my flesh and drinks my blood has eternal life, and I will raise him up at the last day.' Eternal life begins when, in faith, a person identifies himself or herself with the offering of Jesus on the cross.

In the second place, this food sustains life, as we continue to trust in and rely upon the One who gave His life on our behalf: 'For my flesh is food indeed, and my blood is drink indeed.'

Thirdly, this food becomes part of our nature in union with Jesus, transforming our thoughts and emotions and desires: 'He who eats my flesh and drinks my blood lives in me, and I in him.' Jesus likened this to His own relationship with the Father: 'As the living Father sent me, and I live because of the Father, so he who feeds on me, he will also live because of me.' Jesus subsequently taught the same truth by means of a different metaphor, the vine.[2]

Finally there is a physical consequence: 'He who eats my flesh and drinks my blood has eternal life, and I will raise him up at the last day.'

Jesus reminded His hearers that everyone who ate the manna nevertheless died. In fact, they died in the context of much complaining and many acts that stemmed from unbelief, of which the Jewish leaders were now also guilty. Jesus claimed to provide, and actually to be, food that would cause them to live. The language was highly evocative, transporting them back beyond the Exodus event to the Garden in Eden where two alternative types of food were on offer: one that would sustain and perpetuate life and the other that would result in death. The tree of life was accessible only within a relationship of trust in and obedience towards God. Alienation from God and spiritual death were the inevitable outcomes of the choice to eat of the forbidden tree, in consequence of doubting and then defying the words that God had spoken.[3]

Manna sustained physical life on a temporary basis, but it could not renew the hearts of those who ate, and nor could it impart permanent and spiritual life. Following His baptism and anointing, Jesus faced similar temptations to those faced by the man and the woman in the Garden in Eden and also to those that occurred

---

[2] John 15:1-11.
[3] Gen. 2:8-9, 15-17; Gen. 3.

during Israel's wilderness experience. When Jesus was tempted in the wilderness He did not accede to the devil's suggestions because His supreme value was relationship with and obedience to the Father, who continually sustained and nourished His life on earth. Those who followed Jesus would live in a similar way: 'I live because of the Father; so he who feeds on me, he will also live because of me … He who eats this bread will live forever.' The verb forms imply a continuing process of eating rather than an isolated choice or event.

> *6:60-66 Therefore many of his disciples, when they heard this, said, 'This is a hard saying! Who can listen to it?'*
>
> *But Jesus knowing in himself that his disciples murmured at this, said to them, 'Does this cause you to stumble? Then what if you would see the Son of Man ascending to where he was before? It is the spirit who gives life. The flesh profits nothing. The words that I speak to you are spirit, and are life. But there are some of you who don't believe.' For Jesus knew from the beginning who they were who didn't believe, and who it was who would betray him. He said, 'For this cause I have said to you that no one can come to me, unless it is given to him by my Father.'*
>
> *At this, many of his disciples went back, and walked no more with him.*

These events had begun on the mountainside where Jesus had taught a large and varied group of people and had fed them with multiplied bread. A smaller number had pursued Him to Capernaum in hope of further miracles and food, and they had been rewarded with a mixture of rebuke and the offer of something even better: eternal life in relationship with Jesus Himself. The Jewish leaders were offended by His claims to be the bread of life and were ultimately disgusted by His suggestion that eating this bread really meant consuming Jesus' flesh. When He extended this to include drinking His blood, they appear to have been rendered speechless and may actually have left the synagogue in rage and indignation.

This left a sizeable number of people who are described as 'disciples', many of whom were now having second thoughts.

Again, Jesus was aware of their murmuring and recognised that their question was really a complaint. They had become exasperated by His use of obscure symbolic language and were possibly swayed by the opinions of the Jewish leaders whom they considered to be experts in Scripture. They fell into the trap of rejecting what they could not presently understand, as if their ability to do so was the hallmark of truth.

Jesus diagnosed the underlying problem: they did not believe, either in Him or in what He said. He had given abundant evidence of His identity, so they needed to trust Him and await further revelation when He chose to give it. As in the case of the Jewish leaders, Jesus did not make any concessions in the face of complaint and unbelief but instead added a further challenge: 'Then what if you would see the Son of Man ascending to where he was before?' This echoed His previous challenge to Nicodemus: 'If I told you earthly things and you don't believe, how will you believe if I tell you heavenly things?'[4]

Jesus was challenging them to believe in Him as the Son of Man who had come from heaven and to where He would return, His rightful place. His next words, 'It is the spirit who gives life. The flesh profits nothing. The words that I speak to you are spirit, and are life', offered them a key to interpretation of the metaphors, but unless they would trust Him and receive the truth that He spoke, the explanation would fall on deaf ears.

John does not include the institution of the New Covenant in his account, but Jesus' teaching on this occasion complements the descriptions of the Last Supper that are found in the other Gospels. When at Passover a year hence, His true disciples would hear Jesus speak of eating His body and drinking His blood, these earlier words would provide them with an interpretative key. The bread and the wine of the New Covenant are just that, bread and wine, but when we eat and drink in faith, identifying afresh with Jesus' physical and spiritual suffering on our behalf, the Spirit makes the presence of the crucified and risen Jesus real in our hearts and imparts fresh life to us.[5]

---

[4] John 3:12.
[5] Matt. 26:26-29.

John had previously recorded that Jesus knew the hearts of human beings. Jesus now stood in a circle of people who had all aspired to be disciples. An observer could not have separated them into believers and unbelievers. Even those close to Judas had no inkling that he belonged in the latter category, but Jesus knew his heart. Jesus reminded everyone present of what He had previously said to the Jewish leaders: 'For this cause have I said to you that no one can come to me, unless it is given to him by my Father.' His earlier statement appeared to have been a warning against stubborn unbelief, as it would otherwise have merely served to justify their unbelief, rendering them as victims rather than as responsible moral agents. The mystery of divine sovereignty persisted; they did not need to penetrate the mystery, but rather to come to Jesus in faith.

He knew the true state of their hearts, and where this would lead. Unbelief is not an unfortunate condition that we passively experience, but is rather a moral and spiritual evil from which we must turn in repentance. Sadly, many on that occasion turned and walked away, having witnessed more than they could stomach. In a short time Jesus would travel to Caesarea Philippi and the Mount of Transfiguration and would then commence His journey to Jerusalem and the cross. Opposition to His words and actions was rapidly increasing, and the days for uncommitted following were numbered.[6]

> *6:67-71 Jesus said therefore to the twelve, 'You don't also want to go away, do you?'*
>
> *Simon Peter answered him, 'Lord, to whom would we go? You have the words of eternal life. We have come to believe and know that you are the Christ, the Son of the living God.'*
>
> *Jesus answered them, 'Didn't I choose you, the twelve, and one of you is a devil?' Now he spoke of Judas, the son of Simon Iscariot, for it was he who would betray him, being one of the twelve.*

The number of people who listened to Jesus had gradually dwindled from the multitude on the hillside to just His twelve

---

6 Matt. 26:20-30; John 13:18-30; Matt. 16:13–17:13.

chosen apostles, in the synagogue in Capernaum. Of course, there were many other true disciples of Jesus, including women, but they are not mentioned at this point, and may not have been present to hear these words.[7] The initial enthusiasm engendered by the miracle of the loaves and fishes had faded and died in the face of Jesus' increasingly unpalatable pronouncements. Even those who had considered Him a great teacher had left, disillusioned and disappointed, some probably angry at having been deceived by a false prophet or a madman. Jesus made no attempt to humour or placate them; they needed to take Him as they found Him or not at all.

Jesus never counted success in terms of numbers, but rather in the quality of commitment. He had prayed before calling these twelve, and considered each of them to be a gift from His Father. Jesus now made the astonishing statement that one of their number was a devil; this must have sent shock waves through the company. Jesus did not identify the individual concerned and it is evident that until the crucifixion none of the others suspected Judas, who was the unnamed culprit. We are faced with another example of the mystery of divine sovereignty in its interaction with human will and responsibility, for Judas would play a central role in the unfolding drama. Jesus knew that Judas had already given Satan a foothold in his life, through dishonesty among other things. The other disciples were unaware of this but John, in retrospect, informs us that Judas was the group treasurer and that he was a thief.[8]

A central dynamic in John's Gospel is the journey either towards or away from the light that had come into the world. Various people had come near to Him and had seen the evidence that He provided and personified. The Jewish leaders had refused that light and were descending into a darkness that would eventually overwhelm them, and would cause them to offer up their Messiah to the Romans for execution. Judas had become increasingly disillusioned with Jesus and was on the same downhill trajectory. Disciples who were seekers after spectacular signs and

[7] Luke 8:1-3.
[8] Luke 6:12-16; John 12:4-6; 13:2, 10-11, 27-30; 17:12.

who hoped for a political Messiah had melted away. All of these had come and had seen Jesus but had rejected what they had discovered.

Having made no attempt to retain the disillusioned would-be disciples, Jesus now set the twelve free to make their choice, either to go or to stay. Jesus' question suddenly brought the issue into sharp relief. Would the twelve stick with Him in this increasingly isolated and hostile situation? Peter had very recently had a dramatic experience of the power of Jesus' words, when he had walked on the water at Jesus' invitation to come to Him and when Jesus had rescued Him from drowning. Peter now spoke for the others with passion and conviction, anticipating his similar affirmation a little later at Caesarea Philippi. Things might be difficult to understand at present, but Peter realised that Jesus' words were true and life-giving, even if full understanding had to wait. It was one of those choices that was really a no-choice – we have nowhere else to go! For eleven of them the choice would lead to the empty tomb and the outpouring of the Holy Spirit, but for Judas it would lead to betrayal, despair, suicide and eternal loss.[9]

Postscript

Mark paints a different picture of the events that followed Jesus' crossing of the lake after the feeding of the five thousand. He appears to have been describing events subsequent to the departure of those whom John characterised as being offended at or disappointed with Jesus' words. Mark describes another group of people who had heard of Jesus' arrival and began to seek Him as He travelled around the district. Many of them, including those who only touched the hem of His garment, were healed.[10] So it turned out that those who had demanded a spectacular sign to authenticate Jesus' identity missed out on a multitude of such miracles, while those with desperate need and simple faith were blessed. 'He has filled the hungry with good things. He has sent the rich away empty.'[11]

---

[9] Matt. 14:24-33; 16:13-20; 27:3-10; Acts 1:15-19, 25.
[10] Mark 6:53-56.
[11] Luke 1:53.

21

John 7:1-36
A Feast of Mystery and Suspense

> **7:1-10** *After these things, Jesus was walking in Galilee, for he wouldn't walk in Judea, because the Jews sought to kill him. Now the feast of the Jews, the Feast of Booths, was at hand. His brothers therefore said to him, 'Depart from here and go into Judea, that your disciples also may see your works which you do. For no one does anything in secret while he seeks to be known openly. If you do these things, reveal yourself to the world.' For even his brothers didn't believe in him.*
>
> *Jesus therefore said to them, 'My time has not yet come, but your time is always ready. The world can't hate you, but it hates me, because I testify about it, that its works are evil. You go up to the feast. I am not yet going up to this feast, because my time is not yet fulfilled.'*
>
> *Having said these things to them, he stayed in Galilee. But when his brothers had gone up to the feast, then he also went up, not publicly, but as it were in secret.*

The other Gospel writers had described Jesus' extensive Galilean ministry in detail. John did not repeat any of this and referred to the period of six months since the feast of Passover in a single sentence: 'After these things Jesus was walking in Galilee'. Jesus' presence in Galilee had two positive effects: the people in the area received blessing and Jesus avoided premature confrontation with the Jewish leaders who thirsted for His death.

Jesus' brothers remained unconvinced about His identity even though they had been present when He had turned water into wine, and they also knew about His miracle ministry in Galilee. They had never really come to terms with His transformation from a perfectly normal brother into a celebrity who sometimes appeared to be deluded and out of His mind. Everything seemed to have gone haywire since Jesus had visited their crazy cousin John the Baptist in the wilderness.

On one occasion the family had been so worried that they had tried to bring Him back home, hoping to restore His sanity, but He had rejected them, His own flesh and blood, in favour of strangers.[1] Whatever their reasons, they had become cynical about their older brother and may have become resentful because of His altered relationship with them. They did not deny Jesus' miracles, but these seem to have become a source of irritation to them rather than a sign of His identity. They had slipped into the same dangerous mindset as the Jewish leaders, for faith cannot coexist with a bad attitude. In their annoyance they just wanted Him out of their locality so that they would not have to confront the issue and, perhaps, face more personal questions from nosy neighbours.

Anyway, it didn't make sense to them; surely if Jesus was serious about His messianic pretensions He should make His mark in Jerusalem. They appear to have discussed tactics and then issued a united challenge. If He was truly the Messiah then He should gather disciples in the capital city and not restrict Himself to the rural backwater of Galilee where they lived. Jesus' brothers followed the rules of their religion, but the values of the world controlled their attitudes and behaviour. They did not recognise that the same world that treated them with quiet indifference overflowed in hatred and malice towards their brother and thirsted for His death, in order to silence the voice of truth. Jesus, who was light incarnate, understood the nature of the world, and He exposed the darkness that lurked behind the cloak of religion.

Cynicism and rejection within a family can be difficult to handle, but Jesus had a secure and intimate relationship with His Father and was in constant communication with Him. Jesus' response to His brothers was brief and uncompromising: 'My time has not yet come, but your time is always ready.' The first part paralleled His words to Mary at the feast in Cana but the context was very different; Mary obviously believed that Jesus could act to resolve the problem that had arisen. Towards His mother Jesus had

---

[1] Mark 3:20-21, 31-35.

been firm but also gentle and respectful. Now, in the face of His brothers' unbelief, He spoke more sharply. He never submitted to human advice or attempts to control Him, nor did He respond to demands that He must justify His authority or prove His identity.

It is very likely that His brothers also attended regularly the three major feasts, as was required of adult males. Jesus was born under the Law and so attended the obligatory festivals, but He had an additional purpose, for He knew that He had come to fulfil their prophetic significance. He did intend to travel to Jerusalem, but only at the time appointed by His Father.

Jesus is our model of how we should live. He lived in constant relationship and communication with the Father. Through the indwelling Spirit the same possibility exists for us. The Bible describes the principles of our faith, but the outworking is through an intimate relationship with Jesus Himself.[2]

> **7:11-18** *The Jews therefore sought him at the feast, and said, 'Where is he?'*
>
> *There was much murmuring amongst the multitudes concerning him. Some said, 'He is a good man.' Others said, 'Not so, but he leads the multitude astray.' Yet no one spoke openly of him for fear of the Jews.*
>
> *But when it was now the middle of the feast, Jesus went up into the temple and taught. The Jews therefore marvelled, saying, 'How does this man know letters, having never been educated?'*
>
> *Jesus therefore answered them, 'My teaching is not mine, but his who sent me. If anyone desires to do his will, he will know about the teaching, whether it is from God, or if I am speaking from myself. He who speaks from himself seeks his own glory, but he who seeks the glory of him who sent him is true, and no unrighteousness is in him.'*

The Feast of Tabernacles marked the end of the agricultural year. It was also the occasion to pray for rain after the summer drought, which would have lasted for about six months. By the time of Jesus' life on earth, a further significance had been added, and earnest and heartfelt prayers were offered for the coming of the Messiah.

---

2 John 15:1-8.

People were obviously anticipating that Jesus would attend the feast, and the Jewish authorities were on the lookout for Him. Huge crowds thronged the Temple and the place was abuzz with muttered conversations and conflicting opinions about Jesus, conducted in an atmosphere of tension and fear, for the murderous intent of the authorities was well known (see verse 25). Tension had been mounting for several days and then Jesus suddenly appeared and began to teach with an insight and an authority that impressed even the Jewish leaders. They could not understand how a man who had received no formal instruction, having never studied with a rabbi, could teach in this way and without reference to previous religious authorities, as would have been the normal method.

Jesus changed the focus from His facility with words to the content of what He had been saying, His doctrine and its source in the One who had sent Him. Scholars and rabbis repeated the sayings of contemporaries and predecessors in order to authenticate their own interpretations and teachings. Jesus explained that His teaching was independent of human wisdom and traditions and came directly from God. He had previously insisted that human beings were not qualified to pass judgement on His identity as the One whom God had sent, for that was beyond human competence. He did not, of course, expect His hearers to take His claims at face value so He also authenticated His words by means of the works that the Father had given Him to do.[3]

Jesus emphasised the nature of His relationship with the One who had sent Him. He had a single-minded ambition to reveal the Father's glory, seeking none for Himself. He identified the reason why many of His hearers and critics were unable to receive His message. They did not share His unqualified desire to find and do the will of God, and this created a fatal obstruction to receiving the evidence that God had generously provided through the miracle-signs. The conflicting personal agendas that were operating in their minds and hearts effectively blocked their ability to discern and follow the truth. If they were ready to receive and obey God's will,

---

[3] John 5:36-37.

whatever the outcome, He would reward them with inner revelation of truth. This was a tall order, given the entrenched attitudes of the leaders, but not impossible if they were willing to change in pursuit of truth. A similar situation in relation to evidence and faith still exists today.

> **7:19-24** *'Didn't Moses give you the law, and yet none of you keeps the law? Why do you seek to kill me?'*
>
> *The multitude answered, 'You have a demon! Who seeks to kill you?'*
>
> *Jesus answered them, 'I did one work and you all marvel because of it. Moses has given you circumcision (not that it is of Moses, but of the fathers), and on the Sabbath you circumcise a boy. If a boy receives circumcision on the Sabbath, that the law of Moses may not be broken, are you angry with me, because I made a man completely healthy on the Sabbath? Don't judge according to appearance, but judge righteous judgement.'*

In response to a question by the Jewish leaders, 'How does this man know letters, having never been educated?', Jesus had spoken, in general terms, of the need for purity of heart in order to receive truth. Those who heard Him speak were described as 'the people', a crowd that consisted both of those who supported Him and of the Jewish leaders and their followers. Jesus now shocked everyone with a specific accusation that they were seeking to kill Him; this was presumably aimed principally at the leaders and those in the crowd who were following their lead.

In their determination to protect their cherished religious heritage, the religious leaders were prepared to break one of the central precepts of the Law of Moses. This showed how far they had strayed from the will of God in pursuit of their own agendas. They responded to this statement with ridicule and abuse, but what Jesus said was actually true. The hostility of the Pharisees dated from the incident, recorded in John 5, when Jesus had healed the man by the pool on the Sabbath day. They were still smarting at the way He had addressed them on that occasion, accusing them of failing to follow the teaching of Moses. No doubt this grievance had subsequently been intensified by reports from Galilee of further Sabbath breaking and confrontations over the issue of authority.

Jesus referred to that earlier occasion and now offered evidence from Moses in support of His interpretation of the Sabbath. He pointed out that some activities took priority over others within the legal framework. He reminded them that circumcision on the eighth day was an overriding imperative even on the Sabbath, although it involved a type of work. It should therefore be obvious to them that the even greater imperative of healing did not contravene Sabbath law. (Jesus was using an accepted mode of argument, *qal v chomer*, from the lesser to the greater, 'if this, how much more that'.)

The Pharisees focused on external rituals and did not discern the underlying spiritual realities. They were also concerned about outward form because it marked their status within Jewish society. Their priority to protect their privileged positions blinded them to the truth about Jesus that would otherwise have been obvious.

> **7:25-31** *Therefore some of them of Jerusalem said, 'Isn't this he whom they seek to kill? Behold, he speaks openly, and they say nothing to him. Can it be that the rulers indeed know that this is truly the Christ? However we know where this man comes from, but when the Christ comes, no one will know where he comes from.'*
>
> *Jesus therefore cried out in the temple, teaching and saying, 'You both know me, and know where I am from. I have not come of myself, but he who sent me is true, whom you don't know. I know him, because I am from him, and he sent me.'*
>
> *They sought therefore to take him; but no one laid a hand on him, because his hour had not yet come. But of the multitude, many believed in him. They said, 'When the Christ comes, he won't do more signs than those which this man has done, will he?'*

The crowds in the Temple contained both pilgrims and residents of Jerusalem. Some in the latter group were obviously well aware of the attitude and intentions of the Jewish rulers towards Jesus, and they were puzzled at their failure to react to His forthright and challenging words. Surely they could not have done such a rapid about-turn! The leaders seemed uncertain, but one section of the crowd thought that they knew a thing or two. Using a suitably condescending expression, 'this man', with reference to Jesus, they claimed to know His origins, presumably as being from unsophisticated Galilee in the far north. Some of the locals in the crowd claimed that the birthplace of the Messiah was unknown, thus exhibiting their own ignorance of the Scriptures that prophesied the place of birth as Bethlehem, the town of David. Others evidently knew of Micah's prophecy[4] (see verse 42) but had failed to check on the details of Jesus' birth. Many sceptics still reject Jesus on the basis of prejudice, ignorance and misinformation, and are often unprepared to examine the available evidence for themselves.

The leaders had made sneering comments about Jesus' lack of formal education as He engaged in teaching those with hearts to listen. Some other people dismissed Him as a possible Messiah on the basis of His 'known' human origins, making incorrect deductions from inaccurate information, so Jesus paused to repudiate these false conclusions in the first of two loud public statements. He did not mince His words and rebuked their proud attitudes, for He had amply demonstrated His true origins by His words and works. Their problem was the same as that of the leaders: 'He who sent me is true, whom you don't know.' Despite their religious orthodoxy and their punctilious attendance at the feasts, they did not know the God of Moses, the God of Israel.

This opinionated section of the crowd was offended by Jesus' forthright words and, in the absence of determined action by the official leadership, thought they should take matters into their own hands. This still happens in our contemporary world; religious people can quickly be aroused to commit violence, alleging blasphemy. John provided the reason for the failure of their plans: the Father also had a plan, and the time for this had not yet arrived. The sovereignty of God is nowhere more evident than in the events leading to the cross. God's will intersected with and made use of human choice. Others in the crowd took the part of Jesus and received the evidence that Jesus was indeed the Messiah. The former group had spoken derogatively of Jesus as 'this man', but

[4] Mic. 5:2.

164

these others used the same term in a positive way. They believed in Jesus, but we do not know to what extent that commitment was unconditional.[5]

> **7:32-36** *The Pharisees heard the multitude murmuring these things concerning him, and the chief priests and the Pharisees sent officers to arrest him.*
>
> *Then Jesus said, 'I will be with you a little while longer, then I go to him who sent me. You will seek me, and won't find me. You can't come where I am.'*
>
> *The Jews therefore said amongst themselves, 'Where will this man go that we won't find him? Will he go to the Dispersion amongst the Greeks, and teach the Greeks? What is this word that he said, "You will seek me, and won't find me;" and "Where I am, you can't come"?'*

People had been expressing differing opinions about Jesus before He entered the Temple. His words had had the effect of intensifying the debate. It appears that they were engaged in heated but low-volume discussions that had, nevertheless, attracted the attention of the Pharisees. Clearly, the leaders needed to re-establish their authority, lest a riot should ensue and provoke the Romans to intervene. The Pharisees had no jurisdiction in the Temple and so they alerted the chief priests, who then dispatched their guards to arrest Jesus and remove Him from the scene.[6]

Sometimes Jesus spoke in riddles to those who were not open to receive the truth. When the officers arrived He responded in an enigmatic way that baffled the leaders who were present, speaking of some mysterious plans to leave and go elsewhere. Jesus said that He was going to the One who had sent Him. They did not believe that He had been sent by God, and interpreted His words in a way that would solve their problems.[7] The attempt to arrest Jesus was thus frustrated.

This, of course, had an unseen dimension: the Father's purpose and the appointed time for the offering up of His Son. Meanwhile, the Jewish leaders were descending into spiritual blindness, with

---

[5] John 8:30-59.

[6] Acts 21:30-32.

[7] John 5:16-47; 6:41-59.

the spiritual equivalent of a dimmer switch that gradually reduces the light until everything is dark. This contains a solemn warning to all who refuse to believe. They may ultimately be unable to do so.[8]

---

[8] John 12:37-41.

22

John 7:37-52
An Offer and a Challenge

> *7:37-39 Now on the last and greatest day of the feast, Jesus stood and cried out, 'If anyone is thirsty, let him come to me and drink! He who believes in me, as the Scripture has said, from within him will flow rivers of living water.' But he said this about the Spirit, which those believing in him were to receive. For the Holy Spirit was not yet given, because Jesus wasn't yet glorified.*

Tabernacles, or Booths, was the last of the three great pilgrim feasts of the Jewish year. Each of the festivals celebrated a stage in the harvest, each recalled an aspect of the Exodus story and each had prophetic significance concerning the coming messianic Kingdom. Tabernacles was also known as the Feast of Ingathering because it marked the completion of the agricultural year with the harvesting of the fruit crops of the land.[1] The ceremonies and festivities lasted for eight days, the first and last days being observed as Sabbaths. It was a time of rejoicing, involving much music and dancing in thanksgiving before the Creator Lord for His bounty. The people were commanded to live in leafy booths, left partly open to the sky in remembrance of their journey through the wilderness and of how God had protected them and provided them with water and food.

By the time of Jesus another tradition had developed. Each day a priest took a silver pitcher down the hill to the pool of Siloam and filled it with water. He then carried it in procession to the Temple, where the water was poured out at the corner of the altar. This symbolised the longed-for fulfilment of the prophecy of

---

[1] Exod. 23:16; 34:22.

Ezekiel that in the latter days a stream of water would flow from the Temple and would restore the waters of the Dead Sea to freshness and life.[2] The ceremony was accompanied by fervent prayers for rain, to end the six months' summer drought and to prepare the land for the next growing season. There was also passionate intercession for the Messiah to come and pour out the Holy Spirit of God upon Israel, thus bringing to an end the 400 years of silence since Malachi, the last of the canonical prophets.

On this last and great day of the feast the Temple courts would have been filled to capacity. All eyes would have been focused on the vivid and symbolic drama that recalled ancient prophecies about the spiritual and national restoration of Israel. It was a time of intense emotion and heightened hopes that the promised Messiah would soon appear. In the midst of this highly charged atmosphere, and perhaps at the very moment when the water was about to be poured out, a lone voice rang out in the Temple courts: 'If anyone is thirsty, let him come to me and drink! He who believes in me, as the Scripture has said, from within him will flow rivers of living water.' It is impossible to exaggerate the impact and shock that these words would have caused, spoken in that place and on that occasion.

What was the scripture to which Jesus said He was referring? Actually, there is no precise Scriptural text where these words occur. He was using a recognised method of interpretation, where a number of scriptures that relate to a theme were brought together and the essence extracted from each of them. Those present on that occasion would have committed large parts of Scripture to memory and would have identified relevant passages. (This is a challenge to our generation, possessing as we do the Bible in written form but, all too often, with little stored up in our hearts and minds.)

Here are some of the scriptures that were probably in Jesus' mind at the time. When Moses had struck the rock using the rod of God a deluge of water had flowed out, sufficient to quench the thirst of a whole nation and to sustain the lives of very many people. It was a real space and time event but also pointed to the

---

[2] Ezek. 47:1-12.

promised Messiah; Paul subsequently made the connection explicit.[3] Jeremiah and David spoke of God as the spring of living water. God promised through Isaiah that He would pour water on the thirsty and floods on the dry ground, linking this to His promise to pour out His Spirit upon His people. Isaiah also saw a day when Israel would draw water from the wells of salvation. Other scriptures spoke of the Spirit being poured out from on high upon God's people.[4]

The prophets had directed attention away from themselves to God and to His promises and requirements. Jesus was calling attention to Himself as the fulfilment of those prophetic scriptures and as the source of spiritual life and blessing. He was making an unmistakable claim to be the promised Messiah, and even the Lord Himself, come in flesh. Jesus thus confronted the gathered people and their leaders with a stark choice between belief and commitment on the one hand and unbelief and rejection on the other. There could be no middle way. They had come and had seen; how would they (and how will we) respond?

Jesus' words were ambiguous. From whom will the water flow – from Jesus or from those who believe? Frequently, when faced with a choice like this our tendency is to choose a single solution. This analytical approach is sometimes described as 'a Greek way of thinking'. The typical Jewish approach is to say 'both are true', and this seems to work better here. This living water will be poured out on those who believe and will flow into them. It will then overflow from them and bring life to others in the surrounding world. Jesus' encounter with the Samaritan woman and her subsequent witness to her neighbours is a vivid example of this dynamic picture.

John helpfully explained the symbolic language in Jesus' statement, and thus provided the key to understanding the symbolism of water in the rest of the Gospel. When Jesus spoke of water, especially of living or flowing water, He was using it as a symbol of the Spirit. This was the case at the wedding in Cana, in His encounters with Nicodemus and the Samaritan woman, and

---

[3] Exod. 17:1-6, 9; 1 Cor. 10:1-4.
[4] Jer. 2:13; 17:13; Ps. 36:9; Isa. 12:2-3; 32:15; 44:3-4; Ezek. 39:29; Joel 2:28.

also in the healing of the lame man by the pool, where the waters were said to move at times (the context rather than the cause of his healing). Water as a symbol would reappear in the healing of a blind man and at the cross, as blood and water flowed from Jesus' side.

The cross would be a place of humiliation and suffering and also of shame and thirst. Jesus would be the rock that was struck once and for all, the source of living water. The cross was Jesus' route to glory at the Father's side, from where He would pour out the Spirit on His expectant and believing disciples. They would be baptised in the Spirit in a conscious and experiential way, just as John the Baptist had prophesied and as Jesus had promised. When this happened, the symbol of water would give way to the dynamic presence of the Holy Spirit in reality and power.[5] This was not intended only as an initial experience to launch the church, but is a continuing and timeless promise to anyone who is thirsty, and who in faith will come to Jesus and drink.

> **7:40-46** *Many of the multitude therefore, when they heard these words, said, 'This is truly the prophet.'*
>
> *Others said, 'This is the Christ.'*
>
> *But some said, 'What, does the Christ come out of Galilee? Hasn't the Scripture said that the Christ comes of the offspring of David, and from Bethlehem, the village where David was?'*
>
> *So a division arose in the multitude because of him. Some of them would have arrested him, but no one laid hands on him. The officers therefore came to the chief priests and Pharisees, and they said to them, 'Why didn't you bring him?'*
>
> *The officers answered, 'No man ever spoke like this man!'*

Jesus' dramatic announcement provoked further controversy and division among the crowd. His words carried a ring of authority and struck a chord in those with a disposition to believe. Some people identified Jesus as the true successor of Moses who had brought water from the rock; some identified Him as the Messiah who had been promised throughout the Scriptures. Others,

---

[5] Exod. 17:1-6; Num. 20:2-13; Isa. 53:4-5; Heb. 9:25-28; 1 Pet. 3:18; John 1:32-33; Acts 1:4-8; 2:1-4, 16-21, 29-33, 38-39.

appealing to the same Scriptures but failing to check the accuracy of their data, denied that Jesus could be the Messiah. Yet others, having an impulse to lay hands on Him and imprison Him, found themselves mysteriously restrained. The Temple guards, having been sent out again to apprehend Jesus, returned empty-handed to their masters.

The explanation that the guards offered for their failure to arrest Jesus must have sounded very thin, but it was, in fact, both heartfelt and honest. They were so awed by the authority and power of His words that they were willing to disobey the orders of very powerful men who could discipline or dismiss them. The fear of the Lord overcomes the fear of fellow human beings and gives us the courage we need to stand up and be counted.

> *7:47-52 The Pharisees therefore answered them, 'You aren't also led astray, are you? Have any of the rulers believed in him, or of the Pharisees? But this multitude that doesn't know the law is cursed.'*
>
> *Nicodemus (he who came to him by night, being one of them) said to them, 'Does our law judge a man, unless it first hears from him personally and knows what he does?'*
>
> *They answered him, 'Are you also from Galilee? Search, and see that no prophet has arisen out of Galilee.'*

The Pharisees, who were part of the ruling council and who were experts in the interpretation of the law, took their cue from the guards' report. They knew that many of the crowd were impressed by Jesus and His teaching, but disdainfully dismissed them as ignorant peasants whose opinion did not count. After all, the crowds, unlike the Pharisees, did not know and practise all the details of the written and oral law and were therefore living under God's curse.

Two to three years had elapsed since Nicodemus had come to see Jesus, so he had had much time to reflect. No doubt he had followed the reports of Jesus' ministry both in Jerusalem and in Galilee with interest. Nicodemus now re-emerged as a man on a journey, fair minded and open to persuasion but not yet ready to go public with his growing convictions. Many people travel this same path and may not be able to identify a precise moment when they cross the threshold to genuine faith, but nevertheless they know that it has happened.

Nicodemus mildly pointed out an important aspect of the law in relation to evidence and was rewarded with abuse and insult, rather than with a counter-argument from the law, as would have been appropriate. Such was the hypocrisy and duplicity of the leaders whose priority was to protect their own positions, by any means.

The Pharisees of Jerusalem had been proud to be associated with Nicodemus as an honoured teacher, but now a suggestion of sympathy for Jesus and a plea for fair play caused them to despise him. Calling Nicodemus a Galilean, from that unsophisticated primitive backwater in the north, was as much a studied insult as when Jesus was called a Samaritan by the Jewish leaders.[6] In the process the Pharisees actually revealed their ignorance of the Scriptures: a very notable prophet, Jonah the son of Amittai, hailed from Gath Hepher in the vicinity of Cana in Galilee.[7] Another irony is that the Pharisees seemed no better informed about Jesus' place of birth than the people whom they described as ignorant and accursed. Of course, they may have chosen to ignore inconvenient facts that did not fit with the desired agenda. Truth is still often considered relative and malleable, a commodity that can be moulded when expedient.

Nicodemus had discovered the likely cost of making a choice to publicly follow Jesus. When he did so six months later, he must have been keenly aware of the anger and rejection from his fellow Pharisees that would inevitably follow. Many followers of Jesus who leave the religion into which they were born currently suffer very severe persecution, including loss of family relationships, of employment and even of life itself.[8]

---

[6] John 8:48.

[7] Jonah 1:1; 2 Kgs 14:25.

[8] Matt. 10:21-22, 34-39.

23

John 7:53–8:11
Jesus Shames the Pharisees

This section is absent from most of the ancient manuscripts because it does not seem to fit neatly into the flow of the narrative. The events recorded in chapter 7 were in the context of the Feast of Tabernacles, an occasion of great celebration and rejoicing, in keeping with which the Temple was illuminated by enormous candelabras that also lit up the streets of Jerusalem. Jesus had proclaimed Himself to be the source of living water and was now about to identify Himself as the light of the world. The text that begins at John 8:12 continues in a natural way from John 7:52. This, of course, does not deny the veracity of the intervening section. It carries its own internal witness to authenticity, it rings true as a description of the Jesus whom we know from all the Gospel records and it reads convincingly as an eyewitness account of the events. We can safely treat it as authentic and, as will be pointed out, there is a possible and intriguing link between this incident, Jesus' declaration in the Temple and a prophetic word from Jeremiah.

> **7:53–8:6a** *Everyone went to his own house, but Jesus went to the Mount of Olives.*
> *Now very early in the morning, he came again into the temple, and all the people came to him. He sat down and taught them.*
> *The scribes and the Pharisees brought a woman taken in adultery. Having set her in the middle, they told him, 'Teacher, we found this woman in adultery, in the very act. Now in our law, Moses commanded us to stone such women. What then do you say about her?' They said this testing him, that they might have something to accuse him of.*

All we know for certain about the background to this incident is that Jesus had been teaching in the Temple on the previous day, that His hearers had retired to their homes and that He had spent the night on the nearby Mount of Olives. This series of linked events is recorded in the other Gospels only in relation to His final visit to Jerusalem for Passover.[1] This would add poignancy to the incident.

Jesus returned to the Temple and taught once again. Following the custom for a Jewish teacher, He sat down, probably in one of the covered colonnades at the side of the Temple court, and people sat in a circle around Him. The quiet seminar was suddenly disrupted by a group of religious leaders dragging a probably dishevelled and frightened woman. They thrust her into the centre of the circle. She was now the focus of attention.

The leaders claimed that they had come to Jesus because they were confronted with a serious problem, having, innocently and to their horror, observed the woman in the act of adultery. They pointed out that the Law of Moses demanded that she must be stoned to death. As compassionate people they, of course, shrank from this course of action. However, they were mindful of their duty under the Law and were unable to resolve the obvious conflict. Jesus had claimed to have superior authority to interpret the Law, having made statements such as, 'But I say to you' and 'Amen, amen, I say to you'. He obviously considered Himself to be something of an expert, so what could be more appropriate than that He should provide a definitive ruling on the matter?[2]

Of course, Jesus was perfectly aware that this was a trap, and that they had no such high moral or compassionate motives. To them the woman was a mere pawn, part of a strategy to discredit and destroy Him. She was otherwise insignificant to them, and her fate was inconsequential.

The Law required very precise evidence for the sin of adultery. She must be a married woman and two, or preferably three, witnesses must have seen her in the physical act of sexual union. The likelihood of this was quite remote, indicating that this was a

---

[1] Luke 21:37; Matt. 26:30; Luke 22:39.
[2] Matt. 5:21-44; John 5:19-30; 6:35-40.

put-up job, especially in the absence of the other guilty party, as the Law required his death as well.[3]

> ***8:6b-9a*** *But Jesus stooped down and wrote on the ground with his finger. But when they continued asking him, he looked up and said to them, 'He who is without sin amongst you, let him throw the first stone at her.' Again he stooped down and wrote on the ground with his finger. They, when they heard it, being convicted by their conscience, went out one by one, beginning from the oldest, even to the last.*

Jesus gave the appearance of being oblivious to their presence and their words. Scripture teaches that God will not hear or listen to the requests and prayers of the wicked.[4] As was usual, Jesus did not respond to those who acted out of expediency and self-interest rather than in pursuit of truth and conformity to the revealed will of God. He would not allow them to harass or pressurise Him; He would respond in His own time and His own way. Meanwhile He occupied Himself by stooping down to the dust of the earth and writing or drawing with His finger.

We are not informed of what He wrote, but the manner of His writing was reminiscent of the account of the Exodus. The magicians of Egypt had acknowledged defeat and attributed this to the finger of God. The Law given to Moses was engraved by the finger of God on tablets made from hard and unyielding rock.[5] Now, in the Temple, the One who had created humankind from the dust of the earth, and who knows our frame and remembers that we are dust, adopted a posture of humility as the servant of the Lord, and began to write in the soft and yielding dust of the ground.[6]

Thinking that they had succeeded in getting the better of Jesus, the Pharisees pressed home their apparent advantage. They repeatedly demanded an answer, perhaps hoping that Jesus would concede defeat or lay Himself open to the charge of contradicting Moses. Meanwhile, Jesus' chief concern was for the woman, to

---

[3] Lev. 20:10; Deut. 17:6; 19:15.

[4] Ps. 66:18; Isa. 1:15; Jer. 11:11.

[5] Exod. 31:18; Deut. 9:10; Exod. 8:19; Luke 11:20.

[6] Ps. 103:13-14.

raise her up from the place of shame and humiliation and to set her on the path to redemption and recovery. As they continued to demand an answer to their question, Jesus calmly and deliberately raised His eyes and looked at the men who were accusing her. They had done so as a pretext for accusing Him, but now He turned the tables and focused the searchlight of truth on them. If stoning was the order of the day, then the witnesses should throw the stones, but they must first give account of their own lives and behaviour.

With those few words, 'He who is without sin amongst you, let him throw the first stone at her,' Jesus addressed the consciences of these self-righteous men. They had come together, each individual's confidence supported and fuelled by the group dynamic. They thus reinforced their conviction that they were behaving correctly and that their treatment of the woman was justified by the greater good of undermining Jesus' public standing as a man sent by God. Jesus dismantled the protective shield of their group identity and challenged someone to act on his own responsibility, and effectively to claim to be sufficiently holy as to act as God's executioner of the sad and vulnerable woman who crouched at their feet.

John White, a psychiatrist and a Christian pastor, pointed out how a 'lynch-mob' situation can release from moral constraint people who would, as individuals, not otherwise feel free to behave in cruel and violent ways.[7] The history of the past century contains many graphic examples of this on both large and small scales. All hostile action against Jesus was on a corporate basis, from the initial attempt to murder Him in Nazareth to the events of His trial and crucifixion.[8] Stephen's martyrdom was effected by a group of religious men who were inflamed by his testimony. Paul's near-death experience happened in a similar way.[9]

Having implicitly pointed out their guilt, Jesus stooped down and wrote on the ground again. Perhaps He was making a connection between His recent declaration in the Temple at the Feast of Tabernacles and the words of God through the prophet

[7] John White, *Changing on the Inside* (Vine Books, 1991), pp. 58-62.
[8] Luke 4:28-30; John 8:58-59; 10:29-31; 18:2-3, 28-31; 19:12.
[9] Acts 7:54-60; 14:19-20.

Jeremiah: 'LORD, the hope of Israel, all who forsake you will be disappointed. Those who depart from me will be written in the earth, because they have forsaken the LORD, the spring of living waters.'[10] They had rejected the gracious offer from the lips of the incarnate LORD and now their judgement was being written in the earth.

Each man was now rendered naked and alone, facing the searchlight of his own conscience as accusing memories of past misdemeanours surfaced. No one could step out of the group to make a claim that both he and the others knew to be false. Their carefully crafted strategy and apparently foolproof weapon had crumbled to dust in their hands. The finger of accusation that they had pointed towards Jesus and the woman was now pointing back at themselves through their own God-given consciences.

We do not know what issues sprang up in their minds: perhaps memories included sexual sins, and maybe the men were painfully conscious of their shabby behaviour that now contrasted with the calm and measured way in which Jesus had responded. They had encountered holiness incarnate and the shadows in their own hearts cried out in shame. Rendered speechless and embarrassed and looking for the exit, the older men who had most to regret left first.

In relation to this incident, John White makes an insightful distinction between conscience and guilt on the one hand and repentance on the other. The former deals with a particular sin or set of sins, but the latter requires a new understanding of reality. There is no indication that, ashamed as they were of their actions, they had undergone a radical shift in their attitude towards Jesus. They, or others like them, would continue to pursue Him to His death.[11]

---

[10] Jer. 17:13; Jer. 2:13. See also Joe Amaral in 'Understanding Why Jesus Wrote in the Sand', 23 October 2014:
https://www.youtube.com/watch?v=tmWrS86zs4Y (accessed 16th January 2019).

[11] John White, *Changing on the Inside*, pp. 112-115.

8:9b-11 Jesus was left alone with the woman where she was, in the middle. Jesus, standing up, saw her and said, 'Woman, where are your accusers? Did no one condemn you?'

She said, 'No one, Lord.'

Jesus said, 'Neither do I condemn you. Go your way. From now on, sin no more.'

The woman, confused and not knowing what to do, stood rooted to the spot, still surrounded by the seminar group who had just experienced the most dramatic teaching session imaginable. Jesus' entire focus was now on her as if no one else was present. He straightened up, looked at her and asked a question that contained her acquittal. In the absence of accusers, the charge against her was invalid in law and the question of stoning did not arise.

Jesus' words and attitude would have served to restore her dignity and her place in society. However, this did not mean that there were no issues to address. Jesus dismissed her with words that combined comfort and challenge; He neither glossed over the reality of her sin and nor did he leave her in a state of anxiety about her past behaviour. Perhaps He was aware of circumstances that had trapped her in a life of sin and shame.[12] '

It seems that the Law had been unsuccessful in restraining her from sin. She had come unwillingly into the presence of Jesus, in shame and distress and facing possible death. She had seen and experienced His love and grace instead of condemnation and judgement.[13] Now she was walking away in freedom and with words of grace and mercy ringing in her ears. Jesus' words indicated that she now had power to choose the path of righteousness, and His grace had provided her with the opportunity for a fresh start. What would she do with her new-found freedom? A revelation of the goodness of God is designed to lead us to repentance, and often does so more effectively than harsh words.

Jesus had been the real target of attack, as the leaders had been seeking a pretext to accuse Him. The accusers had gone but Jesus

---

[12] Rom. 2:4.

[13] See Appendix 3 for comments on Jesus' attitude to and treatment of women.

remained in the Temple, close to the place of sacrifice. We do not know the content of His thoughts at that moment, but the suffering of the cross was looming on the horizon. His acts of grace incurred a cost to Himself. Each of them anticipated the ultimate sacrifice when He would lay down His life for the sins of the world and all of the consequences that flowed from them.

24

John 8:12-29
The Light of the World

> *8:12-18 Again, therefore, Jesus spoke to them, saying, 'I am the light of the world. He who follows me will not walk in the darkness, but will have the light of life.'*
>
> *The Pharisees therefore said to him, 'You testify about yourself. Your testimony is not valid.'*
>
> *Jesus answered them, 'Even if I testify about myself, my testimony is true, for I know where I came from, and where I am going; but you don't know where I came from, or where I am going. You judge according to the flesh. I judge no one. Even if I do judge, my judgement is true, for I am not alone, but I am with the Father who sent me. It's also written in your law that the testimony of two people is valid. I am one who testifies about myself, and the Father who sent me testifies about me.'*

John 7:45-52 gave details of a private session of the Jewish council while Jesus was in the Temple courts. John 8:12 commences with a Greek word meaning 'again'; this suggests a continuing conversation or debate involving Jesus and the people who had expressed different opinions about His true identity. These included some Pharisees who were not members of the council but who had previously debated with Jesus. Jesus had made no attempt to engage in apologetics, and nor did He ally Himself with those who had named Him as the Messiah. In a short while He would challenge them as to the reality of their faith.[1]

Jesus began this new discourse with an absolute and unqualified claim, one that could be neither modified nor diluted but must be

---

[1] John 7:40-41; 8:30-33.

either received or rejected. His words, 'I am the light of the world. He who follows me shall not walk in the darkness, but will have the light of life', paralleled His previous claim, 'If anyone is thirsty, let him come to me and drink! He who believes in me, as the Scripture has said, from within him will flow rivers of living water.'

Each of these two statements connected with a number of scriptures, and each contained a clear and unequivocal claim that Jesus was Israel's Messiah and also God's answer for the whole human race – 'the world', 'anyone'. Drinking the water and following the light were two descriptions of how to arrive at a single destination: life.[2]

Light was a central theme in the prologue to John's Gospel. John described Jesus as the 'true light', the One who would give light to all men and the light that would vanquish the darkness that pervaded the world. Jesus told the Pharisee Nicodemus about the peril of turning away from that light and of the blessing that would result from coming to that light. In His subsequent encounter with a number of Pharisees following the healing of the lame man, Jesus referred to the light that came through John the Baptist but stated that His own words and works provided a far superior witness.[3] By the time of the recent Feast of Tabernacles there was even more abundant evidence for Jesus' identity, but the Pharisees had stubbornly refused to recognise the light that shone from Him, and they continued in their hostility.

The Pharisees dismissed Jesus assertion, 'I am the light of the world. He who follows me will not walk in the darkness, but will have the light of life', as being legally invalid, probably also implying that it was untrue. Jesus had previously made clear that the works that the Father accomplished through Him provided legally valid witness, and that these works affirmed the truth of His words. He also insisted that because He had personal and first-hand knowledge that the Pharisees lacked, He was competent as a witness and they were incompetent as judges. He pointed out that earthly creatures cannot pass judgement on the One who has been sent by the Father and who will return to Him. The Father's

---

[2] John 7:37-38; Ps. 27:1; 36:9; 118:27; Isa. 9:2; 49:6; 60:1.
[3] John 1:4-9; 3:19-21; 5:33-37.

witness through the works and Jesus' witness by His words provided incontrovertible evidence for His identity.

> **8:19-20** *They said therefore to him, 'Where is your Father?'*
> *Jesus answered, 'You know neither me nor my Father. If you knew me, you would know my Father also.'*
> *Jesus spoke these words in the treasury, as he taught in the temple. Yet no one arrested him, because his hour had not yet come.*

The reason for this question from the Pharisees is difficult to discern, as it must have been perfectly clear that Jesus was referring to the God of Israel, as revealed in the Scriptures. Perhaps it was an innuendo about the circumstances of Jesus' conception, as appears to have been the case later in the passage (see verse 41). Whatever their motivation, Jesus attributed their ignorance about this matter to their failure to recognise Him as the true revelation of God in human form. Their question was a diversionary tactic, so Jesus ignored it and challenged them again about the core issue of His relationship with the Father.

The Pharisees had a false picture of the God whom they studied in their sacred texts. This distorted view was reinforced by self-interest and a perceived threat to the honoured positions that they enjoyed. This was why they failed to recognise Jesus as God's Son and continued to reject Him, refusing even to reassess their dearly held opinions. The same is true of contemporary orthodox Jews who read the Scriptures with a veil over their eyes; Paul understood that one day that veil will be removed and that they will see and receive Jesus as their Messiah and Saviour.[4]

Some Christians have a related problem, thinking that God as revealed by Jesus in the New Testament is different from and more loving than the God of the Old Testament, leading them to neglect that part of the Bible. Even when God was about to judge His people Israel and to send them into exile, He assured them that He loved them with an everlasting love. We need to read the Old Testament through the lens of the person of Jesus, and continually

---

[4] 2 Cor. 3:12-17; Rom. 11:25-32.

understand that the God of Israel is one and the same as the God and Father of the Lord Jesus.[5]

John informs us that this interchange took place in the treasury, which was in the court of the women. This was close to the place of sacrifice, the very centre of religious ritual and power. This very public confrontation probably intensified the rulers' desire to eliminate Jesus, but it seems that there was no immediate opportunity to do so. Once again John gave the true explanation: His 'hour had not yet come'. The Father's invisible hand was guiding events to their appointed destination and on His chosen timescale.

> **8:21-29** *Jesus said therefore again to them, 'I am going away, and you will seek me, and you will die in your sins. Where I go, you can't come.'*
>
> *The Jews therefore said, 'Will he kill himself, because he says, "Where I am going, you can't come"?'*
>
> *He said to them, 'You are from beneath. I am from above. You are of this world. I am not of this world. I said therefore to you that you will die in your sins; for unless you believe that I am he, you will die in your sins.'*
>
> *They said therefore to him, 'Who are you?'*
>
> *Jesus said to them, 'Just what I have been saying to you from the beginning. I have many things to speak and to judge concerning you. However he who sent me is true; and the things which I heard from him, these I say to the world.'*
>
> *They didn't understand that he spoke to them about the Father.*
>
> *Jesus therefore said to them, 'When you have lifted up the Son of Man, then you will know that I am he, and I do nothing of myself, but as my Father taught me, I say these things. He who sent me is with me. The Father hasn't left me alone, for I always do the things that are pleasing to him.'*

Jesus continued to speak to the Pharisees and to warn them of the serious consequences that would result from their stubborn unbelief. They needed to know that this was not inconsequential, but rather a matter of life and death. The door of opportunity

---

[5] Jer. 31:3-6.

would soon slam shut, and they would then look for Him in vain and would die in their sin. His opening words contained four statements, none of which made sense to them, because of their denial of Jesus' true identity. They conjectured (hopefully) that in speaking of 'going away' He might be referring to His death and perhaps at His own hands, but they ignored the accompanying warning that His departure would precipitate their own destruction. The phrase 'die in your sins' was not defined in the Scriptures, but it had overtones of the future judgement to which Jesus would refer a little later: 'I have many things to speak and to judge concerning you.'

As was usual, Jesus ignored the question about Him killing Himself; this was irrelevant to their present and urgent danger of dying in their sins as a result of their unbelief. He and they belonged to two radically different spheres of existence, earth and heaven, and their natures were correspondingly different, both in greatness and glory. They existed in a state of being in sin, whereas Jesus always did those things that pleased the Father. This revelation of Jesus' unique nature, character and role pervades John's Gospel, and is its most important fact on which everything else depends.

Jesus insisted that the Pharisees must believe in Him and commit themselves to Him, for an ominous judgement hovered over them and would come into effect if they died in their sins. Sin[6] is first mentioned in the singular and then in the plural, perhaps connecting the one great sin of proud independence with the many individual sins to which it gives rise. They must repent of that great overarching sin by believing that 'I am he'. The word 'he' is not in the Greek text and nor is there an object for the verb to be.

Jesus was making the stupendous and shocking claim (and even more explicitly in verse 58) to be the eternal God in human form. This being the case, belief in Him was the only to way escape from the consequences of their sins. The enormity of Jesus' claim was so much at odds with their worldview that they did not know how

---

[6] Some English versions, including the WEBBE, translate 'sin' (singular) in v21 as 'sins' (plural), perhaps understanding the Greek word as a collective noun.

to address it, so they treated His sentence as if unfinished, and inquired, 'Who are you?'

Jesus reminded them that, in the course of previous interactions, He had repeatedly answered that question. In brief, He had been sent to act and to speak on behalf of the One whom He described as 'true', and He had been faithfully carrying out that assignment. Perhaps He deliberately avoided speaking of the Father by name in order to give them the opportunity to make the connection for themselves. The fact that they could not identify the One who is true as being the God of Israel, and as the One whom Jesus had recently described as His Father, seems astonishing. This reveals the advanced state of the blindness and unbelief that was pervading their understanding.

Patiently, Jesus now reiterated facts about His presence and purpose in the world. He had been sent by the Father. The Father taught Him, directed Him and was in constant relationship with Him. Jesus knew that following His death people would have to choose whether or not to believe in Him. He knew that many of the Pharisees would persist in unbelief and would die in their sins. (Some, however, including Joseph of Arimathea and Nicodemus, would publicly acknowledge who He was and would be saved.)

Jesus spoke of being 'lifted up' as the Son of Man, accepting this role in obedience to the Father and on behalf of the human race. When He had spoken to Nicodemus, He had not explained who would be responsible for lifting Him up. Now He revealed that the Jewish leaders, some of whom were currently listening to His words of warning, would be responsible for this process. Lifting up would have a double dimension, suffering and glory, for the cross would be a stage in His journey to the Father's immediate presence.[7]

---

[7] John 1:51; 3:13-15; 12:32-34.

25

John 8:30-59
Which Father, Which Freedom?

> *8:30-36 As he spoke these things, many believed in him. Jesus therefore said to those Jews who had believed him, 'If you remain in my word, then you are truly my disciples. You will know the truth, and the truth will make you free.'*
>
> *They answered him, 'We are Abraham's offspring, and have never been in bondage to anyone. How do you say, "You will be made free"?'*
>
> *Jesus answered them, 'Most certainly I tell you, everyone who commits sin is the bondservant of sin. A bondservant doesn't live in the house forever. A son remains forever. If therefore the Son makes you free, you will be free indeed.'*

This interchange involves Jesus and certain Pharisees, here described as 'those Jews who had believed him'. Many (other) people are also said to have believed in Him, so it seems that others had been listening to the conversation as well. All of this appears, at first sight, to have been a major breakthrough in Jesus' ministry, but it is clear that He did not regard it as such. His response goes to the heart of what it means to believe, which is to become a committed disciple of Jesus, one who hears and obeys His word.

Certain forms of evangelism involve efforts to persuade people to agree with a set of doctrinal statements, upon which they are assured that they are now born-again Christians. Of course, no one who denies the fundamental truths of the gospel can be considered to be a follower of Jesus, but true faith includes much more than intellectual agreement. The heart and will must also be engaged in a resolve to remain close to Jesus, whatever the consequences. When He had spoken about eating His flesh and drinking His blood, many would-be disciples had complained and then walked away. Jesus was not interested in popularity or in having a large following, but He was willing to receive those who truly desired to walk with Him along the path of discipleship, and He promised that this path would lead them into true freedom. Jesus did not say, 'If you remain in my word you will be my disciples', but rather, 'you are truly my disciples'. Obedience to Jesus' teaching is the very essence of what it means to be His disciple.

When Jesus spoke to Nicodemus He described this transformation in terms of being born again/born from above and indicated that this was the only means of entrance into the Kingdom of God. Although John only included the term 'God's Kingdom' on that single occasion, the truth itself pervades the whole Gospel. Jesus spoke with absolute authority and He called His would-be followers to radical commitment, to live under His authority as king. Jesus said that the way to freedom was to abide in His word, for His teaching is the true antidote to the false ideas and captivating values of the world. As people walked in relationship with Him, they would learn how to live as children of God and as obedient creatures in God's world. They would thus escape from pressures to conform to the world and would progressively experience freedom from the power of sin. In this way they would experience true freedom and would enjoy the highest form of life that is available to human beings.

The implication that they were not free rankled His hearers, and they responded in a way that revealed the world of illusion in which they were living. Israel had been dominated by a series of empires for hundreds of years, and the land was currently subject to the Roman Caesar. The people groaned under crippling taxes, and pagan symbols desecrated many locations. The Pharisees had retreated into a private religious world that was disconnected from the real one, and they ignored all evidence that conflicted with this worldview. Their mindset thus blinded them to the evidence for Jesus' identity. They were proud of being part of a chosen people that traced its identity back to father Abraham. They had forgotten how God had made a close connection between the nation's faithfulness and obedience to Him and its state of prosperity, whether good or bad. The Pharisees chose to ignore the fact that Israel was currently a nation in bondage.[1]

The Pharisees had interpreted Jesus' words about freedom in physical and national terms. Jesus now drew their attention to an even more terrible form of slavery which was personal and spiritual in nature, and He indicated that this was the slavery to which He had been referring. Being slave or free did not depend on ancestry or religious heritage but was demonstrated in behaviour. Jesus prefaced His response to their foolish, and obviously false, claim with another statement of His absolute authority to speak the truth: 'Amen, amen I say to you'. A person who repeatedly and habitually engages in sin is, by Jesus' definition, a slave of sin. To rationalise sinful behaviour by appeal to religious associations or practices is to engage in self-deception. A person who chooses to remain in slavery by refusing the path to freedom that God has provided through His Son will be excluded from the Father's house. Jesus came in order to bring many children to glory, and those who come to Him must enter His school of discipleship, the only place where true freedom is to be found.[2]

> **8:37-41** *'I know that you are Abraham's offspring, yet you seek to kill me, because my word finds no place in you. I say the things which I have seen with my Father; and you also do the things which you have seen with your father.'*
>
> *They answered him, 'Our father is Abraham.'*
>
> *Jesus said to them, 'If you were Abraham's children, you would do the works of Abraham. But now you seek to kill me, a man who has told you the truth which I heard from God. Abraham didn't do this. You do the works of your father.'*
>
> *They said to him, 'We were not born of sexual immorality. We have one Father, God.'*

Jesus now engaged directly with the claim by the Jewish leaders to be Abraham's children. He made clear the distinction between physical and spiritual relationship. Abraham was related to God by

---

[1] Deut. 11:13-17.
[2] 1 John 3:4-7; Heb. 2:9-11.

faith, and this was demonstrated by his faithfulness and obedience. Abraham's true children will behave in a similar way. Jesus' next statement must have exploded like a bombshell, as He revealed that He knew that they were actively seeking His death. The opportunity to accomplish this had not yet presented itself to them, and their words were designed to conceal their intentions. Jesus not only spoke the truth; He also knew what was going on in their hearts and minds.

Jesus now returned to the subject of parentage, stating that their attitude and behaviour pointed to an as yet unnamed spiritual father. They took this as a gross insult, but significantly they did not deny His assertion that they were plotting to kill Him. Jesus denied their spiritual kinship with Abraham, so now the Pharisees appealed to God Himself as their Father. They seemed to believe that their religious profession and practices would shield them from judgement. The word translated as 'we' in their defensive reply was emphatic, a none-too-subtle slur on Jesus' parentage, the circumstances of which appeared to have generated rumours that His birth was illegitimate.

Character assassination is an unpleasant weapon that is still used to divert attention from, or suppress examination of, the real issues and thus relieve pressure. The Jews probably saw no contradiction in claiming God as their Father while simultaneously seeking to kill Jesus. Like Saul of Tarsus, they considered Jesus to be an imposter and a blasphemer who deserved to die. Many followers of Jesus in our contemporary world are being put to death for a similar reason, for witnessing to the truth that Jesus is the Son of God.

> *8:42-47 Therefore Jesus said to them, 'If God were your father, you would love me, for I came out and have come from God. For I haven't come of myself, but he sent me. Why don't you understand my speech? Because you can't hear my word. You are of your father, the devil, and you want to do the desires of your father. He was a murderer from the beginning, and doesn't stand in the truth, because there is no truth in him. When he speaks a lie, he speaks on his own; for he is a liar, and the father of lies. But because I tell the truth, you don't believe me. Which of you convicts me of sin? If I tell the truth, why do you not*

believe me? He who is of God hears the words of God. For this cause you don't hear, because you are not of God.'

The Jewish leaders claimed that God was their Father. Jesus had come from the Father, so their response to Him gave the lie to that claim. In order to emphasise this, Jesus defined His relationship to the Father in three different ways: He 'came out' (of the Father), had 'come from' (the Father) and was 'sent' by the Father. That they could not believe this truth was not owing to lack of evidence, but was because they did not actually know the God of Israel whom they claimed to know and love.

The reason why they could not understand Jesus' words was because they were out of sympathy with the content of His message. It clashed with their worldview, their perception of reality, their religious traditions, their interpretation and application of Scripture and their place in society. Jesus Himself did not correspond to their prejudiced expectations of what the Messiah would be like. They also realised that He represented a serious threat to their place in society.

People are frequently resistant to ideas that challenge behaviour, status and relationships. Sometimes this is admitted, as in the cases of two prominent atheists. Aldous Huxley wrote that his atheism partly stemmed from a desire for sexual freedom. The philosopher Thomas Nagel confessed that he did not want there to be a God, because he did not want the universe to be like that.[3]

Jesus made an additional startling diagnosis of the process that was at work in their hearts. Evil is not an impersonal force or an atmosphere, but is rather the expression of personal choice and will in opposition to the creator God. Satan, the devil, is a created being who leads this rebellion and entices other creatures to follow his agenda. He has two characteristic features: he is the original and archetypical liar, the father of lies, and he is also a murderer who aims to destroy God's creatures and the creation itself.[4]

---

[3] Aldous Huxley, *Ends and Means* (London: Chatto and Windus, 1941), p. 273; Thomas Nagel, *The Last Word* (Oxford: Oxford University Press, 2001), p. 130. Both are referenced in Andy Bannister, *The Atheist Who Didn't Exist* (Oxford: Monarch Books, 2015, pp. 90-91).

[4] Gen. 3:1-6; 4:8; 1 John 3:8-15; Matt. 4:1-11; John 13:2; Rev. 12:1-17.

Jesus had encountered the devil in the wilderness and had rejected and repelled his advances.[5] The Pharisees had observed Jesus' blameless life and character and the signs that He had performed. All of this should have convinced them that He was speaking the truth but, because this would have disrupted their way of life, they had perversely and persistently refused to believe in Him. This had opened the door to the influence of the evil one and they had become pawns in his hand, sharing in his nature and purposes. They continued to claim God as their Father, but their attitude to Jesus revealed that this was a lie. In fact, despite their religious profession they were not 'of God' at all.

> **8:48-53** *Then the Jews answered him, 'Don't we say well that you are a Samaritan, and have a demon.?'*
>
> *Jesus answered, 'I don't have a demon, but I honour my Father and you dishonour me. But I don't seek my own glory. There is one who seeks and judges. Most certainly, I tell you, if a person keeps my word, he will never see death.'*
>
> *Then the Jews said to him, 'Now we know that you have a demon. Abraham died, as did the prophets; and you say, "If a man keeps my word, he will never taste of death." Are you greater than our father, Abraham, who died? The prophets died. Who do you make yourself out to be?'*

The Pharisees had opened their hearts to the prince of darkness and their course was now out of control and on a rapidly downhill trajectory. They resorted to a double-barrelled insult, calling Jesus a Samaritan and claiming that He had a demon. Jesus dismissed the insult, for He only cared about the Father's opinion and He was content to leave judgement on such matters with Him. Then, once again prefacing His words with the authoritative, 'Amen, amen', He astonished and exasperated them by saying, 'if a person keeps my word, he will never see death'. This sounded totally outrageous. Just who did Jesus think He was – greater than Abraham, and the prophets as well? He was clearly demon possessed and deranged. Although there seemed to be no hope of reasoning with Him,

---

[5] Matt. 4:1-10.

nevertheless their antagonism and their determination to destroy Him drove them on.

> **8:54-59** *Jesus answered, 'If I glorify myself, my glory is nothing. It is my Father who glorifies me, of whom you say that he is our God. You have not known him, but I know him. If I said, "I don't know him," I would be like you, a liar. But I know him and keep his word. Your father Abraham rejoiced to see my day. He saw it, and was glad.'*
>
> *The Jews therefore said to him, 'You are not yet fifty years old! Have you seen Abraham?'*
>
> *Jesus said to them, 'Most certainly, I tell you, before Abraham came into existence, I AM.'*
>
> *Therefore they took up stones to throw at him, but Jesus was hidden, and went out of the temple, having gone through the middle of them, and so passed by.*

The Pharisees had closed their minds to the truth. They had become impervious to the evidence that the Father had provided and to the sublime message that Jesus had spoken. They had fallen prey to the father of lies and had taken on his character. The issue was no longer that they told individual lies, but that they had become liars who believed their own lies. They were convinced that they were God's children and His faithful servants. This was a sad and salutary condition, for the voice of conscience had been silenced. There was now no real prospect of change, for they had chosen darkness, and in the process they had become blind.[6]

Jesus appears to have been speaking in a calm and measured way, but the content of His next statements would have been like adding petrol to a fire. He claimed that father Abraham had known Him and had joyfully anticipated His coming. This confirmed their recent diagnosis of His mental state and they reacted with incredulity and accusation. Jesus was, of course, not claiming to have lived on earth with Abraham, although He had visited with Him on one occasion and in human form.[7]

---

[6] John 9:39-41.
[7] Gen. 18:1-33.

The final straw was when Jesus once again claimed to speak with ultimate authority: 'Amen, amen, I tell you, before Abraham came into existence, I AM.' He had previously hinted at His identity with the God of Abraham, Isaac and Jacob using qualified expressions such as, 'I am the bread of life', but now He claimed the personal name of God for Himself. This was of a different order, being explicit and unambiguous, so they reached for the stones. He might be mad or demonised but now He had surely crossed the line into frank blasphemy.

This, of course, would have been the case if His words were untrue. From their point of view this was clearly impossible. John does not elaborate on how Jesus hid Himself, but we do know why the Pharisees failed in their murderous intent: His time had not yet come.

26

John 9:1-19
A Spectacular Miracle

> **9:1-5** *As he passed by, he saw a man blind from birth. His disciples asked him, 'Rabbi, who sinned, this man or his parents, that he was born blind?'*
>
> *Jesus answered, 'This man didn't sin, nor did his parents; but, that the works of God might be revealed in him. I must work the works of him who sent me while it is day. The night is coming, when no one can work. While I am in the world, I am the light of the world.'*

John probably expected the account of this incident to be read in continuity with the previous one, but this is obscured by the chapter division, without which it reads, 'Jesus was hidden, and went out of the temple, having gone through the middle of them, and so passed by. As he passed by he saw a man blind from birth.'

John informs us that 'the Jews [Pharisees] had already agreed that if any man would confess him as Christ, he would be put out of the synagogue', so some time must have intervened.[1] The Feast of Dedication (Hanukah) was celebrated about eight to ten weeks after the Feast of Tabernacles, so the healing of the blind man must have taken place within the interval between the two feasts.[2] The Pharisees were enraged at Jesus,[3] having just failed to murder Him; this, and the threat of exclusion from social and religious life would have been well known.

The disciples appear to have noticed that Jesus was paying attention to the blind man. Given their past experience with Jesus,

---

[1] John 9:22.
[2] John 10:22.
[3] John 8:59.

this might have led them to expect a miracle, but instead they asked a theological question. The disciples' eagerness to hear Jesus' opinion appears to have taken precedence over proper concern for the man to receive healing from his distressing affliction. How easily this can happen, as we pursue curiosity rather than express compassion.

Sin was widely believed to be the reason for suffering, and some authorities even postulated the existence of sin in utero. Jesus had made a connection between sin and physical infirmity in the case of the lame man, but in the present case He insisted that there was no such connection.[4] Subsequent events would reveal that, although the parents of the blind man were far from perfect, they were in no way responsible for their son's blindness.

Total congenital blindness was a devastating condition that inevitably resulted in poverty and social isolation, reducing the sufferer to life as a beggar. There are no recorded instances in the Jewish Scriptures of people being healed from this condition. The prophets promised that in the age of the Messiah the blind would see, and Jesus had announced that He had come to fulfil these prophecies.[5] Of course, we should not think that Father God had made the man blind in order that Jesus would heal him, and, although the man's affliction was ultimately the consequence of sin, it was not specifically his own sin. Everyone suffers in some way as part of a broken creation, but no one is individually targeted.

What was wonderfully different for this man was that he lived during the precise period when God sent His Son into the world, and he was in the exact place where Jesus was passing by. It was the very day when God purposed to reveal His glory by healing him. That period of special grace was drawing towards its conclusion; in about four to five months' time, Jesus would take upon Himself the sin and suffering of the broken creation, and would then return to the Father. It was still the blind man's day of opportunity and, like the sun, Jesus was shining light that was available to everyone with eyes to see and hearts to obey. The sun of righteousness was about to rise with healing in His wings upon

---

4 Ps. 51:5; John 5:13-14.
5 Isa. 35:5-6; 42:1-7.

this blind beggar, as prophesied by Malachi. He would receive both physical and spiritual sight, and this would be a credible sign to the world that Jesus was the Messiah.[6]

> **9:6-13** *When he had said this, he spat on the ground, made mud with the saliva, anointed the blind man's eyes with the mud, and said to him, 'Go, wash in the pool of Siloam' (which means 'Sent'). So he went away, washed, and came back seeing.*
>
> *The neighbours therefore, and those who saw that he was blind before, said, 'Isn't this he who sat and begged?'*
>
> *Others were saying, 'It is he.'*
>
> *Still others were saying, 'He looks like him.'*
>
> *He said, 'I am he.'*
>
> *They therefore were asking him, 'How were your eyes opened?'*
>
> *He answered, 'A man called Jesus made mud, anointed my eyes, and said to me, "Go to the pool of Siloam and wash." So I went away and washed, and I received sight.'*
>
> *Then they asked him, 'Where is he?'*
>
> *He said, 'I don't know.'*
>
> *They brought him who had been blind to the Pharisees.*

Jesus healed in different ways, depending on individual circumstances and on the Father's leading. The procedure in this case obviously contained symbolism, but its significance is not explained. The use of saliva in healing was a well-known practice. Jesus was working within the current cultural framework but was not giving credence to any magical or chemical properties of the paste that He made. The process enabled Him to communicate with the blind man in a tactile and intimate way. In his turn, the man responded and obeyed the word of Jesus whom he could not see, but who had claimed to be the light of the world. The simplicity of his faith and his willingness to act on the basis of it continues to the end of the account, making this man one of the most attractive characters in the whole Gospel.

Jesus sent the blind man down the hill to the pool of Siloam, whose water flowed along a tunnel from the spring of Gihon (the

---

[6] Luke 4:17-21; 7:19-23; Mal. 4:2.

name means 'sent'). It was the same pool from which the priest had drawn water during the Feast of Tabernacles. The Holy Spirit, flowing in power and love from the person of Jesus, would provide healing, not the clay or the water in which he washed. The man believed and obeyed and came back seeing.

Jesus was not present when the man returned, perhaps having continued on His journey while waiting for events to unfold. The man appears to have returned home, where he encountered his neighbours who responded with a mixture of amazement and confusion. He himself only spoke of what he knew from personal experience, as this was the only subject on which he was an expert. He was a simple but wise man, a not infrequent combination.

The man had turned up on the Sabbath day, able to see and also claiming that Jesus had made clay and had anointed his eyes as part of the process. The neighbours were, no doubt, well aware of the fact that the Pharisees were in conflict with Jesus over issues of Sabbath observance. They also knew about the threat to expel from the synagogue anyone who sided with Jesus as the Messiah. The neighbours therefore took the man to the self-styled experts and left them to sort the matter out. The neighbours may have been unaware that events were rapidly reaching the point where neutrality would be impossible. In our rapidly changing world, the same is increasingly the case.

> **9:14-19** *It was a Sabbath when Jesus made the mud and opened his eyes. Again therefore the Pharisees also asked him how he received his sight. He said to them, 'He put mud on my eyes, I washed, and I see.'*
>
> *Some therefore of the Pharisees said, 'This man is not from God, because he doesn't keep the Sabbath.'*
>
> *Others said, 'How can a man who is a sinner do such signs?'*
>
> *There was division amongst them. Therefore they asked the blind man again, 'What do you say about him, because he opened your eyes?'*
>
> *He said, 'He is a prophet.'*
>
> *The Jews therefore didn't believe concerning him, that he had been blind, and had received his sight, until they called the parents of him who had received his sight, and asked them, 'Is this your son, whom you say was born blind? How then does he now see?'*

These experts now had a problem – opinion among them was divided. The whole group must have accepted the man's testimony of healing, or the issue of Sabbath observance would not have arisen. One part of the group focused exclusively on the issue of Sabbath breaking and chose to ignore the evidence from the unprecedented miracle. Jesus was 'not from God', so any inconvenient facts did not need to be considered. Others were more honest and admitted that the indisputable fact of the miracle needed to be taken into account. It seems that they had misgivings about labelling Jesus as a sinner, even if His unorthodox behaviour did not sit well with their theology. Nicodemus would have been in that camp, although not necessarily present on this occasion.

The next question to the blind man may have been sympathetic and have come from this section, 'What do you say about him, because he opened your eyes?' Alternatively, it may have been a hostile question from the former group, with a view to incriminating Jesus. Either way, they were unwittingly elevating the man to the role of religious expert, and he took up the challenge, replying, 'He is a prophet.' This confession launched the man on a spiritual journey. This journey would climax a little later in worship, when he recognised that Jesus was the Son of God. Meanwhile, the sophisticated Pharisees were stuck in the mire of their prejudice and unbelief. The man exhibited the childlike faith by which we enter the Kingdom of heaven.[7]

The man claimed to have experienced a spectacular and unprecedented healing, and one that was incompatible with the insistence of the Pharisees that Jesus was a sinner. They needed to find a way to contradict the man's testimony and then all would be well; after all, he was only a beggar and probably not to be trusted. They therefore questioned his parents, in the hope that they would settle this vexatious issue in a favourable way and thus permit them to return to the proper calm and peace of the Sabbath day.

---

[7] John 3:3; Matt. 18:3.

27

John 9:20-41
The Blind Who Claim To See

> *9:20-23 His parents answered them, 'We know that this is our son, and that he was born blind; but how he now sees, we don't know; or who opened his eyes, we don't know. He is of age. Ask him. He will speak for himself.' His parents said these things because they feared the Jews; for the Jews had already agreed that if any man would confess him as Christ, he would be put out of the synagogue. Therefore his parents said, 'He is of age. Ask him.'*

The Pharisees asked the parents a two-part question. The first part was straightforward; the parents were expert witnesses in this area and could answer from their own personal knowledge and without danger to themselves. The Pharisees may have been disappointed by their response, for it confirmed that the miracle must somehow have taken place. The subject of the second part of the question was outside the parents' realm of personal experience. They had not witnessed the event, and hearsay testimony would not be legally valid. Like the neighbours, they recognised the danger of saying too much, so they denied having first-hand knowledge of the facts and advised that the issue should be resolved directly with their son. Quite apart from legal technicalities, they were not ready to identify with Jesus on the basis of this amazing miracle, having had little time to process the implications and to count the cost. The one who had benefited from the miracle must deal with the consequences.

> *9:24-34 So they called the man who was blind a second time, and said to him, 'Give glory to God. We know that this man is a sinner.'*

He therefore answered, 'I don't know if he is a sinner. One thing I do know: that though I was blind, now I see.'

They said to him again, 'What did he do to you? How did he open your eyes?'

He answered them, 'I told you already, and you didn't listen. Why do you want to hear it again? You don't also want to become his disciples, do you?'

They insulted him and said, 'You are his disciple, but we are disciples of Moses. We know that God has spoken to Moses. But as for this man, we don't know where he comes from.'

The man answered them, 'How amazing! You don't know where he comes from, yet he opened my eyes. We know that God doesn't listen to sinners, but if anyone is a worshipper of God, and does his will, he listens to him. Since the world began it has never been heard of that anyone opened the eyes of someone born blind. If this man were not from God, he could do nothing.'

They answered him, 'You were altogether born in sins, and do you teach us?' Then they threw him out.

The Pharisees said, 'Give glory to God.' Of course, the irony was that they were doing exactly the opposite themselves. They had become so deluded as to believe that their opinions and conclusions were synonymous with the mind of God.[1] It was now clear to the Pharisees that the man was the only possible source of incriminating evidence, so they, as experts to whose superior knowledge he should submit, began to apply pressure on him. What constitutes true knowledge is central to the dialogue. They claimed to know that Jesus was a sinner simply on the basis of their assumed authority, while ignoring the 'elephant in the room', the undeniable fact of the miracle. Having exhausted all other approaches they now resorted to bullying and demanded that the man should submit to their authority. After all, he was an illiterate beggar; what could he know about the mysteries of religion, in which they were the experts? Religious and political powers still resort to this technique in attempts to enforce conformity.

[1] Acts 4:16-22; 5:26-42.

How did they expect him to respond? Perhaps they hoped that he would submit to their opinion that, despite the miracle, Jesus was a sinner, and then agree to keep quiet. Possibly they hoped that he would alter his account in some way that would fit with their conclusions. This need for support from a powerless man revealed their own sense of vulnerability. The man spoke truth in the face of their opinions and they feared him, for, in fact, he was the expert.

This interchange between the poor, uneducated man and the religious experts is absolutely compelling and needs to be savoured as an exquisite piece of literature. The man prevailed over the overbearing and learned Pharisees because he had personal experience that they did not have. His statements were firmly based on that experience; the Pharisees' arguments were based on a false reading of Scripture and depended on dogma rather than truth. They reasoned that Jesus was a sinner and therefore, unlike Moses, had not been sent by God. It thus followed that He could not have healed the man, so there must be some other explanation. The man knew that Jesus was responsible for this extraordinary miracle, not hitherto known in human experience, and he based his arguments on facts rather than flawed logic. The person who performed such a miracle could not be a sinner and must be from God, as God would not otherwise hear that person's prayers. It followed that Jesus was not a sinner but was a true worshipper of God. It also meant that God must have sent Jesus into the world.

The man was becoming increasingly confident and courageous. Meanwhile, the Pharisees were becoming increasingly frustrated and angry, for he was exposing their arguments as being inconsistent and threadbare. Defeated by a man with no suitable credentials, they now resorted to insults, to pulling rank and perhaps even to physical violence as they cast him out. They said that the man had been 'born in sins', thus denying Jesus' earlier words to the contrary. They arrogantly proclaimed themselves as being in an altogether more exalted category, thus revealing their great sin of pride.

They called on the man to give glory to God and to deny both the miracle and its author. Jesus had said at the outset that the man's healing would be a demonstration of the works of God, and would bring glory to Him. The Pharisees' thinking was corrupted by inflexible interpretation of Scripture and vested self-interest. The man was free from both, and also proved to be superior in his logic and conclusions. Thus the Pharisees continued on their downward trajectory into increasing spiritual blindness. Meanwhile, the man was on an accelerating ascent from physical blindness to spiritual revelation, all within the course of a single day.

> **9:35-41** *Jesus heard that they had thrown him out, and finding him, he said, 'Do you believe in the Son of God?'*
>
> *He answered, 'Who is he, Lord, that I may believe in him?'*
>
> *Jesus said to him, 'You have both seen him, and it is he who speaks with you.'*
>
> *He said, 'Lord, I believe!' and he worshipped him.*
>
> *Jesus said, 'I came into this world for judgement, that those who don't see may see; and that those who see may become blind.'*
>
> *Those of the Pharisees who were with him heard these things, and said to him, 'Are we also blind?'*
>
> *Jesus said to them, 'If you were blind, you would have no sin; but now you say, "We see." Therefore your sin remains.'*

These words record both the wonderful conclusion and the sad finale to that eventful Sabbath day. Jesus chose not to intervene at an earlier stage, but now, as the Good Shepherd, He went in search of His faithful sheep who had been rejected by the false shepherds of Israel. The man looked into the face of Jesus and he recognised the voice that he had heard while he was still blind. Jesus knew that the representatives of organised religion had abused the man, as He himself had experienced. Jesus was confident about how the man would reply to His question, 'Do you believe in the Son of God?'[2]

The man's answer revealed just how far he had come in a single day; it had taken many of the disciples months or years to reach the same level of understanding.[3] He was eager to believe and

[2] John 10:7-8, 11-15; 15:20.

[3] John 6:68-69; Matt. 16:16; John 20:28.

simply lacked the necessary information. The Pharisees had abundant information but refused to believe. The man understood Jesus' question, 'Do you believe in the Son of God?', as an invitation to relationship rather than as an inquiry about his theological beliefs. He responded with his own eager question, 'Who is he, Lord, that I may believe in him?'

Jesus replied, 'You have both seen him, and it is he who speaks with you.' This information was all that the man needed. His physical eyes had been opened in the morning and now, by the evening, the eyes of his heart were also fully open. He responded in worship and was welcomed into the flock of the Good Shepherd. He had discovered the true meaning of Sabbath. The false shepherds, who claimed jurisdiction over the Sabbath, were living in self-imposed blindness because of their stubborn refusal to recognise what was obvious to a simple and unprejudiced mind.[4]

---

[4] John 3:18-21, 35-36; 12:35-41.

28

John 10:1-21
The Good Shepherd and the Sheep

> *10:1-5 'Most certainly, I tell you, one who doesn't enter by the door into the sheep fold, but climbs up some other way, is a thief and a robber. But one who enters in by the door is the shepherd of the sheep. The gatekeeper opens the gate for him, and the sheep listen to his voice. He calls his own sheep by name, and leads them out. Whenever he brings out his own sheep, he goes before them, and the sheep follow him, for they know his voice. They will by no means follow a stranger, but will flee from him; for they don't know the voice of strangers.'*

A chapter division has been inserted at this point in the narrative, but there is no textual evidence for a change of time or place or audience. We know from verse 19 that Jewish leaders were present, and those mentioned in verse 6 do not appear to be disciples. The contrasting way in which Jesus treated the blind man with compassion and the Pharisees with disdain provides an appropriate context for this discourse. Probably Jesus' primary purpose was not to teach His followers but rather to challenge and correct His opponents. Of course, the disciples would also have benefited from the truths that He announced, and this is the case for us too.

The larger context for this discourse is found in the Scriptures, where the role of the shepherd is a common theme. The Patriarchs, Moses and David were shepherds, and the people of Israel were described as God's sheep or His flock.[1] The Lord appointed under-shepherds to rule and guide and care for the welfare of that flock on His behalf. Ezekiel recorded how God sternly rebuked false shepherds who were self-seeking, and who were abusing the sheep:

---

[1] Gen. 13:7; 26:12-14; 37:12-14; Exod. 3:1; 1 Sam. 16:11; Ps. 80:1.

The Lord GOD says: 'Behold, I am against the shepherds. I will require my sheep at their hand, and cause them to cease from feeding the sheep. The shepherds won't feed themselves any more. I will deliver my sheep from their mouth, that they may not be food for them.'

He then promised to come Himself as the true Shepherd: 'Behold, I myself, even I, will search for my sheep, and will seek them out.'[2]

Jesus had now come as the Father's agent to do just that. He began the discourse with the authoritative, 'Amen, amen, I say to you', which is repeated for emphasis a little later, in verse 7. He is the Great Shepherd of the sheep, the Chief Shepherd; in this role He was now standing before the under-shepherds and calling them to account.[3]

The passage contains many intertwining metaphors that we need to understand in order to discover what Jesus intended. The sheepfold represents the Law that was given to Israel at Mount Sinai. The sages of Israel described this as the hedge of the Law, acting as a protective barrier. It was designed to keep Israel separate from the pagan nations and thus guard them from straying into idolatry. God Himself was the doorkeeper; He jealously guarded access to His people and rebuked their attempts to break out into the pagan and idolatrous world. The thieves and robbers were those who tried to entice Israel away from their God, and who often succeeded in so doing. They also included Jewish leaders, both past and present, who abused their positions of trust in pursuit of personal gain.

The sheep represented the people of Israel, for Jesus said that He had been sent only to the lost sheep of the house of Israel. On another occasion He saw crowds of people and had compassion on them, seeing them as sheep without a shepherd.[4] All the people of Israel were potentially His sheep, but Jesus was focusing here on those, His own sheep, who recognised Him as the true Shepherd and were following Him. This corresponds to John's

---

[2] Ezek. 34:10-11.

[3] Luke 15:3-7; Heb. 13:20; 1 Pet. 5:2-4.

[4] Mark 6:34.

introductory statement, 'He came to his own, and those who were his own didn't receive him. But as many as received him, to them he gave the right to become God's children.'[5] The Father had given the flock completely into the care of the true Shepherd and Messiah whom He had sent, and the Law would soon become obsolete in relation to this purpose.

The sheep recognise the shepherd's voice and can distinguish it from the voice of strangers. Words convey information but voice is the key to recognition, as was the case for the blind man. The disciples had recognised Jesus as the true Messiah even though His words often baffled them, and many other people similarly recognised and followed Him. The shepherd calls His own sheep by name, as Jesus did when He called His first disciples. The sheep are not an amorphous and anonymous flock, for the shepherd knows and values each of them.

The shepherd brings the sheep out and goes before them. The confinement and protection of the sheepfold is no longer required because the shepherd is always present to guide them and protect them from danger and temptation. Thus they enjoy freedom under His supervision and care.

This was the fulfilment of one of Micah's prophecies. He described a flock of sheep confined in a sheepfold, as would be the case during the night. The pasture land outside the wall was dangerous and the sheep would have been vulnerable at that time. They were restless and eager to escape but were hemmed in by the surrounding wall. When morning came, the shepherd made a breach in the wall and led them out into freedom, going before them after the manner of a king leading a procession. Micah identified the shepherd as the Lord Himself, and He was now present in the person of Jesus. The confining and protective functions of the Law were thus no longer required.[6]

> **10:6-10** *Jesus spoke this parable to them, but they didn't understand what he was telling them. Jesus therefore said to them again, 'Most certainly, I tell you, I am the sheep's door. All who came before me are*

---

[5] John 1:11-12.
[6] Mic. 2:12-13; Rom. 7:1-7; Gal. 3:21–4:7.

*thieves and robbers, but the sheep didn't listen to them. I am the door.
If anyone enters in by me, he will be saved, and will go in and go out,
and will find pasture. The thief only comes to steal, kill, and destroy. I
came that they may have life, and may have it abundantly.'*

Jesus had spoken in the third person and His hearers were
confused. Why was He giving a lecture in the city of Jerusalem
about keeping sheep? As was often the case, they took His words
in a literal and physical sense, and missed the point. Now, prefacing
His explanation with the emphatic statement of His authority,
Jesus expanded on the illustration that He had just given and
applied it to Himself.

He had used a rather complex metaphor: as the shepherd He
had entered the door that the doorkeeper (the Father) had opened
for Him, but now He pictured Himself as the door itself. The door
exists for two purposes: it excludes the thief and the robber, and it
is the entrance through which the sheep access salvation, provision
and life. There is an atmosphere of freedom as the sheep go in and
out and find pasture. The sheepfold has not been destroyed, but it
is no longer a place of confinement. It has become an integral part
of the pasture lands, for the confining door has gone. The Law is
no longer necessary for its original function to constrain and
control, but the Scriptures that were given to Israel remain as a rich
source of food for believers, Jews and Gentiles alike, and we are
impoverished if we neglect them.[7]

Jesus warned about the activities of thieves and robbers who
continue to pose a threat to the sheep. They sometimes pretend to
be shepherds but they are really strangers who, for their own selfish
reasons, are seeking to entice the sheep away from the true
Shepherd. We need to learn to recognise the voice of the true
Shepherd and flee from those whose desire is to manipulate and
even to fleece the sheep. Genuine sheep have a built in safety
device which distinguishes the false external voices that clash with
the Shepherd's voice within their hearts. In a subsequent epistle,
John described this safeguard as an anointing that we have

---

[7] Matt. 13:52.

received, to teach us what is true and what is a lie. This is an important asset in times of pressure and temptation.[8]

John referred not only to thieves and robbers, but also to the thief. Just as there is a Chief Shepherd, so also there is a chief thief who comes to steal and kill and destroy. He is the father of lies and 'a murderer from the beginning'.[9] His first great lie was that God's intentions for the human race were restrictive and confining and that his own proposals would bring abundant life.[10] This is still one of his major strategies, and it continues to deceive people and set them on the pathway to degradation, despair and death. The Good Shepherd leads His sheep into freedom as they follow Him into the way of life that was the Creator's original plan and purpose.

> **10:11-15** *'I am the good shepherd. The good shepherd lays down his life for the sheep. He who is a hired hand, and not a shepherd, who doesn't own the sheep, sees the wolf coming, leaves the sheep, and flees. The wolf snatches the sheep, and scatters them. The hired hand flees because he is a hired hand, and doesn't care for the sheep. I am the good shepherd. I know my own, and I'm known by my own; even as the Father knows me, and I know the Father. I lay down my life for the sheep.'*

Jesus described Himself as the Good Shepherd. This implied that some shepherds were bad, and perhaps He was hinting that some such shepherds were currently listening to His words. Hirelings regarded shepherding as a way of earning money; when the going was easy, it is possible that many of them did a good-enough job. The real distinction became clear when the wolf turned up and things got tough. The hireling was a professional and did not consider it his responsibility to risk life or limb on behalf of the sheep. 'The sheep will have to fend for themselves; I can always get another job.'

The Good Shepherd has a very different set of values, based on love rather than personal security. To Him, the sheep are not just numbers; He knows them by name, and He is willing to put His

---

[8] 1 John 2:26-27.
[9] John 8:44.
[10] Gen. 2:4-5.

life on the line in order to protect them. David had done just that for ordinary sheep while a shepherd in the Judean wilderness. Jesus would soon do the same for His disciples in the Garden of Gethsemane, where He protected them, the sheep who were about to be scattered.[11] He did not lay down His life out of a sense of obligation but rather in the context of deep and intimate relationships.

Jesus demonstrated His complete love for the Father by offering perfect obedience to His will and purpose. He revealed His unlimited love for His sheep by laying down His life for them. Jesus came from a community – Father, Son and Holy Spirit – in order to enfold us in that community of love. Prior to His death, Jesus taught His disciples to love one another with the same sacrificial love that He was about to pour out for them.[12]

> **10:16-18** *'I have other sheep, which are not of this fold. I must bring them also, and they will hear my voice. They will become one flock with one shepherd. Therefore the Father loves me, because I lay down my life, that I may take it again. No one takes it away from me, but I lay it down by myself. I have power to lay it down, and I have power to take it again. I received this commandment from my Father.'*

Jesus now introduced another element that must have taken His hearers by surprise. If the sheep represented Israel, who, then, were these foreign sheep that He now claimed to have? This was a radical concept that even His close disciples, including Peter, had difficulty in accepting. A Jewish crowd rioted when Paul announced that Jesus had sent him to the Gentiles.[13] Jesus insisted that the other sheep must come to Him and that they would do so in the same way as Jewish sheep, by hearing His voice. Moreover, they would join a flock that would comprise both Jewish and Gentile sheep. Significantly, there would be only one flock. Gentiles do not need to come under the Law nor adopt Jewish rituals, but they can go in and out of the fold and enjoy the treasures of Israel's heritage and history.

---

[11] 1 Sam. 17:34-36; John 18:7-9; Mark 14:27.
[12] John 15:12-13.
[13] Acts 11:1-18; Acts 22:21-23.

Jesus went on to make another surprising statement: 'Therefore the Father loves me, because I lay down my life, that I may take it again.' Of course, the Father's love for Him was eternal and unconditional. There is a mystery here that we cannot fully explain, but there were particular moments during Jesus' earthly life when the Father declared His pleasure and delight in His beloved and obedient Son. Perhaps Jesus was referring to a heightened awareness of the Father's love in the context of His determination to offer ultimate obedience at the cross. Jesus made it clear that He freely chose to obey the Father and that He was certain of the outcome.

> **10:19-21** *Therefore a division arose again amongst the Jews because of these words. Many of them said, 'He has a demon, and is insane! Why do you listen to him?' Others said, 'These are not the sayings of one possessed by a demon. It isn't possible for a demon to open the eyes of the blind, is it?'*

The Jewish leaders were bemused and confused. Some of them dismissed Jesus' words out of hand. After all, He was a Sabbath breaker and could not be expected to talk sense. Jesus spoke in riddles so why listen to His babblings? Others were more perceptive and, in the light of the recent miracle, remained open to the possibility that Jesus was who He claimed to be. We will meet them again, or others like them, who, when confronted with the great miracle of the resurrection of Lazarus, continued to struggle with the cost of commitment to Jesus.[14]

---

[14] John 11:45-46; 12:9-11, 42-43.

29

John 10:22-41
A Setup and an Attempted Stoning

> *10:22-24* *It was the Feast of the Dedication at Jerusalem. It was winter, and Jesus was walking in the temple, in Solomon's porch. The Jews therefore came around him and said to him, 'How long will you hold us in suspense? If you are the Christ, tell us plainly.'*

Jesus appears to have remained in Jerusalem between the Feast of Tabernacles and The Feast of Dedication (Hanukah).[1] This latter festival celebrated an event that took place in 164 BCE. The Temple had been desecrated by a pagan Greek king who had occupied Jerusalem. During a period of persecution some people had compromised with paganism, but others had accepted martyrdom in order to sanctify the name of God. After the Greeks had been driven out, the Temple was cleansed and rededicated to God and the lampstand was lit in the Holy Place. Jewish tradition in the Talmud relates that the available small amount of oil miraculously lasted for eight days. Light was the central motif of this festival, all the more vivid in the context of midwinter darkness.[2]

The Pharisees originated from that period of history, so Hanukah was particularly important to them. They emphasised holiness and strict adherence to the Law, but sadly many had become rigidly legalistic and took pride in their religious traditions and their position within society. As we have seen, the issues of light and darkness loomed large in the clash between Jesus and the Pharisees. Hanukah was therefore an apt setting for this almost

---

[1] See Appendix 4 for possible time-connection between Hanukah and the birth of Jesus.
[2] 1 Maccabees 1:10-64; 4:36-59.

final encounter. It appears that they had been seeking a suitable time to challenge Jesus, so when they saw Him walking in one of the public spaces in the Temple courts they took the opportunity to corner Him, possibly hoping to intimidate Him with their numbers.[3]

Jesus knew that their question about His identity was disingenuous. If He were to say, 'Yes, I am the Messiah,' they would not respond as the blind man had done but would treat His reply as the basis of a formal accusation before the Council. Jesus never gave direct answers to insincere questions of that sort, and nor should we feel under pressure to do so. He simply reminded them of the evidence that should have led them to the correct conclusion, but which they had chosen to discount.

> **10:25-30** *Jesus answered them, 'I told you, and you don't believe. The works that I do in my Father's name, these testify about me. But you don't believe, because you are not of my sheep, as I told you. My sheep hear my voice, and I know them, and they follow me. I give eternal life to them. They will never perish, and no one will snatch them out of my hand. My Father who has given them to me is greater than all. No one is able to snatch them out of my Father's hand. I and the Father are one.'*

Jesus referred them back to His earlier statement – 'I told you' – so these must be the same individuals to whom He had spoken following the healing of the blind man.[4] Jesus explained that their unbelief was a consequence of their being 'not of my sheep'. This could mean that their refusal to believe resulted from God's predetermination: they were not among those chosen to be His sheep and were not enlightened or otherwise assisted along the path to faith. While this is a linguistically possible interpretation, it does not cohere with how Jesus repeatedly challenged them to believe. At the conclusion of this present episode, and in the context of their violent reaction, He reminded them of the evidence provided by the works that the Father had given Him to

---

[3] Matt. 5:20; Matt. 15:1-9; Matt. 23:1-7, 23-25.
[4] John 9:39-41.

do. The Bible does not explain how the sovereignty of God intersects with human choice, but it does teach that both are true. The Pharisees made their choices because they were unwilling to obey the voice of the Shepherd. Those whom He called 'my sheep' listened to His voice and followed Him. Responding in this way is more useful than solving theological puzzles.

Jesus declared emphatically that no one could snatch the sheep out of His hand, or from the Father's hand. The picture is of a fierce predator like a lion or a bear that tries to capture a defenceless sheep. David described two such attacks and how he intervened to save the sheep.[5] Jesus' sheep are even more secure, for He carries them in His arms. This means that an attack on the sheep is also an attack on Him, as some have discovered to their cost.

Jesus may have been thinking about the blind man whom the Pharisees had evicted from the synagogue and had thus excluded from the privileges of religious society. Perhaps He was also anticipating the pressure and violent persecution that His disciples would face following His departure, and also those who would subsequently believe in Him.[6] The devil himself would rage against them like a roaring lion and would sometimes try to seduce them as an angel of light, but they would be safe if they kept close to the Shepherd.[7] Severe persecution is a current reality for many Christians, who are losing everything they possess and even life itself. They die in the certain hope that Jesus has given them eternal life and they have an eternal inheritance. Counted as sheep for the slaughter like Jesus, they are eternally secure.[8]

This promise is underwritten by a double guarantee. Eternal life is a gift from Jesus, who spoke these words in the awareness of the price that He would soon pay for that gift. He will never let go of those whom He has redeemed with His precious blood, His outpoured life. The Father, who is supreme over all things in heaven and earth, is the ultimate guarantor of that promise, for it

---

[5] 1 Sam. 17:33-36.
[6] Matt. 10:16-18; Acts 5:40-42; 7:54-60; 8:1-3.
[7] 1 Pet. 5:8-9; 2 Cor. 11:13-14; Rev. 12:10-13.
[8] 1 Pet. 1:3-9; Rom. 8:35-39.

was He who sent His Son into the world so that whoever believes in Him should not perish but have everlasting life.[9]

Those Pharisees, who already considered Jesus to be mad or demonised, were now confirmed in that belief. The effect on the others is less certain, but Jesus' final words, 'I and the Father are one', may have instantly created a perverse unity among them all. It was a truly explosive statement, perhaps sounding like a parody of Israel's most sacred confession, 'Hear, Israel: the LORD is our God. The LORD is one.'[10]

> **10:31-39** *Therefore Jews took up stones again to stone him.*
>
> *Jesus answered them, 'I have shown you many good works from my Father. For which of those works do you stone me?'*
>
> *The Jews answered him, 'We don't stone you for a good work, but for blasphemy: because you, being a man, make yourself God.'*
>
> *Jesus answered them, 'Isn't it written in your law, "I said, you are gods?" If he called them gods, to whom the word of God came (and the Scripture can't be broken), do you say of him whom the Father sanctified and sent into the world, "You blaspheme," because I said, "I am the Son of God?" If I don't do the works of my Father, don't believe me. But if I do them, though you don't believe me, believe the works, that you may know and believe that the Father is in me, and I in the Father.'*
>
> *They sought again to seize him, and he went out of their hand.*

This was the second occasion on which anger and frustration boiled over into murderous rage under cover of religious zeal. Jesus calmly countered their charge with His usual argument: His works demonstrated His relationship with the Father, hence His claim was true and not blasphemous. The Pharisees' logic worked in the reverse direction: Jesus was a blasphemer and in the light of this His works paled into insignificance and His claims could be ignored.

The accusation of blasphemy remains a deadly weapon in the hands of those who claim the right to define and impose their

---

[9] John 3:16; Rom. 8:31-34; Heb. 6:13-20.
[10] Deut. 6:4.

214

version of truth, or who simply wish to attack an innocent person. Current religious zealots who quote from a different text are in principle no different from these Pharisees.

This logic was perverse, but it fitted with the Pharisees' purpose of maintaining the status quo. Jesus answered them using a form of logic, 'from light to heavy' (Heb. *qal v'chomer*), with which they would have been familiar and which they would have used in their own discussions. Inspired Scripture described human judges as being gods (Heb. *elohim*), in the sense that they stood in the place of God with delegated authority to judge on His behalf.[11] If this was a valid way to speak of ordinary human beings, it was even more valid for Jesus to speak of Himself as the Son of God. The Father had sent Jesus into the world and had provided the authenticating miracle-signs that He had been performing.

Jesus was standing in a circle of men with murder in their hearts and who may still have held stones in their hands, but He did not flinch. He made one last offer to any who had honest hearts. If they would examine His works and give proper weight to the miracles, they would come to see the truth of His relationship with the Father. It was a genuine offer, given in the most unpromising circumstances and requiring both grace and courage. It was also uncompromising, ending as it did with the words, 'the Father is in me, and I in the Father', and this reignited their murderous rage. They were unable to snatch Him out of the Father's hand so He escaped out of their hands.

> **10:40-42** *He went away again beyond the Jordan into the place where John was baptising at first, and he stayed there. Many came to him. They said, 'John indeed did no sign, but everything that John said about this man is true.' Many believed in him there.*

This marks a turning point in Jesus' life. For a prolonged period He had engaged in what we might describe as confrontational apologetics with a group of unbelievers. They were proud of their learning and status and refused to admit any type of evidence that conflicted with their worldview or that was beyond their narrow

---

[11] Ps. 82:6.

field of expertise. Similar attitudes still exist today in the new-atheist camp. Some of Jesus' opponents were also blinded by a form of religious fanaticism and believed that they had a God-given mandate to kill those who deviated from their version of absolute truth. This also has tragic parallels in our contemporary world.

Jesus claimed to be the personification of truth and charged His followers to declare this message, with persuasive words and in ways that demonstrated His love. Many other religions, including those for which the State takes the place of God, make similar truth claims and believe that they are entitled to enforce compliance by law and, if necessary, by force (which in past times the church also did, in direct contradiction to the commands of Jesus). In recent decades followers of Jesus have suffered in a major escalation of persecution because of their faith in and loyalty to Him. The Christian culture that has hitherto protected religious freedom in the West is facing an onslaught from militant secularism on the one hand and radical Islam on the other. Our loyalty to Jesus will be tested more and more within this situation, but this is no more or less than He promised us.[12]

Jesus now left Jerusalem and would not return until Passover, several months hence. The time had come for Him to move on and to devote His attention to those who had left all to follow Him and who would soon be passing through a fierce storm, the greatest crisis of their lives.

Jesus returned to the place where His public ministry had begun, just across the Jordan River to the north of Jerusalem. It was the place where He had been baptised and had been anointed with the Holy Spirit.[13] He now exchanged the place of conflict and controversy for the calm of the wilderness where He could spend time with His disciples and could also welcome others who were open to receive His words. People recalled the words that John the Baptist had spoken about Jesus in that same place, and their faith was strengthened by the knowledge that it had all come true.

---

[12] John 15:18-25; 1 Pet. 4:12-14.
[13] John 1:29-36.

30

John 11:1-31
Mysterious Love

> ***11:1-10*** *Now a certain man was sick, Lazarus from Bethany, of the village of Mary and her sister, Martha. It was that Mary who had anointed the Lord with ointment and wiped his feet with her hair, whose brother, Lazarus, was sick. The sisters therefore sent to him, saying, 'Lord, behold, he for whom you have great affection is sick.'*
>
> *But when Jesus heard it, he said, 'This sickness is not to death, but for the glory of God, that God's Son may be glorified by it.'*
>
> *Now Jesus loved Martha, and her sister, and Lazarus. When therefore he heard that he was sick, he stayed two days in the place where he was. Then after this he said to the disciples, 'Let's go into Judea again.'*
>
> *The disciples asked him, 'Rabbi, the Jews were just trying to stone you. Are you going there again?'*
>
> *Jesus answered, 'Aren't there twelve hours of daylight? If a man walks in the day, he doesn't stumble, because he sees the light of this world. But if a man walks in the night, he stumbles, because the light isn't in him.'*

Jesus probably remained in the wilderness for some weeks between Hanukah in December and Passover in March or April. Verse 54 of John 11 informs us that He subsequently moved further north for a period of time prior to His final journey to Jerusalem.

The incident now to be described would involve people whom John had not previously introduced, so he supplied some preliminary information. A brother and two sisters lived in Bethany, a town located two miles from Jerusalem to the east of the Mount of Olives. In his account, Luke had described a previous visit by Jesus to their home which had led to a close friendship between them, as John confirms in verses 5 and 11. John subsequently detailed the way in which Mary anointed Jesus' feet, but here he pointed out that this incident was already well known from other sources.[1]

The retreat was suddenly interrupted by the arrival of a weary and worried-looking person, with information that would initiate the final series of events in Jesus' journey to His appointed hour of destiny. What had been hidden in the Father's plan was now near at hand. The sequence of these crucial events did not begin in the capital city Jerusalem but in Bethany, a nearby village. Like Bethlehem at the beginning of the story, Bethany was small and insignificant. The central characters in the unfolding drama were not rich and famous but were simple and godly folks who had gladly welcomed Jesus into their home, and who had listened to Him with faith. This is the kind of place and these are the kinds of people that God typically chooses for important purposes.[2] From this unpretentious beginning, a message of glory would spread to gladden the hearts of many. The same report would turn the hearts of others to stone and would provoke the hostile train of events that would lead to the cross. The choices and actions of Jesus' opponents would unwittingly serve the Father's purpose for His Son.

Mary and Martha obviously expected Jesus to respond immediately to their message, 'Lord, behold, he for whom you have great affection is sick.' When the disciple John heard this expression, his own heart must have missed a beat, for this was how he had come to regard his own relationship with Jesus. Jesus assured the disciples as to the final outcome of this disturbing news, apparently ignoring the current and painful situation. He focused on future glory and regarded present circumstances and suffering as stepping stones on that pathway. This sickness, together with all other sicknesses, was part of a broken creation. As in the case of the blind man, this one would be an occasion when God would reveal His glory.

---

[1] John 12:1-8; Luke 10:38-42; Matt. 26:6-13.
[2] Luke 1:26-38, 46-55; 1 Cor. 1:26-31.

Jesus purposely delayed His departure for two days. John's explanation is unexpected: it was because Jesus loved the two sisters and Lazarus. Understandably, neither Martha nor Mary considered Jesus' absence to be an expression of love. At that stage neither they nor the disciples could have imagined that Lazarus would be raised from death after more than three days in the tomb, as a foreshadowing of Jesus' own resurrection, the greatest miracle of all.

Often we cannot see the reason for things that are happening to us or around us. Sometimes in retrospect the purpose becomes clear, but not always during our lifetimes. We need to evaluate everything that happens to us through the lens of the love and the sovereignty of God, rather than viewing Him through the close-up lens of our circumstances.

Presumably the messenger would have described the full details of Lazarus' life-threatening sickness. It is clear from the subsequent account that Lazarus had actually died very soon after the messenger had left Bethany, so Lazarus must have been in extremis at that time. In the light of this, everyone who heard the messenger must have known that the situation was critical and that time was of the essence.

Jesus took no action for a further two days, so the disciples probably concluded that He had wisely decided that, given the circumstances in Bethany, He should not put all their lives at risk. When He said, 'Let's go into Judea again', it must have come as a very unwelcome surprise, and would have been considered to be dangerous and probably futile. The disciples' question sounds more like an objection, designed to remind Jesus of the danger to His life.

Jesus responded with another of His enigmatic sayings, stating the obvious physical truth that it is safer to walk in daylight than after darkness because a person is then less likely to stumble. By now it should have been obvious to them that light and darkness represented spiritual states. The concluding part of Jesus' statement must contain the spiritual application. He did not say, 'because he has no light', but, 'because the light isn't in him'.

Jesus was commenting on the murderous intentions of the Jewish leaders, to which the disciples had just referred. The problem of those leaders was not lack of light, for they had spent much time in the company of the light of the world. Their problem was an inner darkness that had grown thick and dense, to the point where it was total. Consequently, they were stumbling towards eternal ruin, a disaster that was entirely of their own making.

> ***10:11-16*** *He said these things, and after that, he said to them, 'Our friend, Lazarus, has fallen asleep, but I am going so that I may awake him out of sleep.'*
>
> *The disciples therefore said, 'Lord, if he has fallen asleep, he will recover.'*
>
> *Now Jesus had spoken of his death, but they thought that he spoke of taking rest in sleep. So Jesus said to them plainly then, 'Lazarus is dead. I am glad for your sakes that I was not there, so that you may believe. Nevertheless, let's go to him.'*
>
> *Thomas therefore, who is called Didymus, said to his fellow disciples, 'Let's go also, that we may die with him.'*

Next, Jesus turned His attention from the living-dead to His friend Lazarus, whom He described as being asleep. As usual, the disciples interpreted His words in a strictly literal way, even though He had previously used the same metaphor of sleep to describe Jairus' daughter in a state of death.[3] After correcting their misunderstanding, Jesus provided an additional reason for the delay: to strengthen their faith.

Thomas' response made it clear that he saw the likely outcome, not in terms of new life but rather in the deaths of all of them. He expressed the foreboding that they were all probably experiencing. Thomas' words also revealed a dogged loyalty and determination to follow Jesus to the end, whatever the cost, and this encouraged the others to fall in behind their leader. Thomas had his faults, but his devotion to Jesus was not in question, and this was what carried him through in spite of doubts and fears. The company must have felt deeply apprehensive as they journeyed towards Bethany, with a sense of doom rather than destiny, but Jesus was going and so must they.

---

[3] Luke 8:52-53.

At that stage none of the disciples could have imagined that Lazarus would rise from the dead after being in the tomb for four days and that his resurrection would thus become a spectacular revelation of the glory of Jesus and the Father.[4] Nor could they have anticipated that it would act as a prophetic sign of the defeat of death itself through the resurrection of Jesus, and how this would guarantee the resurrection of the dead at the end of the age.[5]

> **10:17-27** *So when Jesus came, he found that he had been in the tomb four days already.*
>
> *Now Bethany was near Jerusalem, about fifteen stadia away. Many of the Jews had joined the women around Martha and Mary, to console them concerning their brother. Then when Martha heard that Jesus was coming, she went and met him, but Mary stayed in the house. Therefore Martha said to Jesus, 'Lord, if you would have been here, my brother wouldn't have died. Even now I know that whatever you ask of God, God will give you.'*
>
> *Jesus said to her, 'Your brother will rise again.'*
>
> *Martha said to him, 'I know that he will rise again in the resurrection at the last day.'*
>
> *Jesus said to her, 'I am the resurrection and the life. He who believes in me will still live, even if he dies. Whoever lives and believes in me will never die. Do you believe this?'*
>
> *She said to him, 'Yes, Lord. I have come to believe that you are the Christ, God's Son, he who comes into the world.'*

We do not know exactly when Jesus heard the details of Lazarus' death and burial. Perhaps He encountered one of the locals as He approached Bethany. Custom dictated that close relatives would stay in the house for a week following the death and that people would visit. Mary and Martha were Lazarus' closest relations so the women of the village gathered around to console them in the great and sudden loss of their beloved brother, on whom they would have relied for many things, including, in the absence of husbands, the legal protection that he would have provided. Many Jewish

---

4 John 11:40-43.
5 1 Cor. 15:20-26.

leaders were also present, emphasising the high regard in which Lazarus had been held in the local community. When the sisters heard that Jesus was approaching, each acted in character. Martha set out to meet Him and Mary remained behind, immobilised by her grief.

Martha offered Jesus no greeting, for her mind and heart were in turmoil. Her first statement was factually true, but it carried an implied reproach and also expressed personal hurt – 'my brother': 'What took You so long? Were You preoccupied with something that You considered to be a higher priority?'

Jesus did not take offence, for He knew that she was hurting and confused. Her next statement showed that although she did not understand, nevertheless she still believed in Him. This is always the safe, fall-back position. Jesus replied with an assurance, but He did not explain exactly what He meant: 'Your brother will rise again.'

Martha's reply seemed to imply, 'I know that, but I need more than doctrine and information at this moment.' Martha, unlike the Sadducees, knew and believed the Scriptures concerning the resurrection.

Jesus' next words took the discussion to a whole new level. Martha had referred to an event that was probably in the far distant future and was difficult to envisage; Jesus spoke of a present reality, embodied in His own person: 'I am the resurrection and the life.' The One who would resurrect and restore the whole creation stood beside her in human flesh. Jesus was making this startling and far-reaching revelation to His friend and disciple Martha, at a moment of acute pain and loss and when all hope seemed to have disappeared. Could she believe such a thing? Jesus' statement had far-reaching implications for never-ending life, eternal life, but if it were true, then Jesus must have power to reverse her brother's death. If He could not raise him to physical life even at this stage, what hope could there be for the universe?

Jesus then asked Martha, 'Do you believe this?' She did not give a straight answer to His question, but she did affirm her belief in His identity as Messiah and Son of God, with all the associated promises in the Scriptures. It was a good reply, but it still fell short of the practical faith towards which Jesus was gently moving her.

Just prior to summoning Lazarus from the tomb, Jesus would remind her of the promise that He made during this earlier conversation: if she believed, in the here-and-now sense, she would see the glory of God.

> **11:28-31** *When she had said this, she went away and called Mary, her sister, secretly, saying, 'The Teacher is here and is calling you.'*
>
> *When she heard this, she arose quickly and went to him. Now Jesus had not yet come into the village, but was in the place where Martha met him. Then the Jews who were with her in the house and were consoling her, when they saw Mary, that she rose up quickly and went out, followed her, saying, 'She is going to the tomb to weep there.'*

Jesus had asked Martha to call Mary to come to Him. He remained on the outskirts of the town, preferring to speak with her in private before being with her in a crowd. He was very sensitive to her needs and her feelings. Mary lost no time in setting out. The Jewish leaders did not know that Jesus was there and they followed her with the intention of continuing to provide comfort as she visited the tomb. Some of the Pharisees had compassionate hearts, and their consideration for the sisters would be rewarded when they also saw the glory of God.

31

John 11:32-40
Grief and Groaning

> *11:32-37 Therefore when Mary came to where Jesus was and saw him, she fell down at his feet, saying to him, 'Lord, if you would have been here, my brother wouldn't have died.'*
>
> *When Jesus therefore saw her weeping, and the Jews weeping who came with her, he groaned in the spirit, and was troubled, and said, 'Where have you laid him?'*
>
> *They told him, 'Lord, come and see.'*
>
> *Jesus wept.*
>
> *The Jews therefore said, 'See how much affection he had for him!' Some of them said, 'Couldn't this man, who opened the eyes of him who was blind, have also kept this man from dying?'*

Mary and Martha were both devoted to Jesus and to their brother and they both approached Jesus with the same words. Otherwise each was very different in how she expressed her emotions, and Jesus was sensitive to this fact. Martha processed her distress by means of words and logic, so Jesus adopted this medium of communication. Mary responded in more physical ways, weeping and falling down at Jesus' feet. Mary's visible expression of her acute emotional pain was echoed in His heart. Jesus was fully human, with all that that implies; He was not merely playing a part, like an actor in a drama.

Words could not convey what Jesus was feeling, and they would have been powerless to alleviate Mary's suffering. Instead, He asked the simple and practical question, 'Where have you laid him?', as the answer would take the process forward towards resolution. The question also anticipated the one that another Mary would subsequently ask in proximity to Jesus' empty tomb, subtly making a connection between Lazarus' resurrection and His own.[1] John tells us that 'the Jews' had accompanied Mary and that they now answered, 'Lord, come and see.' These words are reminiscent of the words that Jesus had used when His first two disciples, Andrew and John, began to follow Him, and also of the words Philip had used when he introduced his friend Nathanael to Jesus.[2] On those two occasions at the outset of Jesus' public ministry, these words marked the end of a quest to find the promised Messiah and the beginning of a journey of hope in company with the Lord of light and life and love. Now, as that journey neared its conclusion, Jesus was being invited into a situation that would illustrate in very graphic terms the problem to which His own death would be the solution.

A torrent of grief swept over Jesus, overflowing in weeping, even though He knew what He was about to do. The Jews who witnessed His tears recognised that they were genuine and spontaneous and unlike the staged weeping of professional mourners who were commonly employed in that culture.[3] The death of Lazarus was not simply a contrivance, designed as a platform upon which to reveal His glory, with Lazarus in the role of an extra. Lazarus was His friend, with whom He had enjoyed conversation and had shared meals around his table, and Jesus knew that Lazarus had experienced sorrow and sickness during his final days. Jesus' empathy with Lazarus and his sisters may have been intensified by His awareness of His own impending suffering and death, and the resulting grief that this would inflict on His own family of faith.

The Jewish leaders appeared genuinely attentive and sympathetic towards the grieving family and they recognised the deep love that Jesus had for Lazarus. The inherent contradiction seemed impossible to explain: why could Jesus, who had given the blind man his sight, not have intervened to heal Lazarus while the opportunity still existed? Of course, their question implied that they were indeed convinced that Jesus had healed the man who

---

[1] John 20:11-16.

[2] John 1:35-40, 45-46 and see footnote on John 1:18.

[3] Luke 7:31-32; Mark 5:35-42.

had been blind from birth. There had also been reports of Jesus raising two young people to life soon after their deaths, but the situation with Lazarus was of a completely different order of magnitude, for he had been dead for four days. This problem was clearly beyond human solution, even for Jesus.[4]

Jesus did not attempt to correct their misconception that He had been unable to prevent Lazarus' death. He did not explain that He could have done this but had chosen not to do so, in pursuit of a higher purpose. He had told His disciples that the death of Lazarus would somehow benefit them and had indicated to Martha that these sad events would climax in a revelation of the glory of God.[5] The Jewish leaders do not seem to have been speaking directly to Jesus, so there was no need for a verbal response; the action that He was about to take would answer their question beyond the power of words and would require them to make a suitable response to Him, one way or the other. After this there would be no room for debate or neutrality.

> **11:38-40** *Jesus therefore, again groaning in himself, came to the tomb. Now it was a cave, and a stone lay against it. Jesus said, 'Take away the stone.'*
>
> *Martha, the sister of him who was dead, said to him, 'Lord, by this time there is a stench, for he has been dead four days.'*
>
> *Jesus said to her, 'Didn't I tell you that if you believed, you would see God's glory?'*

The reason for Jesus' decision to delay His journey to Bethany now became apparent. If it is impossible to restore life and health to this one man, reversing death and corruption, then the prospects for the broken creation are bleak indeed. If Jesus could restore Lazarus to life and health this would be a prophetic sign of the day when the dead will rise again in fullness of life and the whole creation will be renewed. It was for this very purpose that God had intervened in space and time in the person of Jesus, who is the resurrection and the life.

---

[4] John 9:16; Luke 7:11-17; 8:49-56.
[5] John 11:15, 40.

Pointers to this good news had occurred in former times. At the beginning of the story of redemption an elderly and childless couple, Abraham and Sarah, were chosen to initiate the process that would lead to this grand conclusion. They were faced with this same question: can God reverse what seems to be an irreversible process of physical decline? Could God restore vitality to their worn-out bodies and enable them to have a son?[6] The same issue resurfaced just before the birth of the Messiah. An aged priest, Zechariah, and his wife Elizabeth were childless. Zechariah was interceding before God on behalf of the people of Israel, as the nation longed for God to fulfil the promise that He had made to Abraham long ago. Could God rejuvenate his and his wife's elderly bodies, enabling them to produce the forerunner of the Messiah?[7]

The two couples received positive answers in the births of their respective sons, Isaac and John. Of course, an even greater challenge faced Mary, as she was called to believe that God could create a child in her womb without the involvement of a man. Those who reject the virgin birth as impossible can have no reasonable hope for the resurrection of the dead, or the renewal of creation.[8] As Jesus approached the tomb of Lazarus, this issue came centre stage again.

As Jesus responded to the request to 'come and see', He again experienced deep emotions, perhaps now including anger and revulsion. He was entering a scene of death, decay and despair. It portrayed in miniature the condition into which the whole creation had sunk as a consequence of the initial rebellion against the Creator. Everything that Jesus saw, especially the tomb containing the corrupting body of His dear friend Lazarus, was the very antithesis of God's good creation and His purposes for mankind.

It was no wonder that He was grieved to the point of groaning. The sight of the tomb may also have provoked thoughts of another tomb in which He Himself would soon rest in darkness, having given His life to redeem and rescue creation from its bondage to corruption. When He spoke the words that would bring

---

6 Gen. 17:15-21; Gen. 18:9-15; Gen. 21:1-7; Rom. 4:16-21; Heb. 11:11-12.

7 Luke 1:5-20, 57-79.

8 Isa. 7:14; Luke 1:26-38, 46-55; Matt. 1:18-25.

resurrection life into the body of Lazarus, He would anticipate the moment when He Himself would be raised from the dead by the power of the Holy Spirit.

Now He gave an instruction that must have horrified the assembled crowd: 'Take away the stone.' Martha is described as the sister of the dead man, perhaps to emphasise that she was speaking on behalf of a brother who could no longer speak for himself. She protested that Lazarus was not only dead, but was now a fourth-day man. There was a common belief that the spirit tarried around the body for three days after the final breath and then, finally and irreversibly, departed. That period had now elapsed. Martha regarded this as an insurmountable problem, but it was the very purpose of Jesus' decision to delay. No one except the all-powerful Creator God could now solve it. Jesus challenged Martha to move beyond intellectual belief into committed faith, where what is theoretically possible becomes real and immediate. He reminded her of His previous question: 'Didn't I tell you that if you believed, you would see God's glory?'

___

32

John 11:41-53
Glory!

> *11:41-44 So they took away the stone from the place where the dead man was lying. Jesus lifted up his eyes, and said, 'Father, I thank you that you listened to me. I know that you always listen to me, but because of the multitude standing around I said this, that they may believe that you sent me.' When he had said this, he cried with a loud voice, 'Lazarus, come out!' He who was dead came out, bound hand and foot with wrappings, and his face was wrapped around with a cloth. Jesus said to them, 'Free him, and let him go.'*

They had a choice: either to remove the stone in obedience to Jesus' words or to act according to human logic and wisdom. John again emphasised the fact that Lazarus was, beyond contradiction, dead. They may have obeyed with a measure of uncertainty and fear, but they did obey, and left the outcome to Jesus. He did not pray for Lazarus to be raised up, for He knew that His Father had already heard Him and that no further petition was required. By contrast, His subsequent prayer in Gethsemane revealed a soul-wrenching struggle.[1]

The writer to the Hebrews reveals that Jesus' prayed for assurance that He would return to life. He was taking upon Himself the full weight of responsibility for the sin of the whole world, and unless His offering was sufficient there could be no resurrection. Jesus' humanity is emphasised in this passage in Hebrews:

___

[1] Matt. 26:38-44; Luke 22:41-44.

He, in the days of his flesh, having offered up prayers and petitions with strong crying and tears to him who was able to save him from death, and having been heard for his godly fear, though he was a Son, yet learnt obedience by the things which he suffered.[2]

Jesus now publicly thanked God that God had already heard Him, in order that those standing around would be aware of the purpose of the miracle. The raising of Lazarus would act as definitive proof that Jesus' claim to be the One whom the Father had sent into the world was true. Then He shouted, 'Lazarus, come out!' The mourners and onlookers must have been rooted to the spot. Then fear was replaced by amazement and wonder as a figure, swathed in heavy ointment-soaked bandages and with his face concealed by a cloth, emerged awkwardly from the mouth of the cave.

Jesus then instructed any who were prepared to undertake the task to strip away the grave clothes and to remove the cloth from Lazarus' head. As they did so, his face and body must have emerged glowing with life and health. At that moment the light of the glory of God, Father and Son in unity, was evident to all and the darkness of death and mourning was dispelled. Life had returned, corruption had been reversed, and health, cleanness and relationships were fully restored. Touching someone in that condition would have previously rendered those who did so unclean, but physical contact now restored Lazarus to his place within the community with increased honour and respect.

In his prologue to the Gospel John wrote, 'We saw his glory, such glory as of the one and only Son of the Father, full of grace and truth.'[3] This was dramatically enacted in the little town of Bethany on that day. It was a prophetic sign of what would soon be accomplished in nearby Jerusalem, for all mankind.

We might wish that we had a first-hand report from Lazarus concerning life beyond the grave, but this is missing from the account. Scripture does not encourage us to seek such knowledge,

---

[2] Heb. 5:7-8.
[3] John 1:14.

and we need to be wary of reports of that nature. It is enough to know that we shall be with Jesus in the Father's house.

> **11:45-53** *Therefore many of the Jews who came to Mary and saw what Jesus did believed in him. But some of them went away to the Pharisees and told them the things which Jesus had done. The chief priests therefore and the Pharisees gathered a council, and said, 'What are we doing? For this man does many signs. If we leave him alone like this, everyone will believe in him, and the Romans will come and take away both our place and our nation.'*
>
> *But a certain one of them, Caiaphas, being high priest that year, said to them, 'You know nothing at all, nor do you consider that it is advantageous for us that one man should die for the people, and that the whole nation not perish.' Now he didn't say this of himself, but being high priest that year, he prophesied that Jesus would die for the nation, and not for the nation only, but that he might also gather together into one the children of God who are scattered abroad. So from that day forward they took counsel that they might put him to death.*

There is total silence about what happened to Lazarus in the immediate aftermath of his resurrection. The focus is on Jesus and the religious leaders, for this striking and undeniable miracle would have major implications for all of them. John tells us that, as a consequence of what they had witnessed, many of the Jewish leaders believed in Jesus. This is scarcely surprising, given the magnitude of the event and its obvious significance. Some of those present told certain (other) Pharisees what had happened. Since some of those who shared this information were probably also Pharisees, they may have been hoping to influence the others in a positive way. If so, they were to be sadly disappointed. Their account of the events was not disputed but, rather than provoking joy and gratitude to God, it was received as a threat and with a sense of fear and foreboding.

The Pharisees began to formulate a plan, a strategy that would limit the damage and dispel the danger once and for all. An emergency council meeting, including both Pharisees and Sadducees but possibly excluding those known to favour Jesus, was hurriedly called. The two groups were united in a common cause, in a dark parody of the unity of the Father and the Son. The Pharisees had taken centre stage in debate with Jesus and the chief priests had remained in the background ever since their initial confrontation with Him during the first Passover visit of His public ministry. They had re-emerged during the Feast of Tabernacles, when they attempted to arrest Jesus following His dramatic declaration in 'their' Temple.[4]

The council members clearly accepted that Jesus' many miracles were genuine, presumably including this latest and most spectacular one. Significantly, they designated these miracles as signs, implying a purpose beyond the events themselves: that they pointed to the identity of the one who performed them. The Sanhedrin was composed of intelligent and educated men, but at this point emotion took over and panic replaced logic. All they could see was that their whole world was about to fall apart and they were impotent to do anything about it. The possibility that Jesus might actually be the Messiah and the Son of God was too dreadful to contemplate, while the threat to their treasured way of life was all too real and urgent.

This is a classic illustration of the part that desire, ambition and emotions often play in making decisions and choices, even under the façade of apparently reasoned argument. Truth can be made subservient to what we want to achieve or possess, and evidence and facts can be rearranged to fit with this objective.

This recent miracle would have given a huge boost to Jesus' already widespread popularity. The mood of many of the leaders was close to despair, for it seemed that events were slipping out of their control and they could do nothing about it. They were at their wits' end. At this point Caiaphas the High Priest came to the rescue. He was cool, calm and collected, aware of the danger and ready with a solution. He dismissed his colleagues' concerns with a simple but brutal plan: 'it is advantageous for us that one man should die for the people, and that the whole nation not perish'. Caiaphas was both pragmatic and cynical and he used the language of power rather than truth, 'Let's just eliminate the problem, while dressing it up as a noble enterprise.'

---

[4] John 7:44-45.

As High Priest, Caiaphas represented the people before God, but spiritual and moral considerations played no part in his thinking. Reference was previously made to a possible connection between the parable of the rich man and Lazarus and the rich and corrupt family of Annas. In that parable, the rich man in hell requested that Lazarus should be sent back from heaven to warn his brothers not to come to the place of torment. Abraham's words were now proving true in the case of the chief priests, 'If they don't listen to Moses and the prophets, neither will they be persuaded if one rises from the dead.'[5]

Caiaphas was unaware that, on the basis of his office rather than his person, the Holy Spirit was inspiring his speech. The irony in his statement was that the death of the Messiah was the one event that would render the Temple redundant and cause it to pass into history, along with the priesthood that he was so desperate to protect. God would use Caiaphas' evil purpose to serve His own sovereign plan for the salvation of Israel and the world, and to create one new holy people from believing Jews and Gentiles. God had appointed Israel as a nation of priests, and Caiaphas the High Priest would unwittingly offer up the Messiah, the Lamb of God, for the sins of the world.[6]

Jesus had been illegally tried and sentenced in His absence; now all that remained was the issue of how to arrange for the execution.

---

[5] See chapter 8; Luke 16:31.
[6] Exod. 19:3-6; Heb. 8:13.

33

John 11:54–12:19
Anointing and Acclamation

11:54-57 Jesus therefore walked no more openly amongst the Jews, but departed from there into the country near the wilderness, to a city called Ephraim. He stayed there with his disciples.

Now the Passover of the Jews was at hand. Many went up from the country to Jerusalem before the Passover, to purify themselves. Then they sought for Jesus and spoke with one another as they stood in the temple, 'What do you think – that he isn't coming to the feast at all?'

Now the chief priests and the Pharisees had commanded that if anyone knew where he was, he should report it, that they might seize him.

Through the resurrection of Lazarus, Jesus had revealed His glory for anyone with eyes to see, and no further evidence would be added. His public ministry in Jerusalem had begun three years previously in the Temple courts at Passover and it would be completed in the same place, also at Passover. Everything was according to God's timing and fulfilled the prophetic symbolism of the Scriptures. The Jewish leaders, although eager to kill Jesus at the earliest possible opportunity, were also anxious to avoid the period of Passover, as this might cause a riot.[1] (This contradicts the notion that the Jewish nation, as a whole, approved of the crucifixion. Sadly, this false accusation led to centuries of persecution, pogroms and murders of Jews by 'Christians', particularly at Easter.)

Jesus left Jerusalem and travelled north to the mountainous region of Ephraim in order to have uninterrupted time with His

---

[1] Matt. 26:1-5.

disciples. A major movement of population would soon be under way as people would travel from all over the country in preparation for the feast. There was no sign of Jesus, but people were aware that the Chief Priests and Pharisees were looking for Him and that everyone was expected to assist by betraying Him. There was uncertainty and speculation and the population was on tenterhooks about what might happen.

> **12:1-8** *Then six days before the Passover, Jesus came to Bethany, where Lazarus was, who had been dead, whom he raised from the dead. So they made him a supper there. Martha served, but Lazarus was one of those who sat at the table with him. Therefore Mary took a pound of ointment of pure nard, very precious, and anointed Jesus's feet and wiped his feet with her hair. The house was filled with the fragrance of the ointment.*
>
> *Then Judas Iscariot, Simon's son, one of his disciples, who would betray him, said, 'Why wasn't this ointment sold for three hundred denarii, and given to the poor?' Now he said this, not because he cared for the poor, but because he was a thief, and having the money box, used to steal what was put into it.*
>
> *But Jesus said, 'Leave her alone. She has kept this for the day of my burial. For you always have the poor with you, but you don't always have me.'*

John probably included this event in his Gospel because of its proximity to the time of Jesus' suffering, and also because of its symbolic connection with what would soon take place at the Passover meal and beyond. Bethany was a special place for Jesus, a place where He could rest and relax with intimate friends. It was to Bethany that He would return in the evenings of Passover week, following days of confrontation with Jewish leaders in Jerusalem, and it was from Bethany that He would ascend to the Father's presence.[2] Lazarus was simply described as sitting at the table. He was both the catalyst for the decision to destroy Jesus and the living demonstration of Jesus' power over death.

---

2 Mark 11:11; Luke 24:50-51.

Mary may have been aware that her brother Lazarus was now under threat of violent death and that Jesus was also a target for the Jewish leaders. Perhaps this was what stirred her to engage in this uninhibited exhibition of love. When Mary poured the ointment on Jesus' feet and wiped them with her hair, she was disregarding social and religious convention. It was considered improper for a woman to expose her hair, and to let it down carried hints of immorality. Mary had no concern for her reputation, so grateful was she that Jesus had put His own life at risk in order to raise her beloved brother from the corruption of death. She had seen the glory of God and she no longer worried about what people might think about her.

The aroma enveloped everyone, but not everyone was pleased. Sometimes we can be embarrassed, or even offended, when others express worship in ways that we consider extravagant or unduly emotional. Such behaviour can indeed be false or inappropriate, but it can also be true and healthy, as in the present case. Outward expressions of worship involving activities such as music, song, poetry or drama are hollow unless we have walked like Mary in intimate relationship with Jesus. She had sat at Jesus' feet and, as a disciple, she had listened intently to His teaching. Forms of worship to which we are unaccustomed may then create a useful challenge and an opportunity to move out of our own, perhaps too narrow, comfort zones. Such inhibitions are sometimes the product of cultural background and individual personality rather than arising from biblical constraints. We should, of course, also express our love for Jesus by lovingly serving others and being sensitive to them.

Mary may have had a premonition of Jesus' impending death, or perhaps her action was unwittingly prophetic. She had probably been involved in preparing Lazarus' body for burial, using spiced oil in the process. Possibly it was this circumstance that inspired her to anoint Jesus while He still lived, making use of this much more costly perfume. Jesus understood and interpreted her action: 'She has kept this for the day of my burial.'

Jesus would also have been unsurprised by Judas' intervention, for He was well aware of the state of his heart. A year previously, Jesus had informed the disciples that one of them was a devil, without identifying Judas. At this point John was not yet aware of Judas' dishonesty, but he recorded it here in order to explain the real reason why Judas intervened. Unbeknown to the other disciples, he had been descending into an inner darkness through greed, dishonesty and deception. Of course, Jesus saw through Judas' duplicity, and voiced His full support for and approval of Mary's action.

The contrasting responses of Mary and Judas are vivid examples of the theme of light and darkness that is interwoven throughout the text. They had both been present when Jesus revealed His glory through the resurrection of Lazarus, who now sat among them as living evidence of that event. Mary had poured out her treasures at Jesus' feet, but Judas would soon value Him at the price set for a slave.[3]

> **12:9-11** *A large crowd therefore of the Jews learnt that he was there, and they came, not for Jesus' sake only, but that they might see Lazarus also, whom he had raised from the dead. But the chief priests conspired to put Lazarus to death also, because on account of him many of the Jews went away and believed in Jesus.*

News of Jesus' presence in Bethany had spread rapidly in Jerusalem, and many of the Jewish leaders came to investigate. This was a unique opportunity to see Jesus and Lazarus together and to hear the story at first hand. Lazarus had become a major celebrity and Bethany a place of religious pilgrimage. This was causing alarm bells to sound at the Temple, for many religious leaders were making the journey and some, impressed by Lazarus' testimony, were deserting to the enemy, Jesus. Obviously something needed to be done, and soon. Jesus was still inaccessible, because of popular support and also because of His absence from Jerusalem. Lazarus, whose very existence was extremely inconvenient, was a softer target. Perhaps he could be eliminated, thus disposing of inconvenient evidence that did not fit with the official narrative. It may not be a coincidence that in the parable of the rich man and Lazarus the poor man is so named. The possible connection

---

[3] Exod. 21:32; Zech. 11:12-13; Matt. 26:14-16.

between this parable and the family of Annas has already been discussed.

This shocking proposal revealed the depth of the leaders' moral and spiritual darkness. They had become so hardened and corrupted that they could no longer distinguish between good and evil, truth and lies. Good had become whatever sustained their position and truth whatever served their purposes. They knew and did not dispute the facts that had been reported to them, but refused to draw the obvious conclusions that were in conflict with their perceived self-interest. They were determined to hang on to power and prestige at any cost, which for them was the total loss of integrity as human beings. They had lost the ability to distinguish between reality and illusion, truth and falsehood. Others have subsequently made a similar choice, pitting their wills against the purposes of God, with the same outcome.

> **12:12-19** *On the next day a great multitude had come to the feast. When they heard that Jesus was coming to Jerusalem, they took the branches of the palm trees and went out to meet him, and cried out, 'Hosanna! Blessed is he who comes in the name of the Lord, the King of Israel!'*
>
> *Jesus, having found a young donkey, sat on it. As it is written, 'Don't be afraid, daughter of Zion. Behold, your King comes, sitting on a donkey's colt.' His disciples didn't understand these things at first, but when Jesus was glorified, then they remembered that these things were written about him, and that they had done these things to him. The multitude therefore that was with him when he called Lazarus out of the tomb and raised him from the dead was testifying about it. For this cause also the multitude went and met him, because they heard that he had done this sign. The Pharisees therefore said amongst themselves, 'See how you accomplish nothing. Behold, the world has gone after him.'*

In five days' time it would be Passover. Jerusalem was already packed to capacity and tens of thousands of people were encamped on the hills around the city. Many had come from Galilee in the north, the scene of most of Jesus' public ministry, and many others had arrived from the diaspora in the surrounding nations. Passover recalled the deliverance of the people of Israel from bondage in

Egypt and thus struck a chord with the current population that was groaning under the Roman yoke. The Romans and the Jewish authorities both knew that Passover was a potential time of unrest and that it needed to be carefully managed. As a precaution, the governor, Pontius Pilate, moved from Caesarea Maritima on the coast to the north of Jerusalem for the duration of the feast.

When Jesus awoke on the morning following Mary's prophetic anointing, the aroma may still have lingered on His clothing, silently testifying to the climactic events of the coming week. Six months earlier Jesus had slipped quietly into the city and the Temple at the midpoint of the Feast of Tabernacles, but now He was about to make a dramatic entrance, and in a highly symbolic way. He set out from Bethany with a small group of followers and began to climb the eastern side of the Mount of Olives. He had made this ascent many times in the past, but this time it was different in that it was the prelude to His suffering. The unfolding events held no surprise for Him, and He had spoken of them on many occasions. Perhaps we can imagine His thoughts: possibly a mixture of foreboding and anticipation, for He was fully human. Now, as He embraced His appointed destiny, He may have walked in silence and deep in thought.

As He crested the summit, a dramatic vista suddenly spread out before Him, the beautiful city with its magnificent Temple glowing in the morning sun. Bethphage was close by and marked the city limits. It seems that Jesus had made preparations, for the colt of a donkey stood ready to carry the King to His capital city. Jesus was aware of the prophecy of Zechariah to this effect, and was conscious of the messianic symbolism of His action.[4] He had reached the point of no return and, without hesitation, He began to descend towards Jerusalem.

A large and enthusiastic crowd was streaming up the steep side of the Mount of Olives that overlooked Jerusalem. News of the resurrection of Lazarus had spread like wildfire, exciting a hope that this Passover might finally be the time of their longed-for redemption.[5] The behaviour of the crowd suggests that at least

---

[4] Zech. 9:9.
[5] Luke 1:32-33, 51-55, 67-75; 2:25-38; 23:50-51; 24:13-21; Acts 1:3, 6.

some of them understood the symbolism of Jesus' journey, for they waved palm branches that spoke of victory and cried out, 'Hosanna! Blessed is he who comes in the name of the Lord!' These words from Psalm 118 were widely interpreted as referring to the Messiah. The word 'Hosanna' was an ascription of praise, but it also meant 'salvation', and in the present context was probably intended as, 'Save us from the occupying power.' The second part of the cry of the crowd, 'the King of Israel', was connected with the prophecy of Zechariah and was probably applied in a political sense.[6] If Jesus could raise the dead, then surely He could restore the throne of David and drive out the hated Romans.

There was an inherent ambiguity in Zechariah's prophecy, for he described how the King would arrive on a lowly donkey, in meekness and humility. He would also be sold for silver, pierced, wounded in the house of His friends and stricken by God Himself.[7] John notes that the disciples did not fully understand the significance of what was taking place but they were, no doubt, swept along by the enthusiasm of the crowd. Jesus received the acclamation, but when He rode into Jerusalem He turned left into the Temple rather than right towards the Roman fortress. The Lord, the messenger of the covenant, had come to His Temple to cleanse it and to confront the corrupt religious leaders, as Malachi had prophesied. Both Psalm 118 and the words of the prophet Malachi indicated that the Messiah would come at a time when the Temple was standing in Jerusalem. Just forty years later it would lie in ruins.[8]

The leaders, who were desperate to maintain the delicate status quo with the Romans, were very concerned about events on the Mount of Olives. The Pharisees were in despair as the tide of popular acclaim threatened to sweep away everything that they cherished. They were at one with Caiaphas in his desire to eliminate Jesus, but they lacked his ruthless pragmatism and felt helpless in the face of a collapsing situation. The Pharisees gradually faded

---

6 Matt. 21:1-9; Ps. 118:25-26; Zech. 9:9.

7 Zech. 11:12-13; 12:10; 13:6-7.

8 Matt. 21:12-13; Mal. 3:1-3.

into the background and the chief priests assumed leadership in the movement to deal with Jesus. As the Pharisees retreated in dismay, they made an unwittingly prophetic statement: 'Behold, the world has gone after him.'

34

John 12:20-36
Death and Glory

> *12:20-26 Now there were certain Greeks amongst those that went up to worship at the feast. These, therefore, came to Philip, who was from Bethsaida of Galilee, and asked him, saying, 'Sir, we want to see Jesus.' Philip came and told Andrew, and in turn, Andrew came with Philip, and they told Jesus.*
>
> *Jesus answered them, 'The time has come for the Son of Man to be glorified. Most certainly I tell you, unless a grain of wheat falls into the earth and dies, it remains by itself alone. But if it dies, it bears much fruit. He who loves his life will lose it. He who hates his life in this world will keep it to eternal life. If anyone serves me, let him follow me. Where I am, there my servant will also be. If anyone serves me, the Father will honour him.'*

God-fearing Gentiles who were dissatisfied with their pagan gods had come to the feast in order to worship the God of Israel. Apparently they had heard reports about Jesus that resonated with their spiritual hunger, so they were eager to come and see Him. It is likely that He was surrounded by a crowd and was therefore inaccessible. Philip appeared to have connections with Jesus so they approached him in a humble and respectful way, hoping for an introduction. Philip consulted with Andrew and together they brought the request to Jesus. This kind of detail in John's Gospel testifies to its character as a first-hand account.

Philip's hesitation suggests that he was uncertain as to what he should do about the unusual request. Jesus had taught His disciples that He had been sent only to the lost sheep of the house of Israel, and He had confirmed this when He sent them out on mission. More recently, Jesus had spoken of bringing other sheep into His fold, which would have been confusing for them. John does not inform us about how Jesus responded to the request, but it is clear that He interpreted the incident as highly significant, marking the beginning of His hour of destiny. This was the time that the Father had ordained for Him, and what would happen by the end of the current week would have worldwide relevance. The Lamb of God was about to be offered for the sin of the world.[1]

Jesus proclaimed that the hour had come for the Son of Man to be glorified. He had in mind a series of events that would commence at the cross and would climax in His ascension to the throne of God as glorified man. This was a single and indivisible process that would result in a worldwide harvest, of which His visit to the Samaritans at Sychar had also been a prophetic sign. Now these Greeks were a symbolic token of this harvest that would be reaped to the ends of the earth. He could see the vision of abundant life, but He also knew that if a seed was to multiply, it must first die.

When a natural seed falls into the ground it becomes totally vulnerable and is subject to the Creator's purpose. It dies to its previously intact form and structure and there is no way back. Jesus was taking this path of full surrender to the Father's will and purpose, believing in the promise of resurrection life and a multiplied harvest, and He was calling His disciples to follow that same path. Jesus was the one seed through whom all the nations of the earth would be blessed, and His death was vital for that harvest to be realised. What is true in the natural realm is also true in the spiritual realm.

Jesus immediately applied the same principle to His disciples. The difference between serving Jesus and following Him lies in the answer to the question, 'Who is in control?' Service is secondary, being the natural consequence of following Him and being in relationship with Him. We make a choice to surrender to Him and then discover, in the process of living, what it means to take up our cross daily and follow Him. If we retain personal control of parts of our lives, separate from the lordship of Christ, then our service will be unfruitful and we will suffer loss. For those who respond

---

[1] Matt. 15:24; 9:36; 10:5-6; John 10:16; 1:29; 6:51.

to His call there is a double blessing, living in relationship with Jesus and receiving honour from the Father.

> **12:27-33** *'Now my soul is troubled. What shall I say? "Father, save me from this time?" But I came to this time for this cause. Father, glorify your name!'*
>
> *Then a voice came out of the sky, saying, 'I have both glorified it, and will glorify it again.'*
>
> *Therefore the multitude who stood by and heard it said that it had thundered. Others said, 'An angel has spoken to him.'*
>
> *Jesus answered, 'This voice hasn't come for my sake, but for your sakes. Now is the judgement of this world. Now the prince of this world will be cast out. And I, if I am lifted up from the earth, will draw all people to myself.' But he said this, signifying by what kind of death he should die.*

Jesus had known about His destiny for a long time and had frequently spoken about it, but it now provoked deep and troubling emotions. We are familiar with this situation, perhaps in the context of an important examination or interview, or a planned surgical procedure. As the moment draws near our emotions intensify and can almost overwhelm us. Jesus experienced something like this as the reality of His suffering loomed large, for He was fully human. This is the mystery of the eternal Word made flesh, like us.

Jesus did not allow strong emotions to determine His attitude and actions. Like the psalmist, He was determined to trust in God. His supreme ambition was to glorify His Father's name by fulfilling the purpose for which He had been sent. Jesus' death would be the ultimate revelation of God's holiness and love, His righteousness and grace, His wisdom and power. Jesus had affirmed acceptance of that destiny months previously when, with His eyes wide open to the cost, He had set His face like a flint to go to Jerusalem.[2]

The voice from heaven revealed the unity of the Father and the Son in the life and ministry of Jesus, and gave assurance that His work would conclude with glory. The bystanders were only aware

---

[2] Ps. 42–43; 94:16-23; 116; Heb. 5:7-10; Lk 9:28-31, 51-53; Isa. 50:4-9.

of a powerful but unintelligible noise. Some of the crowd attributed the sound to a natural phenomenon and others to angels. This may have been conditioned by theological prejudices. Some people may have been devotees of the Sadducees, who did not believe in angels, and others of the Pharisees who did believe in them. Previously, many people had failed to recognise the significance of the miraculous signs and now they did not think to inquire, 'What was the reason for this noise or voice? What did it signify?'

We, like them, are constrained by our worldviews and are often unaware that this is so. When unusual events happen in our world, we should ask questions such as, 'What is God doing? Where is He in all of this? How does He want us to respond?' The alternative is to accept the humanist/secular view of history, denying or ignoring the activity of God within His creation.

Jesus explained that the voice had been for their benefit rather than for His, as a sign or seal of the truths that they had just heard from His lips. Thunder and loud noise were often associated with God's judgements, and a crucial judgement was imminent. It was the judgement of the ruler of the world, and of the rebellious world order over which he presided.[3] Jesus affirmed the biblical worldview that evil is not merely an influence or an attitude, nor even an accident. It is orchestrated by an evil and unseen being who is implacably opposed to God and His purposes for His creation.

Satan gained access to the world through human choice and disobedience. He, together with the whole evil system that he had spawned, was about to come under judgement through the obedience of the perfect man, Jesus. The lifting up of Jesus on the cross would make a way for people of all nations to come into relationship with Him, to be released from Satan's grip and set free to serve the Creator.

> **12:34-36** *The multitude answered him, 'We have heard out of the law that the Christ remains forever. How do you say, "The Son of Man must be lifted up?" Who is this Son of Man?'*

---

[3] Exod. 9:23; 19:16; 20:18; 1 Sam. 7:10; 12:17-18; Isa. 29:6; Rev. 4:5.

> *Jesus therefore said to them, 'Yet a little while the light is with you. Walk while you have the light, that darkness doesn't overtake you. He who walks in the darkness doesn't know where he is going. While you have the light, believe in the light, that you may become children of light.' Jesus said these things, and he departed and hid himself from them.*

The people had just had an awesome experience and had heard Jesus speak about a world-transforming event that was about to take place. They knew that, in speaking about being lifted up, He was referring to death. Amazingly, they ignored all of this and raised a disputed point of interpretation of Scripture, one that was only obliquely related to what Jesus had just said. Jesus had not, in that context, spoken of Himself either as the Messiah or as the Son of Man. They were possibly referring to a previous occasion when Jesus warned the leaders that they would be responsible for lifting up the Son of Man.[4]

The people who now raised these objections had only a superficial knowledge of Scripture. They had heard certain things from the Law but did not appreciate the overall message of Scripture. This includes prophecies of a Messiah who would suffer as a man, as well as the others that spoke of Him as the glorified Son of Man.[5] Jewish scholars were well aware of this but had not been able to resolve the paradox to their satisfaction. The crowd had missed, or perhaps had deliberately sidestepped, the evidence that Jesus had provided for them through His miracles. Perhaps they were purposely changing the subject in order to avoid implications that they did not want to face. This device is still alive and well at the present time; poorly informed people still raise objections to the Christian faith on the basis of hearsay, without taking time and trouble to make proper investigations.

Jesus ignored their spurious questions, bringing them back to the issue that required an urgent response and impressing on them the danger in which they were living. This was almost the last time that they would hear Him speak, for the fact that His hour had

---

[4] John 8:28.
[5] Is. 52:13–53:12.

come also meant that their time of opportunity was vanishing. He had been with them as the light of the world for several years, but many of His hearers, although they had seen spectacular miracles, had stubbornly refused to accept His word and commit themselves to Him. Jesus warned them of coming darkness, but with even greater emphasis He invited them to come to the light, for light is stronger than darkness.[6]

If they believed in Jesus, the incarnate light, they would not merely understand the truth about Him in a doctrinal sense. They would be transformed into 'children of light', receiving what was otherwise described as new birth from above.[7] If they persisted in their stubborn refusal to receive the proffered light, they would be overtaken by an endless darkness.[8] Jesus then left them to choose, for additional evidence would not now make any difference to their decisions.

[6] John 1:5; 8:12.
[7] John 3:3-7; 11:9-10.
[8] John 3:18-21; 12:37-41.

35

John 12:37-50
Final Offer and Warning

> *12:37-43 But though he had done so many signs before them, yet they didn't believe in him, that the word of Isaiah the prophet might be fulfilled, which he spoke, 'Lord, who has believed our report? To whom has the arm of the Lord been revealed?' For this cause they couldn't believe, for Isaiah said again, 'He has blinded their eyes and he hardened their heart, lest they should see with their eyes, and perceive with their heart, and would turn, and I would heal them.' Isaiah said these things when he saw his glory, and spoke of him. Nevertheless even many of the rulers believed in him, but because of the Pharisees they didn't confess it, so that they wouldn't be put out of the synagogue, for they loved men's praise more than God's praise.*

Jesus had been teaching and performing miracles for several years, but despite this, many people, including leaders and some ordinary people, remained unconvinced of His identity as Messiah. They refused to see, in the face of the overwhelming nature of the evidence, and were descending into a spiritual darkness from which recovery would eventually be impossible. They were losing the ability to distinguish truth from error. Spiritual things can only be understood with the help of the Spirit of God.

Isaiah had been appointed as a prophet at a time in Israel's history when successive generations had ignored God's call to return to Him in sincerity and truth. Spiritual deafness and blindness had crept over the nation: each time they rejected God's call to repentance their hearts became harder. They had now reached the point of no return and would have to live with the consequences of their choice. God had warned Isaiah that his message would only serve to reinforce their blindness.

Nevertheless, the message that he proclaimed and wrote would remain as a permanent witness to future generations, including those who now stood in the presence of Jesus.

John's reference to the prophecy of Isaiah ends with an intriguing statement: 'Isaiah said these things when he saw his glory, and spoke of him.' John appears to have been identifying Jesus as the One who was high and lifted up, the King and the Lord of Hosts. Isaiah also wrote about the Messiah, as the arm of the Lord. He would be God's agent in the world but would be unrecognised by most of those who saw Him.[1] These words were now coming to pass.

In Isaiah's prophetic vision the Lord was lifted up in glory. Jesus was now about to be lifted up in a different way, on the cross, before returning to that exalted glory. He had provided abundant evidence for His identity but He had encountered stubborn resistance. Some people, including many leaders, were actually persuaded that Jesus was the Messiah and were, perhaps, contemplating becoming His disciples, but they would not risk a showdown with the leading Pharisees. Their reputations and their relationships with fellow Pharisees had priority over public recognition of Jesus. As John wrote, 'they loved men's praise more than God's praise'.

Some beliefs are inconsequential as far as behaviour is concerned, but others, if sincerely held, require a radical change in behaviour. Belief in the identity of Jesus is the supreme example of this latter category. A great gulf existed between the Jews' intellectual assent to the evidence and true faith that would motivate them to action. As the apostle James wrote, 'faith, if it has no works, is dead in itself'. Nothing had really changed since the Pharisees had encountered Jesus after He had healed the lame man.[2]

John now explained a startling and mysterious process that was at work, both in past generations and also continuing in the present time. Pharaoh had hardened his heart against the word of God and a moment came when God strengthened Pharaoh in his chosen

---

[1] Isa. 6:1-3, 9-10; 7:14; 9:6-7; 11:1-10; 53:1-3.
[2] Jas. 2:17; John 5:1-47.

course of action, so that he became the agent of his own destruction. The Lord informed Isaiah that He was about to punish the people of the day by hardening their hearts, because they had persistently refused to respond to His word. Isaiah warned that judgement and exile were inevitable, as the people would then be unable to change their fixed attitude of unbelief. God did have a plan to restore Israel, but their unbelief and idolatry was so deeply ingrained that radical surgery needed to precede healing.

Isaiah's warning also applied to the people who heard Jesus' words. God's action in hardening their hearts was not an arbitrary one but was the end stage of a process of stubborn unbelief, and it was also the inevitable outcome of what they had deliberately chosen.[3] Within a few short years Jerusalem would again lie in ruins, the Temple destroyed and the people in exile. Jesus had wept in His grief while predicting the events that would soon take place in consequence of their unwillingness to receive Him.

In the mystery of God's providence, their blindness would play its part in delivering up the Messiah to die for the sins of the world and in the spread of the gospel to the nations of the world. This is not the last word in the story, for God also promised a time when the blindness will be removed and the Jewish people will recognise and receive their Messiah with repentance and faith.[4] The good news is that this has begun to take place. Significant numbers of Jewish people have received Jesus during the past few decades.

> *12:44-50 Jesus cried out and said, 'Whoever believes in me, believes not in me, but in him who sent me. He who sees me sees him who sent me. I have come as a light into the world, that whoever believes in me may not remain in the darkness. If anyone listens to my sayings, and doesn't believe, I don't judge him. For I came not to judge the world, but to save the world. He who rejects me, and doesn't receive my sayings, has one who judges him. The word that I spoke will judge him in the last day. For I spoke not from myself, but the Father who sent me, he gave me a commandment, what I should say, and what I should speak.*

---

[3] Isa. 6:8-13 (note particularly verse 10); 53:1; Exod. 3:19-20; 4:21-23; 8:32; 9:34-10:1.

[4] Matt. 23:37-39; Rom. 11:25-29.

I know that his commandment is eternal life. The things therefore which I speak, even as the Father has said to me, so I speak.'

These are Jesus' last recorded public words in John's Gospel and they contain the essence of His teaching. He called out in a loud voice, aware that His message was urgent and vitally important and that it would never again be heard from His lips. Jesus was the revelation of God the Father in human flesh, so that believing in Him is equivalent to believing in God. He had brought the light of truth into the darkness of the world. If people rejected that light then they would inevitably remain in spiritual darkness. His purpose in coming into the world was for salvation and not for judgement, but those who had heard His word of salvation must face up to the solemn truth that, if they chose to reject the word and the messenger, there would be serious consequences on the coming Day of Judgement.

In these final few words, Jesus re-emphasised the reason why people should believe in His message. The Father, the Creator of the world and the Holy One of Israel, desires that people should share everlasting life with Him forever. The Father sent His Son into the world and had commanded Him to speak this message about eternal life. God now required the appropriate response: faith in His Son. Many of the rulers had recognised with their minds that Jesus was the Messiah but, as we have seen, they were unwilling to risk everything and become His committed disciples.

The focus of John's Gospel is now about to change. Three years have been covered in just twelve chapters, mainly documenting interactions between Jesus and the world. The events contained in the remaining chapters take place during a period of only a few days. Jesus will now spend intimate time with His disciples in private, in order to prepare them for His death and resurrection and for the new situation that they will encounter beyond these climactic events.

36

John 13:1-30
A Unique Passover Meal

> *13:1-5 Now before the feast of the Passover, Jesus, knowing that his time had come that he would depart from this world to the Father, having loved his own who were in the world, he loved them to the end. During supper, the devil having already put into the heart of Judas Iscariot, Simon's son, to betray him, Jesus, knowing that the Father had given all things into his hands, and that he came from God, and was going to God, arose from supper, and laid aside his outer garments. He took a towel and wrapped a towel around his waist. Then he poured water into the basin, and began to wash the disciples' feet and to wipe them with the towel that was wrapped around him.*

Jesus' public ministry was now complete. The last week had been very busy and eventful, involving repeated episodes of controversy with the religious leaders. Jesus was now aware that His hour, the Father's appointed time, had arrived for His suffering, and also for His return to the Father's immediate presence.[1] His love for His disciples had been unwavering, despite their lack of understanding and their somewhat unstable faith. They are described as being His 'own', in a more particular sense than others of His own Jewish people. They were the initial sheep that the Father had given Him and for whom He was about to lay down His life.[2] They were 'in the world' that He had made and had visited in flesh and blood, and which He was about to leave. The Father had given them to Him from out of the world, in another sense of that word – the

---

[1] Heb. 12:2.
[2] John 1:11; 10:14-15, 29.

world as a system ruled by Satan. They had shared with Jesus the opposition from that hostile world.

Jesus loved His own, would continue to love them and would love them to the uttermost extent. Love becomes the dominant word in the next five chapters, whereas light no longer occurs. Jesus' antagonists were now locked in an irreversible spiritual darkness. They had made their choice and He had nothing further to say to them. Jesus would spend the next few hours exclusively with His 'own' and would share His heart with those who had followed Him as Lord. John noted that among them was a traitor, one whose attitude and behaviour had made him vulnerable to deception by the original murderer and the father of lies.[3]

The participants at the Feast would have discarded their sandals at the door and would then have taken up positions around three outer sides of a U-shaped table, each adopting a reclining position and leaning on his left arm. Positions at the table signified rank, and we know from Luke's account that the disciples disagreed among themselves as to who was the greatest.[4] The Gospel writers did not always adhere to strict chronology and it may be that seating arrangements were the occasion of that dispute, provoking Jesus' rebuke. John was probably positioned at one end of a long limb of the table, to the right of Jesus. We cannot be certain where they took their places, but it seems that Judas was to the left of Jesus in what was also considered to be the place of honour. Peter, perhaps chastened by Jesus' words of rebuke, appears to have taken the lowest place at the end of the other side, explaining the subsequent covert communications.[5] It seems that no servant had been provided to wash their dusty feet and, consistent with their sense of dignity, none of the disciples volunteered for this lowly task.

Supper would have begun with the first of four cups of wine, and Jesus as the host would have pronounced a benediction. Following this He, as the head of the Feast, would have ceremonially washed His hands. When Jesus rose from supper the

---

[3] John 8:44; 12:6.
[4] Luke 22:24-27.
[5] Alfred Edersheim; *The Life and Times of Jesus the Messiah, Book V* (Grand Rapids: Wm. B. Erdmanns Publishing Co., 1971), pp. 490-494.

disciples probably remained seated in expectation of this ritual. They must have been shocked when they realised what He was about to do, replacing a ritual that defined a religious elite with one that indicated a lowly servant. Jesus' identity was rooted in His relationship with the Father and was independent of outward circumstances; He brought dignity to the activity of foot-washing rather than deriving His identity from it. This understanding allowed Him to take the place of a servant, so He laid aside His outer garments just as He had laid aside His glory when He came to earth. A little later, both His outer and inner garments would be taken from Him, for He was exposed naked on the cross, bearing our shame.

> **13:6-11** *Then he came to Simon Peter. He said to him, 'Lord, do you wash my feet?'*
>
> *Jesus answered him, 'You don't know what I am doing now, but you will understand later.'*
>
> *Peter said to him, 'You will never wash my feet!'*
>
> *Jesus answered him, 'If I don't wash you, you have no part with me.'*
>
> *Simon Peter said to him, 'Lord, not my feet only, but also my hands and my head!'*
>
> *Jesus said to him, 'Someone who has bathed only needs to have his feet washed, but is completely clean. You are clean, but not all of you.' For he knew him who would betray him, therefore he said, 'You are not all clean.'*

As Peter was probably at the end of the opposite side of the table, it seems that Jesus approached him first. Peter, no doubt along with the other disciples, was confused and discomfited by what Jesus was about to do, contrasting as it did with their own attitudes. Peter probably initially reacted in horror rather than meaning to correct Jesus, as he had previously done. He simply could not understand what was taking place and had never imagined such a thing, Jesus being their Lord and he being merely a disciple. Jesus essentially replied, 'Obedience is for now; understanding will come later.' Peter brushed this aside, no longer addressed Jesus as Lord and substituted his own wisdom, bluntly forbidding Jesus from carrying out His intended action.

Jesus responded by offering Peter a choice that would determine his future. He could cling to his own wisdom and cut himself off from Jesus, or he could recognise Jesus' superior wisdom and submit to Him. This was and is a vitally important lesson to learn. If we only obey God when His word coincides with our wisdom, then we have not made Him Lord of our lives.

Peter was quick to recognise his error and repent. However, not understanding the constraints of the drama, he then went too far in the other direction. Jesus indicated that Peter had had a bath, the spiritual equivalent of the ritual immersion pools with which Jews like Peter were familiar. Later He explained to all the disciples that they had been cleansed by the word that He had spoken to them – that is, by hearing with faith. Peter still had many faults and would soon demonstrate his frailty in a spectacular way, but at the core of his being he was clean and deeply sincere in his commitment to Jesus. Peter was like David; he had also sinned grievously, yet God spoke of him as 'a man after his own heart'. Both men were quick to repent when corrected.[6]

Jesus referred to Judas in a cryptic way: 'You are clean, but not all of you.' Judas was in a different category, for he was a hypocrite, sheltering greed and dishonesty under a veneer of generosity. He had successfully deceived the other disciples but Jesus had understood his true character. Judas had opened his heart to Satan, who was now taking full advantage of that access.[7]

13:12-20 So when he had washed their feet, put his outer garment back on, and sat down again, he said to them, 'Do you know what I have done to you? You call me, "Teacher" and "Lord." You say so correctly, for so I am. If I then, the Lord and the Teacher, have washed your feet, you also ought to wash one another's feet. For I have given you an example, that you should also do as I have done to you. Most certainly I tell you, a servant is not greater than his lord, neither is one who is sent greater than he who sent him. If you know these things, blessed are you if you do them. I don't speak concerning all of you. I

---

[6] Matt. 16:21-23; John 15:3; Eph. 5:26; John 18:15-27; 1 Sam. 13:14; John 6:67-69.
[7] John 6:70-71.

know whom I have chosen. But that the Scripture may be fulfilled, "He who eats bread with me has lifted up his heel against me." From now on, I tell you before it happens, that when it happens, you may believe that I am he. Most certainly I tell you, he who receives whomever I send, receives me; and he who receives me, receives him who sent me.'

Jesus now proceeded around the table and washed the feet of each disciple, including Judas, and then put on His outer garments and resumed His place at the table. Peter had not understood why Jesus had acted in this unconventional way so Jesus now explained. He had been teaching by example and not just with words. They correctly recognised Him as their master and lord, whose 'Amen, amen I say to you' carried final authority. Their appropriate response was to obey His commands and to follow His example. This would be the key to blessing.

Quoting from a psalm, Jesus made a shocking statement. One of those who was sharing table fellowship and whose feet He had washed 'has lifted up his heel against me'. David had composed that psalm in response to the treachery of his counsellor Ahithophel, who had defected to David's rebellious son Absalom. David was a prophet, not only by means of his words but also through the events of his life, many of which foreshadowed the Messiah, the Son of David. In betraying Jesus, Judas was acting in the character of Ahithophel, not consciously but in practice. Both Ahithophel and Judas acted on the basis of their personal choices and values, thus revealing their true characters. Each retained responsibility for his actions and both ended their lives in the same way. When Judas made his choice, the Holy Spirit drew attention to the prophetic nature of that historical event. There was also an irony about Jesus' statement, for He Himself would lift up His heel against the one whom Judas now served.[8]

Satan had quoted another Psalm to Jesus when he tempted Him in the wilderness: 'For he will put his angels in charge of you, to guard you in all your ways. They will bear you up in their hands, so that you won't dash your foot against a stone.' The devil was treading on thin ice, for the very next verse states, 'You will tread

---

[8] Ps. 41:9; 2 Sam. 15:1-12; 17:23; Matt. 27:3-5; Acts 1:15-20; Gen. 3:15.

on the lion and cobra. You will trample the young lion and the serpent underfoot.' Satan had set Jesus on a high place, the pinnacle of the Temple. The same psalm continues, 'Because he has set his love on me, therefore I will deliver him. I will set him on high, because he has known my name.'[9] Jesus' love for the Father, in contrast to the attitude of Judas, was the antidote to all of the devil's blandishments.

Why did Jesus refer to the verse in Psalm 41? He would have been aware that the defection of Judas could subsequently cause difficulties for the disciples. They, and others as well, might wonder whether Jesus had made a mistake in choosing Judas. Was He not aware of his character? The same issue surfaced following Jesus' ascension, and Peter dealt with it in a similar way, quoting from two other psalms.[10] The disciples did not need to be concerned, for Jesus was not deceived, and the Father knew long ago what would take place and had everything in hand. The disciples would soon be able to speak to the world with complete confidence, because they were in relationship with the Father and the Son, and were their appointed representatives.[11]

> **13:21-30** *When Jesus had said this, he was troubled in spirit, and testified, 'Most certainly I tell you that one of you will betray me.'*
>
> *The disciples looked at one another, perplexed about whom he spoke. One of his disciples, whom Jesus loved, was at the table, leaning against Jesus' breast. Simon Peter therefore beckoned to him, and said to him, 'Tell us who it is of whom he speaks.'*
>
> *He, leaning back, as he was, on Jesus' breast, asked him, 'Lord, who is it?'*
>
> *Jesus therefore answered, 'It is he to whom I will give this piece of bread when I have dipped it.' So when he had dipped the piece of bread, he gave it to Judas, the son of Simon Iscariot. After the piece of bread, then Satan entered into him. Then Jesus said to him, 'What you do, do quickly.' Now nobody at the table knew why he said this to him. For some thought, because Judas had the money box, that Jesus said*

---

[9] Ps. 91:11-14; Matt. 4:5-7.

[10] Acts 1:15-20; Ps. 69:25; 109:8.

[11] Luke 7:7-9; John 20:19-23.

to him, 'Buy what things we need for the feast,' or that he should give something to the poor.

Therefore having received that morsel, he went out immediately. It was night.

In the process of applying the recent example and teaching to the disciples, Jesus had digressed to explain that there was one person to whom it did not apply. Now He continued to address the fact of the presence of a traitor among them, no longer on the basis of ancient testimony but rather on the authority of His own independent testimony, 'Amen, amen I say to you'. As He engaged in this much more personal way, Jesus experienced deep and troubling emotions, as had been the case before arriving at the tomb of His friend Lazarus. Jesus was not making a mere objective statement of fact. Judas' treachery was like a wound in Jesus' heart, and He also knew that Judas was travelling into a darkness that would have no exit.

Understandably, this caused renewed consternation among the disciples and was probably the occasion for the question that each of them asked: 'It isn't me, is it, Lord?' Judas, immediately beside Jesus, asked the same question, and Jesus confirmed what both of them already knew. His secret dishonesty and disloyalty had opened a door to Satan, who had then tempted him with thoughts of betrayal and financial gain. Jesus made him aware, without publicly shaming him, that He knew Judas' intentions. This was also his final opportunity to repent and be restored. Perhaps that was why Judas was given a place next to Jesus where private conversation was possible.[12]

Peter, unable to endure the suspense and unable to communicate privately with Jesus, asked John, who was probably sitting directly opposite him, to find out the identity of the betrayer. John was able to lean back against Jesus and whisper the question. Jesus answered by means of a symbolic act that connected with the psalm that He had previously quoted: 'Yes, my own familiar friend, in whom I trusted, who ate bread with me, has lifted up his heel against me.' They had probably reached the point in the Passover

---

[12] Matt. 26:21-25; John 6:70-71; 12:4-6.

meal when Jesus would have dipped a piece of unleavened bread (*matsah*) in a paste (*charoseth*). This He handed to Judas, thus identifying him to John as the betrayer.

Judas received this token of honour and friendship with a cold and unrepentant heart. This demonstrated that he had passed beyond the realms of recovery, for Satan now had complete mastery over him. It is significant that Jesus sent Judas out to accomplish his wicked purpose using words that invoked time: 'What you do, do quickly.' He spoke them as a directive and for all the company to hear, giving Judas the opportunity to exit without raising further anxiety among the other disciples. Jesus remained in control until the end, and even Satan and his willing accomplices had to serve His purposes.

Judas left at this early stage in the Passover celebration and was, therefore, not present during the main part of the meal and the subsequent institution of the New Covenant. The speculations of the disciples emphasise how completely Judas, one of their close associates, had hoodwinked them with his hypocrisy over a long period of time. Their statements also confirm that Jesus had maintained confidentiality when He had spoken to John, and also to Judas.[13]

Passover did not commence until after sunset, so John's comment, 'It was night', appears to be redundant unless there was a deeper meaning. Much earlier in the Gospel, John had described a man who came from the darkness of the night into the presence of Jesus, the light of the world. For the Pharisee Nicodemus, this was the beginning of a three-year journey from spiritual darkness to light. Another man, the erstwhile disciple Judas, had been privileged to walk during the same period with the light of the world, and now he had abandoned Him and was journeying into unending spiritual darkness.

---

[13] Matt. 26:25.

37

John 13:31–14:11
A Temporary Parting

> *13:31-35 When he had gone out, Jesus said, 'Now the Son of Man has been glorified, and God has been glorified in him. If God has been glorified in him, God will also glorify him in himself, and he will glorify him immediately. Little children, I will be with you a little while longer. You will seek me, and as I said to the Jews, "Where I am going, you can't come," so now I tell you. A new commandment I give to you, that you love one another. Just as I have loved you, you also love one another By this everyone will know that you are my disciples, if you have love for one another.'*

The sense of heaviness lifted as soon as Judas left, and Jesus turned from the dark theme of treachery to the bright prospect of glory. During the earlier part of the narrative He had only occasionally spoken about glory, but this theme had become more frequent as He approached the time of His suffering.[1] Now, in company with the disciples with whom He had chosen to share the last hours before that dark experience, He spoke of glory five times in two short sentences. He had referred to death on the cross in ambiguous language as being 'lifted up'. This lifting up, as has been pointed out previously, was not a single incident but was part of a connected series of events. He would first be lifted up in shame and suffering, and then in the glory of the resurrection and the ascension.[2]

Yet, despite appearances, even the lifting up on the cross would be a revelation of glory, for there, as the Son of Man, He would

---

[1] John 11:4, 40; 12:27-28.
[2] Phil. 2:5-11.

reveal the Father's love and also the glory of a life fully committed to the Father's will.[3] Jesus was so fully committed to the task that, from His point of view, the deed was already as good as done, although still in the future. The Father and the Son were totally engaged together in the events that would soon take place and each desired the other's glory, in the unity of their being. This theme would be continued a short time later when Jesus prayed.

Jesus turned to the disciples sitting around the table, their minds no doubt whirling and filled with questions about the many things that Jesus had just told them. He now prefaced His remarks with the tender diminutive, 'Little children', for He was aware that His words would inevitably have engendered a sense of foreboding. The disciples were in a very close relationship with Jesus so the enforced separation of the next few days would be both disorientating and painful. They would still have one another, so He urged, even commanded, them to love one another. Fear and confusion could blow them apart, but they must not allow this to happen. They would need one another as never before and should treat one another as He had treated them.

Of course, this would have more general application in the years that followed, and it is still vital in today's troubled world. Unity and mutual love, especially when directed towards those who are suffering hardship, identify those who are true followers of Jesus.

> **13:36-38** *Simon Peter said to him, 'Lord, where are you going?'*
>
> *Jesus answered, 'Where I am going, you can't follow now, but you will follow afterwards.'*
>
> *Peter said to him, 'Lord, why can't I follow you now? I will lay down my life for you.'*
>
> *Jesus answered him, 'Will you lay down your life for me? Most certainly I tell you, the rooster won't crow until you have denied me three times.'*

Peter had a particular reason for questioning Jesus' cryptic words. He knew that Judas was the traitor and that he was now on the

---

[3] John 3:14-17; 6:62; 8:28; 12:32-33.

loose. Perhaps he still hoped that, even though Jesus had repeatedly spoken of His coming violent death, He might yet seek refuge as He had done previously, when He had retreated to the wilderness.[4] There was no need for Jesus to face this danger alone, for Peter would accompany Him and defend Him with his own life. Jesus did not offer any explanation, but assured Peter that the separation would be temporary and that meanwhile he must be content simply to trust Him.

Jesus knew that Peter loved Him, but also that he lacked the resources to match his words. Satan was seeking to destroy Peter but would not succeed for, unlike that of Judas, his heart was clean. Even in the midst of his despair, having denied his Lord, Peter could take comfort from the fact that Jesus had known in advance about his failure and that He had also promised Peter that he would recover. Moreover, Jesus had specifically prayed that Peter's faith would not be irreversibly damaged and that, after he had recovered, he would be able to help others who were weak.[5]

Here again we encounter the mystery of the sovereignty of God. Peter was responsible for his own sinful actions, but God in His power and love could create an asset out of Peter's negative experience. The same possibility still exists for us. When we repent, the great Redeemer can make use of everything in our history, both good and bad, for His glory, for our good, and for the benefit of others. As in the miracle of the feeding of the five thousand, nothing is wasted.[6]

> **14:1-3** *'Don't let your heart be troubled. Believe in God. Believe also in me. In my Father's house are many homes. If it weren't so, I would have told you. I am going to prepare a place for you. If I go and prepare a place for you, I will come again, and will receive you to myself; that where I am, you may be there also.'*

The insertion of a chapter break at this point is unhelpful, as it interrupts the thought flow of the passage. The Passover meal was still in process and Jesus was continuing to communicate with His

---

[4] John 10:39-40; 11:53-54.

[5] Luke 22:31-34.

[6] John 6:12.

disciples, who must have felt alarmed and insecure as a result of what they had just heard. One of their number was a traitor, Jesus was talking about leaving and going away, and He had also predicted that Peter would soon deny Him. Their emotional state, together with Jesus' enigmatic statements, made it impossible for them to understand, and they were overcome by a paralysing fear of the unknown. Jesus encouraged them to trust Him for the immediate and unknown future, for they were not currently able to process further information about it. They simply needed to know that Jesus was one with the Father, for everything else depended on that.

The next few days would be confusing and chaotic, and they would not know which way to turn as they sought answers to their dilemma. However, there was a great distinction between them and the Jewish leaders, whose searching would lead to death rather than life.[7] Yes, Jesus was going away and leaving them, but, in the case of the disciples, this would be temporary and with a view to a relationship that would never end. He was describing a chain of events rather than a single incident, and this probably added to their bewilderment; naturally, their focus was on the present situation. In relation to that He had repeatedly assured them that He would return to them in the triumph of His resurrection body, at which time their sorrow would be turned into joy. But beyond that, His death, resurrection and ascension would secure a place for them where they would share life with Him forever. He would ascend to His Father's house, to heaven itself, from which there will eventually be an even greater and more glorious return.

In this passage, Jesus used an analogy with a Jewish wedding, where the bridegroom would prepare a place for his betrothed, often in proximity to his father's house, and in due course the bride would be escorted there in joyful procession to enter fully into the marriage relationship. The prepared place is important, but even more so is the person who will receive us to Himself.[8]

14:4-6 *'You know where I go, and you know the way.'*

---

[7] John 7:33-36; 8:21-24.
[8] John 16:16-22; Matt. 25:1-13; Rev. 21:1-4.

Thomas said to him, 'Lord, we don't know where you are going. How can we know the way?'

Jesus said to him, 'I am the way, the truth, and the life. No one comes to the Father, except through me.'

The disciples' reaction to Jesus' provocative statement, 'You know where I go, and you know the way', revealed that they were still not on the same wavelength as Jesus. He had spoken a short time before about going without them and now He was talking about taking them with Him, so it was very difficult to grasp His meaning. On a previous occasion, Jesus had called His disciples to go with Him into the danger zone near Jerusalem, in order to restore life to a dead man, Lazarus. Thomas had been resigned to the possibility that they would all be killed but, out of loyalty, he was prepared to accompany Jesus on what seemed to be a futile and risky enterprise.[9] In that instance, at least they knew the route and the destination to Bethany, but in the present case, Jesus' words were hard to interpret on either score. Once again Thomas vocalised what everyone was probably thinking, 'Lord, we don't know where you are going. How can we know the way?' As was usual, Jesus did not answer with facts or data, but in terms of His identity and their relationship with Him. They did not need a description of the Father's house nor details of how to journey there.

Sometimes we want to know more than has been revealed and end up in a mire of speculation. It is enough to know that Jesus Himself is the way, having opened the new and living way into the presence of the Father. Jesus is the truth as the ultimate revelation of the Father and of His purpose for how His human creatures should live. Jesus is the source and channel of life that will never end. That life is only available in relationship with Him.

Each part of this threefold statement should be read with the initial 'I AM', which evokes the personal and sacred name for God, and this connects with the assertion that follows: 'No one comes to the Father, except through me.' This is extremely important in our modern society, where truth is frequently considered to be

---

[9] John 11:16.

subjective and a matter of tradition or opinion. Jesus was making an exclusive truth claim of the sort that causes offence to many people in our politically correct society. This truth about Jesus is absolute and is not negotiable. If necessary, we must be prepared to 'go out to him outside of the camp, bearing his reproach'.[10]

> **14:7-11** *'If you had known me, you would have known my Father also. From now on, you know him, and have seen him.'*
>
> *Philip said to him, 'Lord, show us the Father, and that will be enough for us.'*
>
> *Jesus said to him, 'Have I been with you such a long time, and do you not know me, Philip? He who has seen me has seen the Father. How do you say, "Show us the Father?" Don't you believe that I am in the Father, and the Father in me? The words that I tell you, I speak not from myself; but the Father who lives in me does his works. Believe me that I am in the Father, and the Father in me; or else believe me for the very works' sake.'*

The disciples had spent about three years in the company of Jesus, had listened to His words and had seen Him act in all kinds of circumstances and perform many amazing miracles. In spite of all this, they did not yet know Him in a way that fully identified Him as the God of Israel. Perhaps their understanding of the nature of God had been shaped, and also distorted, by the interpretations of Scripture to which they had been exposed, and to which Jesus did not completely conform. They needed to understand the God of Israel by interpreting the Scriptures through the life and teaching of Jesus that they had experienced during the previous two or three years. They had not fully grasped the full truth, but events that were about to take place would totally convince them that Jesus and the Father are indeed one.

Each of us comes to the Bible with a cluster of preconceptions, derived from exposure to the opinions of other people and also the filters through which Scripture has been understood by our particular church traditions (both ancient and modern). This is inevitable, and not necessarily bad except that it often goes

---

[10] Heb. 13:13.

265

unrecognised, and thus hinders us from receiving truth that does not conform to the received wisdom. This can lead to a very selective reading of the Bible, and cause us either to ignore inconvenient parts that do not synch with our perceptions, or to try to shoehorn 'awkward passages' to make them fit. It can also lead us to deny the authenticity of experiences that are truly from God because they do not sit comfortably within our framework of orthodoxy. We need to allow the Scriptures to speak to us on their own terms, under the guidance of the Holy Spirit, even if it means that we have to revise our principles of interpretation.

Philip, still mystified, probably spoke for all his colleagues. He wanted Jesus to give some external revelation of the Father, something separate from Jesus Himself. Philip had begun to follow Jesus with the revelation that He was the One promised by Moses and the prophets. Despite all that had happened since that time, he had still not fully grasped that Jesus is one with the Father.[11] To see Jesus is to see the Father, to hear Him is to hear the Father, and His works are the works of the Father.

There was no possible additional way to reveal Him, so Philip's proposition, 'Lord, show us the Father, and that will be enough for us', was simply absurd. Jesus, God incarnate, empathised with Philip's current inability to understand, and offered him a temporary alternative: 'believe me for the very works' sake'. Philip and the others could rely on external evidence until they had the light of inner revelation that transcends, but does not contradict, that evidence. Sometimes we must cling to the truth that we know, in the absence of deep inner assurance, while earnestly praying for the Holy Spirit to be poured out in our hearts to confirm the word that we already believe.[12]

The disciples could not completely and continuously hold on to the reality of Jesus' identity as the eternal Son of God and as being one with the Father. They had encountered the Holy Spirit, who had been present with them in the person of Jesus Himself, but the Spirit had not yet made His home within them. They knew about these relationships chiefly through the works that Jesus had

---

[11] John 1:43-46; 5:39-47.
[12] John 6:5-9; 12:20-33; 20:24-28; Rom. 5:1-5; Eph. 3:14-19.

done in the Father's name and by the power of the Holy Spirit. Jesus now gave them a preview of the amazing transformation that would soon happen when the Spirit came to them in an intimate and personal way.

38

John 14:12-31
The Promise of the Spirit

> **14:12-14** *'Most certainly I tell you, he who believes in me, the works that I do, he will do also; and he will do greater works than these, because I am going to my Father. Whatever you will ask in my name, I will do it, that the Father may be glorified in the Son. If you will ask anything in my name, I will do it.'*

Jesus said, 'He who believes in me, the works that I do, he will do also.' This emphatic statement that they would do even greater works than Jesus must have astonished the disciples and even seemed beyond the boundaries of possibility. If the works are of the same kind, what then is the meaning of 'greater works', since Jesus raised the dead and caused changes in the physical creation?[1] The greater works must be qualitatively similar to those that Jesus did during His life on earth, but they could be greater in other ways. As a man, Jesus accepted the limitations of a body that existed at one point in space and time. Only in exceptional circumstances did He heal at a distance and His ministry was almost entirely to the people of Israel.

Jesus' words present such a challenge to us that we may be tempted to avoid their literal meaning and to confine their application to a distant period in history, or perhaps to remote regions of the world. Some Christians even suggest that for the followers of Jesus to do such things would be to undermine His uniqueness as the Son of God. This is surely a misunderstanding, for the works remain His works. Obviously this can be distorted and obscured by those who attract attention to themselves or who

---

[1] Mark 1:29-34; 4:35-41; 6:54-56; Luke 7:11-22.

make false claims about the success of their activities, but the counterfeit should not deter us from seeking the genuine article. Nor should we, without justification, change the meaning of Jesus' words. Clearly, His own works were supernatural miracles of various sorts, so we are not at liberty to interpret the greater works as being something else.

The records of the early church reveal many similar miracles to those of Jesus, and I am not aware of any indication in Scripture that such things were meant to cease at any subsequent stage. The Body of Christ is present throughout the earth, and there is extensive and credible contemporary evidence that very many such miracles are still happening.[2]

The relative infrequency of such miracles in western countries is linked to a redefinition of these greater works in purely spiritual terms and limiting their physical dimension to a bygone age. Secular humanism is the prevailing worldview in western culture, and it also pervades the mindset of very many Christians. In fact, it is like an atmosphere that we find almost impossible to escape. Jesus encountered similar unbelief in His own country (probably His home town of Nazareth), such that He could do no 'mighty works' there.[3] Perhaps this is where the problem lies; many people believe in a God who intervened in the past and will intervene again at the end of the age but do not, in any practical and meaningful way, believe in a God who will act in power now in response to our faith.

Of course, the fulfilment of Jesus' promise would indeed be impossible if it depended on the disciples' (and our) own wisdom and resources. It is easier to reinterpret Scripture in line with cultural norms. Perhaps we need to admit that the real issue is our failure to cross what often seems to be a very wide chasm between intellectual belief and practical faith. Indeed, we cannot cross it by human effort or by endeavouring to summon up faith, for supernatural power is a gift to be received from the Spirit.[4] The only way to make this journey is to be carried on the wind of the

---

[2] Luke 7:1-10; John 4:46-53; Matt. 15:21-29; Luke 8:26-39; Acts 5:12-16; 8:4-13.
[3] Mark 6:1-6.
[4] Acts 1:7-8; 4:29-31; 1 Cor. 12:8-11; 1 Thess. 1:5; Heb. 2:1-4.

Spirit, like a parascender who floats on warm rising air, having launched from the cliff edge at the prompting of the instructor. This emphasises the need for continuous and intimate relationship with the Spirit, and to cultivate our ability to hear His voice within us. Of course, we only know in part but, if we are willing to take the risk of being wrong at times, we will learn by experience what His voice sounds like within each of us.

Jesus instructed His disciples to ask in His name. This does not, of course, mean simply appending 'in the name of Jesus' to our prayers. It implies that we ask with His authority, which can only happen if we are living in close relationship with Him and are listening to the voice of the Holy Spirit, as He Himself did. His statement, 'apart from me you can do nothing',[5] is actually good news, for it means that there are no alternative strategies or techniques that we need to discover.

> **14:15-18** *'If you love me, keep my commandments. I will pray to the Father, and he will give you another Counsellor, that he may be with you forever: the Spirit of truth, whom the world can't receive; for it doesn't see him and doesn't know him. You know him, for he lives with you, and will be in you. I will not leave you orphans. I will come to you.'*

The Holy Spirit comes as a gift from the Father in response to the prayers of His Son. The precondition is that we should love Jesus and demonstrate this in practical obedience to Him as Lord. It is not uncommon to hear Christians being encouraged to 'fall in love with Jesus'. This idea has its roots in secular romantic expression rather than being derived from the Bible. Love for Jesus does indeed involve our emotions, but it does not operate primarily in that area. Love for Jesus is an attitude of loyalty towards Him and a passionate desire to walk the path of life with Him in trust and obedience, however we may feel at any particular moment. Where this basic attitude is present there is fertile ground for the Spirit to do His work of transformation. Otherwise His coming to us would be pointless.

---

[5] John 15:5.

There is no direct English equivalent for the Greek word *parakletos*, leading to a problem with translation. It is formed from two Greek words meaning 'call' and 'alongside'. It is often translated as 'counsellor', as in this version, or 'helper', but it also includes ideas of advocate, teacher, witness, friend and encourager. When Jesus was present with His disciples, they experienced Him acting in all of these roles. The Holy Spirit is the Spirit of truth, so we must open our lives to Him in transparency and allow Him to transform our thinking and actions. The world had rejected the One who was truth in human flesh, and now they would be unable to receive the Spirit of truth who is invisible and intangible to them.

The Spirit had been with the disciples on a temporary basis, in the person of Jesus. Soon the Spirit would come within them and would remain permanently with them. He would not seem to be a strange or unfamiliar person, for He would be exactly like Jesus and would come in accordance with His promise, 'I will come to you.' Of course, this is a mystery, for Jesus and the Spirit are also distinguished from one another. We should treat this as a paradox that prompts awe, rather than as a puzzle that requires to be solved.

> ***14:19-24*** *Yet a little while, and the world will see me no more; but you will see me. Because I live, you will live also. In that day you will know that I am in my Father, and you in me, and I in you. One who has my commandments and keeps them, that person is one who loves me. One who loves me will be loved by my Father, and I will love him, and will reveal myself to him.'*
>
> *Judas (not Iscariot) said to him, 'Lord, what has happened that you are about to reveal yourself to us, and not to the world?'*
>
> *Jesus answered him, 'If a man loves me, he will keep my word. My Father will love him, and we will come to him, and make our home with him. He who doesn't love me doesn't keep my words. The word which you hear isn't mine, but the Father's who sent me.'*

The world would see Jesus for the last time when He would be put on trial and crucified, and this would promote a sense of relief and satisfaction; however, this would be short-lived. In contrast, Jesus' followers would see Him again after the resurrection, and this would restore and energise them for the next stage of their journey in relationship with Him.

Jesus was looking beyond this glad reunion to the much greater quality of life that they would soon enjoy. They would experience a relationship with Him that would parallel His own unique relationship with the Father. Instead of the visible and physical relationship that they had known during the past few years, they would enjoy an inner revelation of His loving presence. This would be a great privilege and therefore would require a suitable response from them. They could not claim to love Jesus or expect a revelation of His love if, at the same time, they were distancing themselves from Him in disobedience or neglect. While they walked with Him in obedience, in the same way that He had walked with the Father, they would receive continuing personal assurance that both Jesus and His Father loved them.

Judas, perhaps still thinking in visible and physical terms, and wondering how such a revelation could be given to them while excluding the world, asked an important practical question: 'In what way can this happen?'

In His reply, Jesus essentially restated what He had just said and also created a new understanding, by means of a change in pronoun: 'We will come to him, and make our home with him.' The Father, the Son and the Holy Spirit would all be mysteriously present when the Spirit of truth came to the disciples, and this is still the case for us. In the light of this astonishing revelation and privilege, Jesus again emphasised that a profession of love needed to be backed up by a life of obedience, all the more so because the words that He spoke were the very words of the Father Himself.

Jesus related to His Father in perfect trust and obedience and He lived in constant awareness of the Father's love for Him. The Spirit seeks to draw us closer to Jesus and to the Father, for all three persons share the same ambitions for us. We cannot affect the extent of God's love for us but, by our attitude and behaviour, we can determine the extent to which we experience and enjoy the intimacy of the love the indwelling Holy Spirit desires to communicate to us. If we do not really desire to obey God, then we have never truly experienced His grace and we do not truly love Him, regardless of what we say or sing.

> **14:25-28** *'I have said these things to you while still living with you. But the Counsellor, the Holy Spirit, whom the Father will send in my name, will teach you all things, and will remind you of all that I said to you. Peace I leave with you. My peace I give to you; not as the world gives, I give to you. Don't let your heart be troubled, neither let it be fearful. You heard how I told you, "I go away, and I come to you." If you loved me, you would have rejoiced, because I said "I am going to my Father;" for the Father is greater than I.'*

Jesus described the teaching that He had given to the disciples while physically present with them as 'these things'. Their understanding was clouded by preconceptions about what He as Messiah should do, and they were thus unable to make sense of even this limited amount of information. Currently they were extremely anxious and were in no condition to cope with additional data. Jesus now explained that they would benefit from His departure, because the Father would then send the Holy Spirit to act on His behalf and He would teach them 'all things'. The Father, Son and Spirit would continue to act towards them in unity and with a common purpose.

There are two implied reasons why the Spirit would be able to give more comprehensive teaching and how they would be able to receive it. Firstly, the teaching that Jesus had given them about His death and resurrection, which they could not currently comprehend, would have become a historical reality in place of prediction. Secondly, the Holy Spirit would conduct His teaching within their minds and hearts and as revelation rather than mere information. The Spirit would continue to teach them in a way that would fully correspond to the teaching that Jesus had already given them, and He would do so with Jesus' authority. The Spirit would also remind them of what Jesus had previously said to them and would reveal the full significance of that teaching. This helps to explain how the apostolic writers were able to recall and record the material that is contained in the Gospels.

Jesus was well aware of the apprehension that the disciples felt in the context of their troubled circumstances and His repeated statements that He was about to leave them. As had been the case with Mary near the tomb of Lazarus, their emotional state was not conducive to processing more information, so Jesus again spoke words of assurance and peace. The world often defines 'peace' as tranquillity or as the absence of adverse circumstances. When Jesus spoke of peace, He would have been thinking in terms of the Hebrew word *shalom*, emphasising relationship rather than freedom from trouble.[6] When Jesus offered them His *shalom*, the disciples were living in a state of uncertainty that fuelled fear and anxiety. Jesus was instructing them to receive *shalom* by trusting in His word, just as pressures from circumstances were about to increase.

Jesus now repeated and reinforced what He had recently told them. This is an important aspect of His teaching method, but now it was doubly important, for anxiety creates a barrier to receiving what is being taught. He reminded them that He was going to the Father and that He would return to them. Probably the main point of reference is the cross and the resurrection. He would subsequently leave in His ascension and would return, first through the coming of the Holy Spirit and then at the conclusion of the age.[7]

All of these events would depend on the Father. This being so, the disciples should rejoice that Jesus was about to be restored to His place at the Father's right hand, from which they would receive blessing.

> **14:29-31** *'Now I have told you before it happens so that when it happens, you may believe. I will no more speak much with you, for the prince of the world comes, and he has nothing in me. But that the world may know that I love the Father, and as the Father commanded me, even so I do. Arise, let's go from here.'*

Before the climactic events of the cross and the resurrection took place, the disciples already believed in Jesus. They would believe in a more powerful sense when they saw many prophetic scriptures come true before their very eyes, as when the scattered pieces of a complex jigsaw puzzle are assembled to reveal a beautiful picture.

---

[6] Num. 6:22-27; Ps. 4:8; 85:10; Isa. 26:3; 32:17.
[7] Acts 2:32-33; 1:11.

Their faith would be further enhanced when the Holy Spirit would come upon them, thus fulfilling other scriptures and also fulfilling the promises that Jesus had given them. We too can and should grow in faith through believing God's promises to be true, acting upon them and discovering in practice that He is faithful to His word.

Jesus had previously announced that when He would be lifted up (on the cross) then the ruler of this world would be cast out. Satan mistakenly thought that he was on the verge of a great victory, presumably believing that the cross would put an end to the threat posed by Jesus' words and actions. Thus he had put it into the heart of Judas Iscariot to betray Jesus to the religious leaders who aspired to remove Jesus from the scene.[8] The dark prince had no access routes into Jesus Himself for, unlike Judas, He was entirely devoted to the Father and was fully committed to doing His will.

This is the only place in John's Gospel where Jesus explicitly said, 'I love the Father'.[9] He did so now in the context of His determination to confront the evil one with the weapons of love and obedience. Jesus' love for the Father had impelled Him to keep the Father's commandments throughout His life, and now He would not turn back from the ultimate challenge to obey. The world had rejected the evidence of the miracle-signs. If this final act did not persuade the world of His true identity, and that He had come out of love for and in obedience to the Father, then nothing would ever suffice.

---

[8] John 12:31-33; 13:2; 11:49-53.
[9] Leon Morris; *The Gospel according to John*, p. 586.

39

John 15:1-11
The True Vine

> **15:1-5** *'I am the true vine, and my Father is the farmer. Every branch in me that doesn't bear fruit, he takes away. Every branch that bears fruit, he prunes, that it may bear more fruit. You are already pruned clean because of the word which I have spoken to you. Remain in me, and I in you. As the branch can't bear fruit by itself unless it remains in the vine, so neither can you, unless you remain in me. I am the vine. You are the branches. He who remains in me and I in him bears much fruit, for apart from me you can do nothing.'*

The writers of the other Gospels recorded stories and parables that Jesus told in order to illustrate important truths. John did not repeat any of these but instead he recorded visible miracle-signs which then became the basis of much of His teaching. He also painted two word-pictures, of the Good Shepherd and now of the true vine. The latter picture was designed to illustrate Jesus' recent teaching.

The vine and the vineyard were metaphors in Scripture for the nation of Israel.[1] The vine/vineyard belonged to the Lord and He had tended it with great care, guarding, nourishing and pruning the vine. In return He expected to receive fruit – love, worship, loyalty and obedience, but the vine had proved unresponsive and barren. Unfaithful Israel had become a false vine and the nation had thus failed to experience the prosperity and joy of which grapes and wine were symbols.

---

[1] Isa. 6:11-13; 11:1-2; 53:2, 10.

The nation had suffered at the hands of self-serving leaders.[2] Matthew recorded a parable about a vineyard that had been leased to farmers. They exploited it for their own profit and mistreated the servants whom the owner sent to fetch the fruit, and they eventually murdered the owner's son. The Jewish leaders understood that Jesus was referring to them and they would soon do just as He had predicted.[3]

Nevertheless, God's faithfulness continued and He kept His promise to send the Messiah Jesus, who always gave precedence to the Father, here described as the farmer. Jesus was the shoot that was to come out of the stock of Jesse, the branch from his roots that would bear fruit.[4] Jesus thus became the true vine, the embodiment of all that Israel should have been but had failed to be. God was bringing restoration by the action of the man at His right hand (the Messiah).[5]

The life of the true vine had now begun to flow into new branches: the disciples who followed Jesus in committed faith. Branches of a vine are by nature unruly and exuberant with a propensity to grow leaves in abundance, thus diverting the strength of the vine away from fruit-bearing. The vinedresser, being familiar with this tendency, wields His pruning knife to cut back, but not cut off, the living branches. The Father, acting in this role, undertakes this task with infinite wisdom, love and patience. The pruning process may be painful at the time but our loving Father knows what is best for us and has ambitions for us that transcend those that we have for ourselves.[6] The priority is not happiness, but the holiness without which we cannot see the Lord or be in close fellowship with Him.[7]

The heavenly vinedresser uses many and various circumstances to prune the branches and cut away those parts that would detract from the goal of bearing good fruit. To the inexperienced eye, the process of pruning a vine branch might seem destructive and

---

[2] Ps. 80:8-13; Isa. 5:1-7; Jer. 12:7-13.

[3] Matt. 21:33-46.

[4] Isa. 11:1.

[5] Isa. 27:2; Ps. 80:14-18.

[6] Rom. 5:1-5; Heb. 12:5-14; Matt. 6:25-34.

[7] Heb. 12:14; Jas. 4:8; 1 John 1:5-7.

wasteful, but the vinedresser carries out His task with an eye to increased fruitfulness. The story of Peter within John's Gospel is a vivid example of this process. He was opinionated and self-confident; his failure would result in pain, but the ultimate outcome would be for his benefit.

We may be kept waiting for some good thing that we desire, so that we may come to value the Giver more than the gift and learn to seek His Kingdom first. Sometimes submitting to the counsel and correction of wiser and trusted friends, parents or leaders is part of the process of pruning.

Pruning is designed to remove negative factors that reduce the potential for fruitfulness. Pruning by itself will not improve fruit production; the essential requirement is that the branch remains intimately connected with the vine. The branches of a vine draw the sap, the water that sustains their life and the nutrients that support their fruitfulness from that organic union. As disciples we must constantly remain/live/abide in intimate relationship with Jesus, for otherwise there will be no fruit.

The Father sent His Son into the world to reveal afresh how His human creatures should live and also to redeem them and bring many children to glory. The fruit that He desires is a whole new company of men and women who are being progressively transformed into the image of His Son and who, like Jesus, will live with Him in a loving relationship of perfect trust and obedience.[8]

In pursuit of this goal, the Father sent the Spirit to implant the life of Jesus within us. The Spirit imparts both the desire and the determination to live that kind of life from day to day.[9] The expression 'the fruit of the Spirit' is another way of describing likeness to Jesus. The extent to which we produce this fruit depends on how closely and how continuously we live in the consciousness of His immediate presence and in obedience to His words.

> **15:6-8** *If a man doesn't remain in me, he is thrown out as a branch and is withered; and they gather them, throw them into the fire, and*

---

[8] Gen. 1:26-28; 2:7; Heb. 2:5-18; Col. 1:13-23; 2 Cor. 3:17–4:7; Rom. 8:29.
[9] Gal. 5:22-25.

they are burnt. If you remain in me, and my words remain in you, you will ask whatever you desire, and it will be done for you. In this my Father is glorified, that you bear much fruit; and so you will be my disciples.'

Jesus now dealt with the troublesome issue of branches that initially appeared to be growing organically from the vine but were later found to be dead, their true nature having been revealed with the passage of time. It is important to note that these branches did not bear any fruit at all. We should be careful not to extract more from an illustration than may have been intended, but it does seem that these totally unfruitful branches had never been true believers, in spite of initial and hopeful appearances. Being cast into the fire is a symbolic way of speaking of their ultimate fate. There will also be a judgement of fire for believers, not to do with salvation but with the quality of their service as disciples.[10]

Perhaps the case of Judas was in Jesus' mind, and the disciples would soon discover what Judas had done. The words translated 'prune' and 'clean' are very closely related in Greek; 'clean' was used of the disciples when Jesus washed their feet, but He explicitly excluded Judas from this category. To all appearances, Judas was identical to the others, but Jesus knew that this was not the case. Judas did not remain with Jesus but went out into darkness, never to return.[11]

Jesus explained that the relationship is two-way: 'Remain in me, and I in you ... He who remains in me and I in him bears much fruit.' He explained how this dynamic works in practice: 'If you remain in me, and my words remain in you...' The disciples had been made clean by receiving and responding to His word, and now they must simply continue on the same path. The Holy Spirit would remind them of Jesus' words, would interpret their implications and would empower His followers to live accordingly. Two important things would result from this: they would be living as disciples who intentionally follow in the footsteps of their Lord

---

[10] John 13:10-11; 1 John 2:19; Ezek. 15; Matt. 3:10; 1 Cor. 3:8-15.
[11] John 13:30.

and Master, and they would share in His ambition to bring glory to His Father.

> **15:9-11** *'Even as the Father has loved me, I also have loved you. Remain in my love. If you keep my commandments, you will remain in my love; even as I have kept my Father's commandments, and remain in his love. I have spoken these things to you, that my joy may remain in you, and that your joy may be made full.'*

Some of the things that Jesus had just said may have sounded difficult and daunting to the disciples' ears. Depending on temperament, some may have been thinking in terms of a programme of spiritual disciplines to give substance to the teaching. Others may have begun to adopt a more mystical approach, seeking to visualise the presence of Jesus within their hearts. Jesus' next words bypassed both of these, uniting love and commandments in an atmosphere of joy.

There is an unbroken chain of love, from Father to Son and from Jesus to His disciples. The love is freely given but can only be fully received and experienced by keeping the commandments of the love-giver. God's love is not a response to our love, but the full measure of His love can only be experienced in the context of a close relationship with Him. We believe that God is all wise and all loving, and therefore His commands are perfect even when we do not fully understand them. It therefore follows that obedience to His commands will lead to the best possible outcome for us and will bring us maximum fulfilment and joy. His commands are, therefore, not a duty to be performed. Obedience demonstrates that we understand the nature of His love for us, and this response also reveals our love for Him.

40

John 15:12-25
Servants, Friends and Martyrs

> ***15:12-17*** *'This is my commandment, that you love one another, even as I have loved you. Greater love has no one than this, that someone lay down his life for his friends. You are my friends, if you do whatever I command you. No longer do I call you servants, for the servant doesn't know what his lord does. But I have called you friends, for everything that I heard from my Father, I have made known to you. You didn't choose me, but I chose you and appointed you, that you should go and bear fruit, and that your fruit should remain; that whatever you will ask of the Father in my name, he may give it to you. I command these things to you, that you may love one another.'*

If any of the disciples had an unduly mystical or semi-romantic picture of the nature of love and how they should respond to Jesus' love for them, His next statement, repeated a little later for emphasis, would come as a corrective shock: 'This is my commandment, that you love one another, even as I have loved you.' These men had recently argued about their status and position; now Jesus commanded them to love one another to the extent of giving up their own lives. Jesus was a great teacher and leader, for He taught and led by example. On the occasion of His arrest He would protect them and give them the opportunity to escape.[1]

Sometimes people speak casually of being friends of Jesus, but this is actually a high honour bestowed on those who are faithful to Him. Jesus had referred to His disciples as friends on only one previous occasion, and that was in the context of their potential

---

[1] John 18:7-9.

martyrdom for His sake.[2] Friendship with Jesus is contingent on our obedience to His word. This may sound like a strange kind of friendship, like one child saying to another, 'Unless you do what I say, I won't be your friend!', but we need to recognise that friendship with Jesus is a unique and unequal relationship, within which He shares with us His thoughts and plans.

God spoke of Abraham as His friend. Before He judged Sodom, God chose to communicate His intentions to Abraham, thus allowing him to intercede for the city, and this may have played a part in saving Lot and his daughters.[3]

Jesus told His disciples that He no longer called them servants, but this statement contained a paradox. Their status as trusted friends depended on their willingness to obey Him, and that is still the case for us. At the Passover meal He had reminded them that He was their teacher and Lord. Now He was about to call them His friends, but He remained their master as well. This also applies to our relationship with the Father: we must never forget that He is God Almighty.

The Father shared His purposes with His obedient Son and He then shared them with His servant-friends. Jesus had chosen them because the Father had given them to Him. This choice was for a purpose, that they would bear the good and lasting fruit that Jesus had just described.[4] As they did so, they would come to understand more of the Father's purposes and, like Abraham, would be enabled to pray for the very things that He desired to accomplish. Such prayers can be offered confidently in the name of Jesus.

Jesus linked all of this with the command to love one another. He did not mention this as a desirable though unattainable objective, but issued a command to be obeyed and embraced with enthusiasm. No doubt this is also a key condition for answered prayer.

> **15:18-20** *'If the world hates you, you know that it has hated me before it hated you. If you were of the world, the world would love its own. But*

---

[2] 1 Sam. 18:1; 20:30-34; Luke 12:1-12.

[3] Gen. 18:16-33; 19:15; 2 Chron. 20:7; Isa. 41:8.

[4] John 13:12-17; 10:27-29; 17:6; 15:1-8.

because you are not of the world, since I chose you out of the world, therefore the world hates you. Remember the word that I said to you: "A servant is not greater than his lord." If they persecuted me, they will also persecute you. If they kept my word, they will also keep yours.'

Jesus now turned to a contrasting attitude, hatred rather than love, and to a different group of people, the world rather than His disciples. This was the outworking of John's statement in his introduction to the Gospel: 'the world didn't recognise him. He came to his own, and those who were his own didn't receive him.'[5] When Jesus said, 'If the world hates you', He was not suggesting that the world might or might not do so. He also said, 'If they persecuted me', which they certainly did, and, 'If they kept my word', which they certainly did not. 'The world' included religious people who had refused the revelation of God in the person of Jesus. We know that all the apostles subsequently suffered persecution and most of them died as martyrs. Jesus wanted them to know in advance that this hatred was not personal to them, but was entirely owing to their connection with Him.

Jesus reminded the disciples of what He had said in the upper room: 'A servant is not greater than his lord.' They had been chosen out of the world, and rejection and persecution from the world were the other side of a single, indivisible coin. Jesus knew that they would soon proclaim the gospel in Jerusalem, and that the same people who had rejected His word would also reject theirs. Nevertheless, others would receive their word, so their efforts and suffering would not be in vain.[6]

For many years, Christians in western countries appeared to be exceptions to this rule. The church had become a pillar of society. Church membership was considered to be a mark of respectability and often contributed to personal success. We are now waking up to the fact that this was a historical anomaly. The world was still the world, but had adapted to the dominant Christian culture. The church compromised in many ways with the values of the world, creating a kind of ceasefire but not a true peace.

---

[5] John 1:10-11.
[6] Acts 4:1-22; 5:14-42.

During the past few decades, with the rise of secularism, all of this has been changing. Churches have been in decline and true Christianity is disparaged as intolerant and is being progressively excluded from the public space. In many countries where other religions predominate, hatred of Christian believers is rampant, and vicious persecution and martyrdom have reached unprecedented levels. This persecution is largely ignored by the world's media and also meets with indifference among many political and religious leaders.

> **15:21-25** *But they will do all these things to you for my name's sake, because they don't know him who sent me. If I had not come and spoken to them, they would not have had sin; but now they have no excuse for their sin. He who hates me, hates my Father also. If I hadn't done amongst them the works which no one else did, they wouldn't have had sin. But now they have seen and also hated both me and my Father. But this happened so that the word may be fulfilled which was written in their law, "They hated me without a cause."*

Jesus' words are extremely shocking when we consider that the religious leaders of Israel were in the vanguard of those who hated and persecuted Him. Priests and Pharisees, not natural allies, had combined in a conspiracy of malice against Him. Jesus declared that they did not know the Father. Their attitude of hatred towards Jesus, whom the Father had sent, revealed that they actually hated the God of Israel whom they claimed to worship. This they would no doubt have self-righteously denied, for they had become utterly blind to the truth. God incarnate had visited them, had spoken to them and had done miraculous signs before their very eyes, but they had rejected Him.

They could not have sinned in this extreme way had they not had the benefit of direct revelation. Paul said that until Jesus appeared to him, he had acted in ignorance; he then discovered, to his surprise and horror, that to persecute believers was actually to persecute the God of Israel, in the person of Jesus. The leaders who had seen and heard Jesus had no such excuse, for the evidence provided for them was beyond dispute.[7] When they encountered Jesus, the Word made flesh, the outshining of the Father's glory, they hated Him and the threat that He posed to their status and authority. In hating Him, they expressed their true attitude to the One whom they claimed to worship and represent.[8]

Jesus reminded His disciples that this hostile attitude was not new. Similar things had happened to the psalmist many centuries ago. These recorded experiences acted as prophecies of the rejection and suffering of the Messiah. Much later, Peter referenced the example of Jesus who suffered on behalf of others. If His followers lived blameless lives and were made to suffer for His sake, then they would have no cause to be ashamed.[9]

---

[7] Acts 9:3-5; 26:9; 1 Tim. 1:13.

[8] John 8:19; 9:39-41.

[9] Ps. 69:4; 1 Pet. 2:20-25; 3:13-18; 4:12-19.

41

John 15:26–16:15
The Spirit of Truth

> *15:26–16:6 'When the Counsellor has come, whom I will send to you from the Father, the Spirit of truth, who proceeds from the Father, he will testify about me. You will also testify, because you have been with me from the beginning. I have said these things to you so that you wouldn't be caused to stumble. They will put you out of the synagogues. Yes, the time comes that whoever kills you will think that he offers service to God. They will do these things because they have not known the Father, nor me. But I have told you these things, so that when the time comes, you may remember that I told you about them. I didn't tell you these things from the beginning, because I was with you. But now I am going to him who sent me, and none of you asks me, "Where are you going?" But because I have told you these things, sorrow has filled your heart.'*

Jesus had just informed the disciples that He would be sending them out into the hostile world that had been persecuting Him and that they also would be hated and persecuted. This was a daunting prospect, for which they must have felt totally inadequate. His previous explanation about the coming of the Holy Spirit had been in the context of their need to know that they would not be abandoned. The Spirit would comfort and reassure them and keep them aware of the ongoing presence of Jesus Himself. Now Jesus informed them that the Spirit would also come in order to equip them to be witnesses in the world.

The word translated 'helper' does not just mean a supporter or comforter, but also one who strengthens and encourages, and this they would also need. The Spirit proceeds from the Father and would be sent to them by the Son, so all three persons of the

Trinity would be fully engaged with them in their mission. The disciples had personal experience of being with Jesus, and as they shared this with others the Holy Spirit would testify to the truth of what they were saying. He would do this by continuing through them the signs and miracles that Jesus had done.[1]

Jesus did not leave the disciples under any illusions about what lay ahead, as that would have been a recipe for disaster. He repeated some of the things that He had told them only a few days before as they sat together on the hillside overlooking the city.[2] When persecutions arose they would need to remember that they were not the real targets. Their tormenters, in their culpable blindness, were filled with hatred against Jesus Himself and therefore against the Father who had sent Him into the world.[3]

Jesus was aware of the sombre mood of the men around Him. They seem to have been overwhelmed and rendered speechless in their sorrow, not knowing what to think or how to respond to what they were hearing. Under those circumstances we might think that some soothing words would have been appropriate. Jesus knew that they would be devastated by the events of the next few days, and that they needed to know that it was all part of a greater plan.[4]

> ***16:7-11*** *'Nevertheless I tell you the truth: It is to your advantage that I go away, for if I don't go away, the Counsellor won't come to you. But if I go, I will send him to you. When he has come, he will convict the world about sin, about righteousness, and about judgement; about sin, because they don't believe in me; about righteousness, because I am going to my Father, and you won't see me any more; about judgement, because the prince of this world has been judged.'*

Jesus was continuously and completely filled with the Spirit because He was constantly obedient to the Father. The Holy Spirit could not come and make His home within the disciples until Jesus had died and had risen again on their behalf. John the Baptist had described two vital aspects of Jesus' ministry, and Andrew and

---

[1] Heb. 2:1-4; Acts 4:23-31; 5:12-16.

[2] Matt. 24:1-14.

[3] Acts 5:40-41; 9:1-7; 22:1-8.

[4] Heb. 11:24-27; Heb. 12:1-3.

John heard what he said. Jesus was the Lamb of God who would take away the sin of the world, including that of the disciples. He was also the One who would baptise them, and others too, in the Holy Spirit.[5] The two parts were intimately connected, the first being with a view to the second and the second being contingent on the first.

It is clear from the Gospel records that the disciples did not understand the need for either of these events. The prospect of Jesus' death was incomprehensible and unthinkable for them, so they argued with Jesus about it and Peter tried to prevent it. They understood Jesus to be the promised Messiah and He was their teacher and master but, despite John the Baptist's announcement, they could not grasp that Jesus was also the One who would die to remove their sins and also the sins of the world.[6] They were also surprised when Jesus rose from the dead. Their understanding of these matters was delayed until the risen Jesus appeared to them and revealed how His death and resurrection fulfilled God's ancient plan for the salvation of the world, including themselves, just as the prophets had said.[7]

Prior to the crucifixion, the disciples were in a similar position to Abraham and David, and also many others who lived before the incarnation of Jesus. These people from Israel's history, including the prophets who prophesied about His coming, did not understand the details of how God would eventually deal with the problem of sin. They were nevertheless justified by faith in the One who would do it in His own way and in His own time.[8] The disciples initially trusted in Jesus as Messiah and Son of God, but only later as Saviour and Redeemer.

So it was necessary that Jesus should leave the disciples, by means of the cross and then by His ascension to glory. Jesus' death would make them fit to be temples of the Holy Spirit and the Spirit would equip them to be effective witnesses in the world.[9] Through them the Holy Spirit would convict and convince those who heard

---

[5] John 1:29-37.

[6] Matt. 16:21-23; Luke 18:31-34.

[7] Luke 24:13-32, 44-49; John 20:8-10.

[8] Gen. 15:1-6; Ps. 32:1-2; Rom. 4:1-8.

[9] John 1:29-37; 1 Cor. 6:19-20; Acts 1:8.

their testimony. He would still be acting in the role of an advocate, in this case for the prosecution, at the same time pointing to the cross as the means of escape from condemnation.

In the first place, the Holy Spirit would convict of sin, particularly the foundational sin of unbelief and the associated attitude of independence. This sin, which is the basis of all other particular sins, is especially revealed in a refusal to believe in Jesus as God's solution to humanity's sin and rebellion.[10]

Secondly, He will convict people with respect to righteousness, for human beings proudly believe that they can establish their own righteousness rather than receiving it from God. Jesus' resurrection and ascension demonstrated that His offering had satisfied the righteousness of God, and that all other attempts are futile.[11]

Thirdly, His death and resurrection signalled God's judgement and defeat of the prince of this world, and His judgement on the world system that Satan raised up in defiance of the Creator.[12]

On one occasion Jesus gave a solemn warning to some Pharisees who had attributed His miracles to the work of Satan rather than to the power of the Holy Spirit. They were reversing good and evil, calling the Holy Spirit the devil and were, in effect, blaspheming against Him. This is an extremely dangerous sin, for it may cause the Holy Spirit to withdraw His presence. There would then be no possibility of repentance and faith, and therefore no way to obtain salvation through the cross. The religious leaders had moved a long way down that path, preferring to attribute Jesus' power to the devil than admit the evidence for His identity as Messiah and bow before Him.[13]

> ***16:12-15*** *'I still have many things to tell you, but you can't bear them now. However when he, the Spirit of truth, has come, he will guide you into all truth, for he will not speak from himself; but whatever he hears, he will speak. He will declare to you things that are coming. He will glorify me, for he will take from what is mine, and will declare it to*

---

[10] Acts 2:36-39.
[11] Rom. 3:21-26; 10:3.
[12] John 12:30-32; Eph. 2:2; Col. 2:13-15.
[13] Matt. 12:24-32.

you. All things that the Father has are mine; therefore I said that he takes of mine and will declare it to you.'

The disciples were not currently in a fit state to receive and process this important information. The Holy Spirit of truth would explain and illuminate what Jesus had said and done and would apply it to changing circumstances. He would reveal Jesus' glory, just as Jesus had revealed the glory of the Father. Father, Son and Holy Spirit are one and they work together for a single purpose: 'For the earth will be filled with the knowledge of the LORD's glory, as the waters cover the sea.'[14]

---

[14] Hab. 2:14.

42

John 16:16-33
The Father Himself Loves You

16:16-22 'A little while, and you will not see me. Again a little while, and you will see me.'

Some of his disciples therefore said to one another, 'What is this that he says to us, "A little while, and you won't see me, and again a little while, and you will see me;" and, "Because I go to the Father"?' They said therefore, 'What is this that he says, "A little while"? We don't know what he is saying.'

Therefore Jesus perceived that they wanted to ask him, and he said to them, 'Do you enquire amongst yourselves concerning this, that I said, "A little while, and you won't see me, and again a little while, and you will see me?" Most certainly I tell you that you will weep and lament, but the world will rejoice. You will be sorrowful, but your sorrow will be turned into joy. A woman, when she gives birth, has sorrow because her time has come. But when she has delivered the child, she doesn't remember the anguish any more, for the joy that a human being is born into the world. Therefore you now have sorrow, but I will see you again, and your heart will rejoice, and no one will take your joy away from you.'

The next words of Jesus to His disciples increased their bewilderment. They appear to have been reticent about asking Jesus what He meant. They talked among themselves, without reaching any conclusions. Even now, with the benefit of hindsight, it is difficult to be sure to what Jesus was referring. He linked His disappearance and reappearance, each to happen in a little while, with His going to the Father. We usually assume that this did not take place until He ascended visibly to heaven.

There are two possible interpretations, and neither is problem free. The first possibility relates to Jesus' last words from the cross: 'Father, into your hands I commit my spirit!'[1] Peter believed and taught that after His death Jesus visited the spirits in prison, so it is possible that in spirit He also ascended to the Father's presence. Paul described something similar in His own experience.[2]

A second possibility arises from Jesus' post-resurrection encounter with Mary of Magdala. Jesus instructed her not to cling to Him, but rather to go and tell His brothers (the disciples) that He was ascending to His Father and their Father, and to His God and their God. This statement is difficult to explain unless He intended to visit with the Father prior to His appearance to the disciples in the upper room. This interpretation is amplified in chapter 50 of this book.

All we know for certain is that Jesus left the disciples that very night and some of them saw Him again within three days. If taken strictly literally, the phrase, 'because I go to the Father', is enigmatic. Jesus may have been expressing His total confidence that the Father would accept His self-offering and that this would ensure His resurrection and return to the disciples. The world, those who rejected Him, rejoiced at His cruel death on the cross while the disciples were overwhelmed with grief. The disciples rejoiced when He returned to them in resurrection life and the world was discomfited (although this is not mentioned here). Their joy would not be ephemeral, for it would be rooted in an eternal relationship with One who could never again be taken from them, now being beyond the reach of the world.

Jesus likened the coming sequence of events to the process of labour that issues in the birth of a healthy child. This process is associated with pain and distress, which is sometimes very severe. Soon the emotional content of this memory fades as the mother receives her child and relates to him or her. The pain was worthwhile even though it might not have seemed so at the time. The analogy of birth-pain recalls God's response to the disobedience of the first man and woman, but coupled with His

---

[1] Luke 23:46.
[2] 1 Pet. 3:18-20a; 2 Cor. 12:2-4.

promise that another man, born of a woman, would bring to an end the reign of sin and death.[3]

> **16:23-28** *'In that day you will ask me no questions. Most certainly I tell you, whatever you may ask of the Father in my name, he will give it to you. Until now, you have asked nothing in my name. Ask, and you will receive, that your joy may be made full. I have spoken these things to you in figures of speech. But the time is coming when I will no more speak to you in figures of speech, but will tell you plainly about the Father. In that day you will ask in my name; and I don't say to you that I will pray to the Father for you, for the Father himself loves you, because you have loved me, and have believed that I came from God. I came from the Father, and have come into the world. Again, I leave the world, and go to the Father.'*

'In that day' only makes sense here if it refers to the time after He would ascend bodily to heaven, His final going to the Father. Jesus had taught the disciples a prayer beginning with the words 'Our Father', but during the three years that they spent with Him they had had little need to ask the Father for specific things: Jesus was with them in person to hear their requests. This phase would soon come to an end, so He emphatically assured them that His departure would be for their good. They would be able to approach the Father in a more direct way, and with confidence, using the authority of the name of Jesus. He did not explain exactly how this departure would happen, but they would subsequently understand that He was making a way into the Father's presence through His sacrificial death for them on the cross.[4]

There is a beautiful prophetic picture of this when Joseph brought his two sons, Ephraim and Manasseh, to receive blessings from his father Jacob. Joseph's life story has many parallels with that of Jesus, and Jacob the Patriarch represents the Father. When Jacob laid his hands on the lads, he also claimed them as being his own sons and gave each a unique blessing that reflected the will of

---

[3] Gen. 3:14-16; Isa. 9:6-7; Rom. 5:12-21; Gal. 4:4.
[4] 1 Pet. 3:18.

God. Similarly, Jesus desires to bring us to the Father to receive His welcome and to experience His benediction on each of us.[5]

When Jesus said, 'I don't say to you that I will pray to the Father for you', it must initially have sounded disappointing. However the reason He added was glorious: 'for the Father himself loves you.' Jesus had made a similar statement to the Samaritan woman, when explaining that the Father was seeking those who would appropriately worship Him.[6] Jesus was establishing a pattern for prayer that applies to us as much as it did to those first disciples. In prayer we approach the Father through the Son, with the help and guidance of the Holy Spirit. Of course, this does not preclude speaking directly to Jesus, but that is not the norm.

Sometimes people are reluctant to approach God, out of a sense of fear and unworthiness, and feel more comfortable asking Jesus to approach the Father for them – rather like asking a friend to approach an important person on our behalf. This is based on a false premise, for the Father's attitude towards us is exactly the same as that of Jesus. Jesus does not receive our individual prayers and then pass them up to the Father. We ask in Jesus' name, on the basis of our relationship with Him, and His presence as the glorified Son of Man bears constant witness to our open access to the throne.[7]

Jesus completed the statement with words that seem strange, and out of step with many other scriptures: 'For the Father himself loves you, because you have loved me, and have believed that I came from God.' This appears to place the initiative with us, but we know that this is not the case.[8] Surely Jesus must have meant that their committed relationship with Him and their trust in Him as God's agent of salvation had removed all obstacles and opened a door to experience the Father's love in an intimate and experiential way. In other words, our love for Jesus is not the primary cause of the Father's love for us, but it is necessary if we are to enjoy the intimacy of that love.

---

[5] Gen. 48:1-22.

[6] John 4:23.

[7] Eph. 2:18; Heb. 4:14-16; 10:19-22.

[8] John 3:16; 15:16; 17:22-23; 1 John 4:19.

Of course, prayer in the name of Jesus does not merely involve appending His name, as a kind of rubber stamp. All that He had previously said about remaining in Him comes into play. Our task is not to persuade God to do what we choose, but to be in such a relationship with Him that we pray for things that will cause His will to be done on earth as in heaven. The disciples were not yet in a position to understand everything clearly, so Jesus used figurative language. After the cross and the resurrection it would be much easier for them to grasp truths that were currently opaque to them. After those events, they would have a much better understanding of the Father's plan and purpose.

> *16:29-33 His disciples said to him, 'Behold, now you are speaking plainly, and using no figures of speech. Now we know that you know all things, and don't need for anyone to question you. By this we believe that you came from God.'*
>
> *Jesus answered them, 'Do you now believe? Behold, the time is coming, yes, and has now come, that you will be scattered, everyone to his own place, and you will leave me alone. Yet I am not alone, because the Father is with me. I have told you these things, that in me you may have peace. In the world you have trouble; but cheer up! I have overcome the world.'*

The disciples had been confused, but now they felt certain that they saw things clearly. Jesus had said He knew that they loved Him and that they believed He had come from God. Here was a clear and straightforward statement that resonated with what they believed about themselves. We have encountered many occasions in John's record when Jesus knew people's internal thoughts and feelings. The disciples saw Jesus' statement as fresh evidence that He had truly come from God.

Jesus appeared to contradict Himself when He then asked them, 'Do you now believe?' On one level the disciples did believe, but this belief would not be sufficiently robust to prevent them from deserting Jesus in His hour of trial and fleeing for fear of their lives. Jesus was warning them against the kind of self-confidence they had recently expressed. Their protestations of loyalty were sincere, but they did not yet have the resources to back them up.

Jesus' prediction of their failure was intended to keep them from despair when it happened, for that failure would not be final. The trouble from the world would be eclipsed by the greater truth that, despite current and troubling circumstances, Jesus had overcome the world.

43

John 17:1-12
Father and Son Are One

> *17:1-5 Jesus said these things, then lifting up his eyes to heaven, he said, 'Father, the time has come. Glorify your Son, that your Son may also glorify you; even as you gave him authority over all flesh, so he will give eternal life to all whom you have given him. This is eternal life, that they should know you, the only true God, and him whom you sent, Jesus Christ. I glorified you on the earth. I have accomplished the work which you have given me to do. Now, Father, glorify me with your own self with the glory which I had with you before the world existed.'*

It seems John wants us to know that Jesus spoke this prayer aloud in the presence of His disciples. He concluded the extended teaching session with final words of comfort, and then turned His eyes away from them and looked up to heaven. His words, now directed to the Father, would have continued to assure them that they would not be abandoned during the coming days of crisis and uncertainty. The Gospels do not include any other long prayers of Jesus. His prayer times were usually in private locations, so this extended prayer was probably a unique experience for the disciples.[1] They would no doubt have been impressed by the deep reverence and the complete intimacy with which He addressed His Father God.

Unity is often regarded as the central focus of this prayer. It is indeed a vital component, but the primary theme is glory. The prayer begins and ends with glory and everything else connects with it. Jesus' hour of destiny had come, and with it unimaginable

---

[1] Mark 1:35; Luke 5:16.

anguish and suffering, but He was looking beyond to the glory that would follow.

Greek pilgrims had recently come requesting to see Jesus, and He had understood this as confirmation that the appointed time had come. A shadow had passed over His soul, but He had dismissed it with the words, 'Father, glorify your name!'[2] Now, in the presence of His disciples, He prayed, 'Father, the time has come. Glorify your Son, that your Son may also may glorify you.' Jesus' overriding purpose on earth was to glorify God in everything He did, describing it as His food.[3] As He now reflected on the journey of His life, He knew that He had fulfilled that ambition in every detail. The last stage of that journey would be the most challenging, like the final ascent of a steep mountain. He had set His face to go to Jerusalem and He would not turn back, whatever the cost. He had a baptism with which to be baptised and He longed to accomplish it. It was the hour for which He had come.[4]

In his first epistle, Peter said that the Spirit of Christ had testified beforehand through the prophets of 'the sufferings of Christ, and the glories that would follow them'. Jesus now prayed that the Father would complete the process by raising Him from the dead. A little later in Gethsemane, Jesus would pray with strong cries and tears to the One who was able to save Him from death.[5] Through the answer to this prayer the Father and the Son would both be glorified and eternal life would be made available to people everywhere ('all flesh').

Jesus defined eternal life in terms of intimate relationship with the Father and the Son. This is an absolute and exclusive definition, for there is only one Creator God and only one Saviour and Redeemer who can give eternal life, as was promised in the Scriptures. This way of restoring the broken relationship would reveal the wisdom, love and power of God, and would thus bring glory to the Father and the Son. This glory would be seen on earth in the lives of His followers and after Jesus' restoration to the

---

[2] John 12:20-28.
[3] John 4:32-34.
[4] Luke 9:51-53; Isa. 50:7; Luke 12:50; John 12:27.
[5] 1 Pet. 1:10-11; Heb. 5:7-9.

eternal glory that He had laid aside in becoming man. This theme is revisited later in the prayer.

> **17:6-8** *'I revealed your name to the people whom you have given me out of the world. They were yours, and you have given them to me. They have kept your word. Now they have known that all things whatever you have given me are from you, for the words which you have given me I have given to them, and they received them, and knew for sure that I came from you. They have believed that you sent me.'*

The disciples must have listened intently at this juncture, for now Jesus was talking to His Father, the Holy One of Israel, about them! The disciples, as creatures, belonged to the Father, and He had given them into the care of His Son. Jesus had called them in response to the Father's specific instructions. They were neither a random group of men nor a self-selected company of volunteers. Jesus implied that the Father was still primarily responsible for them. God is faithful and actually likes to be reminded of His commitments and promises; He is glorified in responding to prayers of this kind.[6]

Jesus described how He had fulfilled the Father's commission by teaching the disciples everything that the Father wanted them to know up to that point in time. They were convinced that Jesus was the true Messiah and they had received His words as the very words of God who had sent Him. They had not only heard the Word and agreed with it in theory, but they had also demonstrated the reality of their faith by leaving their previous pursuits and faithfully following Him as disciples.

> **17:9-12** *'I pray for them. I don't pray for the world, but for those whom you have given me, for they are yours. All things that are mine are yours, and yours are mine, and I am glorified in them. I am no more in the world, but these are in the world, and I am coming to you. Holy Father, keep them through your name which you have given me, that they may be one, even as we are. While I was with them in the world, I kept them in your name. I have kept those whom you have*

---

[6] Luke 6:12-16; Exod. 32:11-14; Deut. 9:25-29.

given me. None of them is lost except the son of destruction, that the
Scripture might be fulfilled.'

Jesus emphasised the distinction between His chosen disciples and others, whom He described as 'the world'. He had recently spoken of 'the world' as those who hated Him and who also hated His followers, so 'the world' would include the hostile Jewish leaders who were currently plotting His death.[7] He had made many offers to them through the signs He had performed and the words He had spoken, but they had stubbornly rejected Him. Now He turned His attention from them to those whom the Father had given Him, and who belonged equally to the Father and the Son in a bond of intimate love.

Jesus now used 'the world' as a place that He and His disciples shared with the world that hated them. He was 'no more in the world', for in His mind He had moved beyond the phase of dealing with these hostile people and into His hour of destiny. At the same time, He was acutely aware of how that world would treat the disciples whom He loved. They were far from perfect, but they had stayed loyal to Jesus in the face of fierce opposition and in the process they had changed in ways that had begun to reflect His glory.[8] Now Jesus, in order to obey the Father and fulfil His purpose, must necessarily leave them. This prospect would have been a matter of great concern for the listening disciples, so Jesus now prayed aloud for them. He reminded the Father that He had faithfully discharged His responsibility to guard these men and that, for a time, He would be unable to do so. During this period the Father should assume direct responsibility to care for them.

At first sight, this way of praying may seem artificial or contrived, but it is often found in Scripture.[9] Jesus was praying as we are encouraged to pray, holding God to His word. This kind of prayer glorifies God by appealing to His faithfulness in keeping His promises, and He delights to answer such prayers. Jesus' approach was determined and definite, but it was also deferential: 'Holy

---

[7] John 15:18-24; Luke 22:1-2.

[8] John 13:1; Matt. 19:27-28; Luke 22:28-29.

[9] Exod. 32:7-14; Isa. 63:7-19.

Father'. We must be careful not to confuse intimacy with informality and inappropriate familiarity.[10]

Jesus' concern for the disciples involved more than their physical survival. They needed to be preserved in faith and love so that they could participate in the unity and love of the Father and the Son for all eternity. They were about to be confronted by an evil power that was much greater than the visible power of their opponents, and one that aimed at their total destruction. Peter was vulnerable because of his self-confidence, so Jesus had specifically prayed that his faith would not fail.[11]

Judas had already succumbed to Satan's blandishments. Perhaps all the disciples were by now aware that Judas was a traitor, and they must have wondered at the fact that he had been chosen as an apostle. They needed to know that the choice of Judas was not a mistake but was in the foreknowledge of God.[12]

---

[10] Gen. 18:17-33.
[11] Luke 22:31-34.
[12] Ps. 41:9; Acts 1:16-20.

44

John 17:13-26
Eternal Glory and Love

> *17:13-19 'But now I come to you, and I say these things in the world, that they may have my joy made full in themselves. I have given them your word. The world hated them, because they are not of the world, even as I am not of the world. I pray not that you would take them from the world, but that you would keep them from the evil one. They are not of the world even as I am not of the world. Sanctify them in your truth. Your word is truth. As you sent me into the world, even so I have sent them into the world. For their sakes I sanctify myself, that they themselves also may be sanctified in truth.'*

Jesus used the expression 'the world' nine times in this short section. Thus, He strongly emphasised the clear-cut distinction between Himself and His followers on the one hand and the hostile and unbelieving world on the other. On three occasions He used the term 'sanctify' or 'sanctified' in relation to Himself and His disciples, indicating that both He and they have been set apart and separated from the world.

At the beginning of the prayer Jesus stated that He had finished the work that the Father had given Him to do, even though the crucial and most demanding part still lay before Him. He had also described Himself as being 'no more in the world'. At the level of His determination and commitment this was as good as done. Now when He said, 'I say these things in the world', He was referring to His continuing physical presence in the world, in company with His beloved disciples. Jesus was coming to the Father on their behalf and His spoken prayer was designed to encourage them in their present and uncertain situation.

Jesus had taught the disciples about the source of total joy: relationship with Him and obedience to His word, which is identical to the Father's word.[1] Twice He explained that they were not of the world, in the same sense that He was not of the world. Their relationship with Him had radically changed their relationship with the unbelieving world of their contemporaries. They had become new people with new identities and altered loyalties. This had two kinds of consequences: inner joy and external opposition.

Jesus was aware that they were about to experience a major onslaught from the evil one and his agents in the world. He knew that the Father could easily lift them out of the physical world into a comfortable and safe environment elsewhere, but that would negate the purpose for which they had been called out of the unbelieving world. They too must go through the stressful times that lay ahead, in order to fulfil the purpose for which the Father had sent Jesus into the world and for which purpose Jesus would soon send them into the world.

Jesus prayed that, in the midst of all this pressure, the Father would guard the disciples from the evil one, protecting them by setting them apart by the truth. They would survive the next few days by remaining convinced of the truth that Jesus had taught, even when the evidence of current experience pointed to a different conclusion. Then Jesus would reappear to them. The antidote to fear and despair, in the context of adverse circumstances, is to cling to unchanging truth. Jesus was about to set Himself apart to do the will of God in radical trust and obedience. The disciples would see the outworking of this, when God in His faithfulness would raise Jesus from the dead. In consequence, they would be inspired to stand for the truth with faith and courage, in the face of implacable opposition from the unbelieving and persecuting world.

> **17:20-23** *Not for these only do I pray, but for those also who will believe in me through their word, that they may all be one; even as you, Father, are in me, and I in you, that they also may be one in us; that*

---

[1] John 15:9-11; 17:8, 13-14.

the world may believe that you sent me. The glory which you have given me, I have given to them; that they may be one, even as we are one; I in them, and you in me, that they may be perfected into one; that the world may know that you sent me and loved them, even as you loved me.'

For a period of forty days following His resurrection, Jesus would visit His followers and teach them more about the Kingdom of God. He would thus complete His own personal mission in the world and would ascend to the Father. Jesus knew that, after they were baptised in the Spirit, the disciples would become effective witnesses to Him and would raise up many other disciples, creating more communities of faith and love.[2] Jesus now prayed for all those who, generation after generation and throughout the world, would believe in Him and become His committed disciples. It is very reassuring that Jesus, when He was about to suffer on the cross, was thinking of all His believing people to the end of time. Jesus still intercedes before the throne of God for His suffering people.

The first disciples had had significant issues with competition and disunity. Jesus realised that this would continue to cause problems as numbers increased and His Kingdom continued to spread among diverse groups of people.[3] He emphasised unity at this point in His prayer, but in the context of glory rather than in terms of human structures or organisations. Glory is the realised presence of God, when His invisible presence becomes tangibly real. This happened in a dramatic way when the Spirit fell at Pentecost and it has happened in similar ways throughout the church age.[4]

God's glory is also revealed in supernatural answers to prayer. It is revealed most vividly in communities of believers who bear the fruit of the Spirit as they live as branches in the vine, loving one another and expressing this in acts of kindness, forgiveness and mercy. This unity reflects the unity of love that has existed

---

[2] Acts 1:1-3, 8; 2:1-4, 22-47.

[3] Mark 10:35-37; Luke 9:46; 22:24; Acts 6:1; 1 Cor. 1:11-13; Phil. 2:1-4; Phil. 4:2.

[4] Acts 2:1-11, 41-47.

eternally within the Godhead. It is an organic unity rather than a contrived uniformity and, like happiness, is a by-product rather than being the primary goal.

We will toil in vain to manufacture this unity through church councils and adjustments in organised religion. Unless we enter deeply into relationship with the Lord and with one another, it will not happen at all. Denominations and structural divisions of the church are not the real issue: competition, criticism, pride and unwillingness to forgive and to be forgiven are the real impediments. These problems were all present to some extent in the early church, but the dominant feature was love and an awareness of the presence of the Lord.

Jesus still expects that kind of unity among His people and, where it is visibly present, the world of ordinary human beings still recognises that the Father did indeed send His Son into the world. People are attracted to communities of faith where, through His people, they experience Jesus' love for them. In this way they come to know in a real way the love of the Father for the Son.

> **17:24-26** *'Father, I desire that they also whom you have given me be with me where I am, that they may see my glory, which you have given me, for you loved me before the foundation of the world. Righteous Father, the world hasn't known you, but I knew you; and these knew that you sent me. I made known to them your name, and will make it known; that the love with which you loved me may be in them, and I in them.'*

Finally, Jesus turned His attention to those who had walked with Him on earth, longing for the day when they will see Him in the fullness of His glory. No doubt subsequent generations of disciples were also included in this part of the prayer. Jesus had spoken of the glory that, in consequence of His nature as God, He shared with the Father before the world was. Now that glory is being expressed in an additional way, for Jesus is man as well as God. He is the glorious Son of Man to whom the Father has given the title of Lord, and He is uniquely qualified to judge the world at the end of time.[5]

Jesus, as God and fellow man, has a special relationship with His faithful people. They will share eternity with Him and will see and be included in the eternal love that flows between the Father and the Son. Then, at last, they will fully understand the destiny for which they were created and to which they are called. All the suffering and persecution that they experience in this world will be seen as nothing in comparison to the glory then being revealed.[6]

Jesus addressed God reverently as 'Righteous Father'. He is righteous and will reward those who have been faithful to Him. The great reward will be to see Him and to be in His immediate presence, and to know and experience fully what was previously known only in part. Meanwhile, the Spirit is the Father's gift to us, purchased through the costly obedience of the Son.[7] The Spirit is equivalent to the presence of Jesus within us, pouring out His love in our hearts and giving fullness of joy and a foretaste of glory.[8]

---

[5] 1 Tim. 2:5; Dan. 7:13-14; Mark 14:61-62; Phil. 2:5-11; Rev. 1:13-16, c.f. 5:6-10.
[6] Matt. 19:27-30; 2 Cor. 4:7-11, 16-18; 1 Pet. 1:6-9.
[7] Acts 1:4-8; 2:22-24, 29-36.
[8] Eph. 3:14-21; Rom. 5:1-5; 1 Pet. 1:3-9.

45

John 18:1-27
Jesus Is Betrayed and Denied

> **18:1-8a** *When Jesus had spoken these words, he went out with his disciples over the brook Kidron, where there was a garden, into which he and his disciples entered. Now Judas, who betrayed him, also knew the place, for Jesus often met there with his disciples. Judas then, having taken a detachment of soldiers and officers from the chief priests and the Pharisees, came there with lanterns, torches, and weapons. Jesus therefore, knowing all the things that were happening to him, went out, and said to them, 'Who are you looking for?'*
>
> *They answered him, 'Jesus of Nazareth.'*
>
> *Jesus said to them, 'I am he.'*
>
> *Judas also, who betrayed him, was standing with them.*
>
> *When therefore he said to them, 'I am he,' they went backward, and fell to the ground. Again therefore he asked them, 'Who are you looking for?'*
>
> *They said, 'Jesus of Nazareth.'*
>
> *Jesus answered, 'I told you that I am he.'*

Jesus and the disciples had left the city, made their way across the valley of the Kidron and climbed part-way up the Mount of Olives. Their destination was a garden of ancient olive trees known as Gethsemane. The name meant 'olive press', thus symbolising Jesus' soul-crushing distress when He agonised in prayer. John witnessed this event at close quarters but did not leave a record of it, presumably because it had been described in the other Gospels and the details were already well known.

Instead, John concentrated on the closing events in the long conflict between Jesus and the religious authorities. Recent events, including the raising of Lazarus and a series of confrontations with them in the Temple, had added a sense of urgency to their plans to eliminate Jesus. Passover was an extremely sensitive time, and thousands of people who had recently demonstrated their great enthusiasm for Jesus were currently living in and around Jerusalem. The Jewish leaders had already condemned Jesus to death at a private (and illegal) hearing.[1] They now faced the problem of implementing their decision. Arresting Jesus publicly could trigger civil unrest, which the Roman authorities were likely to suppress with overwhelming force. This could upset the delicate balance between the Romans and the Jewish leaders, who might in consequence lose their privileged positions in society.

At this point, Judas turned up with a surprising proposition.[2] It may have seemed to the leaders as an act of providence, for Judas offered to lead them discreetly to Jesus in the dead of night. Jesus could then be processed rapidly through the religious courts, and surely Pilate would not challenge their decision in favour of a troublemaker. There was every prospect that Jesus would be safely dispatched before the commencement of the Sabbath. The wheels were rapidly set in motion and their optimism was rewarded when the Roman authorities provided a detachment of troops to supplement the Temple guard.

The full moon of Passover shone brightly overhead, but the officials carried lanterns in case a search among the trees was required. Jesus was not known to be violent but the soldiers carried swords in case His disciples put up a fight. Judas was merely noted as being present.

Jesus immediately stepped forward and took control of the situation with a question: 'Who are you looking for?' He would act in a similar way during the subsequent trials. Jesus, apparently in a weak and vulnerable position, repeatedly unnerved His captors and judges, shaming and confounding them with His questions and answers, and also with His silences. He held the moral high ground at every stage in the proceedings, thus demonstrating the truth of His identity.

---

[1] John 11:47-53.
[2] John 10:31-39; 11:47-50; Luke 22:1-6.

When the officials replied, 'Jesus of Nazareth', Jesus responded with, 'I am'.[3] This statement appeared artless and innocent, but it was clothed in ambiguity. He seemed to be merely affirming His human identity as Jesus of Nazareth, but He was actually breathing the unspeakably holy name of God that had been revealed to Moses from the burning bush.[4] His words had awesome power, causing the armed band to recoil and perhaps even to stumble and fall.

Jesus chose to ignore their dramatic reaction to His words and asked the same thing again, while remaining calmly in control. His renewed question contained a challenge to the effect, 'Why are you not arresting me, since I have identified myself as the person whom you are seeking?' He included the same word 'I am' that had caused fear, but now as reported speech to confirm His identity rather than as a claim to be the God of Israel, and no untoward effects followed.

> **18:8b-18** *'If therefore you seek me, let these go their way,' that the word might be fulfilled which he spoke, 'Of those whom you have given me, I have lost none.'*
>
> *Simon Peter therefore, having a sword, drew it, struck the high priest's servant, and cut off his right ear. The servant's name was Malchus. Jesus therefore said to Peter, 'Put the sword into its sheath. The cup which the Father has given me, shall I not surely drink it?'*
>
> *So the detachment, the commanding officer, and the officers of the Jews seized Jesus and bound him, and led him to Annas first, for he was father-in-law to Caiaphas, who was high priest that year. Now it was Caiaphas who advised the Jews that it was expedient that one man should perish for the people.*
>
> *Simon Peter followed Jesus, as did another disciple. Now that disciple was known to the high priest, and entered in with Jesus into the court of the high priest; but Peter was standing at the door outside. So the other disciple, who was known to the high priest, went out and spoke to her who kept the door, and brought in Peter.*

---

[3] 'He' is not part of the Greek text.
[4] Exod. 3:13-14.

> *Then the maid who kept the door said to Peter, 'Are you also one of this man's disciples?'*
>
> *He said, 'I am not.'*
>
> *Now the servants and the officers were standing there, having made a fire of coals, for it was cold. They were warming themselves. Peter was with them, standing and warming himself.*

Jesus' sole concern was for His disciples and He protected them, in line with His recent prayer, by giving them an opportunity to escape. John wrote that Jesus was fulfilling His own previous words, thus equating Jesus' words with the Scriptures.[5]

Jesus' statement, in peaceful defence of His disciples, was immediately followed by Peter's violent action. Given the presence of the Roman soldiers, his intervention appears reckless and hopeless, but it does demonstrate his sincerity in promising to lay down his life for Jesus.[6]

Peter was wrong in thinking that he knew better than Jesus, whose recent teaching, admonition and example he was ignoring. Jesus only rebuked him briefly before healing Malchus' ear, for Peter would have to experience a deep valley of personal failure before he could recognise his own weakness. This miracle should have caused the arrest party to reconsider what they were about to do, but they carried on regardless, as others had done when Jesus had previously performed the miracle-signs.

Just before He allowed the group to lead Him away, Jesus referred to 'The cup which the Father has given me'. The cup is a common metaphor in the Jewish Scriptures and is used in two contrasting ways. It sometimes speaks of blessing, joy and salvation.[7] Much more frequently it is used in connection with God's anger and judgement on wicked people and nations.[8] It was this latter cup that Jesus accepted from His Father's hand, as in Psalm 75:8, 'For in the LORD's hand there is a cup, full of foaming wine mixed with spices. He pours it out. Indeed the wicked of the earth drink and drink it to its very dregs.' This, in love and

---

[5] John 19:24, 26-37

[6] John 13:37-38.

[7] Ps. 16:5; 23:5; 116:13.

[8] Ps. 11:6; 75:8; Isa. 51:22; Jer. 25:15-28; Hab. 2:16.

obedience, He did for us, in anticipation that He would drink the cup of joy with us in His Father's Kingdom.[9]

The accounts in the other Gospels describe Jesus' agony as He prayed to the Father, even asking if it was possible that 'this cup' could pass from Him. In obedience Jesus had taken the cup from the Father's hand and He would drink it until it was fully drained. In accepting His role as the second man, the last Adam,[10] Jesus had said, 'Behold, I have come to do your will, O God.' Adam, the first man, had used His God-given body to rebel against His Creator, leading to the reign of sin and death. Jesus, in human flesh, offered perfect obedience to the Father both in life and in death, and held true to His promise in the face of every kind of temptation and pressure. In His recent prayer He had truly said to His Father, 'I glorified you on the earth. I have accomplished the work which you have given me to do.'[11]

Earlier that night in Gethsemane, Jesus had faced the ultimate challenge of faith and obedience, graphically described by the writer to the Hebrews. He informs us that Jesus, in His human body, offered up prayers and petitions with strong crying and tears to Him who was able to save Him from death, and that He was heard on account of His godly fear. He was not praying that He would not die, but rather that death would not be final. Jesus was aware that He would soon take responsibility for the sins of the world. If the offering of His life was insufficient then there could be no resurrection. Only in utter trust could He pray 'not my will, but yours, be done', while committing His soul to the faithful Creator.[12] Jesus allowed Himself to be bound, just as Isaac had willingly submitted to His father Abraham, in trust and obedience.[13]

Peter followed to see what would happen, possibly reflecting on his risky action and puzzling over the fact that Jesus, who had so much power, had allowed Himself to be bound and taken away. John recognised the name of the high priest's servant whose ear

---

9 Matt. 26:27-29.
10 1 Cor. 15:45, 47.
11 Matt. 26:37-44; Heb. 10:5-10; John 17:4.
12 Heb. 5:7-9; Luke 22:41-44; 1 Pet. 4:19.
13 Matt. 26:36-44; Gen. 22:9.

Peter had cut off and knew his name, so he was probably the one who was able to enter with the arrest party and later to vouch for Peter.

The doorkeeper, a servant girl, was suspicious and asked Peter a tentative question, 'Are you also one of this man's disciples?' Peter, who had faced down a troop of soldiers, was suddenly caught off guard. The adrenaline rush had subsided and he was probably deflated and stressed. He was totally unprepared to make a measured response, and he could not retreat, for that would have given the game away. Perhaps he thought that the girl was of no account in the larger scheme of things, so what he said to her wouldn't matter, would it? Peter's reply, 'I am not', was the beginning of a slippery slope, and contrasted with Jesus' previous words, 'I am'.

> **18:19-27** *The high priest therefore asked Jesus about his disciples and about his teaching.*
>
> *Jesus answered him, 'I spoke openly to the world. I always taught in synagogues, and in the temple, where the Jews always meet. I said nothing in secret. Why do you ask me? Ask those who have heard me what I said to them. Behold, they know the things which I said.'*
>
> *When he had said this, one of the officers standing by slapped Jesus with his hand, saying, 'Do you answer the high priest like that?'*
>
> *Jesus answered him, 'If I have spoken evil, testify of the evil; but if well, why do you beat me?'*
>
> *Annas sent him bound to Caiaphas, the high priest.*
>
> *Now Simon Peter was standing and warming himself. They said therefore to him, 'You aren't also one of his disciples, are you?'*
>
> *He denied it and said, 'I am not.'*
>
> *One of the servants of the high priest, being a relative of him whose ear Peter had cut off, said, 'Didn't I see you in the garden with him?'*
>
> *Peter therefore denied it again, and immediately the rooster crowed.*

Jesus was being interrogated by Annas who, although no longer the official High Priest, was probably still the senior figure and wielded power behind the scenes. Annas questioned Jesus about His teaching and also about His disciples' activities. This was entirely illegal, as it was the court's responsibility to produce witnesses. Jesus pointed out that the Jewish leaders who had heard Him speak on many occasions could fulfil this role. He did not have two contrasting messages (although He did share additional insights with His committed disciples).[14]

One of the officials struck Him on the face,[15] which was also illegal, and Jesus protested, for He had done nothing wrong. He did not turn the other cheek because this was a judicial situation and not just a personal one. He would not tolerate injustice at the hands of one who claimed to act on behalf of God and who was presently abusing his office.

Annas realised that he was getting nowhere and passed Jesus on to Caiaphas, his son-in-law and current High Priest. John recalled the occasion when Caiaphas had convicted Jesus in absentia, and had cynically but also prophetically spoken of Jesus dying for the nation.[16]

Meanwhile, Peter had moved to the open fire in the courtyard and was facing the same question that the girl at the door had asked him. This setting was more dangerous, for he now found himself in the company of those who had taken part in the arrest. He could have run away on the previous occasion but he was now confined in the courtyard and was among enemies. Only a convincing denial could avert the imminent danger; and Peter, already compromised, did not hesitate.

One of the group then took a closer look at Peter, by the light of the fire, and asked the question yet again. This man was a servant of the High Priest and was also a relative of the injured Malchus, so Peter must have felt extremely vulnerable. Jesus had surrendered and was now in custody. All Peter's attempts to save Him had been rejected and had come to nothing. He was now deeply compromised by his repeated denials and was close to complete emotional collapse. He simply caved in, denying Jesus for the third time. Satan was indeed seeking to sift him as wheat, as Jesus had warned and as Peter had discounted, relying on his own resources of wisdom and courage.[17]

---

[14] Mark 4:33-34.
[15] Luke 22:64.
[16] John 11:49-53.
[17] Luke 22:31-34.

As has been noted, John rarely recorded incidents that had been described by the other Gospel writers. This raises the question of why John chose to repeat the account of Peter's denial of Jesus, as it had already been included in the Synoptic Gospels. John and Peter were close friends and associates, both as fishermen and as two of only three disciples who were privileged to share special experiences with Jesus. John would surely not, without good cause, have wanted to remind people about Peter's failure, and he was merciful in omitting reference to Peter's oaths and curses. Probably the reason why he recorded this well-known failure was to provide context for the final incident in his Gospel, where he described how Jesus graciously restored and recommissioned Peter.

46

John 18:28-40
Jesus Confronts Pilate

> **18:28-32** *They led Jesus therefore from Caiaphas into the Praetorium. It was early, and they themselves didn't enter into the Praetorium, that they might not be defiled, but might eat the Passover.*
>
> *Pilate therefore went out to them, and said, 'What accusation do you bring against this man?'*
>
> *They answered him, 'If this man weren't an evildoer, we wouldn't have delivered him up to you.'*
>
> *Pilate therefore said to them, 'Take him yourselves, and judge him according to your law.'*
>
> *Therefore the Jews said to him, 'It is illegal for us to put anyone to death,' that the word of Jesus might be fulfilled, which he spoke, signifying by what kind of death he should die.*

Up to this point, John had concentrated on the conflict and controversy between Jesus and the religious leaders, whose authority He had challenged. Having decisively rejected Jesus, they had now delivered Him to Pilate, the representative of the imperial political power, in order to destroy Him and also to delegitimise Him in the eyes of the people. Crucifixion was the ideal means by which to achieve this, for God had placed a curse on anyone who was hanged on a tree.[1] As they brought Jesus to the Praetorium, the chief priests were probably confident that Pilate would rubber-stamp their verdict and sentence and would process Jesus in short order. This would leave them with plenty of time for Passover preparations (which appears on the surface to conflict with the fact

---

[1] Deut. 21:23; Gal. 3:13.

that Jesus had celebrated Passover on the previous evening[2]). John hinted at the irony of the situation: the leaders had no scruples about hounding an innocent man to death, but were concerned about ceremonial purity and religious observances.

The religious leaders were dismayed when Pilate required them to specify the charges against Jesus. Pilate had provided soldiers to ensure His arrest, so they assumed that he considered Jesus a troublemaker who needed to be eliminated. Although cruel and ruthless, Pilate was also Caesar's representative to administer law and justice, and he believed that he must follow due process. He was also stubborn and was determined not be directed by these turbulent priests.

When the priests protested that Jesus was a bad man who did bad things, Pilate assumed that they were speaking about some moral or religious issue that was of no concern to him, and he bounced the ball back to them. They now revealed their reason for involving Pilate: he alone could impose the death penalty by crucifixion. Attempts had already been made to stone Jesus to death. Stephen was subsequently killed by this method and Paul was also stoned, so this was an option, but only crucifixion would achieve their present goal.[3] They were unaware that by so doing they were serving the Father's plan for His Son and that they were fulfilling the Scriptures.

> **18:33-36** *Pilate therefore entered again into the Praetorium, called Jesus, and said to him, 'Are you the King of the Jews?'*
>
> *Jesus answered him, 'Do you say this by yourself, or did others tell you about me?'*
>
> *Pilate answered, 'I'm not a Jew, am I? Your own nation and the chief priests delivered you to me. What have you done?'*
>
> *Jesus answered, 'My Kingdom is not of this world. If my Kingdom were of this world, then my servants would fight, that I wouldn't be delivered to the Jews. But now my Kingdom is not from here.'*

---

[2] See Appendix 5.
[3] John 8:59; 10:30-31; 11:8; Acts 7:54-60; 14:19-20.

John seems to assume that his readers were familiar with the other Gospels, for otherwise Pilate's question to Jesus is unintelligible. Luke informs us that the question 'Are you the King of the Jews?' was prompted by accusations that Jesus had been perverting the nation, and claiming to be the Messiah and also a king. These were political crimes and therefore within Pilate's jurisdiction. Another serious accusation recorded by Luke was that Jesus had forbidden people from paying taxes to Caesar. Of course, this was untrue, and they deliberately twisted what Jesus had actually said, 'Then give to Caesar the things that are Caesar's [money], and to God the things that are God's [people who bear his image].'[4]

Jesus' responded to Pilate's question with His own question. This reveals that Jesus was not intimidated by Pilate, despite his official position and power, and this fact determined the course of the subsequent trial. Jesus appears to have challenged the validity of the trial, since His accusers had offered no supporting evidence. Mark tells us that Pilate was well aware of the priests' motives: they had delivered Jesus to him out of envy, presumably on account of His popularity with the people.[5]

Pilate seemed to be on edge, for Passover was problematic at the best of times and he could have done without this intrusion. Ignoring Jesus' challenge, and wanting to avoid complicated arguments with these troublesome Jews, he replied to Jesus with more than a hint of impatience. He resorted to a simple question, hoping that a simple answer would short-circuit a prolonged legal process: 'What have you done?' Jesus declined this improper invitation to incriminate Himself and reverted to the former question about His identity as a king.

Luke records that Jesus agreed that He was a king and that Pilate responded by pronouncing Jesus as innocent.[6] This appears contradictory, but John provides more of the dialogue, explaining why Pilate did not consider Jesus to be guilty of any political crime against the Roman Empire. Although Jesus confirmed that He was indeed the King of the Jews, He qualified His answer by explaining

---

4 Luke 23:1-2; 20:20-26.

5 Mark 15:9-10.

6 Luke 23:3-4.

the nature of the Kingdom over which He ruled. Jesus had no political objectives and, when being arrested, had deterred His followers from violent action. He had done so because His Kingdom differed in kind and in order from the kingdom that Pilate represented. Jesus' Kingdom was from beyond this world. 'Not of this world ... not from here.'

John only recorded one other occasion where Jesus referred to the Kingdom: in a conversation with the Pharisee scholar and teacher Nicodemus. He, like Pilate, had been mystified. Human power, reason and learning cannot interpret the things of the Spirit or the spiritual world. God reveals Himself to those who are humble and receptive like little children.[7]

> **18:37-40** *Pilate therefore said to him, 'Are you a king then?'*
>
> *Jesus answered, 'You say that I am a king. For this reason I have been born, and for this reason I have come into the world, that I should testify to the truth. Everyone who is of the truth listens to my voice.'*
>
> *Pilate said to him, 'What is truth?' When he had said this, he went out again to the Jews, and said to them, 'I find no basis for a charge against him. But you have a custom, that I should release someone to you at the Passover. Therefore, do you want me to release to you the King of the Jews?'*
>
> *Then they all shouted again, saying, 'Not this man, but Barabbas!' Now Barabbas was a robber.*

Jesus appeared to be talking in riddles. Pilate had no way to understand what He was talking about, because his worldview was completely different from that of Jesus. Pilate was baffled and so returned to his earlier question, 'Are you a king then?' Jesus treated this as a proposition rather than a question, and then qualified it in a way that made no sense to Pilate. Jesus claimed that He was born as a king, having come from another world in order to proclaim a message of truth. Those who had a disposition to hear would recognise and receive His words.

There was no meeting of minds, for Pilate did not think about truth in this apparently abstract and philosophical sense. The

---

[7] John 3:3-11; Matt. 18:2-4; 1 Cor. 2:1-14.

Roman Empire, like most empires, was founded on another principle, which was the pre-eminence of power. The military might of Rome moulded societies to conform to the will of the emperor, and this was treated as ultimate truth. To Pilate it would have seemed that this young man, on trial for His life, was obviously a harmless dreamer of dreams. He was living in an illusory world and had no plan or strategy that would threaten Caesar in this remote province of the empire.

Pilate's famous question, 'What is truth?' signalled the end of the conversation. It was really rhetorical in nature, and probably dismissive or sneering in tone. Jesus' words were nonsense in Pilate's ears and he was incapable of understanding the detailed explanation that Jesus could have added to His brief statement.

Jesus had come from another sphere of reality, from which this world had been created and on which it depends for its continuance. He was truth incarnate in a world that had been corrupted by lies and deception, and which was in a continuing state of rebellion against the Creator God who still sustained it. He completely trusted and obeyed the Father, and His life and behaviour revealed the truth of how people had been designed to live. Power had corrupted human beings; in laying down His life as an obedient offering, Jesus would restore them, God's creatures, to the God of truth. None of this would have made sense to Pilate, the representative of ultimate and almost absolute power on earth.

Pilate was obviously frustrated with Jesus. He also had no love for the Jewish religious leaders who had sent a petition to Caesar when he had tried, more than once, to install pagan symbols in the holy city. The emperor had ordered him to retract the order, resulting in a humiliating climb-down before the Jewish leaders. He knew that they were trying to use him to get rid of Jesus in a painful and degrading way, and he had no wish to facilitate them. The prisoner was strange and was rather unnerving in His apparent complacency about His possible fate. Nevertheless, He seemed to be a harmless and deluded fool rather than a danger to the existing regime.

Pilate stepped out and gave his official verdict, and sweetened it by offering to release Jesus instead of Barabbas, a robber and notorious murderer. If they were sincere in their desire to prosecute someone who threatened public order and also threatened the delicate balance between their nation and Rome, here was the way to demonstrate it. To Pilate's dismay, the Jewish leaders rudely threw the suggestion back in his face, with the words 'Not this man, but Barabbas!', thus revealing their true characters and motives.

Barabbas' name meant 'son of the father', and he was elsewhere called Jesus Barabbas. The choice between Jesus and Barabbas represents the choice between the true Messiah and false ones.[8] In a similar way Jesus referred to Himself as the Good Shepherd when addressing the bad shepherds, and as the true vine in contrast to the false vine that Israel had become. Jesus also described His Father as the farmer, distinguishing Him from the wicked ones, the Jewish leaders who featured in the parable of the vineyard and who were now seeking to destroy Him.[9]

[8] Matt. 27:16 (NKJV alt. reading, NU Text); 24:23-25; Acts 5:35-37.
[9] John 10:11; 15:1; Matt. 21:33-44.

47

John 19:1-16
No King But Caesar

> ***19:1-7** So Pilate then took Jesus, and flogged him. The soldiers twisted thorns into a crown, and put it on his head, and dressed him in a purple garment. They kept saying, 'Hail, King of the Jews!' and they kept slapping him.*
>
> *Then Pilate went out again, and said to them, 'Behold, I bring him out to you, that you may know that I find no basis for a charge against him.' Jesus therefore came out, wearing the crown of thorns and the purple garment. Pilate said to them, 'Behold, the man!'*
>
> *When therefore the chief priests and the officers saw him, they shouted, saying, 'Crucify! Crucify!'*
>
> *Pilate said to them, 'Take him yourselves, and crucify him, for I find no basis for a charge against him.'*
>
> *The Jews answered him, 'We have a law, and by our law he ought to die, because he made himself the Son of God.'*

Pilate did not intend to suffer another defeat at the hands of these impossible people, so he now took decisive action that was intended to awaken Jesus to the peril of His situation and bring Him to His senses. It should also satisfy the bloodlust of the associated crowd that the priests had assembled for the occasion. John ignored any reference to these others, for he knew that the leaders were the real culprits and that their followers did not represent the people who had acclaimed Jesus less than a week previously.[1] Roman scourging was a brutal punishment that could bring the victim to the brink of death, and this he now authorised. Humiliation was part of this process, for scourging was carried out

---

[1] Matt. 27:20-25; John 12:12-19.

in public view. The soldiers then added to both the suffering and the humiliation by their mockery of Jesus, in parody of His claims to be king of the Jews. John repeated this title over and over again, emphasising that Jesus suffered and died with that identity. He was the suffering Messiah, as described by the prophet Isaiah.[2]

Pilate then presented Jesus to His accusers, still dressed in a purple robe and with His battered and disfigured face visible beneath the crown of thorns. Perhaps Pilate was hoping to evoke sympathy for Jesus, whose condition visibly contradicted any claim to kingship. Pilate presented Jesus to them in this way in order to emphasise that this was his final verdict: 'I find no basis for a charge against him.' The statement 'Behold, the man!' has been appropriately transformed into a statement of wonder and worship, but clearly Pilate would not have intended it as such. He was pointing to a figure whom his soldiers had ridiculed and tortured and whose claims had been thoroughly discredited. Jesus could now be safely released to live out His short and broken life in obscurity, another failed and forgotten messianic pretender. Later, when advising the Sanhedrin Council not to take precipitate action against the apostles, Gamaliel, who was a Pharisee and a mentor of Saul of Tarsus, made reference to two such pretenders: Theudas and Judas of Galilee.[3]

In the face of Jesus' immense and visible suffering, the chief priests and their followers insistently cried out, 'Crucify! Crucify!' This demonstrated that their hearts had turned to stone in their determination to destroy Him in the cruellest available way. Affirming for the third time his verdict according to Roman law, 'I find no basis for a charge against him', Pilate challenged the leaders to crucify Jesus themselves. By so doing, he was demonstrating his disdain, for he knew that it was beyond their power to crucify anyone.

The priests did not hesitate to defy the decision of Caesar's appointed judge. They had a trump card to play, but were keeping it concealed until the final move. They first argued that Jesus had committed a crime according to their law and that this should take

---

[2] Isa. 50:6; 53:5-8a.
[3] Acts 22:3; 5:33-39.

precedence over the Roman code of law: 'We have a law, and by our law he ought to die, because he made himself the Son of God.'

The Roman governor was a pagan and was superstitious. The priests played on that weakness by referring to Jesus' claims to be the Son of God. Pilate's concerns were reinforced by his wife, who had sent him a message in which she described a disturbing dream about the prisoner. She had advised her husband, 'Have nothing to do with that righteous man, for I have suffered many things today in a dream because of him.'[4] The leaders were becoming more strident, believing that they were gradually undermining Pilate's self-confidence and also aware that he was anxious to avoid public disorder at this very sensitive time of the Feast of Passover.

> **19:8-11** *When therefore Pilate heard this saying, he was more afraid. He entered into the Praetorium again, and said to Jesus, 'Where are you from?' But Jesus gave him no answer. Pilate therefore said to him, 'Aren't you speaking to me? Don't you know that I have power to release you and have power to crucify you?'*
>
> *Jesus answered, 'You would have no power at all against me, unless it were given to you from above. Therefore he who delivered me to you has greater sin.'*

John stated that Pilate became more fearful. This was not only because of the unforeseen complications of the trial, but also because of some possible involvement of the gods. Rational and irrational fears were mingling and he was beginning to panic. He returned to where Jesus was standing, bloody but unbowed, and sought some way to escape from a situation that was spiralling out of his control. He asked Jesus, probably in an agitated manner, 'Where are you from?' Pilate appears to have been spooked, and Jesus' silence further unnerved him and increased his inner tension.

Pilate was struggling with the frustrating anomaly of the situation. He was supposed to be in charge but was being manipulated by the Jewish priests. The accused man was facing crucifixion but seemed sublimely unconcerned, and a suggestion had been floated that He was one of the gods in disguise. In

---

[4] Matt. 27:19.

desperation, Pilate tried to shake Jesus out of His silence by bluntly reasserting his power, in contrast with Jesus' seeming vulnerability: 'Don't you know that I have power to release you and have power to crucify you?'

Jesus' reply, 'You would have no power at all against me, unless it were given to you from above', contradicted the assumption on which all world empires are built: that power derives from the ability to control human resources and military might. He dismissed the premise of Pilate's statement and insisted that, contrary to present appearances, power flowed from the place of absolute and universal truth from which He Himself had come. This truth continues to challenge us as we try to understand geopolitical events in the context of the sovereign purposes of God.

The prophet Daniel had intimate experience of two great world empires: Babylon and Media Persia. By means of dreams and visions, God revealed to him the dynamics of their rise and fall. Each empire aspired to absolute and permanent power, but each was doomed to fall and to be replaced. This is still inevitable because such empires are built on false beliefs that human beings are in control of their own destiny and that human power can dictate the course of history. Daniel understood that the succession of empires would eventually be brought to an end and would be replaced by the Kingdom of God. In the sequence of empires that Daniel saw, Greece followed Media Persia and therefore the fourth beast represented Rome. In the vision, Rome was portrayed in the form of a beast with hideous and apparently invincible strength. It was revealed to Daniel that this beast also represented the final empire in world history, which would also possess overwhelming power. The Son of Man, God's agent of truth, will appear in glory to destroy that empire and inaugurate His eternal Kingdom.[5]

It was this self-same Son of Man who now stood before Pilate and denied Pilate's claim to ultimate power. Pilate needed to know that power is a gift from the One who is infinitely higher than Caesar. Pilate did indeed have power to crucify the man Jesus; nevertheless, that power flowed from heaven and not from Rome

---

[5] Dan. 2:26-45; 7:1-27.

and would have a very different outcome from the one that Pilate intended. God the Father was giving His beloved Son to die for the sins of the world, and Pilate, in pursuit of his own aims, would be part of the process in fulfilling God's eternal plan. God makes even the wrath of man to praise Him and uses ungodly rulers to do His will.[6]

Pilate would receive no credit for his actions and would be judged on the basis of his motives and desires, but he was much less culpable than those who had sinned despite having been given light and revelation. Caiaphas, the High Priest of Israel, had orchestrated the whole process and was thus supremely guilty.

> **19:12-16** *At this, Pilate was seeking to release him, but the Jews cried out, saying, 'If you release this man, you aren't Caesar's friend! Everyone who makes himself a king speaks against Caesar!'*
>
> *When Pilate therefore heard these words, he brought Jesus out and sat down on the judgement seat at a place called 'The Pavement', but in Hebrew, 'Gabbatha.' Now it was the Preparation Day of the Passover, at about the sixth hour. He said to the Jews, 'Behold, your King!'*
>
> *They cried out, 'Away with him! Away with him! Crucify him!'*
>
> *Pilate said to them, 'Shall I crucify your King?'*
>
> *The chief priests answered, 'We have no king but Caesar!'*
>
> *So then he delivered him to them to be crucified. So they took Jesus and led him away.*

Pilate made further strenuous efforts to persuade the Jewish leaders that Jesus should be released, hoping to regain control of the situation. Then they made their penultimate move towards checkmate, using a thinly veiled threat: 'If you release this man, you aren't Caesar's friend! Everyone who makes himself a king speaks against Caesar!' Pilate would have remembered that the religious Jews had previously reported his actions to Caesar, and he knew that they would not hesitate to do so again if it suited their purposes. They were using Pilate as a pawn in their sinister game,

---

6 Ps. 76:10; Isa. 10:5-11; 44:28; 45:1; Exod. 9:16; Rom. 9:17; Acts 4:24-28.

with the King Himself, Jesus, as their target. Caiaphas knew his opponent's weakness and which string to pull.

Pilate was being pulled and pushed in different directions, by his loathing and fear of the Jewish leaders, by his judicial responsibility under Roman law and by his superstitious fears and the unsettling character of his prisoner. Jesus, who should have been reduced to a state of desperation, remained calm and dignified and seemed to possess an unworldly peace and assurance, such as Pilate had never seen.

In a final attempt to find a way through the impasse, Pilate brought Jesus out again. His previously dismissive 'Behold, the man!' now became 'Behold, your King!' Perhaps he hoped that the priests would somehow change their attitude, but if he did entertain that hope he was to be sadly disappointed. They renewed their bloodthirsty cries with increased venom. When Pilate responded with the question, 'Shall I crucify your King?', which was probably designed to shift all the blame to their shoulders, they made their final move with the assertion, 'We have no king but Caesar!' Now it was checkmate!

In making this statement, Caiaphas was reversing the earlier assertion in which he had implied that the law of God was higher than Roman law. Caiaphas had previously revealed himself to be a cynical pragmatist who was willing to take the course of action that seemed to be currently expedient. Once again he was acting in character. The statement, 'We have no king but Caesar!' was astonishing, coming as it was from the lips of the chief priests, who were the supreme representatives of God to the Jewish people.

Jesus had previously said, 'Then give to Caesar the things that are Caesar's, and to God the things that are God's.' Caesar's image was stamped on the coins with which taxes were paid. God the Creator had imprinted His image on His human creatures, but now the leaders were surrendering their identity and their inheritance in the Messiah to Caesar, just as Esau had sold his inheritance for a bowl of stew.[7] By so doing they had sealed their own fate, as well as the fate of the nation on whose behalf they had spoken. Within forty years, Jerusalem would lie in ruins, the Temple destroyed and

---

[7] Luke 20:25; Gen. 25:27-34.

multitudes crucified or carried away as slaves to Rome, as captives of their chosen king.[8]

John tells us that Pilate delivered Jesus to them to be crucified. This is curious and significant, for they were not physically His executioners. At the beginning of the trial they had handed Jesus over to Pilate, and now, symbolically, he handed Jesus back to them, even though his soldiers would do the dirty work. God had appointed Israel as a priestly nation and now, in the person of the corrupt and worldly Caiaphas, they fulfilled their destiny to offer up the Lamb of God for the sins of the world. Jesus also suffered as the Passover Lamb, whose death would open the door to freedom and life.

All of this fulfilled the purpose of the Lord of the universe.[9] Once again we are confronted by the mystery of the sovereignty of God, worked out through history over many centuries, and now consummated in the free choices of His creatures. We cannot understand how this intertwining of human and divine purposes works, but we know that it is true. Unlike Pilate and the priests, we must align our lives with God's revealed will, and serve His purposes with glad and willing hearts. God can and will use the choices of wicked people to accomplish His eternal purposes. They will receive no credit for those choices or for their behaviour.

---

[8] Dan. 9:24-26.
[9] Luke 23:23-25; Acts 2:22-24; 4:8-12, 24-28.

48

John 19:17-37
Finished!

> *19:17-22* He went out, bearing his cross, to the place called 'The Place of a Skull', which is called in Hebrew, 'Golgotha', where they crucified him, and with him two others, on either side one, and Jesus in the middle. Pilate wrote a title also, and put it on the cross. There was written, 'JESUS OF NAZARETH, THE KING OF THE JEWS.' Therefore many of the Jews read this title, for the place where Jesus was crucified was near the city; and it was written in Hebrew, in Latin, and in Greek.
>
> The chief priests of the Jews therefore said to Pilate, 'Don't write, "The King of the Jews," but, "he said, 'I am King of the Jews."'"
>
> Pilate answered, 'What I have written, I have written.'

John is very economical in his description of the events of the crucifixion, which again indicates that the accounts in the other Gospels were widely known. He selected incidents that focus on the identity of Jesus and the purpose of His life and death, and those that connect these crucial events with the previous Scriptures. Thus John described the journey to the place of crucifixion in a few words: 'He went out, bearing his cross'. It was indeed His cross, for Jesus, as the suffering Son of Man, had voluntarily chosen this path to glory. John retained the Hebrew word Golgotha, perhaps as a reminder that Jesus travelled there as the Jewish Messiah. Archaeological evidence suggests that the Church of the Holy Sepulchre was subsequently built on this site.

John simply stated the facts of the crucifixion without its brutal details. Other sources reveal that it was designed to inflict prolonged and extreme suffering and humiliation, partly as a warning to others. What John does highlight is that Jesus did not suffer alone, but was crucified between two other people. The other Gospels document the contrasting ways in which each of these two men regarded Jesus, having been brutally thrust into His company. One man recognised who Jesus was and responded in faith. The other saw only a weak and helpless victim of the power of Rome and continued to ridicule Him, in company with the religious leaders, passers-by and soldiers. The world was thus united in contempt for the Lord of glory.[1]

The words placarded on the cross described the crime for which Jesus was accused and for which He was being executed. Pilate had presented Jesus to the religious leaders with the words, 'Behold, your King!' The chief priests had exerted maximum pressure on Pilate with their statement, 'We have no king but Caesar!' Perhaps he was now reinforcing the symbolism of washing his hands during the trial and indicating to the Jewish leaders that they, rather then he, were responsible for the execution of Jesus.[2]

The notice was written in Latin, Greek and Hebrew. One possible version of the Hebrew script, illustrated in a painting by Fra Angelico (1434 CE), would have resulted in an acronym for the ineffable covenant name of God.[3] If this was the case, the inscription would have caused the greatest possible offence to the Jewish leaders. Pilate may have been unaware of the significance of the particular wording, but the possibility is intriguing. Pilate took the opportunity to reassert his superior position by refusing to alter the inscription. Thus the words, 'What I have written, I have written', corresponded to John's assertion that all the details of the crucifixion were to fulfil the (written) Scriptures. The use of the three languages emphasises that Jesus died not only as the King of the Jews but also as the Lamb of God for the sin of the world, including the other sheep that were not of the Jewish fold.[4]

> **19:23-24** *Then the soldiers, when they had crucified Jesus, took his garments and made four parts, to every soldier a part; and also the coat.*

---

[1] Luke 23:35-43; Matt. 27:38-44; Mark 15:27-32; John 1:10-13; 1 John 3:1.
[2] Matt. 27:21-26.
[3] Eli Lizorkin-Eyzenberg, *The Jewish Gospel of John: Discovering Jesus, King of All Israel* (2015), pp. 260-269.
[4] John 10:14-16.

Now the coat was without seam, woven from the top throughout. Then they said to one another, 'Let's not tear it, but cast lots for it to decide whose it will be,' that the Scripture might be fulfilled, which says, 'They parted my garments amongst them. For my cloak they cast lots.' Therefore the soldiers did these things.

It appears that four soldiers were responsible for each crucifixion and that they were entitled to keep the bloodstained clothes which in this case comprised five items, one of which was a long, closely woven garment worn close to the skin (a chiton). The chiton was considered to be of greatest value, so they cast lots for it. John emphasised that the soldiers' actions were in order to fulfil Scripture.[5] Of course, they would have been innocent of this fact and were simply following the usual practice. God weaves His tapestry from such unlikely materials, thereby revealing His glory.

19:25-27 *But standing by Jesus' cross were his mother, his mother's sister, Mary the wife of Clopas, and Mary Magdalene. Therefore when Jesus saw his mother, and the disciple whom he loved standing there, he said to his mother, 'Woman, behold, your son!' Then he said to the disciple, 'Behold, your mother!' From that hour, the disciple took her to his own home.*

Four women followed the grim procession to Golgotha, remaining faithful to the end. The beloved disciple, assumed to be the apostle John, accompanied them but there is no indication that any other male disciples were present. The religious leaders who mocked Jesus had no concern for those who, in quiet and dignified sorrow, watched Him suffer. There are obvious parallels in the modern world where religious fanatics still trample on the followers of Jesus, and even crucify them in imitation of His suffering.

Jesus' attitude was very different from the mockers. He who had said 'Father, forgive them' in relation to the soldiers, and 'today you will be with me in Paradise' to the dying thief, now looked at His mother with compassion and concern, and committed her to the care of His faithful disciple with the words, 'Behold, your

---

[5] Ps. 22:18.

son … Behold, your mother'.[6] At the marriage in Cana, Jesus had indicated a new relationship with Mary. As far as we know, Mary's other sons did not yet believe in Jesus. He had previously described His disciples in this way: 'Behold, my mother and my brothers!'[7] Mary was His mother in a double sense, both as His birth mother and as His disciple, so Jesus entrusted Mary to the care of His spiritual brother John. After Jesus ascended, Mary was with the other disciples in the Upper Room, now including her other sons who had previously been among the sceptics but who now believed that Jesus was the Son of God.[8]

> **19:28-30** *After this, Jesus, seeing that all things were now finished, that the Scripture might be fulfilled, said, 'I am thirsty.' Now a vessel full of vinegar was set there; so they put a sponge full of the vinegar on hyssop, and held it at his mouth. When Jesus therefore had received the vinegar, he said, 'It is finished.' He bowed his head, and gave up his spirit.*

John does not describe the three hours of darkness and the other phenomena that Matthew had already recorded in detail, but we can safely assume that his readers were conversant with this information and that they would have known that it was now the ninth hour (3pm). This corresponded with the time of the evening sacrifice in the Temple. Jesus said, 'I am thirsty', because He was fully human and, by this stage, He would certainly have been experiencing a raging physical thirst.

Jesus, as a Jewish man, would have been very familiar with Psalm 22, and the words would have been a natural way to describe His distress. The psalm was originally a poetic way in which David expressed his own painful experiences and his inner turmoil, but it was also prophetic of the suffering of the Messiah. Jesus was not simply ticking off items that were necessary in order to fulfil biblical prophecy, but He would have been aware of the many detailed connections with His crucifixion, including the intense

---

[6] Matt. 27:41-43; Luke 23:32-34, 39-43.
[7] Mark 3:34.
[8] John 2:3-5; 7:2-5; Acts 1:12-14.

thirst that He experienced. There was a double significance, for He also thirsted to drink the cup that His Father had given Him.[9]

The soldiers only understood the physical component of His thirst, and they offered Him hyssop soaked in sour wine; in so doing they also were unwittingly fulfilling Scripture. Hyssop had been used to apply the blood of the Passover lamb to the lintels and doorposts of the Israelites' houses in Egypt, in order to protect the firstborn sons from death. Jesus, the true Passover Lamb, was slain to deliver His people from death and from slavery to sin.[10] Hyssop was also used to sprinkle water in situations of ritual uncleanness, and David recognised that this symbolised the need for cleansing of the heart. Jesus shed His blood for our forgiveness, to deliver us from the penalty and the power of sin, and also to cleanse us from its shame and pollution.[11]

The climax had now arrived, emphasised by the triple use of the same Greek word root (*teleo*), once translated 'fulfilled', and twice translated 'finished'. Jesus cried out and released His spirit to the Father. This statement has several connections and applications. Firstly, it applied to Jesus in a very personal way. He had lived His life in perfect trust and obedience to His Father and now surrendered that life to Him in an ultimate act of obedience. By so doing, Jesus fulfilled the description by John the Baptist, for He offered Himself as the Lamb of God who takes away the sin of the world.[12]

In the second place, it marked the completion of the long journey that had begun in Eden with the promise of the seed of the woman who would bruise the serpent's head. That journey had continued through the Patriarchs and the prophets of Israel and had remained intact, notwithstanding the repeated disloyalty and failure of the covenant people. Now the story of salvation history had successfully reached its goal in the suffering of the Messiah. He shouted in triumph over the powers of darkness that He had decisively defeated. This paralleled the events at the Red Sea, and

---

[9] Ps. 22:15; John 18:11.
[10] Ps. 69:21; John 17:4; Exod. 12:22; Matt. 26:29.
[11] Lev. 14:4-6, 49-52; Num. 19:17-19; Ps. 51:7; Heb. 9:18-28; 1 John 1:7-9.
[12] John 1:29; 10:17-18.

marked the beginning of a new Exodus into freedom and covenant relationship with God for all who would follow Him.[13]

Finally, in draining the bitter cup of suffering, Jesus now looked forward to drinking the sweet fruit of the vine, along with His redeemed followers, in His Father's Kingdom. The cross was a climax in the story, but not the final one. In John's vision in the book of Revelation he records similar words from the throne of God: 'It is done! I have become the Alpha and the Omega, the Beginning and the End. I will give freely to him who is thirsty from the spring of the water of life.' Jesus' suffering, thirst and experience of abandonment will have this final outcome for all His people. The ultimate goal will have been reached, when God will once again be present among His people and everything will be made new.[14]

John was an eyewitness of the crucifixion and he alone recorded this cry. That declaration of completion set in motion a series of events that Matthew and Mark recorded. The great curtain that concealed the Most Holy Place in the Temple was torn from top to bottom, an earthquake shook the district and a number of deceased saints were raised to life.[15]

Three rabbis referred to events that happened during the year of Jesus' crucifixion and forty years before the destruction of the Temple. The heavy doors swung open, the western lamp was extinguished and from that time the sacrifices lost their efficacy. One of the rabbis lamented that these events were portents of the coming destruction of the Temple: 'Temple. O Temple, why do you grieve? I know that they will come to destroy you, for the prophet Zechariah had foretold of you, "Open your doors O Lebanon, that the fire may devour your cedars."'

---

13 Gen. 3:15; John 12:30-32; Col. 2:15; Exod. 14:26–15:18; 19:4-6; Matt. 2:13-15.
14 Matt. 26:29; Rev. 21:6, NKJV (quotation omitted in M-Text and in WEBBE).
15 Mark 15:37-39; Matt. 27:51-53.

Another rabbi said, 'It [the Temple] is called Lebanon, because it whitens Israel's sins.'[16] Truly, the old order was finished and would soon disappear.[17]

> ***19:31-37*** *Therefore the Jews, because it was the Preparation Day, so that the bodies wouldn't remain on the cross on the Sabbath (for that Sabbath was a special one), asked of Pilate that their legs might be broken, and that they might be taken away. Therefore the soldiers came, and broke the legs of the first, and of the other who was crucified with him; but when they came to Jesus, and saw that he was already dead, they didn't break his legs. However one of the soldiers pierced his side with a spear, and immediately blood and water came out. He who has seen has testified, and his testimony is true. He knows that he tells the truth, that you may believe. For these things happened that the Scripture might be fulfilled, 'A bone of him will not be broken.' Again another Scripture says, 'They will look on him whom they pierced.'*

For the third time John referred to the Jewish leaders' concern about the fact that the crucifixion was on a day when they needed to prepare for Passover, also described as a high day of Sabbath. John made a clear connection between the slaying of the Passover Lamb and the suffering and death of Jesus. The apostle Paul wrote that 'Christ, our Passover, has been sacrificed in our place'.[18] Jesus was crucified both on the day of Passover and on the day of preparation for Passover.[19]

Once again, the Jewish leaders emerged in their true colours. The breaking of legs would shorten the duration of the ordeal. The brutal intervention would not actually cause sudden death and was only requested in order to avoid ritual contamination on the ensuing holy day. Having disposed of Jesus, this was their only remaining concern.

---

[16] Talmud Yoma 39b, Shabbat 22b, and Minhoth 86b; quoted in Risto Santala, *The Messiah in the New Testament in the Light of Rabbinical Writings* (Jerusalem: Keren Ahvah Meshihit, 1992), pp. 231-232.

[17] Heb. 9:6-8; 8:13.

[18] 1 Cor. 5:7.

[19] See Appendix 5, 'Did Jesus Die at Passover?' for an explanation of this paradox.

John emphasised that he was writing as a first-hand witness of what took place. He also provided an interpretation of what he saw, although this may have been on the basis of a subsequent reflection rather than an immediate revelation. He connected the two events with two scriptures, one a historical incident and the other a written prophecy. Prophecy can take the form of words or actions, as we have seen in the life and writings of David.

The first connection was with the Passover lamb. The Israelites who were about to escape from bondage in Egypt were instructed to roast the lamb and to preserve its bones intact. Unlike the other two victims, Jesus' legs were not broken, and John understood the significance of this fact. He had heard John the Baptist proclaim, 'Behold, the Lamb of God', and now he saw this identity graphically enacted in the suffering of Jesus. The Israelites had been instructed to eat the lamb just before the Exodus from Egypt. The blood of the lamb had been instrumental in saving them from slavery and death. As Jesus contemplated His imminent death on the cross, He said, 'Now is the judgement of this world. Now the prince of this world will be cast out.'[20]

The flesh of the lamb nourished the Israelites as they commenced their journey to the Promised Land. Jesus said, 'He who eats my flesh and drinks my blood has eternal life, and I will raise him up at the last day. For my flesh is food indeed, and my blood is drink indeed. He who eats my flesh and drinks my blood lives in me, and I in him.'[21]

The second connection was with the daily morning and evening sacrifices in the Temple. The book of Exodus reveals that these two sacrifices were required to make it possible for the Lord to continue to dwell among His people.[22] When Jesus was crucified, He offered Himself for the sins of the world, just as John the Baptist had revealed.[23] A lamb was offered in the Temple at the third hour (9 am) when Jesus was nailed to the cross. Jesus declared that His work on the cross was complete and committed His spirit

---

[20] Ex. 12:11-14; John 1:36; John 12:30-33.
[21] Exod. 12:8-10, 46; John 6:54-56.
[22] Exod. 29:38-46.
[23] John 1:29.

to His Father's care at the ninth hour (3 pm), approximately the time when the second lamb was being offered.[24]

Jesus died as the Passover Lamb, thus setting us free (redeeming us) from bondage to sin and death. As the burnt offering, He removed the guilt and uncleanness of sin that separated us from God. When Jesus died, the veil of the Temple was torn apart from top to bottom, opening the new and living way into God's presence.[25]

The apostle John witnessed the piercing of Jesus' side and the outflowing of blood and water. Blood symbolises life, poured out for our redemption and for the forgiveness of sins. The prophet Isaiah foretold that the Messiah would be pierced for our transgressions.[26] Jesus subsequently showed His pierced hands and side to Thomas as evidence of the truth of who He was and of what He had done.[27] Water speaks of cleansing and also functions as a symbol for the Holy Spirit, as is the case throughout John's Gospel. The Holy Spirit would be given on the basis of Jesus' death and resurrection.[28]

The prophet Zechariah spoke of a time, yet to come, when the people of Israel will recognise the identity of the Messiah, whom they pierced. This will result in national repentance and an outpouring of the Holy Spirit upon them, and in unprecedented blessing for the world.[29]

---

[24] Matt. 27:45-50.

[25] Matt. 27:51; Col. 1:13-14; Eph. 1:7; Heb. 10:19-22.

[26] Exod. 12:21-23; Lev. 17:11; Isa. 53:5.

[27] John 20:24-29.

[28] John 1:29, 33; 7:37-39; 16:7; 20:21-23; Acts 2:22-33.

[29] Zech. 12:10–13:2; Luke 13:34-35; Rom. 11:15, 25-32.

49

John 19:38-42
Secret Disciples No More

> *19:38-42 After these things, Joseph of Arimathaea, being a disciple of Jesus, but secretly for fear of the Jews, asked of Pilate that he might take away Jesus' body. Pilate gave him permission. He came therefore and took away his body. Nicodemus, who at first came to Jesus by night, also came bringing a mixture of myrrh and aloes, about a hundred Roman pounds. So they took Jesus' body, and bound it in linen cloths with the spices, as the custom of the Jews is to bury.*
>
> *Now in the place where he was crucified there was a garden. In the garden was a new tomb in which no man had ever yet been laid. Then because of the Jews' Preparation Day (for the tomb was near at hand) they laid Jesus there.*

Before retiring with His disciples to celebrate the Passover, Jesus had made a last appeal for His hearers to abandon their unbelief and follow Him. The audience had contained a significant number of Jewish leaders, many of whom were convinced in their minds but were unwilling to take a public stand with Jesus, because they feared loss of approval from their fellows. We do not know if Joseph of Arimathea was present on that occasion, but he was certainly a believer. The other Gospels provide additional information about him: he was wealthy, he was a member of the ruling council and he was waiting for the Kingdom of God. He had not consented to the decision to kill Jesus, nor had he participated in the deed itself.[1] He was a secret and private disciple. He may therefore have avoided situations where he would have

---

[1] John 12:42-43; Matt. 27:57; Mark 15:43; Luke 23:50-51.

been required to make his position clear, in this way quieting his conscience.

We may criticise Joseph for this, not having walked in his shoes, but a similar situation faces many believers at the present time, living as they do in situations of extreme persecution. They need our prayers and support and not our disapproval. The Lord knows how to protect such people until they are strong enough to face their enemies, and in His own time He may bring them into circumstances where they must nail their colours to the mast. We who live in the West may also be tempted to keep silent in situations when our beliefs conflict with those of others whose opinion we value or whose criticism we fear.

Like Simeon, who had been 'looking for the consolation of Israel', Joseph had been 'looking for God's Kingdom'; these terms are probably synonymous.[2] Simeon had found his answer in the tiny infant Jesus; Joseph now found the same answer in the crucified Messiah. Each had a revelation that demanded a public response, Simeon by his prophetic words and worship and Joseph through his decisive action. Joseph's act revealed a deep faith and loyalty, even though he may not have been able to resolve the apparent contradiction between Jesus' identity and the ignominy of His crucifixion. Joseph engaged in what may have seemed like an irrational action, but it was one that revealed his love, just as Mary had done when she poured out the expensive ointment in anticipation of Jesus' burial. Jews are very eager to show respect for the dead. Joseph wanted to spare Jesus the further disgrace of being cast into a criminal's grave.

Joseph had little time to think, for the authorities would soon be disposing of Jesus' body, and also the Sabbath was at hand. It required courage and resolution to approach the governor, who might rebuff him, having had more than enough from the troublesome members of the Jewish council. Joseph's mind was made up and he was now off the fence, whatever personal consequences might ensue. He would face the unpleasant task of handling the mangled body, which would render him unclean for the whole period of Passover and Unleavened Bread. He would

---

[2] Luke 2:25; Mark 15:43.

then have to submit to a process of ritual purification. Pharisees had similar concerns about defilement as the priest and the Levite in the Good Samaritan story.[3] Joseph's courage and disregard for personal convenience were rewarded, for Pilate agreed to his request. This may have been out of respect for Jesus, but perhaps also to annoy the truculent priests.

Another secret disciple and fellow Pharisee and council member now came out of the closet and joined him. Nicodemus had been on a long journey for the past three years since he had visited Jesus by night. He had briefly put his head above the parapet at a council meeting about six months previously, but had had to retreat under heavy and disdainful attack.[4] Joseph's resolute decision now propelled him into action.

We should not underestimate the importance of obeying the voice of the Holy Spirit, even if the action seems foolish and unlikely to succeed. This risky obedience may be just the encouragement that another vulnerable person needs, and it may prove to be the spark that ignites a spiritual fire in the hearts of many other people. Joseph would probably have found the physical effort more than he could manage, and it would have been very lonely and emotionally exhausting to attempt this by himself. Nicodemus added his physical strength and also supplied material assistance, in the shape of one hundred pounds of myrrh and aloes to preserve the body. By their joint enterprise, Joseph and Nicodemus fulfilled the prophecy that was symbolised by the wise men's gift. As wealthy men, they also performed the words of the prophet Isaiah.[5]

Jesus was born of a Jewish mother, He was circumcised and dedicated as a Jewish infant, He lived as an observant Jewish man, He kept the Jewish festivals and fulfilled their prophetic symbolism, He was condemned by a Jewish council, He died as Jesus of Nazareth and as the King of the Jews, and He was buried in accordance with Jewish practice. Salvation is truly from the Jews.[6]

---

[3] Num. 19:11-21; Luke 10:30-32.

[4] John 3:1-2; 7:50-52.

[5] Matt. 2:11; Isa. 53:9.

[6] Luke 1:26-36; 2:21-32; Gal. 4:4-5; Matt. 17:24-27; John 4:22.

It seems clear that Joseph and Nicodemus had no expectation of the resurrection, for they were thoroughly wrapping the body. There was no possibility that Jesus could walk from the tomb as Lazarus had done, given the weight and nature of the bandages. Matthew informs us that this procedure was carried out under the watchful eyes of two women who had been Jesus' close followers and disciples, and who had been at the cross.[7]

Time was of the essence as the Sabbath was at hand, so the nearby tomb that Joseph had prepared for his own burial seemed to be the providential and obvious place to lay Jesus' body. Joseph did not look for an alternative solution, for he had the means to supply it himself and he gladly made the tomb available for the purpose. Matthew records that Joseph's final action was to roll a large (flat) stone over the entrance. The chief priests had gained Pilate's permission to seal the tomb and place a guard, in order to prevent the disciples from stealing the body and claiming that Jesus had returned to life. This would be the ultimate deception and must be prevented at all costs.[8] If they had known how demoralised, confused and fearful the disciples were at that time, they would not have bothered.

---

[7] John 11:43-44; Matt. 27:55-61.
[8] Matt. 27:60-66.

50

John 20:1-18
Who Are You Looking For?

> *20:1-2 Now on the first day of the week, Mary Magdalene went early, while it was still dark, to the tomb, and saw the stone taken away from the tomb. Therefore she ran and came to Simon Peter and to the other disciple whom Jesus loved, and said to them, 'They have taken away the Lord out of the tomb, and we don't know where they have laid him!'*

Jesus was buried in Joseph's tomb just before the commencement of Sabbath, at sunset on (our) Friday. The Gospel records give precise information that the tomb was empty by sunrise on the first day of the week, the beginning of the third day from Jesus' death. The resurrection could thus have taken place at any time after the end of Sabbath, this period also corresponding with the three days and three nights of the Hebrew idiom that Jesus had used.[1] The important lesson is that Jesus rested in the tomb during the Sabbath, having perfectly completed the task of obedience and the work that would issue in a new creation. The resurrection was the Father's powerful seal of approval. It also coincided with the Feast of First Fruits, when the first sheaf of the barley harvest was presented to God in the Temple, in anticipation of the full harvest at Shavuot (Pentecost) and Succoth (Tabernacles). Paul taught that Jesus, by His resurrection, became the first fruits of those who sleep, the great harvest of resurrected believers when He will return in glory.[2]

---

[1] Matt. 28:1; Mark 16:1; Luke 24:1; Matt. 12:40; 16:21.
[2] Gen. 2:2; Ps. 16:7-11; Acts 2:25-35; Lev. 23:9-22-44; 1 Cor. 15:20-28.

We know that at least three women came to the tomb, but John chose to focus on Mary Magdalene for reasons that will appear later. She was on a definite mission to anoint the body of Jesus, so the discovery that the stone had been moved came as a great shock to her. She interpreted the circumstances through her current worldview, having personally observed Joseph and Nicodemus carrying out the burial procedure. Mary would undoubtedly have heard Jesus speak about His death and resurrection, but this possibility had not entered her troubled mind. Two questions, occupied her mind: the identity of the grave-robbers and the current location of the body. Not knowing what to do next, she ran back to find help and encountered Peter and John.

> *20:3-9 Therefore Peter and the other disciple went out, and they went towards the tomb. They both ran together. The other disciple outran Peter, and came to the tomb first. Stooping and looking in, he saw the linen cloths lying, yet he didn't enter in. Then Simon Peter came, following him, and entered into the tomb. He saw the linen cloths lying, and the cloth that had been on his head, not lying with the linen cloths, but rolled up in a place by itself. So then the other disciple who came first to the tomb also entered in, and he saw and believed. For as yet they didn't know the Scripture, that he must rise from the dead.*

Peter's last memory of Jesus was from the courtyard of the High Priest, where Jesus had looked into his eyes following his threefold denial and the crowing of the cock. John had spent several harrowing hours at the cross, witnessing the excruciating suffering of the man who had meant so much to him. It is unlikely that many words passed between Peter and John as they walked together, each deep in his own thoughts. Suddenly Mary, anxious and agitated, burst into their private worlds, and her news shocked them out of their introspection and into action. We do not know what they made of the words that Mary had blurted out and whether they raced to the tomb in hope or fear, or even a combination of both. John was fleeter of foot; he looked through the entrance and saw the grave clothes lying there, but hesitated to go in. Peter, acting in character, went straight in and John then followed close behind. John carefully recorded the details of what he observed, just as he did at the cross, and in each case he recorded the presence of more than one witness, as required for valid testimony.

John's description is brief but seems to imply that the grave clothes, including the head piece, were lying in an undisturbed position where the body had lain. What they observed seemed incompatible with Mary's suggestion that the grave had been robbed. John said that when he saw (the arrangement of the cloths) he believed, but he does not comment on Peter's reaction. John had previously used the word 'believe' in various ways, sometimes in a tentative or conditional sense, sometimes in a superficial and factual sense and sometimes in the sense of committed faith.[3] On those occasions, as an external observer, John was commenting on the responses of other people. Here John stated that he himself believed, but this seems out of keeping with his subsequent statement: 'For as yet they didn't know the Scripture, that he must rise from the dead.' Probably John and Peter simply believed that what Mary had told them about the absence of Jesus' body was true. In this state of mind John and Peter returned home, uncertain of what it all meant and of what they should do.

The Greek word here translated 'know' can also be rendered 'understand', which makes more sense. Their failure to understand was a result of their inability to understand the Scriptures that foretold the resurrection of the Messiah, despite Jesus' repeated teaching on that subject. Perhaps they were influenced by the prevailing expectation of a triumphant and reigning Messiah.

Jewish scholars were also aware of prophecies of a suffering Messiah. They had difficulty in reconciling the two pictures and some even postulated two separate people: Messiah ben Joseph who would suffer, and Messiah ben David who would reign.[4] In the context of the Roman occupation there was, understandably, a focus on the reigning Messiah, to the exclusion of the suffering one. Unlike us, they were unaware that the one and only Messiah would come on two separate occasions.

---

[3] John 2:23-24; 4:39; 6:66-69; 8:3-37; 9:35-36; 12:42-43.
[4] Raphael Patai, *The Messiah Texts: Jewish Legends of Three Thousand Years* (Avon Books, 1979), p.166.

We now read the Bible in the light of the first appearance of Jesus, so our problems with interpretation concerning His second coming are greatly reduced (as we can eliminate the prophecies that have been fulfilled). Nevertheless, we also may read the Scriptures in a selective way, biased by the prevailing paradigms within our religious cultures.

At the time when Jesus was born there was an expectation that the words of the prophets would be literally and physically fulfilled, and so they were. Scholars had no difficulty in identifying the place of Messiah's birth as Bethlehem, and many other prophecies about Jesus' life were fulfilled in a literal and physical way.[5] During the post-Apostolic period a new approach was introduced, a metaphorical or allegorical method of interpretation, and this remains popular.[6] Peter and John can be excused for failing to understand that the Messiah would come to earth and to Jerusalem on two separate occasions. If we substitute allegory for literal interpretation in relation to Jesus' return, we are abandoning the method by which the details of His first coming were correctly interpreted, and without scriptural warrant.

> **20:10-16** *So the disciples went away again to their own homes. But Mary was standing outside at the tomb weeping. So as she wept, she stooped and looked into the tomb, and she saw two angels in white sitting, one at the head, and one at the feet, where the body of Jesus had lain.*
>
> *They asked her, 'Woman, why are you weeping?'*
>
> *She said to them, 'Because they have taken away my Lord, and I don't know where they have laid him.'*
>
> *When she had said this, she turned around and saw Jesus standing, and didn't know that it was Jesus. Jesus said to her, 'Woman, why are you weeping? Who are you looking for?'*
>
> *She, supposing him to be the gardener, said to him, 'Sir, if you have carried him away, tell me where you have laid him, and I will take him away.'*

---

[5] Mic 5:2; Matt. 2:1-6.

[6] Matthew Allen, 'Theology Adrift: The Early Church Fathers and Their Views of Eschatology', 2004, https//bible.org/article/theology-adrift-early-church-fathers-and-their-views-eschatology (accessed 28th January 2019).

Jesus said to her, 'Mary.'
She turned and said to him, 'Rabboni!' which is to say, 'Teacher!'

Mary had apparently followed them back, but not into the tomb. She was in a state of deep distress, and was weeping as she peered through the entrance of the tomb. It seems that only a brief time had elapsed since Peter and John had left, but meanwhile two visitors had arrived and were sitting, one at either end of the grave shelf.

Luke informs us that the women had seen the angels previously on their first visit to the tomb and that they had told them that Jesus was alive. The angels had also quoted Jesus' previous words to that effect. Luke further indicates that when the women informed the apostles, they dismissed it as nonsense and that Peter and John soon set off to investigate.[7]

John recorded that the angels were not present (or visible) when he and Peter visited the tomb. Perhaps this was in consequence of their own failure to believe the Scriptures and the words of Jesus. John's description of the angels must have been based on information from the women. He only referred to Mary Magdalene, but we know from Luke's account that other women were also present.[8]

It is difficult to make a single coherent narrative from the four Gospels, as each writer selected particular items from the complex series of events and they did not always place them in the same chronological order. We need to realise that writers in those days were not as interested in this as are modern historians. Matthew appears to have compressed two visits by the women into one, and also highlighted different parts of the sequence than those selected by John.[9] John's single focus on Mary Magdalene is typical of the way he crafted his narrative in order to emphasise Jesus' relationships with individual people.

Mary does not seem to have been over-impressed by the reappearance of the angels. Her problem remained the same: Jesus

---

[7] Luke 23:54–24:12.
[8] Luke 24:22-23.
[9] Matt. 28:1-10.

was not there and she did not know where He was. Neither angels nor explanations were enough to relieve her emotional pain, for only the immediate presence of Jesus would suffice. Turning away, she saw the figure of a man. Mary did not recognise Jesus in the midst of her confusion and distress, and she saw Him through the veil of her tears. She wanted Jesus, even if it was only the body that He had inhabited, in order to express her undying devotion in any way that was possible under the circumstances.

Jesus resolved Mary's disturbed condition in a single moment and with one word: 'Mary'. The Lord spoke, and she recognised His voice. The shepherd called one of His own dear sheep by name and she followed Him. Mary realised that she was in the presence of Jesus, alive again and now accessible to her. When she spoke, she was probably using the name by which she had previously addressed Him. *Rabboni* means 'my teacher, my great one', and indicates that Mary Magdalene regarded herself as a disciple of Jesus. She had been one of a group of women who had followed Jesus from Galilee and had provided for His material needs. She had followed Him to the cross and to the place of burial and had now returned to honour Him.

> **20:17-18** *Jesus said to her, 'Don't hold me, for I haven't yet ascended to my Father; but go to my brothers and tell them, "I am ascending to my Father and your Father, to my God and your God."' Mary Magdalene came and told the disciples that she had seen the Lord, and that he had said these things to her.*

It must have seemed to Mary that everything had returned to normal, but Jesus needed her to know that the cross and the resurrection had begun a new chapter. Soon Jesus would return in glory to the Father. Mary must not cling to Him because His future mission would be universal and would be directed from the throne of God. Jesus' words, 'I am ascending to my Father', may refer to His visible ascension forty days later, but the more natural reading suggests that He would initially ascend to the Father before appearing to the disciples as a group. If this interpretation is correct, then Mary's devotion was being richly rewarded by Jesus' unique visit with her in the garden.

When Jesus sent Mary with this message, He was about to be glorified with the Father, yet He affirmed His continuing humanity and His intimate relationship with the disciples as His brothers. This was an amazing truth for them and it is true for us as well. The writer to the Hebrews subsequently explained that Jesus' high priestly ministry on our behalf depends on the fact that He 'was obligated in all things to be made like his brothers', and that 'he is not ashamed to call them [us] brothers'.[10]

Jesus also referred to the Father as His God. In His incarnation He had accepted a relationship with the Father that corresponded to creature and Creator, and this will continue forever.[11] Jesus did not say, 'Our Father and our God', for there is an essential and unbridgeable gulf between His relationship with the Father and ours. Jesus is the eternal and only begotten Son of the Father. We must never blur that distinction or treat Him in an inappropriately casual way.

Mary, now filled with joy, brought glad news and conveyed the Lord's message. She became a prototype for all the devoted women who have been Jesus' spokespersons ever since then, although they have often not been acknowledged or encouraged to take on this role.

---

[10] Mark 3:33-34; Heb. 2:14-18, 10-12; 4:14-16.
[11] Eph. 1:3; Heb. 2:17, 12-13a; Acts 17:30-31; 1 Tim. 2:5.

51

John 20:19-31
My Lord and My God

> *20:19-20 When therefore it was evening on that day, the first day of the week, and when the doors were locked where the disciples were assembled, for fear of the Jews, Jesus came and stood in the middle, and said to them, 'Peace be to you.' When he had said this, he showed them his hands and his side. The disciples therefore were glad when they saw the Lord.*

The opening words of John's Gospel described the eternal Word by whom all things were made, echoing the opening statement in Genesis. Now, near the end of the Gospel, Jesus the true light who had come into the world has, through His death and resurrection, become the author of the new creation. All of the Gospel writers emphasise that Jesus rose from the dead on the first day of the week.[1]

Approximately twelve hours had elapsed since the tomb had been discovered to be empty. The disciples had had time to ponder and to discuss the strange and bewildering events of the day. Mark and Luke revealed that the disciples did not believe the women's account. John, who was present, recorded that they met behind locked doors because they were afraid of the Jewish leaders. Luke tells us that during that same day two depressed and disappointed members of the company had set off from Jerusalem to go to Emmaus. Jesus had met them on the road and had taught them and revealed Himself to them. They then returned to Jerusalem

---

[1] 2 Cor. 5:17; Rom. 8:18-25; Gal. 6:15; Rev. 21:1; Matt. 28:1; Mark 16:2; Luke 24:1; John 20:1.

and told of their experiences, but were met with scepticism.[2] Those in the locked room were astonished and possibly alarmed when Jesus suddenly appeared and stood in their midst. His first words were in the form of a typical Jewish greeting: 'Peace be to you.' This became the word of life that banished the turmoil, grief and unbelief of the previous few days.

In His grace, Jesus provided them with substantive evidence by exposing the wounds on His hands (wrists) and on His side. Mark tells us that Jesus also rebuked them for their stubborn refusal to believe the witnesses.[3] We can only hope that they apologised to the two Marys for treating them as deluded and hysterical women whose word could not be trusted. Unsurprisingly, the mood and atmosphere within the room was transformed: 'The disciples therefore were glad when they saw the Lord.'

> **20:21-23** *Jesus therefore said to them again, 'Peace be to you. As the Father has sent me, even so I send you.' When he had said this, he breathed on them, and said to them, 'Receive the Holy Spirit! If you forgive anyone's sins, they have been forgiven them. If you retain anyone's sins, they have been retained.'*

This series of events must have been an emotional roller coaster. Jesus had more to say and needed their undivided attention, so again He spoke peace into their hearts. The disciples were overjoyed to see Him again and this consumed their attention, but Jesus needed them to know that things would never be the same again. Their relationship with Him was changing and He would not be constantly physically present with them. They would become visible witnesses to Him in the world.

The Father had sent Him into the world on a mission, and He had completed His work. Jesus' death and resurrection was the goal and climax of His public ministry, but the previous two to three years had also been essential to what would happen next; during that time Jesus had been training the disciples for their role in the next phase in the Father's plan. He had done so by modelling

---

[2] Mark 16:9-11; Luke 24:8-43.
[3] Mark 16:14.

the way in which they would function and operate. Now He commissioned them for this task with these words: 'As the Father has sent me, even so I send you.'

Jesus laid aside the prerogative that He had as eternal God and did not make use of this power. The Father sent Him into the world to act on His authority and anointed Him with the Holy Spirit. Jesus was totally dependent on the Father for instructions and guidance, and on the Holy Spirit for the power to perform signs and miracles.[4] The disciples had observed Him speaking and acting in this way and now they were to continue in a similar way, totally dependent on the Holy Spirit to energise and guide them.

Jesus breathed on them, just as the Creator had breathed life into the first man whom He had shaped from the dust of the earth.[5] We do not know exactly what the disciples experienced at that time, but it was a foretaste of what they would receive in abundance at Pentecost. Jesus also authorised them to proclaim forgiveness of sins to some and to deny it to others, in keeping with what He had said at Caesarea Philippi. 'Binding' and 'loosing' were technical terms referring to the way religious leaders interpreted and applied the Law in particular circumstances. The disciples would have wisdom and discernment to enable them to proclaim forgiveness of sins to those who truly believed. They would also identify insincere claims to faith in the absence of repentance and would warn people of the consequences. There are examples of this in the life of the early church. Obviously Jesus was not giving permission to dispense forgiveness in an arbitrary fashion or for personal gain, or simply on the basis of hierarchy. Plurality of leadership and the guidance of the Holy Spirit are essential safeguards in the process.[6]

> **20:24-29** *But Thomas, one of the twelve, called Didymus, wasn't with them when Jesus came. The other disciples therefore said to him, 'We have seen the Lord!'*

---

[4] Matt. 12:28; John 3:34; Luke 4:14; Acts 10:38.
[5] Gen. 2:7.
[6] Matt. 16:19; 18:18; Acts 5:1-11; 13:6-12; 1 Cor. 5:1-7; 2 Cor. 2:3-11.

> *But he said to them, 'Unless I see in his hands the print of the nails, put my finger into the print of the nails, and put my hand into his side, I will not believe.'*
>
> *After eight days again his disciples were inside and Thomas was with them. Jesus came, the doors being locked, and stood in the middle, and said, 'Peace be to you.' Then he said to Thomas, 'Reach here your finger, and see my hands. Reach here your hand, and put it into my side. Don't be unbelieving, but believing.'*
>
> *Thomas answered him, 'My Lord and my God!'*
>
> *Jesus said to him, 'Because you have seen me, you have believed. Blessed are those who have not seen, and have believed.'*

The company in the locked room contained disciples other than the apostles. Thomas is described as being 'one of the twelve', emphasising the incongruity of the fact that he was missing. We know that Thomas was deeply loyal to Jesus and that he had previously demonstrated this in his determination to remain faithful even when his own life was at risk. Perhaps he felt a sense of personal disappointment at having deserted Jesus in the Garden of Gethsemane and had retreated into private grief and recrimination. Whatever the reason, and despite any positive rumours that he may have heard in the meantime, his distress may have been unnecessarily prolonged because of lack of communication with the other disciples.

Thomas' choice contains a lesson for those of us who respond to times of stress and difficulty by withdrawing from fellowship and thus miss opportunities for healing. Thomas is derived from the Hebrew word for 'twin'; he was also called Didymus, the Greek word for 'twin'. John was the only Gospel writer to use this double name for Thomas and also to highlight Thomas' unique contributions to the narrative.[7] Using this compound name does not seem to have been a device to identify Thomas for, unlike James, he did not share his name with any of the other disciples. John appears to have been purposeful in his selection of material.

Perhaps this detail is intended to remind his readers of the sovereignty of God in choosing people for particular purposes.

---

[7] John 11:16; 20:24; 21:2.

Twins have much in common, whether identical or otherwise, and the Bible contains accounts of at least two other sets of twins whose lives turned out to be very different from one another.[8] Each person, even in the case of identical twins, has a unique calling. This can only be discovered in individual relationship with God and should then be pursued in faith.

We might criticise Thomas for his refusal to believe, but the other disciples had also refused to accept the testimony of reliable witnesses. They had actually seen Jesus' wounds, whereas Thomas had only their word for evidence. They were all meeting in a room with a locked door, so their confidence was not exactly brimming over. In that context Jesus reappeared and spoke the same words of peace as on the previous occasion. He did not begin with words of reproach, for He understood Thomas' temperament and also his sincere desire to have a reliable basis for faith. Jesus had rebuked the others for not receiving the testimony of their fellow disciples, but His invitation to Thomas was gentle. Jesus was willing to provide him with the evidence that He had previously given to the other disciples. Thomas' response was immediate and as emphatic as his previous refusal to believe: 'My Lord and my God!'

Thomas had received direct visual evidence and, on this basis, had believed. This faith was valid, as was faith that resulted from seeing the former signs that Jesus had performed, but Jesus now referred to people who would believe without seeing such things. He told them that people who would not see Him in a physical sense would be blessed through believing (on the basis of others' testimony, the witness of the Scriptures and the enlightenment of the Holy Spirit). We may wish that we also could meet Jesus in human form, but He insisted that it was better that He should go away and that the Holy Spirit should come and bring revelation and understanding to our hearts and minds.

During the succeeding few weeks Jesus would spend much time with the disciples, demonstrating how His life, death and resurrection had fulfilled the Scriptures. Although they had believed that Jesus was the Messiah and were familiar with passages

---

[8] Gen. 25:23-26; 38:27-30.

that described a Messiah who would suffer, they had somehow managed to exclude this unpalatable truth from their minds. We might criticise them for this, but do we not all have blind spots, often ignoring parts of the Bible that do not sync with our current worldviews?

The disciples had to adapt to a different kind of relationship with Jesus, for He was the same person and yet strangely different. John, in a subsequent revelation on Patmos, had vivid personal experience of this truth. He saw Jesus as the glorified Son of Man, as the Alpha and the Omega, the First and the Last and the Amen. We too must learn to relate to Jesus as He is now; in His ascended glory He is incomparably different from us and yet He is still our brother, one like us. He is immeasurably far above us and yet is simultaneously near and accessible, in the person of the Holy Spirit. This truth defies our categories of thought and imagination but inspires us to worship.[9]

> **20:30-31** *Therefore Jesus did many other signs in the presence of his disciples, which are not written in this book; but these are written, that you may believe that Jesus is the Christ, the Son of God, and that believing you may have life in his name.*

John is alerting us to the fact that he is bringing his account of the life of Jesus to a conclusion. It has included only a few selected miracles, signs that pointed to Jesus' unique identity as the Son of God and as the Messiah who had been prophesied in the Scriptures. John's purpose was not merely to write an interesting biography of a truly great man or to give an account of His teachings and wisdom. He challenges us to come and see Jesus as much more than this, as God in human flesh walking on planet Earth in the same reality of space and time that we experience. This is the unique and vital distinction between Jesus and all other great religious leaders who have ever lived.

One of John's opening statements, 'The Word became flesh, and lived amongst us. We saw his glory, such glory as of the one and only Son of the Father, full of grace and truth', expressed his

---

[9] John 16:7; Rev.1:8-18; 5:13-14.

core conviction and was based on what he himself had seen and experienced. John may have been recalling the occasion of the Transfiguration, an overwhelming revelation of Jesus as the Son of God. Peter had also been present and it was indelibly printed on his memory. Many years later he wrote:

> For we didn't follow cunningly devised fables when we made known to you the power and coming of our Lord Jesus Christ, but we were eyewitnesses of his majesty. For he received from God the Father honour and glory when the voice came to him from the Majestic Glory, 'This is my beloved Son, in whom I am well pleased.' We heard this voice come out of heaven when we were with him on the holy mountain.[10]

We cannot put the text down as we picked it up, for John's Gospel demands a response. The nature of that response will determine our destiny for life or for death, both in this life and in the next. John wrote as an evangelist who sought a response from his readers, and he also seeks a response from us.

---

[10] John 1:14; Luke 9:28-37; 2 Pet. 1:16-18.

52

John 21:1-25
Feed My Sheep

> ***21:1-3** After these things, Jesus revealed himself again to the disciples at the sea of Tiberias. He revealed himself this way. Simon Peter, Thomas called Didymus, Nathanael of Cana in Galilee, and the sons of Zebedee, and two others of his disciples were together.*
>
> *Simon Peter said to them, 'I'm going fishing.'*
>
> *They told him, 'We are also coming with you.' They immediately went out, and entered into the boat. That night, they caught nothing.*

If John had ended his account at the conclusion of chapter 20 it is unlikely that anyone would have considered it to be incomplete. We might have noticed the absence of any reference to the ascension, but John had included this in his own way through Jesus' teaching at the Last Supper, and also through His interaction with Mary Magdalene at the garden tomb.[1] We also might have wondered why John, who rarely repeated events contained in the other Gospels, included another reference to Peter's great failure when he denied Jesus three times.[2]

This incident probably provides the answer. Luke recorded Jesus' assurance to Peter that his failure would not be final, but none of the Synoptic Gospels included the account of how Peter was restored.[3] John and Peter had been close friends and associates. Perhaps John wanted to honour Peter by recording this final episode, while also revealing Jesus' faithful love for him.

---

[1] John 14:1-3; 20:17.
[2] John 13:36-38; 18:15-18, 25-27.
[3] Luke 22:31-34.

The events in this chapter have a different atmosphere from the previous one where Jesus seemed to relate to the disciples in a more formal way. Now there are many reminders of past times when the disciples were on very intimate terms with Him, and the ambiance becomes almost domestic in character. Jesus is very different from those earlier days and yet still the same.

At the empty tomb the angels had told the women that Jesus would meet the disciples in Galilee.[4] Jesus had appeared to them on two occasions while they were in Jerusalem, and now seven of them travelled to Galilee to await a further encounter with Him. They included three former fishermen and two others who are not identified by name. Jesus had not made an appearance and they did not know when or where to expect him. He was unpredictable and, like the Spirit, did not adhere to human timetables.[5] Peter was a man of action and seems to have been restless. Perhaps he was still ill at ease, remembering his recent failure, and was somewhat apprehensive about meeting Jesus again. Perhaps he experienced a wave of nostalgia, remembering how Jesus had called him on the lakeshore in the context of a fishing expedition.[6]

Peter decided to go fishing again that night and his friends, whether fishermen or not, volunteered to join him. The previous time that Peter had fished all night and caught nothing had turned out to be the occasion of his call to follow Jesus. He had failed in that calling and now, once again, he was failing in the area of his natural talents and training. Peter was probably wet and cold and hungry and wondering where his life was heading. His mood must have been pretty low and depressed. Sometimes we are tempted to try to recreate circumstances where we had a special encounter with God but, as He takes His own creative initiatives, this is usually disappointing.

> **21:4-11** *But when day had already come, Jesus stood on the beach, yet the disciples didn't know that it was Jesus. Jesus therefore said to them, 'Children, have you anything to eat?'*

---

[4] Mark 16:6-7.

[5] John 3:8.

[6] Luke 5:1-11.

They answered him, 'No.'

He said to them, 'Cast the net on the right side of the boat, and you will find some.' They cast it therefore, and now they weren't able to draw it in for the multitude of fish.

That disciple therefore whom Jesus loved said to Peter, 'It's the Lord!' So when Simon Peter heard that it was the Lord, he wrapped his coat around himself (for he was naked), and threw himself into the sea. But the other disciples came in the little boat (for they were not far from the land, but about two hundred cubits away), dragging the net full of fish. So when they got out on the land, they saw a fire of coals there, with fish and bread laid on it.

Jesus said to them, 'Bring some of the fish which you have just caught.' Simon Peter went up, and drew the net to land, full of one hundred and fifty-three great fish. Even though there were so many, the net wasn't torn.

Just then a 'déjà vu' moment occurred. A figure on the shore called out, they followed His instructions and suddenly their net was filled to overflowing with fish. Strangely, Peter did not realise the significance, but John remembered the previous incident and, in that moment of revelation, he called out, 'It's the Lord!' The seven of them were having difficulties dealing with the fish but Peter, impetuous as ever, left them to cope. His priority had changed and he was determined to get to Jesus even if they lost the whole catch. Material gain and astounding miracle were no match for the opportunity to be with Jesus again.

On a previous occasion, when His popularity seemed to be vanishing before their eyes, Jesus had challenged the disciples with a question, 'You don't also want to go away, do you?' Peter had spoken for them all, 'Lord, to whom would we go? You have the words of eternal life. We have come to believe and know that you are the Christ, the Son of the living God.'[7] His experience with Jesus had spoiled him for anything else, for he knew that he had encountered 'the real thing', besides which anything else was hollow. The same is true for all who have truly known Jesus and, for whatever reason, have become estranged from Him.

---

[7] John 6:66-69.

Peter threw his cloak around himself, presumably out of respect for Jesus, plunged into the water and swam about a hundred yards to shore. This was in stark contrast to his response to the similar miracle when he had first encountered Jesus on that selfsame beach. Then, his fearful reaction had been to keep away from Jesus. Peter had spent two to three years with Jesus since that day and he knew that, despite his appalling sin and failure and his sense of shame, the risen Saviour would not now turn him away. When we fail Him we may feel uneasy about coming near, but if we cast off our cloak of shame and pride we will find Him ready to receive and restore us too.[8]

There is no record of any conversation between Jesus and Peter at that time and he soon turned back to help his colleagues to land the net, perhaps feeling awkward and ill at ease. John was a keen observer of detail and the text reads as a first-hand account, and he included two interesting details as he described the huge catch of fish. One was that, apparently to their surprise, the net had not broken. The other was the unusual precision about the number of fish in the catch. The disciples had just encountered Jesus in a very dramatic way and yet their priority was to count the fish – 153! Why would they have taken the time to do so under such circumstances? John and his Jewish readers would have been familiar with the use of Gematria as a method of interpreting Scripture. Each Hebrew letter has a specific numerical equivalent, and 153 has the numerical equivalent of 'sons of God'.[9]

The unusual number of fish may thus have symbolic significance, and this possibly connects with one of Jesus' parables. He likened the Kingdom of heaven to a dragnet that was drawn up on the beach and contained good fish and also bad ones that were discarded, representing the fate of the righteous and the wicked at the end of the age. In His prayer to His Father, Jesus had said that He had lost none of those that He had been given, the one 'bad fish', Judas, having voluntarily left the company.[10] Perhaps with this in mind, Jesus had instructed the disciples to count the fish.

---

[8] 1 John 1:5–2:2; Heb. 10:19-22

[9] Richard Bauckham, 'The 153 Fish and the Unity of the Fourth Gospel', *Neotestamentica* 36 (2002): pp. 77-88.

[10] Matt. 13:47-50; John 17:11-12; 6:70-71.

Jesus had performed a similar miracle before calling the fishermen from their livelihood to become His full-time disciples. On that occasion also they had landed a great number of fish, and Jesus had promised Peter and Andrew that in future they would catch people. In response, they had left everything and followed Him.[11] Perhaps the fish were also symbolic of those who would believe in Him through their witness and would thus become children of God, fulfilling the promise that John had penned in his prologue to the Gospel: 'But as many as received him, to them he gave the right to become God's children, to those who believe in his name.'[12]

> **20:12-14** *Jesus said to them, 'Come and eat breakfast!'*
>
> *None of the disciples dared enquire of him, 'Who are you?' knowing that it was the Lord.*
>
> *Then Jesus came and took the bread, gave it to them, and the fish likewise. This is now the third time that Jesus was revealed to his disciples after he had risen from the dead.*

Jesus seems to have been aware of their physical discomfort and hunger. They were probably also tense and possibly embarrassed, not knowing what to do or say. Jesus recognised how difficult it is for people who are physically and emotionally stressed to hear and process information. He had already asked them to add some of their fish to those He was already cooking on the fire, perhaps in order to make them feel more at ease. He now invited them to breakfast and served them bread and fish. Jesus had some vitally important things to communicate to them, and especially to Peter, but first He attended to their physical and emotional needs. In this respect Jesus was totally unchanged: perceptive, wise and compassionate. We should learn from this example when we encounter vulnerable people in need of guidance, or even of correction.

---

[11] Matt. 4:18-19; Luke 5:4-11.
[12] John 1:12; 20:30-31.

20:15-17 *So when they had eaten their breakfast, Jesus said to Simon Peter, 'Simon, son of Jonah, do you love me more than these?'*

He said to him, 'Yes, Lord; you know that I have affection for you.'

He said to him, 'Feed my lambs.' He said to him again a second time, 'Simon, son of Jonah, do you love me?'

He said to him, 'Yes, Lord; you know that I have affection for you.'

He said to him, 'Tend my sheep.' He said to him the third time, 'Simon, son of Jonah, do you have affection for me?'

Peter was grieved because he asked him the third time, 'Do you have affection for me?' He said to him, 'Lord, you know everything. You know that I have affection for you.'

Jesus said to him, 'Feed my sheep.'

Perhaps Peter had been uncharacteristically quiet during breakfast, and he may have been painfully aware of the time when he had stood around another fire in the High Priest's courtyard.[13] Jesus was about to show His love to Peter. He had done this in a physical way when He had washed his feet, and now He would wash Peter's feet in a spiritual way. This act of grace, although painful for Peter, would allow him to put the past behind him and progress into a new calling.

Jesus knew that Peter was clean and had indicated this when He was about to wash his feet. He and the other disciples, apart from Judas, were clean because they had received the word that Jesus had spoken to them.[14] They were clean in the sense that they were in genuine relationship with Him. Jesus' intention now was to wash Peter's feet in a spiritual sense, in relation to a recent and specific failure, but one that had not broken relationship with Himself.

Jesus did not confront this failure in a direct way, and there was no accusation in His words or in His voice. The interview had to be in public, not to shame Peter but rather to restore him in the presence of the disciple band. Jesus had not discarded Peter and He had a big job for him to do. Jesus' prayers for him had been effective, and the experience of failure would change Peter's outlook in ways that would enable him to fulfil this new calling.

---

[13] John 18:18.
[14] John 13:3-15; 15:3.

Jesus knew that Peter had already repented with bitter tears. What he needed now was the opportunity to reaffirm his love for Jesus and his loyalty towards Him. Jesus turned to him and perhaps their eyes met, as they had done in the court of the High Priest.[15] Significantly, Jesus addressed him as Simon son of Jonah, going back to the time when they had first met and before Jesus had given him a new name and a new identity.[16] Much had happened since that day, and Peter now had an opportunity to reaffirm what was central to his life.

We do not know exactly what Jesus intended or what Peter understood by 'these'. It cannot be that Jesus was encouraging Peter to boast that his love was greater than that of the other disciples, as this attitude had been part of his problem. Perhaps Jesus was hinting at Peter's promise to lay down his life for Him. He may have been referring to Peter's previous occupation as a fisherman, to which he had recently returned. He had probably made an impulsive decision in a state of boredom and tension, a dangerous combination that can make the world seem like an attractive alternative. Would Peter prefer to continue in that course? Peter knew that he could never settle for that option.[17]

Probably Jesus' question was open-ended: 'Do you love me more than anything else?' It was a question about the ultimate values and loyalty that are the essence of love. Jesus deliberately asked the question three times so that Peter could affirm his love just as emphatically as he had voiced his denial, and Peter got the message. This was a painful process, and probably also painful for Jesus, but He knew that it was necessary. Sympathy is not the same as compassion: sympathy can sooth emotions without addressing the issues, and thus leave a deep, unhealed wound in the soul.

In the first and second questions, Jesus used the Greek word *agape* to express love, implying a deep and committed love, but Peter responded with *phileo*, a lesser word that has the sense of affection or brotherly love. In the light of his recent failure, Peter could not bring himself to claim the depth of love that Jesus'

---

[15] Luke 22:61.

[16] John 1:40-42.

[17] John 6:66-69.

question implied, and perhaps he was unable to forgive or trust himself. At the third asking, Jesus used Peter's word *phileo*, and this seemed to burst open a dam in Peter's heart, expressed in the plaintive words, 'Lord, you know everything; you know that I love [*phileo*] you.' Wisely, he left Jesus to answer his own question from His treasure-house of understanding.

As Peter replied to each question, Jesus responded by giving him a new responsibility, emphasising that He had not rejected him. Peter would still be a fisher of people, an adventurous evangelist, but the deep and dark experience of failure, coupled with the healing that he was now receiving, would qualify him to be a shepherd, a pastor and a healer of souls.[18] An additional string had been added to his bow, for he would be able to better understand, from his own experience, the things with which other people struggle. The Good Shepherd trusted Peter, as an under-shepherd, to heal and to guide and to lead the sheep into green pastures.

In the divine economy, nothing is lost or wasted. The deepest failures in our lives can become the threads with which God weaves a tapestry for His glory, and also the means that He uses to bring healing and life to others. The outcome depends on how we respond when He calls us back to Himself. Peter heard, was restored and was recommissioned.

> ***20:18-19*** *'Most certainly I tell you, when you were young, you dressed yourself and walked where you wanted to. But when you are old, you will stretch out your hands, and another will dress you and carry you where you don't want to go.' Now he said this, signifying by what kind of death he would glorify God. When he had said this, he said to him, 'Follow me.'*

For the final time, Jesus used the authoritative introduction, 'Amen. Amen I say to you'. Peter had proclaimed his willingness to die for Jesus, but he had lacked the inner resources to fulfil his promise, and nor was it his time to be a martyr. Jesus assured Peter that one day he would redeem that earlier pledge of ultimate

---

[18] 1 Pet. 5:1-4.

loyalty, but only after many years spent serving his Lord. Peter and John would experience persecution and James would be killed at the whim of Herod, but Jesus solemnly assured Peter that he would have many years to live and follow Him on earth.[19] Peter would ultimately die as a martyr, but then it would be for the glory of God and not to fulfil a reckless vow. Meanwhile, he must simply continue on the journey that had begun when Jesus called him three years before, on that very same beach, with the words, 'Come after me.' This is the general requirement for disciples, the foundational command that undergirds our lives and upon which all specific callings rest.[20]

> **20:20-23** *Then Peter, turning around, saw a disciple following. This was the disciple whom Jesus loved, the one who had also leaned on Jesus' breast at the supper and asked, 'Lord, who is going to betray you?' Peter seeing him, said to Jesus, 'Lord, what about this man?'*
>
> *Jesus said to him, 'If I desire that he stay until I come, what is that to you? You follow me.' This saying therefore went out amongst the brothers, that this disciple wouldn't die. Yet Jesus didn't say to him that he wouldn't die, but, 'If I desire that he stay until I come, what is that to you?'*

It seems that at some point during the conversation Jesus had led Peter away in order to complete the process in private. As the interview drew to a conclusion, Peter noticed his friend John following just behind. Perhaps sensing an opportunity to change the subject and divert the focus from himself, Peter inquired about John's future. Peter had just received a new commission and news about a challenging role; what plans did Jesus have for John?

It was dangerous to ask Jesus this kind of question, for He always returned focus to the questioner.[21] Essentially, what Jesus said to Peter was, 'Mind your own business,' an instruction we would all do well to follow. It is enough for us to know what God requires of us and not to be inquisitive about His plans for our brothers and sisters. Of course, we should be involved in each

---

[19] Acts 5:40-42; 12:1-11.
[20] Mark 1:16-18.
[21] Luke 12:13-15.

other's lives, share as we see fit, pray for one another and give help and advice when requested, but we do not need to inquire inappropriately about the details of their lives.[22]

Jesus answered with a hypothetical question. What if it was His purpose to keep John alive until He returned from heaven? Even in this extreme case, Jesus did not need to discuss such matters with Peter or reveal His intentions. Information of this kind is given on a need-to-know basis. What Jesus said as a rebuke to Peter was, almost inevitably, interpreted as a statement of fact, such is the power of human beings to misinterpret situations. It is easy to start rumours, making two and two add up to five, six or seven, or anything that fits with the imagination, but it is impossible to call back the false information after it has been circulated. This is all the more so in our age of instant communication.

> ***20:24-25*** *This is the disciple who testifies about these things, and wrote these things. We know that his witness is true. There are also many other things which Jesus did, which if they would all be written, I suppose that even the world itself wouldn't have room for the books that would be written.*

John affirmed his credentials as a faithful witness of all that he had recorded. Much more could have been said, because the evidence for the identity of Jesus as the Son of God was almost inexhaustible in its scope. John's purpose in highlighting this particular selection of material was not merely to inform or entertain, or even to engage in controversy, but as he had previously stated:

These are written, that you may believe that Jesus is the Christ, the Son of God, and that believing you may have life in his name.

---

[22] 2 Thess. 3:11.

APPENDIX 1

Inverse Parallelism: The Literary Structure of John 2:1-12

Inverse parallelism is a device that illustrates by literary structure how transformation has taken place. The initial condition is described, followed by a number of steps to the critical point. This launches a parallel series of steps in reverse sequence. The steps can be summarised using a notation similar to the one below, where F denotes the pivotal point where Jesus gave a command that signalled His personal authority. John's readers would not need to discern the structure in a conscious way. The arrangement will act unconsciously to emphasise the truth that he is seeking to convey. The medium and the message are in full accord.

A The third day. Mother invited to wedding; Jesus and disciples follow.

  B Wine has run out; sign of old religious system, and social disaster.

    C Mother says, 'No wine'. Jesus says, 'My hour has not yet come.'

      D Mother tells servants, 'Whatever He says to you, do it.'

        E Water pots empty.

          F Jesus tells servants, 'Fill the water pots with water.'

E¹ Water pots full.

D¹ Jesus tells servants, 'Draw some out and take it to the master of the feast.'

C¹ Master says, 'You have kept the good wine until now.'

B¹ Abundant wine; sign of Jesus' glory; the disciples believe in Jesus.

A¹ Not many days; Jesus now the leader of the group as they leave.

APPENDIX 2

John 1:14
The Only Begotten Son of God

> *The Word became flesh, and lived amongst us. We saw his glory, such glory as of the one and only Son of the Father, full of grace and truth.*

The WEBBE, in common with a number of other English versions (including the RSV, NIV and ESV), omits the term 'begotten' when translating the Greek word *monogenes*, preferring the phrase 'one and only Son'. When I shared this part of the manuscript with others there was a lack of enthusiasm about it. It seemed like an exercise in archaic language, with emphasis on an abstruse point of theology; why not be content with the translation, 'one and only Son'? This is, of course, a true description of the relationship of the Son to the Father, but it does not carry the full weight of its meaning and can lead to a serious misunderstanding of the God who is revealed in the Bible. On the one hand it can lead to a false picture, not far removed from the concept of three gods in a kind of council or consortium. Another aberration is the idea of a God who manifests Himself in three different ways towards His creation. A third consequence, common in contemporary church life, is to prioritise Jesus in expressions of worship, whereas the Father has the supreme position. The Son and the Spirit are the same in essence as the Father, but Jesus and the apostles taught that He is first in honour, and is the ultimate source of creation and redemption.[1]

Monogenes is a compound word, from *mono* ('only, one') and *genes* ('kind, species, offspring'), giving rise to the English words gene

---

[1] John 5:30; 10:28-29; Acts 2:32-36; 17:30-31; 1 Cor. 15:24-28; Phil. 2:9-11; 1 Tim. 6:13-16; Rev. 4:1-11.

and genetic. When *monogenes* otherwise occurs in the Gospels it is with reference to an only child of his/her parents.[2] On two occasions Isaac was described as the only son of Abraham, although Abraham had another son, Ishmael. The relationship between Abraham and Isaac was unique because the promised seed was transmitted to Isaac, and he was considered to have the same 'spiritual genes' as Abraham, becoming a second person of the same kind. Isaac's life story serves to illustrate this, for, in many respects, it was a mirror image of Abraham's life, even including his failure when he concealed his relationship with his wife Rebecca.[3]

The word 'begotten' is sometimes used to describe a father's biological contribution to the life and nature of a child. This analogy has some value in helping us to understand the relationship between the Father and the Son, in the sense that the Son's life flows from the Father. However, the analogy is also weak, for the Son is uncreated and eternal. Jesus is the *monogenes* (the only begotten) of the Father, eternally arising from Him and sharing His nature and essence.[4] He is begotten in a completely different and unique sense, unlike all others who are called sons of God.[5] Arius pushed the analogy too far and produced a heresy of the Son as a created and secondary god. This was decisively rejected at the first Christian council at Nicaea in AD 325, which produced the following creed:

> We believe in one God, the Father almighty, maker of all things visible and invisible; And in one Lord, Jesus Christ, the Son of God,
> begotten from the Father, only-begotten, that is, from the substance of the Father,
> God from God, light from light, true God from true God, begotten not made,

[2] Luke 7:12; 8:42; 9:38.

[3] Gen. 12:14-20; 20:1-17, c.f. 26:6-11; 21:22-32, c.f. 26:15-33.

[4] For more detailed treatment see Michael Marlowe, The Only Begotten Son (2006), http://www.bible-researcher.com/only-begotten.html (accessed 28th January 2019).

[5] Gen. 22:2 c.f. Heb. 11:17; Gal. 4:29; John 20:17; Gal. 3:26; 1 John 3:1.

of one substance with the Father, through Whom all things came into being, things in heaven and things on earth,

Who because of us men and because of our salvation came down, and became incarnate and became man, and suffered, and rose again on the third day,

and ascended to the heavens, and will come to judge the living and dead,

And in the Holy Spirit.

But as for those who say, There was when He was not, and, Before being born He was not, and that He came into existence out of nothing, or who assert that the Son of God is of a different hypostasis or substance, or created, or is subject to alteration or change – these the Catholic and apostolic Church anathematizes.[6]

An explanation by C S Lewis is helpful at this point:

One of the creeds says that Christ is the Son of God 'begotten, not created'; and it adds 'begotten by his Father before all worlds.' Will you please get it quite clear that this has nothing to do with the fact that when Christ was born on earth as a man, that man was the son of a virgin? We are not now thinking about the Virgin Birth. We are thinking about something that happened before Nature was created at all, before time began. 'Before all worlds' Christ is begotten, not created. What does it mean?

We don't use the words begetting or begotten much in modern English, but everyone still knows what they mean. To beget is to become the father of: to create is to make. And the difference is this. When you beget, you beget something of the same kind as yourself. A man begets human babies, a beaver begets little beavers and a bird begets eggs which turn into little birds. But when you make, you make something of a different kind from yourself. A bird makes a nest, a beaver builds a dam, a man makes a wireless set – or he may make something more like himself than a wireless set: say, a statue. If he is a clever

6 'The Creed of Nicaea' available at
https://earlychurchtexts.com/public/creed_of_nicaea_325.htm (accessed 4th February 2019).

enough carver he may make a statue which is very like a man indeed. But, of course, it is not a real man; it only looks like one. It cannot breathe or think. It is not alive.

Now that is the first thing to get clear. What God begets is God; just as what man begets is man. What God creates is not God; just as what man makes is not man. That is why men are not Sons of God in the sense that Christ is. They may be like God in certain ways, but they are not things of the same kind. They are more like statues or pictures of God.

The First Person is called the Father and the Second the Son. We say that the First begets or produces the second; we call it begetting, not making, because what He produces is of the same kind as Himself. In that way the word Father is the only word to use. But unfortunately it suggests that He is there first – just as a human father exists before his son. But that is not so. There is no before and after about it. And that is why I have spent some time trying to make clear how one thing can be the source, or cause, or origin, of another without being there before it. The Son exists because the Father exists: but there never was a time before the Father produced the Son ... In the same way we must think of the Son always, so to speak, streaming forth from the Father, like light from a lamp, or heat from a fire, or thoughts from a mind. He is the self-expression of the Father – what the Father has to say. And there never was a time when He was not saying it ... Naturally God knows how to describe Himself much better than we know how to describe Him. He knows that Father and Son is more like the relation between the First and Second Persons than anything else we can think of. Much the most important thing to know is that it is a relation of love. The Father delights in His Son; the Son looks up to His Father.[7]

Jesus' role in creation, His anointing as Messiah, His atoning death, His resurrection and His enthronement are all described in the context of His identity as the only begotten Son and are direct consequences of it. The Scriptures speak of the Messiah in three interconnected way: begotten, beloved/chosen and firstborn.

---

[7] C S Lewis, *Mere Christianity* (Fontana Books, 1955) pp. 133-134, 146-147.

Jesus is the one through whom God the Father made the worlds. He is described as 'the firstborn of all creation', with the rights of the firstborn son and, in consequence, the authority to reign over all creation.[8]

When the Holy Spirit came upon the Virgin Mary and the power of the Most High overshadowed her, Jesus was conceived as a fully human person, but He did not lose His identity as God. The Christmas carol says it well, 'True God of true God, Light from Light Eternal, lo, He abhors not the virgin's womb'.[9] He voluntarily laid aside the prerogatives and powers of deity and depended on the anointing of the Holy Spirit for all that He did. Jesus, the only begotten Son, became the physical and visible revelation of the invisible God. As the only begotten Son, Jesus, sharing the nature of the Father, revealed, in unique and intimate and tangible ways, the glory of the God of Israel.[10] That glory is connected with His goodness, including His grace and His compassion.[11] We have seen many examples of this grace in action in the picture John has painted of Jesus.[12]

Such was the Father's love for the world that He not only sent His beloved and only begotten Son into the world, but also gave Him to death on the cross so that we, unworthy and rebellious as we are, should not perish but have everlasting life. This was prefigured when God requested Abraham to offer Isaac, whom He described as 'your son, your only son, Isaac, whom you love', later defined as Abraham's only begotten son.[13] A Jewish commentary likens Isaac's ascent of Mount Moriah 'as one who carries his own cross on his shoulders',[14] a vivid portrayal of the Father and the Son, beloved and only begotten, acting in perfect harmony.[15] When Jesus died as the sacrifice for the sin of the world, God was

---

[8] Heb. 1:1-2; Col. 1:15.

[9] 'O Come All Ye Faithful' (Public Domain).

[10] John 4:8-26; Exod. 33:12-23; 34:5-9; 2 Cor. 4:6; John 14:9; 17:6; 8:1-11.

[11] Exod. 33:18-19; 34:6, Ps. 103:1-14.

[12] Luke 1:31-35; Heb. 1:5-6; Heb. 10:5-10; John 5:5-15; 9:1-7, 35-38; 10:30; 11:32-44; Phil. 2:5-8.

[13] John 3:13-18; Gen. 22:1-2; Heb. 11:17 (NKJV); Gen. 22:9.

[14] The Babylonian Talmud, quoted in Chaim Potok, *Wanderings: Chaim Potok's History of the Jews*, (New York: Fawcett Crest, 1978), pp. 309-310.

[15] Isa. 42:1; John 1:32-34; Luke 3:22; 9:28-36.

crucified: 'God ... reconciled us to himself through Jesus Christ ... God was in Christ reconciling the world to himself.'[16]

The resurrection was a further and dramatic revelation of Jesus as the only begotten Son. In the second psalm, God the Father said to His anointed king, 'You are my son. Today I have become your father [begotten you].' Paul, speaking to fellow Jews, explained that this prophecy was connected with the resurrection of Jesus. It was the moment when the Father declared Him 'to be the Son of God with power, according to the Spirit of holiness, by the resurrection from the dead, Jesus Christ our Lord'.[17]

Psalm 2 records a second declaration about the only begotten Son: '"Yet I have set my King on my holy hill of Zion." ... Ask of me, and I will give the nations for your inheritance, the uttermost parts of the earth for your possession.' The Messiah's resurrection is with a view to His reign; He is described as 'Jesus Christ, the faithful witness, the firstborn of the dead, and the ruler of the kings of the earth'.[18] He will return at the conclusion of this age to rule over the earth in peace and righteousness.[19]

As creatures, our understanding of the nature of God is inevitably limited, but He has given us permission and revelation to enable us to enter a little way into the divine mystery, and we should go as far as we can with humility and reverence. The incarnation of Jesus has greatly increased the potential for us to do so, for He is the ultimate revelation of the Father and He has also sent the Holy Spirit to us to aid our understanding. Nevertheless, it has added a paradox to the mystery, for now the eternally begotten Son is also a fellow human being who is not ashamed to call us His brothers and who joins us in our worship of the Father.[20] He is at one and the same time a fully human person and the eternal God whom angels worship, and whom Thomas and John and the other apostles also worshipped.[21] How should we relate to Him? The typical Jewish answer to such a question is 'both

---

[16] 2 Cor. 5:18-19.

[17] Acts 13:26-37; Ps. 2:7; Rom. 1:4.

[18] Ps. 2:6, 8; 89:24-29; Rev. 1:5 c.f. Acts 13:30-33.

[19] See, for example, Ps. 72:8, 12-17, Isa. 9:7-8.

[20] Heb. 2:10-13.

[21] Heb. 1:6; John 20:27-28; Rev. 1:12-18; Matt. 28:16-20.

ways'. So we approach the Son with awe and intimacy, confidence and humility, gratitude and faith, always remembering that His highest ambition for us is to bring us to the Father, whom we worship through the merits of the Son and in the energy of the Holy Spirit.[22]

---

[22] Eph. 2:18.

APPENDIX 3

Jesus' Attitude to and Treatment of Women

John's account of how Jesus related to the woman who was accused of adultery is consistent with many other occasions, recorded in all four Gospels, when He interacted with women.[1] He always treated them as having equal value to His male disciples and with special consideration in view of their lower social status and greater vulnerability. The incidents in John's Gospel make this fact very clear.

Jesus' response to His mother Mary at the wedding in Cana may seem at first sight to be an exception to this but, as explained in chapter 7 of this book, there were special circumstances and He was not being disrespectful to her. From the cross, in the midst of His agony, Jesus compassionately committed Mary into the care of the apostle John.[2]

Jesus treated the Samaritan woman with great sensitivity, conscious of her vulnerable position as a woman and also her perception of being despised by Jews. He engaged with her in intelligent discourse and she became His agent to alert her neighbours in Sychar to the presence of the Messiah. By contrast, Jesus' disciples had made no spiritual impression on the villagers and were surprised that He had been talking with a woman.

Jesus recognised Martha as a woman who believed in Him, to the extent that He was confident to challenge her to rise to a new level in her faith. He revealed Himself to her as the resurrection and the life and called on her to believe that her brother would rise again.

---

[1] Matt. 9:20-22; 13:33; 27:55; 28:5; Mark 7:24-30; 15:41; Luke 1:42; 7:11-15, 36-50; 8:1-3; 10:38-42; 13:11-16; 23:27, 55.
[2] John 19:25-27.

Mary of Bethany was a less resilient character than Martha, and Jesus treated her in an empathetic manner, sharing her emotional state and weeping in empathy with the grief that she and others were experiencing. Subsequently Jesus defended Mary in the face of criticism at her prophetic act of love in anointing Him with perfumed oil and expressed appreciation for what she had done. John recorded that Jesus loved both Martha and Mary, two very different but devoted women who served Him in their separate ways.

John records that four women made the harrowing journey to the crucifixion of Jesus: His mother Mary, Mary's sister, Mary the wife of Clopas and Mary Magdalene. John was the sole representative of the male disciples.

John records that Mary Magdalene was first at the tomb on the first day of the week (Mark mentions two other women: Mary the mother of James and Salome[3]). She evidently did not interpret what she discovered – the empty tomb – as evidence for Jesus' resurrection but instead suffered a deep sense of grief and loss. Mary was granted the honour of being the first human being to see the risen Lord. He announced this fact by calling her by her personal name, and she immediately responded in worship. Jesus appointed her as His first emissary to convey the news of His resurrection and to communicate His instructions to the disciples. John 21 records the consequences of their following those instructions.

The way in which Jesus treated women was in sharp contrast with the attitudes of some of the religious leaders of His day. He did not see them as subservient to men or existing for their convenience. Jesus set the standard for teaching and practice in the early church, where women were honoured members of the Christian communities and considered to be fellow heirs with their husbands of the grace of life.[4] Jesus' example, when fully appreciated, has played a major role in raising the status and dignity of women within societies that have been influenced by the

---

[3] Mark 1:16.
[4] Acts 1:14; 9:36-43; 12:12-16; 16:13-15, 40; 18:1-3, 24-26; 21:8-9; Rom. 16:1-7, 12-15; 1 Cor. 1:11; 7:1-16; Gal. 3:28; Eph. 5:21-33; Phil. 4:2-3; 2 Tim. 4:19; 1 Pet. 3:7; 2 John 1:1-6, 12-13.

Gospel, and this persists as an (often unrecognised) legacy in post-Christian areas in the world.

All of this is in stark contrast with many societies, past and present, within which women have been and are still sometimes viewed and treated as inferior. Under these circumstances, men may regard them as chattels who exist for their personal convenience and pleasure. Thank God for the example of Jesus.

APPENDIX 4

Was Jesus Born at the Feast of Hanukah?

Hanukah had its origins in the period between Malachi and Matthew. In 164 BCE the people of Judah succeeded in freeing their land and their capital city Jerusalem from several years of Gentile occupation. During those years the Temple had been defiled and a pagan altar had been introduced. After cleansing the Temple, worship of the Lord was reinstituted and the Menorah (Lampstand) was lit again.[1] Jewish tradition refers to a miracle: there was only sufficient oil for one day but it lasted for eight days. Light is a central feature in the celebration of Hanukah, lamps being lit for eight consecutive days at the darkest time of the year.

John's reference to this festival functioned as a time marker on Jesus' journey to the cross, but this was possibly neither the only nor the main reason for highlighting the event. A little earlier, Jesus had proclaimed Himself as the light of the world, with the implication that those who did not follow Him were walking in darkness. This incident had concluded with an attempt by the Jewish leaders, in their blindness, to stone Him to death. Now, at Hanukah, the festival of light, Jesus claimed to be one with the Father, and the leaders again took up stones to stone Him.[2]

Is there any evidence that Jesus had a special connection with Hanukah that might have led John to highlight this event? Hanukah is celebrated in December, varying in dates from year to year in keeping with the lunar calendar. Very early Christian tradition, from before the end of the second century, dates the birth of Jesus as occurring in mid-winter, and the Christian Feast of the Annunciation takes place on 25th March, nine months before 25th December. This has been contested as being simply a

---

[1] 2 Maccabees 10:1-8.
[2] John 8:12, 54-59; 9:39-41; 10:22-33.

device to replace mid-winter pagan practices with the Christian festival of Christmas, but there does not appear to be any firm historical evidence to support this claim.

So what is the evidence that the date for the Feast of the Annunciation was actually the date when Jesus was conceived? The strongest evidence is based on a calculation of the time when the angel Gabriel appeared to Zechariah in the Temple. Zechariah, the father of John the Baptist, belonged to the division of Abijah that was on duty at that time. The original sequence of priestly divisions, as prescribed in 1 Chronicles, was disrupted by the exile in Babylon, from which the division of Abijah returned but not all of the other priestly divisions,[3] and also by the events prior to the first celebration of Hanukah. This made accurate calculations of dates impossible on the basis of the original plan.

However, Josephus gave first-hand information concerning the priestly division that was on duty when the Temple was destroyed by the Romans on 9th–10th Ab (5th August) in 70 CE. He recorded that the division of Jehoiarib was serving at that time. Working backwards, it can be calculated that in 6 BCE the division of Abijah, Zachariah's division, would have been serving during the period of the Feast of Tabernacles, 3rd–10th October.[4]

Zechariah was old and had hitherto been unsuccessful in the selection procedure for who should officiate. Now at last, in the Lord's time, his lot came up. It is probable that Elizabeth conceived soon after this angelic visit, as happened also with Mary a little less than six months later, following Gabriel's message to her.[5] This would place the conception of Jesus in late March of 5 BCE, corresponding with the traditional date of the Christian Feast of the Annunciation, and Jesus' birth would then have taken place in late December.

Josephus recorded that a lunar eclipse occurred shortly before the death of Herod the Great. Calculations from astronomy indicate that this took place on the night of 12th–13th March 4

---

[3] 1 Chron. 24:10; Neh. 7:39-42; 12:1-21.
[4] A Edersheim, *The Life and Times of Jesus the Messiah* (Grand Rapids : Wm.B Eerdmans Publishing Co., November 1971), Appendix VII, p. 705.
[5] Luke 1:5-80; 26-57.

BCE.[6] Herod's death is assumed to have taken place during the following lunar month, during which the Feast of Passover would have been celebrated, close to the date of the subsequent Feast of the Annunciation. Thus, available historical data suggests that the birth of Jesus took place late in 5 BCE, possibly coinciding with the Feast of Hanukah. The true light, which gives light to everyone, had indeed come into the world.

These calculations necessarily make some assumptions, but they are based on contemporary and documented evidence as well as some early traditions. The conclusion is consistent with the belief that the Festivals of Israel had prophetic significance in relation to the coming of the Messiah. As we have seen, John's Gospel puts great emphasis on God's timing in relation to the life of Jesus, and the time circumstances of His birth appear to fit with this.[7] The coincidence of these miraculous events with three of the Feasts of Israel serves to highlight Jesus' unique identity as the light of the world, as the revelation of the Father's glory and as the One who came to save and deliver His people.

---

6 Edersheim, *The Life and Times of Jesus the Messiah*, Appendix VII, p. 704.
7 Gal. 4:4.

APPENDIX 5

Did Jesus Die at Passover?

The Synoptic Gospels agree that Jesus ate the Passover meal with His disciples on the evening prior to His crucifixion. However, John indicates that the priests were preparing to eat the Passover on the Friday evening, following Jesus' trial and crucifixion, and that, for the same reason, they wanted His body removed from the cross before evening.[1] One commentator states that this issue has been much debated by scholars, without a consensus solution, and this invites criticism from those who have an inclination to cast doubt on the veracity of the New Testament records.[2]

Recent discoveries from the Essene community in Qumran have been used in an attempt to explain this apparent contradiction. The Essenes followed a different calendar from the one used in the Temple and observed Passover two or three days earlier. The Essenes in Jerusalem lived in community in the upper city area, the probable location of the Last Supper and, unusually, men carried water pots. In the knowledge that He was to die just before Passover on Friday evening, Jesus might have chosen to make use of the alternative calendar, which would have left more time for the arrest and subsequent trials. However, the Synoptic Gospels contradict this theory, stating that it was the day when the Passover lamb was killed (according to the Temple calendar).[3]

The simplest explanation for John's threefold reference to the Passover that would follow the events of the crucifixion is probably along the following lines: contemporary use of language did not make a clear distinction between the Passover (a single meal) and the Feast of Unleavened Bread (a seven-day festival).

---

[1] Matt. 26:2; Mark 14:1, 12-16; John 18:28; 19:31.

[2] See Morris, *The Gospel according to John*, pp. 684-695.

[3] Mark 14:12-17; Luke 22:7.

Unleavened bread was eaten with the Passover lamb, but the seven-day Feast of Unleavened Bread did not actually commence until the following day. Jesus' disciples referred to the Passover itself as the first day of Unleavened Bread, and Luke stated that 'the feast of unleavened Bread, which is called the Passover, was approaching'.[4] John's repeated reference to the Preparation, and specifically to the Preparation day for the Passover, should be interpreted in the context of this contemporary convention.

John recorded the Jewish leaders' concerns that the bodies should be removed before the commencement of the Sabbath, at sunset, and He also stated that this particular Sabbath was a high day. In 30 CE, Nisan 14th (the designated day for Passover) began on Thursday evening at sunset and ended on Friday at sunset. Nisan 15th, the first day of Unleavened Bread as prescribed in the Torah, commenced at that time, making it a high Sabbath with particular emphasis on ritual purity.

During that Sabbath Jesus rested in the tomb, rising on the morning of the first day of the week as the first fruits of the new creation. Almost simultaneously, the Feast of First Fruits was being celebrated in the Temple, immediately followed by the fifty-day countdown to the Feast of Shavuot (Pentecost).[5] All of these events, from Passover to Pentecost, were intimately interconnected, and Jesus thus fulfilled in precise detail the prophetic timetable of these Feasts.

---

[4] Exod. 12:8-20; Lev. 23:6; Matt. 26:17-19; Luke 22:1.
[5] Lev. 23:4-21; Acts 2:1.

APPENDIX 6

What Were the Times of the Morning and Evening Offerings?

Exodus 29:38-39 gives the regulations for the daily offerings as follows:

> Now this is that which you shall offer on the altar: two lambs a year old day by day continually. The one lamb you shall offer in the morning; and the other lamb you shall offer at evening.

No precise times are specified. Edersheim stated, 'According to general agreement, the morning sacrifice was brought at the 'third hour', corresponding to our nine o'clock'.[1] This would have been at the conclusion of the morning offering, similar to the occasion when Zechariah was burning incense.[2] Jesus was nailed to the cross at the third hour. The Holy Spirit came at the third hour on the Day of Pentecost.[3]

The second lamb was offered at evening; more literally this is 'between the evenings' (Hebrew: *beyn ha'arbayim*). The account in 1 Kings 18 of Elijah's contest with the prophets helps us understand how to interpret this:

> They [the false prophets] took the bull which was given them, and they dressed it, and called on the name of Baal from morning even until **noon**, saying, 'Baal, hear us!' But there was no voice, and nobody answered ...

---

[1] Edersheim, *The Temple* (London: James Clarke & Co. Ltd, 1959), p. 143.
[2] Luke 1:8-11.
[3] Mark 15:25; Acts 2:15.

When midday was past, they prophesied **until the time of the evening offering**; but there was no voice, no answer, and nobody paid attention …

At the time of the evening offering, Elijah the prophet came near, and said, 'LORD, the God of Abraham, of Isaac, and of Israel, let it be known today that you are God in Israel, and that I am your servant, and that I have done all these things at your word. Hear me, LORD, hear me, that this people may know that you, LORD, are God, and that you have turned their heart back again.' Then the LORD's fire fell, and consumed the burnt offering, the wood, the stones, and the dust, and licked up the water that was in the trench. When all the people saw it, they fell on their faces. They said, 'The LORD, he is God! the LORD, he is God!'[4]

A significant period of time must have elapsed between noon and Elijah's offering. The subsequent events involving the capture and execution of the false prophets, Elijah's prayer for rain and his fourteen-mile run to Jezreel would have taken several hours before darkness would have overtaken him.[5] All of this points to the time of the evening offering being early- to mid-afternoon and fits with the understanding of 'between the evenings' as referring to the midpoint between the times when the sun began to decline and when it set, i.e. the ninth hour (3 pm).

Edersheim stated that, according to the rabbis, the lamb was slain at the eighth hour and a half and was laid on the altar an hour later. He also referenced Josephus as giving the ninth hour as the time for the offering. Peter and John went to the Temple at the hour of prayer, the ninth hour (3 pm), probably at the conclusion of the evening offering.[6]

This information suggests that the times of commencement and conclusion of the process of Jesus' crucifixion paralleled the first and second offerings of lambs at the Temple, a further instance of how Jesus, the Jewish Messiah, fulfilled the Jewish Scriptures.

---

[4] 1 Kings 18:26-39 (emphasis added).

[5] 1 Kings 18:36-46.

[6] Edersheim, *ibid* p 144; Josephus, *The Jewish Wars*, Ant. xiv. 4, 3; Acts 3:1.